Cover Illustration:
Nuestra Señora del Parral, Segovia, claustro procesional

(From a slide provided by Antonio Ruiz Hernando)

LEEDS IBERIAN PAPERS

Series Editor: M.A. Rees

LEEDS IBERIAN PAPERS

Published Titles

LEEDS PAPERS ON LORCA AND ON CIVIL WAR VERSE
1988
Second, extended edition
1990

LEEDS PAPERS ON HISPANIC DRAMA
1991

LEEDS PAPERS ON ST JOHN OF THE CROSS
1991

LEEDS PAPERS ON THRILLERS
IN THE TRANSITION
1992

AFTER CERVANTES: 75 YEARS OF IBERIAN
STUDIES AT LEEDS
1993

LEEDS PAPERS ON SYMBOL AND IMAGE
IN IBERIAN ARTS
1994

SOULS IN ANGUISH
RELIGION AND SPIRITUALITY IN LORCA'S
THEATRE
1994

PORTUGUESE AT LEEDS: ESSAYS FROM THE
ANNUAL SEMANA PORTUGUESA
1995

CROWN, COURT AND CHURCH IN GOLDEN AGE IBERIA
1996

CONVIVIUM: CELEBRATORY ESSAYS FOR RONALD CUETO

Edited by John Macklin and Margaret A. Rees

Published 1997 by   Trinity and All Saints
University College
Brownberrie Lane
Horsforth
Leeds
LS18 5HD

Copyright   Trinity and All Saints 1997

ISBN   0 9525636 2 2

British Library Cataloguing in Publication Data
A catalogue record for this book is available from the British
Library

Produced in Great Britain
by
Trinity and All Saints University College
and
University Print Services
A division of Media Services at Leeds

CONTENTS

Our thanks are due to Gillian Goodwin for preparing the material for publication, to Michael O'Brien, Ruth Beetham and Gareth Rees for assistance with word-processing, and to Gwilym Rees for his editorial help.

The editors acknowledge with gratitude a generous grant towards the publication of this volume from the Cañada Blanch Foundation

FOREWORD

Ronald Cueto was born on 4 October 1932 in Maryport, Cumbria. Following his early education at Workington Grammar school, he gained a State Scholarship in 1950 and continued his studies at St Catharine's College, Cambridge. After graduating in 1954, he began his career teaching in Santander in northern Spain. Between 1959 and 1962 Ronald conducted research at the University of Madrid under the supervision of Professor Manuel Ballesteros. Having completed his doctoral thesis, he returned to England where he taught in Bromsgrove.

In 1966 he became the first Head of the Spanish Department at Trinity and All Saints College, Leeds. This was a new venture in what was then known as a College of Education. Trinity and All Saints was the first institution of its kind to provide initial training to intending teachers of Spanish by offering jointly a degree of the University of Leeds and qualified teacher status. As such, it had no precedent. Ronald met this challenge with characteristic imagination, style and scholarly rigour. His philosophy was that the teaching of Spanish could only be undertaken effectively by those who had been exposed to Spanish scholarship of the highest standard. This culminated in a course which was rigorous and wide-ranging whilst at the same time encouraging in his students an appreciation of Spanish culture in the broadest sense.

The continued respect and prestige which this Department enjoys owes a great deal to the vision and energy which Ronald devoted to its establishment.

In 1974, Ronald was appointed to the Department of Spanish and Portuguese at the University of Leeds where he was subsequently promoted to Reader in Spanish History in 1986. He retires from this post in September 1997. In addition to his outstanding academic record, Ronald contributed to the administration and management of the Department in numerous ways including holding the post of Acting Head of Department from 1987-1988.

A perusal of his publications and the courses he has taught indicates the diversity of Ronald's academic and scholarly interests. The breadth of his scholarship and his ability to treat a wide variety of themes are outstanding. He has published studies in areas as diverse as Art, Lorca, Cervantes, Golden Age, 19th-century and more recent Spanish history.

As a teacher, Ronald's contribution has been as wide as his academic interests. The courses he has offered to several generations of students have ranged from Golden Age and 19th- and 20th-century Spanish literature and history to a rare contribution as genuinely bilingual scholar to the teaching of the Spanish language.

However, Ronald's abiding interests and the ones to which he has devoted the greatest part of his endeavours are twofold. The first is an investigation of ecclesiastical history, especially in so far as Roman Catholicism has formed an integral part of Spanish history, politics and culture. The second is the history of the Castilian town of Segovia which, as those who know him well will testify, is where Ronald chooses to spend much of his time in Spain. Particularly in recent years, Ronald has been increasingly in demand as a visiting lecturer. Invitations have been forthcoming from bodies as diverse as several universities in Great Britain and elsewhere, the media, and the Ministry of Defence.

As a teacher Ronald made of his students the same demands of intellectual endeavour, honesty and integrity which characterise his own work. At the same time he was always understanding of, and sympathetic to, the gap between himself and those he taught. Whilst he has been known to modestly attribute this to the difference in age and academic experience between himself and his (mostly) very young students, the reality is, of course, very different. Few of us who had the privilege to be taught by Ronald Cueto could ever hope to emulate his erudition, breadth of knowledge or commitment to scholarship. Nevertheless, his personal and intellectual integrity have provided an unforgettable example to those of us who are fortunate to count him as a teacher, colleague or friend.

Monica Tomkiss

TERENCE O'REILLY

University College Cork

JORGE DE MONTEMAYOR AND THE POETRY
OF THE PSALMS

Jorge de Montemayor has long been associated with the origins of
modern fiction in sixteenth-century Spain, but if he had not
written *La Diana* he would probably be remembered today for his
pioneering work in another genre, poetry inspired by the psalms:
'fue uno de los primeros que sintieron la grave música de los
Salmos, y el primero, sin duda, que intentó hacerla cantar en
castellano con el ritmo nuevo del hendecasílabo'.[1] His familiarity
with the psalter is apparent in one of his early works, *Exposición
moral del psalmo LXXXVI* (1548), in which a prose commentary
on conventional lines accompanies a version of the psalm in
octosyllables, the traditional metre that Juan del Encina had used
in his earlier rendering of Psalm 50.[2] At this point in his life there
was no sign of an ambition to imitate the poetry of Scripture in the
new Renaissance metres that the works of Garcilaso and Boscán
were currently making popular. Six years later, however, in 1554,
he published in the new style a long sequence of poems on the
fourth penitential psalm, *Miserere mei Deus*, which he reissued in
1558, corrected and revised.[3] To create it he took as a model a
prose meditation by Savonarola that was being read throughout
Europe at the time, the *Expositio in Psalmum quinquagesimum*,
composed by the Dominican in prison shortly before his death in
1498. The Spanish translation of 1511, patronised by Cardinal
Cisneros, was reprinted often in the early sixteenth century, and
Montemayor had it before him, it seems, as he worked.[4] The
pages that follow examine in detail the ways in which he adapted

1

his source, and relate his poetic practice to the literary theories of the time.

Imitatio

Montemayor's decision to use the new style in his *Miserere* sequence ensured that it was influenced by contemporary notions of *imitatio*. As Anne Cruz has shown, the poetry of Garcilaso and Boscán was shaped by the debate in Italy between Pietro Bembo and Gianfrancesco Pico della Mirandola in which Bembo defended the imitation of a single model and Pico that of many.[5] Boscán followed Bembo, taking as his guide the *Rime*, and through them the *Canzoniere*, of Petrarch. Garcilaso followed Pico, drawing together in his works classical, Italian and *cancionero* sources. In the *Miserere* sequence Montemayor chose to imitate a single model, like Boscán before him. His attention was therefore focused on *elocutio*, the articulation of his model in verse.[6] However, a comparison of the sequence with its source shows that he also gave thoughtful attention to *inventio*, the selection of materials, and to *dispositio*, their ordering.

Inventio

In the course of writing his sequence Montemayor altered in two ways the material his model contained. First, he omitted certain passages, the most important of which were concerned with Savonarola himself and the circumstances in which his meditation had been composed. In the opening section he left out all the allusions to the prison cell in which the Dominican was awaiting execution, and in the concluding section he excised a mention of martyrdom that could have been interpreted as a reference to the author's impending end.[7] It may be, as some have suggested, that he omitted these passages in order to conceal his source, for Savonarola was a controversial figure and rapidly becoming a *persona non grata* at the time. In some Spanish editions of the meditation the author's identity is obscured, no doubt with such concerns in mind.[8] Other editions, however, make no attempt to conceal Savonarola's name and, since the prose meditation was so widely known, it is hard to believe that contemporary readers of the poem would have been unconscious of where its inspiration lay.

An alternative explanation may perhaps be found in Montemayor's practice of *imitatio*. Juan Luis Vives had argued that when imitating a single model a writer should study it carefully in order to create not a mere copy but a separate work with a distinctive intention of its own:

> Proposito autem ante oculos exemplari attentissime aemulator contempletur, ac consyderet qua tandem arte ac ratione ab autore id putet confectum ut simili artificio et ipse *quod animo destinarit*, perficiat.

> The zealous imitator should examine closely the proposed model before him and consider the art and procedure by which it was seemingly fashioned by the author, so that he too by similar means may produce *what he inwardly intends*.[9]

The omission of all references to the historical and biographical circumstances in which the original meditation was composed means that the poetic subject in Montemayor's sequence is anonymous. As a result the reader is free to identify with the lyric self it presents and to apply to his own situation the heartfelt prayers that it voices.

If such was the distinctive intention of Montemayor it indicates that he wished to imitate in his poem one of the most important features of the psalms in Christian tradition: their capacity to become in prayer a mirror of the religious self, one in which a reader could find reflected his own spiritual experience:

> in an age in which emphasis on a personal religion was renewed, the individual required models for self-examination, and standards for self-assessment... meditation on the psalms helped the individual to define the responsibilities of his position, to articulate his spiritual problems and to realise his relationship with God.[10]

It was this capacity that ensured their central place in the liturgy, as well as in the private devotions of individuals, both clerical and lay.

Other omissions made by Montemayor are consonant with such a purpose. One is a passage in which it is lamented that in the world at large Christians form a minority greatly outnumbered by pagans (f.72r), words written by Savonarola shortly after the New World was discovered and before the initial impact of Christian missions. Another is a section in which the enterprise of obtaining a plenary indulgence is warmly commended (f.56v). Neither passage would have seemed controversial when Savonarola was writing, but in Montemayor's day both would have seemed dated and struck a jarring note. The same may be said of Savonarola's lengthy commentary on the parable of a father and his hungry son which Montemayor left out also (f.63). The various foods mentioned (bread; an egg; a scorpion) are interpreted by the Dominican allegorically, in a scholastic mode that the exegesis of the humanists had made unfashionable, and that was associated in Spain with the poetic conventions of the fifteenth century rather than with the new Renaissance style.

The second way in which Montemayor altered his model was by adding to it passages of his own. His additions amount to approximately 260 lines, or *circa* 15% of the total, a higher figure than has generally been supposed.[11] Some additions are designed to replace omissions. In the opening section, for instance, the allusions to Savonarola's incarceration are replaced in part by an imitation of Manrique's famous *coplas* on his father's death.[12] Others serve to make explicit for the reader references to Scripture that Savonarola felt no need to explain. Most of them, however, underscore or expand theological themes that are already present, though less pronounced, in Savonarola's work. Foremost among them are the omnipotence of God; the weakness of fallen man; the sinner's dependence on grace; the need for faith in divine mercy; and, above all, the importance of gratitude for the salvation that Christ's Passion obtained. By such means, it may be argued, Montemayor developed the theology of Savonarola in order to bring it in line with the spirituality of the *beneficio de Cristo* that was current in his day.[13]

Dispositio

Apart from occasional cuts and additions Montemayor's poem normally follows the sequence of material in its model. It differs from it, however, in the way in which the text is subdivided and presented. In the Spanish version of Savonarola's meditation the reader is confronted with continuous prose in which the translated words of the *Miserere* psalm are usually, though not always, in bold type. Montemayor's poem, by contrast, is divided into twenty numbered sections, termed 'cánticas' in the first edition and 'omelías' in the second, which correspond to the twenty versicles of which the psalm is composed. At the head of each section Montemayor placed the text of the versicle in Latin, and beneath the Latin he supplied a version in Spanish, sometimes reproducing the one provided in his model, but more often reworking it to eliminate archaisms or to make it more accurate and complete.

These changes in presentation throw further light on the 'distinctive intention' that informs his poem. The reader's

5

attention is drawn by them, initially, to the literal text of the psalm, and is then focused on a spiritual interpretation of their sense in which the wisdom of the psalmist is appropriated by the anonymous lyric self, and applied in a prayerful fashion to its anguish. In this way, one might say, the poem offers the reader a practical demonstration of how the psalm may properly be read.

Contemporary reformers in Spain were much concerned to help people recover the psalter's spiritual sense. The Spanish translation of Erasmus' *Enchiridion* had warned against a reading of the psalms that went no deeper than the letter:

> Mejor te sabrá y mejor provecho te terná el entendimiento de un versico, si, quebrada la cáscara, sacares el meollo de dentro y rumiares bien en él, que si todo el psalterio cantases de boca, solamente atendiendo a la letra.[14]

In the same vein Montemayor's older contemporary Constantino Ponce de la Fuente lamented that although the psalms were recited by Christians in every walk of life few understood how to penetrate their interior sense:

> Entre los libros sagrados ninguno anda tan ordinario ni tan en las manos de todos como es el salterio. De toda suerte de gente por maravilla hay quien no reze salmos. No puede ser cosa mas acertada, y muchas vezes he mirado en ello. Mas quanto ella es mejor, tanto pone mayor lastima, ver quan friamente se passa por ellos, quan sin sentimiento y sin inteligencia de cosas tan grandes.[15]

It was to show people how to find a spiritual reading that Constantino composed his commentary on the psalm *Beatus vir*, following in this the example of Erasmus whose exegesis of the same psalm was already available in Spanish:[16]

Averiguadamente creo que, si, con ser tan común la lección de los salmos, uviesse juntamente guia de verdadera inteligencia, seria medio para alcançarse notable fruto y para que muchos que tienen oficio o devocion de rezarlos, sintiesen en sus corazones grande consuelo de la mano de Dios para los trabajos espirituales y corporales.[17]

An analogous concern to renew prayer based on the psalter is apparent in the various translations of the psalms into Spanish that were printed between 1529 and 1559, and it may have been one of the factors that made Savonarola's psalm meditations so popular among the contemporaries of Montemayor.[18]

Striking though it is, the respect for Scripture that Montemayor's poem reveals should be distinguished from the more learned approach of his humanist contemporaries who strove to renew appreciation of the psalms by studying them in Hebrew. The precedent set in this respect by Juan de Valdés, who was the first humanist to translate the Hebrew psalter into Spanish,[19] was carried further in the next generation by a group of scholar poets among whom Arias Montano and Luis de León were prominent.[20] Montemayor's poem stems from another tradition, based on the Gallican Psalter of St Jerome that was used in the public liturgy of the Church, a tradition that may be traced back before him to Juan del Encina, and that was continued after him in the psalm poems of later writers, notably San Juan de la Cruz and Lope de Vega.

Elocutio

Study of the process by which Montemayor transformed into hendecasyllables the prose meditation before him shows that he worked with varying degrees of fidelity to his model. In some parts the changes he made were minimal. One example is the passage in which Christ is invoked as the good Samaritan:

O ven, ven dulce Samaritano, y al llagado medio muerto
levantalo, cura mis llagas, vino y azeyte derrama sobre mi,
pon me sobre tu mula, trahe me al meson, encomienda me al
mesonero, dale dos dineros, y mandale que me cure.

(f.55r)

From this Montemayor shaped poetry by simply altering the order
of words and adding a few of his own:

Pues ven, Samaritano, dulce y bueno,
y levanta al llagado medio muerto.
Cura, señor, sus llagas, y derrama
sobre este pecador aceite y vino.
Ponme sobre tu mula, y tráeme luego
al mesón de tu gracia, y encomienda
mi ánima cuitada al mesonero.
Dale dinero, y manda que me cure,
y aun promete pagar lo que gastare,
que jamás sin pagar dexaste cosa.

(p.315)

Sometimes the adjustments made, though minor, have the
significant effect of creating a tone that is direct and informal,
even colloquial:

pues verdadero señor eres, cumple lo que prometiste, heme
aqui, yo peccador gimo, y te llamo, gimo porque se tornaron
a corromper mis llagas, las que ya curado señor me auias.

(f.51v)

Pues, ¡sus! ¡Heme aquí! Vengo a demandarte
que cumplas la palabra que nos diste.
Mis llagas me curaste, mas volvieron
por mi mal regimiento a renovarse.

(p.309)

In other parts Montemayor reworked his model more extensively. At one point, for instance, Savonarola reflects that Peter's bitter repentance for having betrayed Christ did not spur him to intervene in the Passion:

> Quien no creera que el dolor que de la negacion tiene le hara salir en medio del mundo, y en el consistorio de pilato entre los bozes de los Judios, entre aquel crucificalo, entre aquel su sangre sobre nos y sobre nuestros hijos, entre aquel si a estas dexas no seras amigo de Cesar, en aquella persuasion en que los pontifices al pueblo dezian que pidiessen a Barrabas y al redemptor matassen, en aquellas mayores agonias y acusaciones, quien no creera que saldras Pedro...
>
> (f.65r)

Montemayor's version is faithful to the sense, but expresses it in different terms and more vividly:

> Pues tras la fe cayó allí la noticia,
> mas no salió por eso entre las vozes
> de aquellos phariseos, quando pedían
> que su sangre sobre ellos se esparziese,
> ni allí se halló al tiempo que dixeron
> que a Barrabás soltasen, y que Christo
> crucificasen luego como a malo.
>
> (p.334)

At such moments Montemayor's version becomes a paraphrase in which, using his own words and *quasi uixta loquens*,[21] he interprets Savonarola's thought succinctly. Sometimes, admittedly, the paraphrase attains concision by sacrificing lively images and ideas, such as the comparison of divine wisdom with a nursing mother:[22]

Da me coraçon de niño porque si yo no me tornare como niño, no podre entrar en el reyno delos cielos. Haz me señor como vno delos tus niños que maman, porque siempre este yo colgado delas tetas de tu sabiduria, las quales muy buenas son, muy hermosas son, muy mas dulces que el vino.

(f.69r)

Pues dame una humildad, señor, tan grande,
que pueda bendecirte y alabarte,
y que me vuelva niño en la inocencia,
para que mejor hable en tus loores.

(p.341)

On the whole, however, the poem remains remarkably close to the spirit of its model, so close, in fact, that one modern reader has wondered, 'whether such a degree of capitalisation on another's work might be ethically dubious'.[23] Such scruples, it must be said, do not make sense in terms of sixteenth-century *imitatio* which allowed the relationship between the model and the new work to be 'as close or as distant as the imitator wished'.[24] If the model was a religious text, moreover, fidelity was more likely than invention. What mattered was that the imitation should have a distinctive intention of its own and therefore resemble its model 'not as a picture resembles its original for a picture is a lifeless thing', but 'as a child resembles its father'.[25]

The Literary Self

The Italianate style made accessible to Montemayor a number of techniques associated with what Paul Julian Smith has called a 'rhetoric of presence'.[26] One of them is the device known as *enargeia* (in Latin, *evidentia* or *illustratio*) which in its three modes of person, time and place may be observed in several passages, including the following:

Pues ves aquí, señor, ante tu cara
suplícote que no me alances de ella.
Ante tu gran bondad estoy en tierra,
en tí vengo a buscar misericordia,
y no espero de ti mala respuesta.
Pues no me eches, señor, avergonçado
delante de tu cara y confundido.
¿Quién vino a ti, mi Dios, que triste fuese?
¿Quién nunca te pidió que no le dieses?

(p.326)

Here immediacy of person is created by the use of apostrophe, heightened by *interrogatio*, in which what is signified by the subject pronouns 'tu' and 'yo' is both general and particular, universal and private. Through it the reader is drawn into an interior monologue directed by the poetic self towards the Other. Immediacy of time is realised by the use of the present tense, to which past and future are subordinate; and immediacy of place is conveyed by the use of 'aquí', as well as by small but vivid details that sketch the poet prostrate on the ground. By such means the passage may be said to fulfil the objective of *enargeia* as the manuals defined it: to so express something that is seen rather than heard; to place it before the reader's inner eye.[27]

Other techniques are connected with metre. Montemayor's decision to write his poem in hendecasyllables involved him in echoing in its pages the cadences of conversation. As F.J. Avila has shown, Garcilaso's notion of style was derived in part from Castiglione, whose *Cortegiano* he read with enthusiasm and persuaded Boscán to translate.[28] In the heated discussion of language described in the opening book a distinction between writing and speech is acknowledged, but the written language praised is one that resembles the spoken as much as possible. As one of the characters puts it in the version of Boscán:

> lo escrito no es otra cosa sino una forma de hablar que queda
> después que el hombre ha hablado... lo que se requiere en lo
> que se escribe se requiere también en lo que se habla.[29]

The ideal to which such words pointed was not confined to the
court and its concerns but also inspired writers involved in
religious reform, among them Juan de Valdés who observed in a
well known passage of the *Diálogo de la lengua*: 'el estilo que
tengo me es natural, y sin afetación ninguna escrivo como
hablo'.[30]

The new eleven-syllable line made it possible to realise the
aspiration in poetry, for unlike the medieval *canción* or *romance* it
did not involve, necessarily, regularity of stress or of rhyme. It
could therefore be used to imitate the inflexions of prose rather
than song, as understood by Aristotle in the *Art of Rhetoric*:

> The form of diction should be neither metrical nor without
> rhythm. If it is metrical, it lacks persuasiveness, for it
> appears artificial, and at the same time it distracts the
> reader's attention, since it sets him on the watch for the
> recurrence of such and such a cadence... wherefore prose
> must be rhythmical, but not metrical, otherwise it will be a
> poem. Nor must this rhythm be rigorously carried out, but
> only up to a certain point.[31]

It is clear from the *Miserere* sequence that by 1554
Montemayor was familiar with the poetic possibilities that the
new style had opened up as well as with the technical problems to
which it could give rise. The patterns of stress in the
endecasílabos sueltos that he chose to use enabled the imitation
of feelings and thoughts in a flowing, discursive style, as
Garcilaso had shown in the *Epístola a Boscán*, where such lines
are employed to create the easy, intimate tone expected in an

Horatian epistle.[32] At the same time the absence of patterned rhyme and of the strophic forms associated with it meant that the structure of individual lines required the closest attention:

> La renuncia a la rima y, por consiguiente, a la disposición estrófica más común permite formalmente la expresión de las ideas en forma más inmediata, y en las traducciones facilita una mayor fidelidad al original. La falta de rima y sus funciones, sin embargo, tiene que compensarse por una estructura rítmica especialmente cuidada y fluida de los versos.[33]

Montemayor rose to the challenge by combining in his poem features both regular and variable. In the *endecasílabo a maiore* that he normally used the fixed stress on the tenth syllable is accompanied by another on the sixth which is followed, in turn, by a *caesura*. The further main stress, by contrast, falls unpredictably on the first, second and third syllable, and sometimes on the fourth. The resulting metrical variety, which Montemayor was careful to sustain, is reinforced in his sequence by the use of enjambement and on occasion by the ending of a sentence in the course of a line rather than its end. By such means his poem creates the impression of a personal voice, intimate, confiding and emotional, an impression that may be said to spring from the interplay between speech and metre, 'between the sound the words would make if read as prose and the notional metrical pattern that constrains them'.[34]

The representation of the self that such techniques enabled had an acknowledged place in Renaissance poetic. In his debate with Pico, Bembo had affirmed that the activity of imitation involved reproducing not only another's style but 'that very temperament present in him whom you have chosen as a master',[35] and in his contribution to the same debate, the *Dialogus Ciceronianus*, Erasmus had urged that style should be the mirror of the mind:

> Quum tanta sit ingeniorum dissimilitudo, quanta vix est formarum aut vocum, mendax erit speculum, nisi nativam mentis imaginem referat, et hoc ipsum est, quod in primis delectat lectorem, ex oratione scriptoris affectus, indolem, sensum ingeniumque cognoscere, nihilo minus quam si complures annos cum illo consuetudinem egeris.

> Minds differ far more than voices and physical features do, and the mirror will lie unless it reflects the true born image of the mind. The very thing which the reader enjoys is getting to know the writer's feelings, character, disposition and type of mind from the way he writes, just as he would by living on familiar terms with him for several years.[36]

In the *Miserere* sequence the writer whom the reader comes to know is not Savonarola, whose meditation inspired it, nor Montemayor, whose poetic skills shaped it, but the 'implied author', the anonymous lyric self, whose voice is an imitation of the psalmist.

NOTES

1. Marcel Bataillon, *Erasmo y España. Estudios sobre la historia espiritual del siglo XVI* (Mexico: Fondo de cultura económica, 1966), p.608.

2. Michel Darbord, *La poésie religieuse espagnole des Rois Catholiques à Philippe II* (Paris: Institut d'Etudes Hispaniques, 1965), p.396.

3. The first edition (1554) has been published in *El cancionero del poeta George de Montemayor*, edited by Angel González Palencia (Madrid: La Sociedad de Bibliófilos Españoles, 1932), pp.304-351, from which all quotations in this article are drawn.

4. Marcel Bataillon, 'Une source de Gil Vicente et de Montemor: la méditation de Savonarole sur le *Miserere*' in his *Etudes sur le Portugal au temps de l'humanisme* (Coimbra: por ordem da Universidade, 1952), pp.197-217. The quotations from the meditation in the present article are drawn from the Spanish edition published in Antwerp in 1550, a copy of which is held in the British Library.

5. Anne J. Cruz, *Imitación y transformación. El petrarquismo en la poesía de Boscán y Garcilaso de la Vega* (Amsterdam and Philadelphia: John Benjamins, 1988).

6. Thomas Greene, *The Light in Troy* (New Haven: Yale University Press, 1982), pp.175,177.

7. Darbord, pp.406,413.

8. Marcel Bataillon, 'Sur la diffusion des oeuvres de Savonarole en Espagne et en Portugal (1500-1560) in *Mélanges de philologie, d'histoire et de littérature offerts à M. Joseph Vianey* (Paris: Les Presses Françaises, 1934), pp.93-103.

9.   Quoted in Rivkah Zim, *English Metrical Psalms. Poetry as Praise and Prayer 1535-1600* (Cambridge: Cambridge University Press, 1987), p.9.

10. Zim, p.203.

11. The figures are based on a comparison of Montemayor's poem with the meditation of Savonarola, the results of which I hope to publish in a forthcoming edition of the *Miserere* sequence.

12. Darbord, p.406.

13. This aspect is examined in detail in my article 'The Religious Context of Montemayor's *Omelías sobre Miserere Mei, Deus*', forthcoming in *Crown, Court and Church in Golden Age Iberia*, edited by Margaret A. Rees (Leeds: Trinity and All Saints College).

14. Quoted in Bataillon, *Erasmo y España*, p.195.

15. From the *dedicatoria* to his *Exposición del primer salmo* (Seville, 1546), quoted in María Paz Aspe Ansa, *Constantino Ponce de la Fuente. El hombre y su lenguaje* (Madrid: Universidad Pontificia de Salamanca and Fundación Universitaria Española, 1975), p.113.

16. Bataillon, *Erasmo y España*, pp.308-309.

17. Aspe Ansa, *loc.cit.*

18. Bataillon, *Erasmo y España*, pp.389; 596-597.

19. Juan de Valdés, *Diálogo de doctrina christiana y El Salterio traducido del hebreo en romance castellano*, edited by Domingo Ricart (Mexico: Universidad Nacional Autónoma, 1964).

20. Bataillon, 'Une source de Gil Vicente et de Montemor...', p.200.

21. Zim, p.12.

22. 'Il semble gêné par le réalisme ingénu': Bataillon, 'Une source de Gil Vicente et de Montemor...', p.208.

23. Bryant L. Creel, *The Religious Poetry of Jorge de Montemayor* (London: Tamesis, 1981), p.91.

24. Zim, p.15.

25. 'Etiam si cuius in te comparebit similitudo, quem admiratio tibi fixerit altius, similem esse te volo quomodo filium, non quomodo imaginem; imago res mortua est': Seneca, Epistle LXXXIV, in *Ad Lucilium Epistulae Morales*, edited and translated by Richard M. Gummere, 3 vols (Cambridge, Massachusetts and London: Harvard University Press, 1917), vol. 2, p.280.

26. Paul Julian Smith, *Writing in the Margin. Spanish Literature of the Golden Age* (Oxford: Clarendon, 1988), p.43.

27. Smith, pp.44-45.

28. See the introduction by Bienvenido Moros to his edition of Garcilaso de la Vega, *Obra poética y textos en prosa* (Barcelona: Crítica, 1995), pp.xliii, xlvi.

29. Baltasar Castiglione, *El Cortesano. Traducción de Juan Boscán* (Madrid: Saturnino Calleja, 1920), pp.64-65.

30. Juan de Valdés, *Diálogo de la lengua*, edited by José F. Montesinos (Madrid: Espasa-Calpe, 1926), pp.154-155.

31. Aristotle, *The 'Art' of Rhetoric*, translated by John Henry Freese (London and Cambridge: Heinemann, 1947), p.383. I am grateful to my colleague Anne Walsh for drawing my attention to this passage.

32.   Garcilaso de la Vega, pp.115-119; 452-456.

33.   Rudolph Baehr, *Manual de versificación española*, translated into Spanish by K. Wagner and F. López Estrada (Madrid: Gredos, 1970), p.78.

34.   John Stevens, *The Old Sound and the New. An Inaugural Lecture* (Cambridge: Cambridge University Press, 1982), p.16.

35.   Quoted in Thomas Greene, *The Light in Troy*, p.174.

36.   Greene, p.184; Erasmus, *The Ciceronian: A Dialogue on the Ideal Latin Style*, translated and annotated by Betty I. Knott, Collected Works of Erasmus, vol. 28 (Toronto, Buffalo and London: University of Toronto Press, 1986), p.440.

A.D. WRIGHT

University of Leeds

THE ENGLISH CATHOLIC COMMUNITY:
ALTERNATIVES TO MARTYRDOM?

The canonisation in 1970 of the Forty Martyrs of England and Wales was rightly a cause of rejoicing. The forty Recusants were themselves drawn from 199 beatified in, variously, 1886, 1895, 1929, and those in turn from a potential figure, 357, of those executed between 1535 and 1680 for whom causes had formally been opened. At the head of this band of witnesses, as it were, stand More (beatified 1886) and Fisher, both canonised in 1935. But to celebrate such official ecclesiastical declarations of sanctity, finally delivered, is not necessarily to pursue the most fruitful path to historical analysis and understanding. The tasks of hagiography and historiography are necessarily distinct.

In 1591, Robert Parsons, writing to the Cardinal Nephew, Sfondrato from Seville, recalled warmly the hospitality of Charles Borromeo at Milan, which he and Edmund Campion had received years before, on their way to England.[1] Famously Campion was martyred, Parsons was not. Yet Parsons, until his death in Rome in 1610, kept up a literary discourse designed to deter English Catholics from accommodation with the Protestant regime, urging the necessity of absolute Recusancy. But at a not much later date, the impressive achievement of the English Catholic community was celebrated at Milan with a subtly but crucially different emphasis. The successor-but-one to Charles Borromeo in the archbishopric of Milan, his younger relation Federico Borromeo, wished to confront the casual and careless inattention of Italians in church with the admirable devotion of a

19

contrasting Catholic community, in a vernacular sermon for the feast of All Saints, posthumously published, as the Second Sermon in Book IX of his collected sermons, at Milan in 1646. The archbishop tells of a live witness to conditions as they were in England in the recent past, where the Catholic community could only worship clandestinely, in fear and danger. Such necessarily private worship brought the faithful together in obscure prisons, harsh confinement, in conditions of detention, among criminals, amid stocks and chains. Certainly the cries of the tortured might be heard, the shedding of blood and the wounding and breaking of bodies might suggest the ever present threat of death. But what was in this account held up for admiration was the perseverance, the constancy, the unfaltering devotion of the Catholic community, their continuity in the faith, not precisely their deaths.[2] This passage might indeed be compared with letters written by Federico in 1595, at the time he first became archbishop of Milan. In one, of 2 September, he gratefully acknowledges receipt of relics of an English martyr, Saint Thomas of Canterbury, and promises continued help at Milan to English Catholics.[3] In the other, of 8 November, he acknowledges the arrival of portraits of More and Fisher, heroic figures, clearly, but not at this date canonised saints; commemorated in portraits, not venerated in relics.[4] Since Milan was one of the most important centres of the Italian Counter-Reformation, and a place where British Catholics were known and sometimes worked, under both Charles and Federico Borromeo, a further investigation of these responses to the condition of Catholicism in the British Isles might prove worthwhile.[5]

William Warmington was born about 1566 and died in 1612. He followed a path from Oxford to Douai which John Bossy, some time ago, well established as typical of an initial style of response to the problem of religious proscription in Elizabethan England.[6] Indeed he eventually became chaplain to the leader of this first 'programme' of response, Cardinal Allen, and by the time of the latter's death in 1594 was noted as his *maestro di casa*. But he should not be seen as utterly distinct from the next wave of English Catholic exiles, those preparing for mission rather than awaiting better times in studious preparation in extended residence abroad. For after being priested at Douai in 1580, he did indeed return to England, from where he was deported by 1585. The death of Cardinal Allen left the English Catholics on the continent in some state of uncertainty, deprived of a clear source of native leadership and patronage, especially when the papacy did not appoint another native as 'Cardinal of the English' in succession to Allen, who had been a cardinal since 1587.[7] Warmington himself found, as British Catholic exiles on occasion did, a place in which to serve the Church, precisely at Milan. Indeed he entered the elite body of diocesan clergy founded by St. Charles, the Oblates of St. Ambrose, whose special vow of obedience to the Milanese archbishop of the day thus paralleled the extra, fourth vow of absolute obedience to the papacy taken in the universal Church by the inner elite of the Society of Jesus. Since this body of clergy, the Oblates, was precisely diocesan, it was rare for the archbishops to release any for service outside Milan. Yet Warmington was, unusually, given leave, in order to return to England. He was thus a figure who had been at the heart of the English Catholic community in exile, and at the heart of the Italian Counter-Reformation. But after he was apprehended in 1608, he was not martyred, but eventually died in the household of Thomas Bilson, bishop of Winchester, to which he had been directed by James I, after appealing to the king for some material support. What led to this unexpected conclusion was not, however, apostasy, at least as commonly understood. His arrest confronted him sharply with the practical problem then dividing the English Catholic community, the legitimacy of taking an oath of allegiance to the monarch. It was this specific issue, not his faith as such, which divided him from others (though by definition not all) in the community, especially after in 1612 he published in defence of taking the oath, was released on indeed taking it, and then published other reflections on the policies of Sixtus V and the death of Henri III of France.[8]

It should not, however, be thought the continental, non-British leaders of the Counter-Reformation were naive about Catholic exiles from the British Isles. The possibility of double-agents, for example, seems to have been understood. Henry Constable was also recommended to Federico Borromeo, but the archbishop seems to have avoided further contact with him. Constable (1562-1613) was indeed a very different figure from Warmington. From Cambridge he moved to Paris, leading a Catholic life as a lay author. His apparent interest in detaching English Catholics from reliance on Spain, moving them to a greater connection with France again, in itself, represents a clearly defined alternative attitude among the English Catholic community, well identified some years ago by John Bossy.[9] In that context his visit to Edinburgh in 1598-99, seeking an interview with the Scots king, alleging that he came with papal authorisation, might possibly be regarded as largely plausible. After his return to Paris he ventured to England uninvited, in 1603-4, was arrested and released, and died at Liège in 1613. But more suspect contacts, from a Catholic point of view, included correspondence with Walsingham in 1584-85, and by 1595 with Anthony Bacon, secretary to Essex.[10] His case is nevertheless a reminder that not all Catholic exiles from Britain were priests. The scholar Thomas Dempster was born, possibly, in 1579, and before his death in 1625 his career began with a move, once again, from Cambridge to Paris. His desire to study in a Catholic environment was further confirmed by his move to Louvain. Yet he did not initially remain there, but was sent on to Rome by the president of the Scots College, the Jesuit William Crichton, in response to a papal scheme for providing such education for Scots. Ill health however brought him back to Douai, with a pension from the Spanish authorities. Nevertheless his first teaching posts were in the alternative exile of France, at Paris and Toulouse. Visits to Scotland and England allowed him, in the latter case, to marry, but he returned to Catholic territory, to Rome and Florence, despite further visits to London. Tuscan patronage had given him a chair at the university of Pisa, but he moved on to Bologna, in the papal states, to a chair to which he was appointed by the papal authorities there. His precocious classical scholarship and antiquarian erudition established his reputation. But he had to clear himself at Rome on a charge, brought by an Englishman, concerning heretical books. Moreover in 1621 his intended publication on Roman antiquities was placed on the Index, in the category of works awaiting necessary correction, and in 1623 a volume entitled 'Scotia Illustrior' was prohibited. Yet he remained in Bologna until his death, during the pontificate of the learned Urban VIII. Unlike Constable, then, he might perhaps be more surely considered a Catholic layman who chose to live in a Catholic society. For behind the denunciation which appeared to initiate his troubles over his publications may well have been personal, indeed domestic, rather than religious infidelities. At the time of his death his wife was fleeing from him, accompanied by her lover; and she had already left him once, during his Pisan professorship, precisely for an Englishman.[11]

If in Warmington we find a seemingly conscientious Catholic priest, willing to return to serve in England, but among those who thought a legitimate path for the Catholic community lay through an oath of allegiance, in Dempster we arguably have a Briton who was more than willing to lead the life of a Catholic lay scholar, even at the cost of exile from Scotland. In neither case did martyrdom follow, and yet both were in some sense part of a Catholic community which was in the end preserved, whether at home or abroad. Moreover those British Catholics who in the end remained in exile, and did not return to the British Isles, who therefore ran no risk of martyrdom, included those clearly appreciated by leaders of the continental Counter-Reformation, who evidently did not regard exile as a totally unacceptable alternative to potential martyrdom on mission. Griffith Roberts was already in exile from Wales when he took his M.D. at Siena. He contributed to the attempt to maintain Catholic allegiance in Wales by publishing in Welsh, at Rouen in 1585, 'The Christian Mirror', but had prepared for this by publishing a tripartite treatise on Welsh grammar in 1567. The latter was published at Milan, and his subsequent priestly service there may have included his acting (c.1590) as confessor to the young Federico Borromeo, and appeared to culminate, by 1611, in the important post of canon theologian at Milan cathedral.[12] In this way he was following in the footsteps of a major Welsh servant of Charles Borromeo, Lewis Owen (1532-1594), whose career began at Winchester and New College, before the typical move to Douai. As part of Allen's circle he was involved in the direction of the English colleges in exile, but from Rome went to Milan to act as a major diocesan official for Charles Borromeo, prior to his employment by the pope himself, in canonic visitation of the Rome diocese, and his appointment as bishop of Cassano, in Southern Italy, from 1588. He was also sent as papal nuncio to the Swiss, and for a while, during the archiepiscopate of the immediate successor of St. Charles, Archbishop Visconti, helped to keep an eye at Rome on the then rather troubled affairs of the Milanese diocese.[13] During the subsequent archiepiscopate (1595-1631) of Federico Borromeo, the scholarly abilities of a Scots priest, David Colvil, were welcomed by the archbishop, in his promotion of Arabic studies at Milan.[14] From the circles of British priests in exile also came Daniel Halsworth (or Holdsworth), who from Douai and Rheims came to the English

College, Rome, and was priested by another exile, Thomas Goldwell, in 1583. By the agreement of Cardinal Allen he did not return on mission to England, but continued his studies in Italy. He was thus sufficiently well qualified to act as a theological adviser to Charles Borromeo apparently, before the latter's death in 1584, and also provided tuition for the young Federico Borromeo.[15] A parallel figure, William Shepreve (or Shepery, 1540-98), left Oxford for Rome, where he apparently was awarded his D.D. Certainly his learning enabled him to advise the post-Tridentine bishop (subsequently archbishop) of Bologna, the colleague of Charles Borromeo, Gabriele Paleotti.[16] Bologna and Milan had been distinguished as the two great examples, outside Rome, of the implementation of Conciliar reform, in the restoration of Catholic life after the Council of Trent, by the learned exile Gregory Martin, best known for his biblical scholarship. His career had of course taken him, from the Saint John's College, Oxford, of the young Campion, to Allen's Douai, to his visit to Rome in 1577, before his death at Rheims in 1582.[17]

Such figures, it might be argued, merely confirm the point, well established by John Bossy, that an initial form of Catholic reaction to the facts of the Elizabethan succession in England, as they emerged, was typified by but not confined to the response of Allen, involving prolonged exile and the employment of Catholic learning, as opposed to a second generation committed to immediate mission and therefore the very real risk of martyrdom. So much, indeed, is obvious, but the necessary and valuable classification of such positions was perhaps clearer by accident than design. Thomas Goldwell, after all, was involved both with the Marian Catholic restoration in England itself and with the Theatines as they evolved in Italy. After participation in the Council of Trent in 1562 he was by 1563 acting in the service of Borromeo at Milan, and later assisted the Cardinal Vicar of Rome. But though his career in that sense seems to place him entirely with the long term exiles, not among the missioners, it was age and ill health which caused him to drop out of Campion's mission, at Rheims in 1580, before his death in Rome in 1585. On the other hand the pattern of prolonged exile in the service of the Catholic Church did not simply end with the passing of an initial generation. William Gifford (1554-1629) moved from Oxford to Louvain where the young Bellarmine taught, and then to Paris, Rheims and Rome. Recalled to Rheims by Allen, in 1582, he taught there and took his D.D. at Pont-à-Mousson. When Allen became a cardinal he too moved to Rome until Allen's death in 1594, and then apparently assisted the Milanese Church, by virtue of his connection with Lewis Owen, in an epoch when the affairs of the English College, Rome, had been distinctly troubled. But given his own entry into the Benedictines (from 1608), he was soon involved in the parallel dispute over the right of English Benedictines to play their part in mission in England itself, and, so, the issue of their status and organisation. From 1611 he himself headed the English Benedictines in Paris, and from 1617 was president of the Benedictine English Congregation. He was thus eminently involved with provision of some native Benedictines for service in England, despite his appointment as archbishop of Rheims from 1622.[18]

Moreover, the path of exile chosen by those who remained abroad and did not therefore risk martyrdom, was evidently accepted by leaders of the Italian Counter-Reformation as honourable and in its own way valuable. Catholic communities in the British Isles, for their preservation, needed constant supplies of priests, not least in a time of possible martyrdom; but such priests could only be educated abroad. For those vowed to go immediately on mission, the danger was of course known and calculated, as the depictions on the walls of the chapel at the English College, Rome, reminded them. But while the martyrs were admired without doubt, they were not, at the time, canonised. Perhaps a more fruitful historiographic, as opposed to hagiographic, category relevant to that time itself would thus be heroism rather than canonic sanctity. Exiles as well as martyrs, and above all the clandestine worshipping communities of the faithful in England, might all perhaps have been seen as heroic. More and Fisher were clearly heroic, though not canonised, for Federico Borromeo. His relation, Charles, was canonised in 1610, but was not a martyr. Philip Neri (died 1595), Ignatius Loyola (died 1556), Teresa of Avila (died 1582), Francis Xavier (died 1552) were not canonised until 1622, but none were martyrs, any more than Isidore Agricola, canonised with them, was a martyr of Protestant repression. Before that, Francesca Romana, canonised in 1608, was not a martyr, and the few canonisations prior to that, after a resumption of canonisations in 1588 following a sixty-three-year interval, involved figures like Raymond of Peñaforte, who was not a martyr. In 1588 the pope also set up the Congregation of Sacred Rites, which thenceforth controlled the rigorous procedures for canonisation, a legal process which became more stringent still under Clement VIII, Paul V, Gregory XV and above all Urban VIII. Certainly these same popes were taking steps to control the movement of authentic relics too, but these were essentially relics from the Roman catacombs of saints who were regarded as such because they were presumed to be martyrs.[19] The varieties of heroism demonstrated by the English Catholics of the era certainly included martyrdom, but clandestine conditions hardly favoured the precise legal authentication of relics and of witness statements, concerning candidates for canonisation, which Roman procedure now demanded. In the later sixteenth and early seventeenth century English Catholic martyrs were perhaps a striking example of heroism, but they had to await twentieth-century declaration of sanctity.

Yet it is ultimately arguable that it was the totality of the forms of heroism which preserved the English Catholic community. The case for the necessary role of the so-called Church Papists in allowing the preservation of faith and practice in the British Isles has now, arguably, been made more convincing than ever by recent scholarship.[20] It could certainly be suggested that for England and Scotland at least, even if Ireland presents a different case, the wider community of Church Papists allowed not only lay Catholicism as such to avoid cumulative eradication, but also preserved those opportunities out of which fresh generations of candidates for the Catholic priesthood could come, for their necessary training abroad. For a continued supply of priests was of course vital for the survival of a Catholic community in any meaningful sense, irrespective of deaths precisely from martyrdom. The contrast with the case of Japan, where exclusion of Europeans came too soon for the successful establishment of a self-perpetuating native clergy, and a clandestine lay community therefore remained deprived of all sacraments except baptism, surely remains valid. The presence of the penumbra of Church Papists, even if by a paradox, enabled a Catholic priesthood to survive which could, and did, minister both to absolute Recusants and, on occasion, to Church Papists themselves.[21] In the late sixteenth and early seventeenth century the Catholic Church of the European Counter-Reformation was promoting the cult of the relics of those who were regarded as early Christian saints because they were presumed to be martyrs. But for contemporary British martyrs, there was no corresponding immediate assumption of canonic sanctity. Historians of these events might perhaps be nearer to the range of views held at the time if they were to enlarge their vision to the varieties of heroism exemplified by the British Catholic communities, rather than confine their attention to the undoubtedly outstanding category of the martyrs.

NOTES

1. Letter of Parsons to Card. Sfondrato, Seviglia alli 18 d'Aprile 1591: Archivio Segreto Vaticano: Segreteria di Stato: Spagna [A.S.V. Spagna]: Vol. 38: f.420 r; cf. J. Bossy, 'The Character of Elizabethan Catholicism', *Past and Present*, xxi (1962), 39 sqq.: p.45.

2. *I Sacri Ragionamenti Sinodali* – Vol. Nono – In Milano – MDCXLVI: Nel Giorno di tutti i Santi – Rag. II, pp. 407 sqq.: p.412.

3. Biblioteca Ambrosiana, Milan [B.A.], MS G.260 inf., Mins. of letters of Federico (under date, f..284 r, adi 2 di 7bre 95): Al Cardl. Pinelli; A Monsr. di Cassano [Owen], f.284 r – v; cf. A.A. King, *Liturgies of the Primatial Sees* (London 1957), p.335.

4. Portraits of both at Federico's foundation, the Ambrosiana: Minute of letter of Federico (under date, f.319 v, adi 8 di Novre. [15] 95): Al Sr. Ugo Grissone: Ambrosiana, Milan, MS G.260 inf., f.319 v.

5. *Calendar of State Papers – Milan* (London 1912) [C.S.P. Milan] sub anno 1560 sqq.; cf. *Storia di Milano* (Fondazione Treccani degli Alfieri), X (Milan 1957), p.162; Gregory Martin, *Roma Sancta* [1581]. First ed. from the MS by G.B. Parks (Rome 1969), pp. 255 sq.; Federico Borromeo, *Patentes Litterae* [s.l.n.d.; Mediolani post 1629], p.12: Universis Angliae Regni Catholicis — Mediolani. Non. Augusti MDCXXIII; L.von Pastor, *History of the Popes* (London 1891 sqq.), xxix, 29; cf. H.O. Evennett, *The Spirit of the Counter-Reformation* (Cambridge 1968), pp.85, 144.

6. Bossy, 'The Character'.

7. Letter from Rome, alli 8 Agosto 1587: Archivio Arcivescovile, Milano: Carteggio Ufficiale: Vol. 65: Q.15 [f. 4 r], from Owen; cf. Visconti to Allen: ibid., Vol.115: f.60 v; cf. P.Hughes, *Rome*

and the Counter-Reformation in England [London] (1942), p.293.

8. *Dictionary of National Biography* [D.N.B.] (63 vols., London 1885-1900), s.v.; *C.S.P. Milan,* pp.610 sq.; E. Fustella, 'Biografie dei Sacerdoti che si fecero oblati dal 1586 al 1600', *Memorie storiche della diocesi di Milano,* xiii (1966), 47 sqq.: pp. 97 sq.; Permission in Archivio Arcivescovile, .Sezione VIII.

9. J. Bossy, 'Rome and the Elizabethan Catholics: A question of geography', *Historical Journal,* VII, i (1964),135 sqq.; cf. 'The Character', pp.55-6.

10. *D.N.B.* s.v.; Min. of Federico, Ambrosiana G.261 inf., f.519 v [1600?].

11. *D.N.B.* s.v.; cf. *Storia d'Italia,* ed. R. Romano and C. Vivanti, V, ii [I Documenti] (Turin 1973), 1454.

12. *D.N.B.* s.v.; cf. A.Turchini, *La fabbrica di un santo* (Casale Monferrato 1984), pp. 73, 75, 104, 109; A. Rimoldi, 'Gaspare Visconti, I Seminari e gli Oblati', *Studia Borromaica,* I (1987), 57-73: p.63.

13. Letter of Owen to Seneca from Rome, 22 Agosto 1587: Arch. Arcivesc. Cart. Uff.: Vol. 65: Q.14[f.6r]; Letters of Owen to Morra from17 di Maggio 1587 to 10 Ott. 1587, all from Rome: ibid., Q.5[f.2r], Q.11 [f.3r,f.6r-7r], Q.12[f.1r-v,f.4r], Q.14[f.4r], Q.15[f.4r]; Letter of 17 di Maggio 1587: Q.5 [f. 2r]; Letter of 10 Ott.1587: Q.11 [f. 6r – 7r]; Nuncio in Spain, (Bishop of Novara), to Card. Montalto: Di Madrid li V. di Marzo MDLXXXViii: A.S.V. Spagna: Vol.34: f.196 r sqq.; C. Marcora, 'Serie cronologica dei vicari generali della diocesi di Milano', *Memorie storiche della diocesi di Milano,* vi (1959), 252 sqq.: p. 275; cf. *D.N.B.,* xi, 1073; *Decadis Quartae Historiarum Mediol. Ecclesiae Sive de Pontificatu Gasparis Vicecomitis Libri Duo — ab auctore Petro Paulo Bosca* — Mediolani MDCLXXXII, p.104; Hughes, *Rome and the Counter-Reformation in England,* pp.162 sq., 199, 212; J. Bossy, *The English Catholic Community 1570-1850* (London 1975), pp.25-8.

14. Rivola, *Vita di Federico Borromeo* (Milan 1656), p.660; Petri Pauli Boschae, *De Origine. et Statu Bibliothecae Ambrosianae* (Mediolani MDCLXXII), p.142.

15. *D.N.B.* s.v.; C. Castiglioni, *Il cardinale Federico Borromeo* (Turin 1931), p.59; C. Marcora, 'La biografia del card. Federico Borromeo scritta dal suo medico personale' *Mem. stor. della dioc. di Mil.*, xv (1968), 125 sqq.: p.136.

16. *D.N.B.* s.v.; cf. Augustini Bruni De Vita Cardinalis Gabrielis Paleoti —: f.53r: Biblioteca Vallicelliana, Roma, MS E.48; P. Prodi, *Il cardinale Gabriele Paleotti*, II (Rome 1967), 235 n. 55; Gregory Martin, *Roma Sancta*, pp.263 sq.; cf. pp.251 sq.

17. *D.N.B.* s.v. *Roma Sancta*, chapter 34, esp. p.253; cf. Bossy, 'The Character', p.45; P. Guilday, *The English Catholic Refugees on the Continent 1558-1795 i: The English Colleges and Convents in the Catholic Low Countries 1558-1795* (London 1914), pp. 76 sq.

18. *D.N.B.* s.v. Goldwell; for Gifford: *D.N.B.* s.v; Rivola, *Vita*, p.643; Federico Borromeo, Letter to unknown recipient, s.l.n.d.: *Patentes Litterae* cit., p. 29; cf. D. Knowles, *The Religious Orders in England*, III (Cambridge 1959), 444 sqq.; *C.S.P. Milan*, pp. 611 sqq.; Bossy, *English Catholic Community*, pp.28; 33.

19. Ditchfield, *Liturgy. Sanctity and History in Tridentine Italy. Pietro Maria Campi and the Preservation of the Particular* (Cambridge 1995).

20. A.Walsham, *Church Papists: Catholicism. Conformity and Confessional Polemic in Early Modern England* (Woodbridge 1993).

21. A.D.Wright, 'Catholic History, North and South' *Northern History*, XIV (1978),126-51; 'Catholic History, North and South, Revisited', ibid., XXV (1989), 120-34.

JOHN A. JONES

University of Hull

'CON LA PLUMA EN LA MANO': THE BOND OF WORDS BETWEEN BENITO ARIAS MONTANO AND PEDRO DE VALENCIA

As every student of the Renaissance knows, letter-writing was a favourite pastime of Renaissance humanists. This is substantiated by the many large collections of letters that survive and which constitute a most valuable source of information on all kinds of subjects.[1] A recurring element in many of these letters either implicitly or explicitly is the friendship that unites the writers and the addressees. Examples of this are numerous, and we need look no further for illustration than the letters of the humanist *par excellence*, Erasmus himself. The bonds of friendship forged by the pen, however, were not restricted to letters but also found expression in other forms of writing which linked scholars to each other, for example, poems, prologues and dedications to books. It is some examples of these that this paper aims to highlight in relation to the friendship that existed between the two key Spanish humanists, Benito Arias Montano and Pedro de Valencia.

The friendship between the two men is well known.[2] It has many different facets which shed valuable light on intellectual life in Spain at the time. What interests us here, however, is how the friendship that united them was initiated and nourished through the pen and words. As with many other humanist friendships, what we find in Arias Montano and Pedro de Valencia is a relationship which is the fruit of the two men's command of language, of their thirst for reading and of their devotion to writing. It was these common humanist skills and interests that brought them together in the first place.

The initial contact between Valencia and Montano was made through the written word, in fact through the Word of God, namely, the Polyglot Bible that Arias Montano edited and published in 1572.[3] Valencia's admiration for this monumental work of biblical scholarship was essentially what motivated him to visit Arias Montano at La Peña de Aracena, Montano's retreat near Seville which Valencia could reach relatively easily from his nearby home-town of Zafra. It would be writing and words which from then on would link the two permanently, for Pedro de Valencia soon became Arias Montano's amanuensis. Montano had been looking for someone who could help him with his many scholarly undertakings but he had not had much luck in finding a suitable person. In Pedro de Valencia, however, he found the spiritual and intellectual qualities he was looking for, and, in fact, Valencia then devoted a large part of his life to acting as amanuensis for the scholar who became his friend and mentor and whom he would come to regard almost like a father. The task of transcribing would later develop so that their friendship, which lasted until Montano's death in 1598, also led Valencia into other areas such as translating, editing, explaining and defending what Montano had written. Words and writing were therefore at the centre of the friendship, and there are many illustrations of this in the large body of manuscript and published material that has survived. A good example is Valencia's defence of passages from Arias Montano's works censored in the Roman Expurgatory Index of 1607, or his defence of the Polyglot Bible against the proposed emended reprint that Andrés de León wished to publish.[4] These and other manuscripts give some idea of the sheer physical effort involved simply in sitting with pen in hand transcribing or composing. More interestingly, many of these works also show how this close contact provided a channel of influence and led to the transmission of ideas and views. Pedro de Valencia's writings are often informed by what he has learned from his friend and mentor, and he frequently openly acknowledges this. The writings of both Valencia and Montano contain many comments relating to their deep friendship. In particular, we find clear acknowledgements of this relationship and of the attitudes which nourished it in many of the letters they wrote to diverse friends and colleagues.

In the case of Arias Montano, these contacts were wide-ranging and included Christopher Plantin, the French printer, Justus Lipsius, Abraham Ortelius and many others.[5] Fewer letters survive in the case of Pedro de Valencia, but these comprise extremely interesting ones written to Montano and Valencia's common friend and colleague and librarian at El Escorial, fray José de Sigüenza. This group of letters constitutes one of the best illustrations of the spirit of friendship that linked Arias Montano and Pedro de Valencia to each other as well as to others. In these letters, we find numerous comments that Valencia makes about his relationship and collaboration with Montano which also point to the close connection between Montano and Sigüenza, as well as with others. However, it is not upon this evidence that we wish to focus but on three other pieces of writing which were the result of the friendship between Montano and Valencia. These texts are two prefaces written by Valencia for collections of poems by Montano, and a dedication that the latter wrote to his commentary on Psalm XXXI in his book, *In XXXI Davidis Psalmos Priores Commentaria* (Antwerp, 1605). The first two of these have been mentioned briefly in other studies, but the third, the dedication, has hardly received attention, hence the transcription of it which is included below.

The works for which the prefaces were written were Montano's *Poemata in Quatuor Tomos Distincta* (1589) and *Hymni et Secula* (1593), collections of poems on biblical themes.

The two prefaces are of interest in several ways. Juan Alcina has already written briefly but usefully on the preface for *Hymni et Secula.* His comments relate to the place of Arias Montano's poems in the general context of Latin poetry in the peninsula.[6] Pedro de Valencia's most recent biographer, Luis Gómez Canseco, has echoed Alcina's comments.[7] My purpose is to highlight aspects of the prefaces, so far only available in the original published volumes, which are interesting in relation to the friendship between Montano and Valencia but which also point to aspects of the contemporary debate about the nature and role of poetry.

Pedro de Valencia's best-known views on poetry are those relating to Góngora since they have been closely scrutinized by *gongoristas.*[8] More recently, Gómez Canseco has reminded us of Valencia's approval of Fernando de Herrera's *Versos emendados i divididos por él en tres partes* (Seville, 1619) which Valencia welcomed 'por la estimación que se deve a la buena memoria d'el Autor, y la elegancia de sus Poesías: que en ingenio, erudición y lenguaje se pueden comparar con las que más, en este género, celebró la antigüedad, i preferir a muchas de las que oi se precian las naciones estrangeras'.[9] Well before writing either of the above, Valencia had written the prefaces for Arias Montano's books of poems which we wish to highlight here.

Valencia begins his preface to *Poemata* by sounding a word of warning. This immediately relates to the general context of the debate about poetry and the negative views of it deriving from Plato's *Republic* which 'claim that it is better for men to do without any utility it may have, and its delights, however great these may be, than seduced and captivated by its charm to be pierced unawares by its dart and indeed infected and destroyed by its vain and poisonous teaching'.[10] Valencia counters this view by drawing a distinction between good and bad poetry, recalling Pythagoras's defence of the useful and true Muses. He acknowledges the existence and circulation of bad poetry which he agrees lacks divine inspiration and contains foolish, empty superstitions, and temptations and incitements to depravity. Alluding to the issues of appearance and reality, instruction and entertainment, he, however, rejects the defence of such poetry on allegorical grounds which point to a hidden meaning for it. The element of teaching such poetry contains is usually very small; rather than sweet honey it contains venomous poison, and it is certainly dangerous for young boys to read it even though perhaps experienced men may not be harmed by it. The issue of appearance and reality, of the external covering and the inner message, leads him to consider the matter of myth which he says many claim is essential to poetry. Valencia rejects this, raising the necessity of truth as a central element in good poetry together with simple language, albeit full of sweetness and elegance. He directs us to the Bible for examples of poetry which 'contains true benefit and unalloyed pleasure, and is such as may be studied with profit and without any risk by unsophisticated readers'.[11] This last comment is interesting in relation to his previous reference to the reading of poetry by boys, for Valencia has in mind poems which may be read with profit not only with regard to content but also to the rules and grammar of the Latin language. He therefore sets a specifically didactic aim which he, in fact, later encouraged in Zafra. Unsurprisingly, the types of poems he commends may be found in the poems of Arias Montano whom he describes as 'a man outstanding in piety and learning, one such as no one can find wanting in Latinity, or poetic grace and metre, or in style and elegance'.[12] Valencia's praise of the poems is high, and strongly emphasises their didactic purpose and, indeed, certain utilitarian aspects:

> There is no reason ... why these poems should not take their place in the hands of Christian men, and certainly no others ... are more suitable for boys to read, and learn

and commit to memory. Examples may be taken from them to illustrate the elements of grammar, the refinements of the Latin language, the principles of rhetoric and the various verse forms, so that without noticing it (and this is the golden rule in teaching boys) they are in the process imbued with the teaching which will be of greatest practical use to them when they grow up.[13]

Valencia's words provide us with valuable hints on teaching and the contemporary syllabus, and they certainly show him to be a good promoter of Montano's book. In fact, he openly acknowledges his awareness of the danger he runs in saying too much about the poems of a man who is so close to him:

I would go on to commend these poems further, if they were not immediately about to commend themselves, and if I were not liable to be accused of too great an affection for the poet. And indeed I admit that he is greatly revered and loved by me, but I cannot be satisfied that he is yet loved as much as he deserves, considering all I owe him.[14]

In commending both the poet and the poems, Valencia thus openly acknowledges his debt to Montano. These comments, however, go beyond the mere personal level and are probably also conditioned by a desire to defend the position of Montano who, since the publication of the *Biblia Regia*, had been under attack and whose image was therefore somewhat tarnished. The more idealistic elements alluded to by Valencia therefore need to be complemented by more down-to-earth, more mundane preoccupations resulting from rivalries and tensions of the time which might lead to further criticism of Montano for indulging in a dubious practice such as the writing of poetry. Similarly, a mixture of elements may be detected in the reasons given for publishing the volume. On the one hand, there is certainly a genuine concern with and love for learning and truth. On the other, however, there is also a more concrete, material element involved in a publishing venture which was potentially lucrative.

Valencia expresses the concerns that motivated him in this project: firstly, a desire that no one should be deprived of the benefit and charm of the poems, and secondly, his concern that teachers of Latin should choose them instead of secular poems for boys in the literary high schools. It is interesting to note that the impetus for publishing the volume seems to have come from Valencia, and that this enterprise was a direct result of his intimate involvement with Arias Montano's writings. In fact, Valencia tells us, it was the fact that the poems were scattered amongst Montano's papers that impelled him to bring them together and make them accessible in the suitable format of a small, handy volume which would be relatively inexpensive and easy to carry around and to be used by boys. In these comments, he reveals some familiarity with the publishing business. This was an inevitable result of his collaboration in the work of Montano and the latter's association with the printing-house of Christopher Plantin in Antwerp. In fact, in the choice of Plantin as the publisher, Valencia again finds a happy combination of spiritual and material elements:

> I thought that no one would satisfy this desire of mine better than Plantin, both because of his large stock of most elegant type-faces and because I knew that though I was not known to him, even by name, he was very well acquainted with what was good for people, and cared much about it.[15]

It is surprising that Valencia should say he was not known to Plantin even by name. Considering the close contact with Montano for a period of nearly ten years by the time he wrote this first preface, it is difficult to imagine that Plantin knew nothing of Montano's closest friend and helper. Yet, there is certainly no available evidence of any contact between them so Valencia's comment, though surprising, may be correct. But clearly Valencia, for his part, knew much about Plantin, and so he arranged for an approach to be made to him.[16] Plantin readily agreed to the project provided Valencia edited the texts, a task which the latter carried out as speedily as possible. The volume of poems thus came into being as a joint venture between the poet, Montano, the printer, Plantin, and the editor, Valencia.

The preface concludes with an assertion of the Christian nature of the poems and an exhortation to discover the hidden message in them:

> But I thought that you should also have this advice from me, consistent with the love I know I should bear towards all men: in reading this man's poetical writings, do not be delighted mainly by the sweetness of the diction and fail to look further, rather seek to discover for your good the hidden meaning in them; for they are full of true wisdom, and if you examine them deeply they will cast a great light before you to lead you to the shrines of sacred literature.[17]

Valencia also looks to the future and promises a possible further collection which will contain a variety of verse forms and which, within the confines of a small volume, will provide variety, truth, simplicity and genuine Christian teaching.

This promise was fulfilled with the publication of Montano's *Hymni et Secula*. In the preface for this volume,

Valencia again emphasizes the biblical basis of the poems and the Christian teaching they contain, asserting that 'there is in the whole of these poems no sentiment which has not been derived from the open interpretation of the word of God'.[18] He, in fact, claims a biblical basis for everything that Montano has ever written, and he expresses the hope of being able to substantiate this through an annotated edition of his poetry some time in the future.

After establishing this well-grounded basis for the poems, Valencia then extols Montano's selfless reasons for publishing these poems: he is not seeking renown but simply that 'the glory of the divine name and the advantage of the Christian Church might be promoted day by day'.[19] Valencia also attempts to forestall possible criticism from those who might consider poetry an unworthy pursuit, particularly for a man of advanced age and of serious and sober character such as Montano. He thus continues the defensive line of the *Poemata* preface against criticisms which reveal the dubious light in which poetry was seen by many moralists in the continuing tensions and debates concerning imaginative literature in post-Tridentine Spain.[20] Valencia, however, is reluctant to engage in a polemical defence of poetry which he, in any case, describes as 'a most ancient, most enjoyable and indeed most beneficial and, if not quite divine, then certainly a sacred art'.[21] He also commends the soothing and civilizing effects of harmony. But he checks his growing indignation which he dismisses as not fitting for a civilized man, and he focuses instead on the difference between true art and debased, counterfeit, specious imitations which pass themselves off as the real thing, and which are responsible for provoking the type of criticism he has mentioned. He therefore feels it necessary to define poetry:

> For us poetry is none other than a decorated form of
> expression, elevated above the common discourse,

tempered and fitted to the use of music, suitable for the exposition of weightier subjects and the expression of loftier feelings.[22]

He goes on to suggest that for this type of writing what is required is not common, pedestrian language but rather language that is musical, that takes wing and soars. The aspect of musicality leads him to consider the question of harmony alluding, on the one hand, to the Pythagorean music of the spheres and, on the other, to well-known examples of poetry in the Bible and the writings of the Church Fathers. He also avails himself of Plato's view that 'harmony, kin and sister to the mind, was granted by the Muses to us ... so that we can reduce to order and consonance the discordant and disorderly motions of the mind persuaded and tamed by its aid and assistance'.[23]

But Valencia checks himself: he has strayed too far, he says. His task is not to commend or defend poetry in general. He is merely concerned with Arias Montano and his poetry, and, with regard to this, he considers it sufficient to establish that Montano's themes are serious and sacred ones; they have ancient, divine precedents; they cannot be expressed better than in poetic form since, because of their content, they require eloquent expression and song to celebrate 'the day that the Lord made'.[24]

Valencia's further comments relate more directly to his relationship with Montano. He refers to the latter's practice of writing poems on holidays almost as a kind of hobby or relaxation, but he emphasizes that these are nevertheless important, serious works. Valencia's formation as a Renaissance humanist scholar enables him to evaluate the worth of the poems which he can compare with the best Classical models: 'Certainly in their artistry and elegance, and in their use of all manner of poetic ornament, they are comparable to none but the best Greek and Latin poetry'.[25] As with *Poemata*, Valencia feels his comments may be weakened in the eyes of critics because of his friendship with Arias Montano:

> I see very many make a great fuss and object that my great love for the poet has influenced my judgement. That love indeed we admit while not excessive (for none could be that) is yet as great as it is possible for love to be.[26]

Indeed, Valencia indicates that his evaluation is based upon comparison and consideration of the poems themselves, not upon second-hand reports. His considered opinion is that in learning, artistry and genius, Arias Montano's poems are to be highly commended. He outlines Montano's breadth of knowlege which encompasses theology, philosophy, an exceptional command of almost all languages and liberal arts, as well as a knowlege of the mechanical ones. The poems are therefore demanding, and require an erudite reader if they are to be properly understood. With these comments, Valencia points to the important relationship between writer, reader and text, and raises questions of intentionality and reception of the text.[27] With regard to the form of the poems, Valencia praises the economical style in which they are written, without any of the superficial supports and props of bad poetry such as redundant expressions put in merely for purposes of sound. The content of the poems is grounded in sacred authority. The volume has a three-fold division reflecting a time before the beginning of the world, then a review of the ages of creation, and lastly the dawn of the new age of Christ. The poems are therefore conducive to piety and learning, and they offer a celebration of the freedom and light brought to mankind by the coming of Christ.

This second preface therefore reveals interesting points which are linked with and extend comments made in the first one.

It shows us Valencia's continuing involvement in the work of Montano. Valencia's awareness of how his views might be interpreted as a result of their friendship are interesting, particularly in relation to the subsequent occasions on which he would speak out on behalf of Montano in much more open fashion and in situations which were far more polemical. The emphasis placed by Valencia on the religious content of the poems and the benefits to be derived from them points to the presence already of this defensive line and also to the dubious status of poetry at the time.

The two prefaces taken together therefore provide further material concerning Valencia's views on poetry which usefully complement the better-known comments he made in the case of Góngora. They also furnish important illustrations of the strong bonds that united Arias Montano and Pedro de Valencia, in particular, revealing Valencia's views and attitude to his mentor. These views can be complemented by the third text we have mentioned, Montano's dedication to Valencia of Psalm XXXI, in which Montano himself takes up the pen to express in carefully chosen words a memorial of the friendship and collaboration that existed between them.

In his commentaries on the psalms of David, Montano included a series of dedications to different friends as a kind of testimony of the friendships he had enjoyed during his lifetime. In last place, as a way of highlighting the special quality of the relationship, he placed the dedication to Pedro de Valencia which is both sufficiently brief and important to quote in full:

> Commentary on Psalm XXXI. To Pedro de Valencia, Greeting.
> I am happy to recall with praise the example of your past, and with greater pleasure I congratulate you upon your fortune in the present, my dearest Peter, and indeed my

faith in divine blessings leads me to look forward with eagerness to congratulating you most joyfully upon the fulfilment of our expectations for you: since I know that in your devotion since boyhood to the study of the humanities, in the daily increasing strength of your character, you have made such great progress that in our time no one of your age has set a more distinguished example in either respect (may no element of fulsomeness in a father's praise for his son – for that is the nature of the love I bear you – nor any cause for jealousy be detected in what I say): next, indeed, in the very flower of youth itself, having acquired the knowledge of divine prophecies, – and that [is] neither the common knowledge nor that received from the extravagant fabrications of the human intellect – initiated in the mysteries of true devotion as soon as you have entered the first courts of the sacred temple, you will have thanked the one God, and the same true genius of the place, publicly and openly because he has revealed the clearest and purest fountain-head itself of all those streams whose sources you have long followed in various ways; from which you will have drawn more true and reliable and most wholesome teaching in a short time than you had acquired by long and assiduous labour throughout many years before, and not without a confusing mixture of misconceptions from the minds of those who taught you. Finally, you will have gained that goal above all which, however it may be sought out, no effort or skill of human wisdom can ever discover and show and lay open for itself: this is that most holy mystery of the salvation of man, promised and furnished by God, which [having been] once concealed throughout the ages and generations, will be revealed, extended to and shared by the saints at the end of the ages. Now that you have happily absorbed its beginnings and first principles, your earnest wish and endeavour is to gain an absolute knowledge of it, the like of which neither eye has seen nor ear heard and which we have understood has not risen into the heads of ordinary mortals; but we believe that it comes prepared and freely bestowed by divine blessing upon those who have taken the trouble to cultivate true piety in a due and pure manner. This belief is based upon the most weighty and abundant testimony of those who to mark their attainment of a share in so munificent a gift have both offered substantial praise to God, its original source, and in speech and writings made everlasting proclamation of it for the benefit of people in present and future times. Our psalmist David along with the other prophets, as they pondered in their souls and minds the abundance of their divine blessing, longed for and perpetually sought after by themselves and by all devout men, were wont to burst out in praises, prayers, shouts of joy, in short in various kinds of thanksgiving. And it is one of these which is to be found in the next Psalm.[28]

The above text speaks for itself. However, it is particularly interesting, in the context of this paper, to note some of the points it contains. The evidence it provides of the close relationship between the two men is important. Arias Montano mentions qualities of Pedro de Valencia which, in part, explain why he accepted him as amanuensis and helper: he alludes to Valencia's devotion to study of the humanities since boyhood, his strength of character and the outstanding example he offered in this respect. The reference to the father-son relationship also points to the way the collaboration developed. Montano's comment concerning his praise of Valencia as objective and not simply the result of friendship also parallels Valencia's own comments to this effect. But of considerable interest too because of their enigmatically mystical tones are some of Montano's words. They can perhaps be read at face value but, given Montano's connections with the Family of Love and his resulting visionary approach to the Bible towards the end of his life, they raise doubts. His references to Valencia as 'initiated in the mysteries of true devotion', as having 'entered the first courts of the sacred temple' and having gained 'true, reliable and most wholesome teaching', as having gained 'that most holy mystery of the salvation of man' which comes to those who 'cultivate true piety', all of these are somewhat enigmatic phrases and susceptible of several interpretations. However, be this as it may, Valencia's orthodoxy was never in doubt in his own lifetime, and it has not been seriously questioned since, and in all of his defences of Montano he is at pains to establish that Montano himself never deviated from orthodox views. Whatever interpretation may be possible of these comments, and this is a matter which goes beyond the limits of this paper, the questions they raise nevertheless serve to focus our attention on the importance of the written text in the context of a relationship that was constantly sustained and nourished by paper, pen and the many words which still bear witness to it.

NOTES

1. The source of this Spanish phrase is a letter written by Arias Montano to Gabriel de Zayas from Antwerp on 27 February 1573 in which he says: 'Y sepa v.m. entre nos, que allende de los demás motivos é impulsivos que he tenido, fué recísimo el del papa, que la segunda vez que le hablé, me dijo que mas servicio haría á Dios y á la Iglesia con la pluma en la mano, que con cuantos otros negocios hubiese en el mundo, y nunca se me ha quitado de la imaginación esta sentencia, y loque me añadió sobre ella', in *Colección de documentos históricos para la historia de España*, ed. by Sres. Marqueses de Pidal y de Miraflores y D. Miguel Salvá, 112 vols (Madrid: 1842-95; repr. Vaduz: Kraus Reprint Ltd., 1966), 41, 288.

2. For some letters of Arias Montano and Pedro de Valencia, see respectively: *Colección de documentos históricos para la historia de España*, 41, 127-418; Guillermo Antolín, 'Cartas inéditas de Pedro de Valencia', *La Ciudad de Dios* (1896-97), 41, 341-50; 490-503; 42, 127-35; 292-96; 43, 364-68; 437-41; 44, 354-58.

3. See J. A. Jones, 'Some Aspects of the Friendship and Collaboration between Benito Arias Montano and Pedro de Valencia', in *'A Face not Turned to the Wall': Essays on Hispanic Themes for Gareth Alban Davies*, ed. by C.A. Longhurst (Leeds, 1987), 67-84.

4. This was: *Biblia Sacra, Hebraice, Chaldaice, Graece & Latine, Philippi II Reg. Cathol. Pietate et Studio ad Sacrosanctae Ecclesiae Usum*, 8 vols (Antwerp: Officina Plantiniana, 1569-73).

5. See J.A. Jones, 'Pedro de Valencia's Defence of Arias Montano: the Expurgatory Indexes of 1607 (Rome) and 1612 (Madrid)', *Bibliothèque d'Humanisme et Renaissance*, 40 (1978), 121-36, and 'Las advertencias de Pedro de Valencia y Juan Ramírez acerca de la *Biblia Regia*', *Bulletin Hispanique*, 84 (1982), 328-46.

6. This is amply substantiated in the following: *Correspondance de Christophe Plantin*, ed. by M. Rooses and J. Denucé, 9 vols (Antwerp-Ghent, 1883-1918); *Epistolario de Justo Lipsio y los españoles*, ed. by Alejandro Ramírez (Madrid, 1966).

7. Juan Alcina, 'Tendances et caractéristiques de la poésie hispano-latine de la Renaissance', in *L'humanisme dans les lettres espagnoles*, ed. by Augustin Redondo (Paris, 1979), 131-49 (pp.140-41, 146).

8. Luis Gómez Canseco, *El humanismo después de 1600: Pedro de Valencia* (Seville, 1993), 276-77.

9. See, for example, Eunice Joiner Gates, 'An Unpublished Letter from Pedro de Valencia to Góngora', *Modern Language Notes*, 66 (1951), 160-63; C.C. Smith, 'Pedro de Valencia's Letter to Góngora (1613)', *Bulletin of Hispanic Studies*, 39 (1962), 90-1.

10. Gómez Canseco, *Pedro de Valencia*, 63.

11. 'Potius enim esse hominibus aiunt, eius aut utilitate quapiam aut quantumvis magna oblectatione carere, quam dulcedine illectos & delinitos ipsius interim aculeo incautos pungi, vanaque imo et venenosa doctrina inflari et perdi', *Poemata*, 3. I gratefully thank Mr. J.C.G. Strachan for his help with the Latin texts.

12. 'ea nempe veram utilitatem, sinceramque voluptatem continet, & quae sine ullo periculo a simplicibus peti percipique possit', *Poemata*, 6.

13. 'ea sunt viri pietate & doctrina egregij Benedicti Ariae Montani, in quibus nec Latinitatem, nec poeticum leporem & numerum aut stylum & elegantiam quisquam desiderarit ...', *Poemata*, 7.

14. 'nihil demum excipi possit ... haec potius poemata in Christianorum hominum manibus sint, saltim non alia

pueris legenda & ediscenda, memoriterque tenenda tradantur. ex quibus & Grammaticorum rudimentorum, & Latini sermonis elegantiarum, & Rhetoricarum praeceptionum, carminumque diversorum generum exempla peti possunt, puerisque imitanda proponi, ita etiam ut interim ea disciplina tacite imbuantur (quae puerilis institutionis lex est) qua viros effectos uti & exerceri maxime expedierit', *Poemata*, 7.

15. 'Ulterius poemata haec commendare pergerem, nisi ea se statim essent commendatura, egoque plus nimio poetam diligere iudicandus forem, quem valde quidem a me coli & amari fateor, nondum pro suo merito meoque debito dilectum mihi satisfacere possum', *Poemata*, 8.

16. 'Huic meo desiderio neminem Plantino melius satisfacturum sum arbitratus, & propter elegantissimorum typorum copiam, & quia etsi me nomine etiam tenus ignotum ipsi, tamen publicam utilitatem notissimam charissimamque sciebam', *Poemata*, 9.

17. Plantin's reply is indicated in his letter to Arias Montano of 27 March 1587: 'Proinde cupio ut virum illum ut pium ita P. de Valentia illa nobis curet ut concepit in ordinem redigere et ad nos mittere', *Correspondance de Christophe Plantin*, VIII, 193: [Therefore, I should like such a pious and learned man as P. de Valencia to see to the editing of them for us as he thinks fit and to send them to us']. Pedro de Valencia, in fact, gradually developed strong connections with Plantin's printing-house. See, for example, his letter to Jean Moretus written on the death of Arias Montano and published in Alejandro Ramírez, 'Una carta inédita de Pedro de Valencia', in *Filología y crítica hispánica*, ed. by A. Porqueras Mayo and C. Rojas (Madrid, 1969), 63-67.

18. 'Sed & illud te moneri a me deberi existimavi, pro ea qua homines omnes prosequi charitate debere me scio, ne in viri huius poeticis scriptis legendis dictionis tantum suavitate

delectatus, ulterius quaerere desistas, sed potius quid
reconditi sensus in illis sit, ad tuam utilitatem inquiras; sunt
enim vera sapientia plena, & quae penitus introspecta
magnam lucem praeferent ad sacrarum litterarum adita
adeunda', *Poemata*, 10.

19.   'Nihil enim sententiarum est totis his carminibus, quod non
ex aperta sacrorum oraculorum interpretatione sit petitum',
Hymni et Secula, 3.

20.   'ut divini nominis gloria & Christianae Ecclesiae utilitas in
dies promoveantur', *Hymni et Secula*, 4.

21.   For a discussion of views concerning the role and status of
poetry see Bernard Weinberg, *A History of Literary
Criticism in the Italian Renaissance*, 2 vols (Chicago –
Toronto, 1961), I.

22.   'poeseosque antiquissimum, iucundissimum, atque
utilissimum, ac pene divinum usum, certe sacrum
probemus, nunc non est', *Hymni et Secula*, 4.

23.   'Nobis poesis non aliud est quam ornata quaedam ac supra
vulgarem rationem sublimis, ad musicesque usum
temperata aptaque oratio, grandioribus rebus dicendis &
maioribus animis sensis exprimendis opportuna', *Hymni et
Secula*, 5.

24.   'harmoniam, quae menti cognata sit atque germana, a Musis
concessam ... ut inconcinnos ac perturbatos animi motus
ipsius ope & auxilio persuasos & cicuratos in ordinem &
congruentem ornatum redigere possimus', *Hymni et Secula*,
9.

25.   'dies quam fecit Dominus ...', *Hymni et Secula*, 9.

26.   'artis vero & elegantiae poeticorumque omnium
ornamentorum ratione cum nulla non Graecorum &
Latinorum eximia poesi componenda', *Hymni et Secula*, 10.

27. 'Video tumultuantur plurimi, nostroque iudicio maximum nostrum erga poetam amorem obiiciunt;quem quidem nos non nimium (nam nullus fuerit) sed quam fieri potest maximum fatemur', *Hymni et Secula*, 10.

28. These questions, which are perhaps most often discussed in relation to imaginative literature, also arise in many of the polemical writings of Arias Montano and Pedro de Valencia in which matters of intention and interpretation are central to the nature of the controversies in which they were involved.

29. 'Commentarium in Psalmum XXXI. Petro Valentiae Salutem. Et praeteriti tibi temporis exemplum libens laudansque recito, & praesentis vicem libentius gratulor, Petre carissime, atque expectationis de te nostrae usum laetissime gratulaturus mihi iam ex divinae benignitatis fide videor & gestio: cum te a puero humanioribus disciplinis deditum, & honestis moribus in dies auctum, tantum profecisse noverim, ut nullus (absit adulatio patri erga filium, quo te amore complector, absit quoque invidia verbo) nostra aetate in utriusque, exempli laude tibi coaevus excelluerit: Deinde vero in ipso adeo iuventae flore, divinorum oraculorum notitia contingente, eaque nec vulgari nec ex humani ingenii luxuriosis commentis accepta, pietatis verae arcanis initiatus, quamprimum sacrosancti templi prima ingressus es atria, uni Deo atque eidem vero loci genio gratias publice ac palam egeris, quod tibi eorum omnium, quorum diu ac varie confectatus fueras rivulos, caput fontemque ipsum limpidissimum & purissimum demonstraverit; unde plus verae & solidae atque saluberrimae doctrinae brevi tempore hauseris, quam multis antea annis longo assiduoque exceperas labore, non sine eorum ingeniorum, per quae illa deducebatur, commixto vario nec nihil turbidi habente vitio: Demum vero id potissimum fueris consecutus, quod nulla humanae sapientiae industria aut solertia, quamlibet conquisitum, tamen repertum sibi vere ostendere & patefacere potuerit: hoc est, humanae salutis a Deo promissae & praestitae

arcanum illud sanctissimum, quod a seculis & generationibus quondam absconditum, in seculorum finibus demum revelatum ac sanctis creditum communicatumque constat. Cuius initiis et elementis feliciter iam imbutus, absolutam confectari voves & pergis notitiam, qualem nec oculus vidit, nec auris audivit, nec in communis aleae mortalium cor ascendisse intelleximus; sed plane divino beneficio iis, qui veram pietatem rite ac pure curant & colunt, paratam & ultro donatam contingere credimus, testimonio gravissimo & frequenti edocti eorum, qui tanti muneris ac doni participes evadentes, & laudem solidam Deo tribuerunt auctori ac parenti, & praeconium aeternum voce & scriptis ad praesentium posterorumque temporum publicam utilitatem mandarunt. Cuius quidem divini beneficii optatam sibi atque piis cunctis & perpetuo expetitam copiam, David noster una cum Vatibus aliis dum animo ac mente secum agitabant, in laudes, in petitiones, in exclamationes, in varia denique gratulationis prorumpere solent genera. ex quibus unum id est, quod proximo celebratur Psalmo', *In XXXI Davidis Psalmos ...* , 381-82.

JOÃO MANUEL SARAIVA DE CARVALHO

Arquivo da Universidade de Coimbra

D VICENTE NOGUEIRA
Courtier, Diplomat and Scholar

From time to time, people are born whose destiny is to leave a very personal mark in history. Such people are often ignored by all but specialist researchers, although their lives are well worth knowing. This is the case of D Vicente Nogueira, one of the greatest scholars of his age and today practically unknown.

The notes you are about to read hardly do justice to their subject matter; D Vicente Nogueira's life is worth a doctoral thesis. But we hope that they will inspire a reader to write the biography of a man who, like Oscar Wilde would do two and a half centuries later, put all his genius into his life.

***

D Vicente Nogueira was born in Lisbon in 1586, when Portugal already was under Spanish rule. His father was Dr Francisco Nogueira, a distinguished lawyer whose acceptance of the new situation made him a member of the Council of State of Portugal in the Madrid Court, and of D Maria de Alcáçova, a lady of noble descent. He had an older brother, Paulo Afonso Nogueira, who never married and died in Madrid early in November 1647.

D Vicente Nogueira was twelve when he was accepted by Felipe II as a Young Gentleman of the Royal Household. During his stay in the Spanish Court, he applied his brilliant mind and energy to studying, and became a regular customer of the Court librarians from the age of 14[1]. His most powerful and distinguished friends – particularly Don Bernardino de Mendoza, Constable of Castile, and Don Lorenzo Suárez de Figueroa, Duke of Feria – understood his potential and encouraged him to be selective: to concentrate on the more recent works of the best authors, leaving no place for the old-fashioned religious treatises. Don Bernardino de Mendoza, he recalled many years later,

> "se impacientava contra seu sobrinho o Duque de Alcalá de vello gastar dinheiro em liuros scolasticos, e dizerlhe que elles os haveria queimado, se forão seus; porque não soo erão liuros improprios de hum grande senhor mas inda desnecessarios no mundo, e que se havião de prohibir e se concedessem ao menos soo a frades ociosos, que perdessem nelles o tempo e o miolo"[2].

Pursuing his studies, D Vicente Nogueira obtained a Bachelor's degree in Canon Law in the University of Salamanca on 20 April 1606, and moved to Portugal at the end of the Summer, being incorporated in the University of Coimbra on 3 November[3]. The Faculty of Canon Law elected him Councillor on 10 November[4], and he registered in the same Faculty on 15 October 1607 in order to prepare for a Licentiate's degree. At the same time, he applied to become a boarder in St Peter's University College, but later withdrew his application. It was rumoured that this was because his grandmother on his mother's side was partly of New Christian descent; but such rumours were wholly groundless. The truth was that he had a yearly income of 700 cruzados, far above the limit of 125 cruzados set by the College Statutes, and his request for a dispensation was apparently turned down by the Collector General[5].

He was already respected for his superior intelligence and scholarship, but there was another side to his personality. Those who knew him well could not ignore his tendencies: the young man was becoming notorious as an active homosexual. His tastes knew no class barriers: among his known partners were Spanish Grandees, choirboys, students and valets. It is hard to understand how his astonishing lack of inhibitions did not get him into serious trouble at this time.

D Vicente Nogueira obtained his Licentiate's degree *nemine discrepante* on 21 July 1608, but went no higher in the University, much to the astonishment of some of his teachers, who expected him to pursue an academic career. He went to Madrid, where he remained for a few months and committed his favourite sin with at least four people. He returned to Portugal in 1610 and lived in Oporto, Miranda do Douro and Évora before going to Lisbon, where he was a guest of Cristóvão de Almada for about a month and seduced various grooms and pageboys of his host. He returned to Coimbra in the Autumn, accompanied by his brother Paulo Afonso, and rented a house in the Rua da Moeda. He did register in the University on 21 October 1610; but his studies no longer monopolised his attention. He seduced various students and the 24-year-old valet of D Luís de Meneses, Count of Tarouca. In 1612 he was a guest of Paulo de Santa Maria, in his house near the Monastery of the Most Holy Trinity, where he continued to give in to his tendencies with various boys and young men, from his host's page to students, at the same time maintaining intimate relations with a 14-year-old schoolboy, Manuel Rodrigues. His family connections earned him an appointment as Senator of the House of Appeals in 1613[6], which he eventually exchanged for a canonry in Lisbon Cathedral. He settled in the capital in early 1614.

D Vicente Nogueira's career was ruined by his scabrous private life. On 15 November 1614 he voluntarily confessed to Inquisitor D Rodrigo da Cunha that he had committed the sin of sodomy since at least 1607, when he lived in Coimbra. He avoided a prosecution but did not change his life. In June 1618 he applied for a charter of Familiar of the Holy Office, which was denied him, and calmly went on sinning. He maintained intimate relations with his page Clemente de Oliveira since 1624, when the boy was still under 14.

A few years went by, and D Vicente Nogueira earned a reputation as a learned jurist – and as a connoisseur of the best food and wine. In 1626 he was promoted to Magistrate of the House of Appeals, but never was particularly concerned about mending his ways. It was his interest in the choirboys of Lisbon Cathedral that caused his downfall. Infatuated by 17-year-old Manuel Pereira, he seduced him and in mid-November 1630 had intimacies with him in the Chapterhouse itself, on two occasions; but the young man did not enjoy the experience and told his uncle Francisco Peres Godinho, who reported the matter to the Inquisition. On 27 November, in fear of being arrested, D Vicente Nogueira made a spontaneous confession to Inquisitor Manuel da Cunha; but this time he had gone too far. The Inquisition obtained statements against him from 17 people[7] before he was arrested on 17 June 1631. For a sensitive man like him, the time he spent in prison was a nightmare: "eu choro lagrymas de sangue quando me lembra o que vy naquelles horrendos carceres", he wrote from Rome eighteen years later[8]. But he was never tortured.

His defence, a masterpiece of jurisprudence, saved him from the secular arm; he was sentenced in private to the suspension of his Holy Orders and to life deportation to Príncipe island. He appealed but lost; and on 28 August he was handed over to the custody of Agostinho Freire, master of the "Nossa Senhora dos Remédios".

Being a shrewd man, he never reached his destination. He landed in Brazil, where he lived for a few years as a lawyer, under an assumed name, and continued to give in to his tendencies. He finally boarded a ship for the Peninsula, caused some moderate scandal on board, and landed in Galicia with a young boy, whom he left in Santiago de Compostela. He then left for Rome, where the love of youths was an established tradition, where he was taken into Cardinal Barberino's household, and soon became known as a first-class scholar and bibliophile[9]. He received the title of Referendary of His Holiness, and was also Gentleman of the Chamber of the Archduke Leopold of Austria and a member of the Council of the Two Majesties, Caesarean and Catholic. He was honoured by the highest dignitaries of the Vatican and by the best writers and scientists of his time, who benefited from his protection and sang his praises in their works. One of them was Lope de Vega, who wrote of him in his *Laurel de Apolo*:

> "Que libro se escrivio, que no lo viese?
> Que ingenio florecio, que no le honrase?
> En que lengua se hablò, que no supiese?
> Que sciencia se inventò, que no alcançasse?"[10]

He liked Lope de Vega both as a poet and as a friend. He wrote about him years after his death:

> "Era o mayor Poeta que teve nem terá Espanha, mas inda melhor homem que poeta, e tirado alguma fragilidade da carne, a que commumente são sogeitos os taes grandes engenhos, no mais não tinha tanta malicia, com hum minino de cinco annos, e a sua pena bendita não hauendo nunca escritto hua satyra e chovendo contra elle muitas cada dia"[11].

D Vicente Nogueira made a point of being in touch with the best minds of his time. One of them was the celebrated Menasseh ben Israel, his correspondent for many years:

"Menasse ben israel, envergonhado de ver que val tanto o que lhe mando cadanno, a titulo de não querer comissão, como os mesmos livros que me compra: porque de nenhuma parte são os liuros taõ caros como de hollanda, me presentou a sua biblia castelhana enquadernada em taboas e couro vermelho [...] liuro, impresso em Ferrara de muito ruim letra gottica"[12].

He even visited the Rome synagogue on the feast-day of *Sukkoth* of 1648, to listen to a sermon by a famous rabbi. The sermon was long – two and a half hours – and he was rather uncomfortable, having arrived late ("fiquei em pee, e taõ estreito que naõ podia moverme"), but he was very well impressed, both with the rabbi's accent ("No toscanismo he outro Boccaccio") and with his learning ("não passou daly Demosthenes ou Cicero"). He even compared this 45-year-old rabbi, whose name he did not mention, with certain Portuguese ecclesiastics of his day – which would be unthinkable in his own country[13]. He understood the Jewish culture and admired their friend, the Jesuit Father António Vieira, with whom he became acquainted in Rome[14]. All the same, he was realistic about the Portuguese New Christians he met:

"Entre os christaons novos eu me serviria dos mais baixos e mais cominheyros, porque em sendo empolados, quando os buscais mercadores os achaes fidalgos, e quando os buscais fidalgos os achaes mercadores"[15].

D Vicente Nogueira's cultural activities in Rome are known to us through his letters to his friend the Admiral D Vasco Luís da Gama, first Marquis of Nisa and a descendant of the great navigator[16], although they have never been studied in detail. He was, for instance, one of the first to note the harmful effects of tobacco:

"Dominico belli mestre de ceremonias do Papa [...] esteue tomando tabaco com huns amigos muito contente, e cahio morto hauerá duas horas: o que seja advertencia para V. S. prohibir o tal tabaco a todos seus subditos e criados, porque quasi nenhuma destas mortes supitas que taõ frequentes andaõ se vee senaõ nos tabaquistas [...] e para ter todos os tabaquistas, por mais viciosos que os bebedos de vinho, que o que tomado huma vez em jejum, ao levantar da cama pode ser medicina, he baixesa e infamia, tomarse alguma outra vez de dia, e naõ ha entrado em nenhum Cardeal tal abuso, antes o Papa prohibindoho a os clerigos da sua Igreja de Saõ Pedro"[17].

His political comments were always interesting and showed a fairly deep understanding of the international scene:

"Homens roins crescem no desaforo quando lhes saem bem os primeiros atreuimentos, e eu desde que ui a Carlos Rey de Inglaterra consintir ao Parlamento lançar de sy os Bispos, que sempre ali tiueraõ lugar, e depois disso condemnar hum innocente, como o era o Vizo Rey de Irlanda só por afagar e ter beneuolo o tal Parlamento ia dei por perdido o dito Rey, ainda que o auer de ser degolado num cadafalso naõ podia imaginar naõ achando em toda a antiguidade exemplo semelhante"[18].

Knowing that the Marquis Admiral wanted to have a good private library, he volunteered to help him obtain the best available books, which he bought and sent him in regular batches. He thus learned all there was to know about transport by sea, export duties and packing:

"Cada caixa destas he de sette palmos de comprido, tres de largo e mais de tres de alto, das que se não movem senão com quatro mariolas [...] alem dos encerados vão cubertos de palha e calhamaço em modo que lhes não chegue agua alguma"[19].

He also became deeply in debt, because the Marquis Admiral, hard pressed for money from various sides, was not always in a hurry to pay him, and in any case communications were handicapped by the state of war between Portugal and Spain. His letters have frequent appeals for money:

"Estou tão cheyo de dividas que me envergonho, dandome elRey tanto dinheiro. E assi quando V. S. tiuesse comodidade de soccorrerme seria obra de misericordia, e não de soo justiça, como as dividas ordinarias. V. S. me fara nisto toda a merce e pressa que sem perda sua puder usar"[20].

Three years later, the situation had not changed much:

"Por todos quantos respeitos de amizade houve, ha e haverà entre nós queira contar antes de acabarse este anno de 52 os seiscentos mil reis que inda deve da letra aceitada a Hieronimo nunez Perez, para que demos fim a debito taõ tresnoitado com que lido desde 48"[21].

D Vicente Nogueira worked as an unofficial agent of King João IV in the Vatican. His reports, sent through the Marquis Admiral, were greatly appreciated in the Portuguese Court and helped him obtain the protection of the King himself and eventually a Royal pension of 30 cruzados (12,000 réis) a month, later raised to 50 cruzados[22]. Always a realistic man, he never let this token of royal munificence interfere with a very personal view of all things Portuguese: "Os prelados em Portugal", he wrote on 2 February 1647, "não tem de pastores mais que o nome, que tudo o mais he pura vaidade e cuidarem que consiste em terem melhores tapecerias e melhor pratta".

He was a lonely man: "Deos me fez taõ solitario que me não deixou neste mundo parente algum, e nem inda amigo senaõ V. S. em grao mais preeminente"[23]. His health was no longer what it used to be:

> "Inda que cuidava haverme o azeyro curado da dor de estomago, que me durava ha tantos meses: estes tres dias a hei tido passante de tres horas e amenhaã mo começão a dar de novo [...] agora pago os 30 ou 40 annos dos excessos de Madrid [...] Estou tal, que temo morrer em pee, segundo a fraqueza e dores que se me renovão, na mayor dieta que pode imaginarse: e hoje que jantei as dez horas, quanta mongana faria o tamanho de tres castanhas ordinarias e não provei agua alguma, e de vinho soo tres onças que he a quarta parte de hum quartilho, sem fruta nem conserva alguma: são as seis da tarde sem me deixar a dor que me começou quando jantava [...] parece me estaõ mettendo hum punhal pello estomago" [24].

> "Cada dia me parece o ultimo, porque em subir da missa estes 84 degraos faço muitos pousos e o ultimo que he na minha sala me tem muitos credos despaço a tomar follego" [25].

More than anything else, he wanted to spend the last years of his life in Portugal. But on his own terms; he was a proud man.

> "Se V. S. não julgar que em Portugal posso viver muito honrado, não se lembre haverlhe remoqueado cousa alguma [...] nestes quinze anos de Roma não houvi nunca, nem no

rosto, nem nas costas, palaura de que me fizesse vermelho: habituado a tanta estimação, rebentaria se ahi achasse o contrario e quereria mais pouca saude e inda morte, que muito pequena ignominia, principalmente sendo eu quem por minha vontade e pés me fosse a buscalla"[26].

What he asked was more than the King himself could grant, but he did not know it. For the Holy Office, he was a convict, a fugitive, and his scholarship could not change it. But he did try:

"Esteja V. S. certo, que se me negociasse algum officio e occupação, lhe seria eu de grande honra, mostrando seu grande acerto. E ja disse a V. S. que nem minha idade e disposiçaõ. nem meu animo, se applicaria ja a nenhum officio de judicatura, inda que fosse chanceller da supplicaçaõ, ou desembargador do Paço: mas si a qualquer dos tribunaes de consciencia, fazenda ou ultramarino, nos quaes naõ seria inferior a nenhum dos que se ali achaõ, antes bem igual a os melhores, e isto quanto a officios de Lisboa.

Mas quando S. Magestade tiver tanta abundancia de sojeytos que venha eu a sobejarlhe, se me honrasse com algum beneficio pingue, com que eu pudesse, sem vaidades sustentarme e ter quatro tostoens que dee de esmolas, quiça me seria melhor [...] Mas quando não houvesse occasiaõ de nada disto, nem antes que eu fosse vagasse Obidos ou Sedofeita, que soo resultaõ da provisaõ dos bispados, neste caso me podia S. Magestade prover em alguma commoda igreja na qual eu esperasse a vagante das ditas ou de alguma outra equivalente, digna de hum pastor velho [...] Mas quando V. S. achar que El Rey me tem algum fastio ou nojo, por teremno ganhado os inquisidores, e que lhe pareça melhor morrer eu neste desterro, V. S. naõ se opponha contra a corrente de taõ caudaloso Rio; nem gaste sua valia em opporse a minha ruim fortuna, mas cedendo sabiamente ao tempo: entaõ pode dizer al Rey, que supposto minha grave idade e doenças, naõ seria grande perda sua mandarme dar aqui em Roma sessenta escudos ao mes, e inda cento, pois pouco lhe poderaõ durar estas más fadas [...]

Na materia de officios ou beneficios, naõ tenho que acrescentar a o ja dito: senaõ que se V. S. achasse vago ou proximo a vagar, o de guarda mor da torre do tombo, que naõ seria dos que eu peyor serviria, principalmente se me desse a habitaçaõ nas casas da mesma torre, donde sempre a estivesse cultivando, e ordenando"[27].

"Assegure V. S. que o pensamento de repatriar he soo polla saude e vida, que todo o homem deseja estender, hauendome os medicos avisado muito tarde e para mi muito fora de tempo, pois não tivera lançado aqui minhas raizes e sepultura"[28].

"E V. S. me faça merce de constituirme seu bibliothecario in capite, por achar em mi os requisitos da sua licença e em quanto eu não for a Portugal per modum provisionis o proveja em algum seu capellão ou clerigo não idiota, mas exprima que servirá soo durante a minha absencia"[29].

"Naõ crerei da suma bondade e fineza de V. S., que aja deixado de sondar este vao e sabido a esta hora a vontade de S. Magestade no ponto de hauer eu de tornar a Portugal e como, e a que: que inda que para a saude me será utilissimo; todavia por ella soo nua e crua; sem ser de prestemo para alguma occupaçaõ de servir a Deos, ou el Rey, ou ambos, naõ acometteria viagem, tanto sconmoda e perigosa: e a ocupaçaõ ja vaga, que naõ he esta grande idade a proposito para pretensaoens, mas para da nao, despois de Beijada a maõ al Rey, ir a ella em direitura"[30].

Knowing how difficult to obtain a pardon could be, the Marquis Admiral tried to persuade him to request from the Holy See a suitable dignity in Rome, but that was not that simple:

"Beijo as maons a V. S. pollo conselho de que procurasse pensaõ beneficios ou alguma boa dignidade para renunciar, com a qual tiuesse melhor sustento nesta ultima velhice, mas V. S. está muito desinformado desta curia [...] e como me naõ vio, fallou, nem conhece, mais que de cartas, e inda mal scrittas, cuida que sou como os mais dos homens, que trazem sempre diante dos olhos, o que lhes he mais util"[31].

As next Spring approached, D Vicente Nogueira's hopes were at their lowest ebb:

"Se totalmente naõ ha que esperar ajame V. S. licença de S. Magestade para conservandome em sua boa graça me retire clerigo em algum mosteiro ou congregaçaõ em Roma ou fóra a quietarme e trattar soo de minha alma, Já que naõ presto para servir em minha patria"[32].

He sadly wrote, "Naõ vejo ja a hora de desempenharme e irme metter num monte, onde soo falle com os meus livros, ja que vejo irseme desfazendo as esperanças de ir acabar nesse Reyno"[33].

True enough, D Vicente Nogueira never saw his country again. He died in Rome in 1654, far better known and respected in Italy than in Portugal. The question remains: did he change his tastes, or was he just more cautious? One thing we do know: he had two teenage pageboys, Marco Antonio and Sacchetti, who read to him when he was tired, "e he cousa maravilhosa, que deleite he taõ grande". One of the boys was "hum mocete de tivoli de quinze annos ja mui adiantado no latim, raro saber modestia e vergonha, excellente leytor". D Vicente Nogueira even recommended him to his friend the Marquis Admiral:

> "Entre tantos pagens luzidos e bem affigurados de V. S. escolha algum que naõ passe de catorze annos e com a sua estantinha em pee façaho lerlhe"[34].

Perhaps it was just as well that he never returned to Portugal.

NOTES

1. Letter dated 22 November 1649.

2. Letter dated 2 February 1647.

3. AUC, *Actos e Graus, 1606-1607*, fl. 26v-27. The incorporation meant that his Salamanca degree was accepted in Coimbra as if it were obtained there, and was taken into consideration for future advancement in his career.

4. AUC, *Conselhos, 1606-1607*, fl. 20v-21.

5. AUC, *Colégio de S Pedro. Capelas*, Vol. 2, fl. 74.

6. AUC, *Acordos do Cabido*, Vol. 9 (1609-1614), fl. 190v-191.

7. Cf. ANTT, *Inquisição de Lisboa*, Processo Nº 4241.

8. Letter dated 19 December 1649. Not unsurprisingly, he bore a grudge against the Holy Office for the rest of his life. When the banker Duarte da Silva was arrested on a charge of judaising – which, incidentally, was quite true – he wrote to the Marquis Admiral on 11 May 1648: "Deus alumie entendimentos taõ cegos, que eu não quero crer que soo se peque de malicia, e desejo de roubar, ou de ganhar bispados". About King João III, who introduced the Holy Office in Portugal, he had this to say: "El Rey Dom Joaõ 3° era huma posta de carne ou hum homem de Palha sem saber, sem valor e que soo com a capa de fradenho e reformador de frades ganhava credito na plebacha" (1.6.1648).

9. See, for example, FATIO, Alfred Morel – "Vicente Nogueira et son discours sur la langue et les auteurs d'Espagne", in *Zeitschrift für Romanische Philologie*, Vol. III (1879).

10. *Laurel de Apolo*, Silva III.

11. Letter dated 30 March 1648

12. Letter dated 10 February 1648.

13. This letter was first published by RÉVAH, I S – "D Vicente Nogueira et la Synagogue de Rome", in *Arquivo da Bibliografia Portuguesa*, Year I (1955), p. 235-238.

14. "Pareceme hum prodigio, e como no que atqui hei vivido, lhe naõ conheço igual" (letter dated 5 March 1650).

15. Letter dated 19 December 1649.

16. Codex CVI/2-11 of the Évora Public Library and District Archive (BPADE), which contains these letters, was transcribed by SILVA, A J Lopes da – *Cartas de D Vicente Nogueira, publicadas e anotadas pelo Director da Biblioteca Pública de Évora*, Coimbra, 1929, and later in Vol I of the *Arquivo de História e Bibliografia*.

17. Letter dated 30 April 1650.

18. Letter dated 8 May 1651.

19. Letter dated 30 March 1648.

20. Letter dated 26 June 1649.

21. Letter dated 12 October 1652.

22. From January 1649. It was just a symbolic allowance, occasionally supplemented by gifts. For example, according to D Vicente Nogueira's letter dated 15 May 1649, King João IV gave him a Christmas gift of 300 cruzados.

23. Letter dated 7 December 1648.

24. Letter dated 19 October 1648.

25. Letter dated 7 December 1648.

26. Letter dated 15 May 1649.

27. Letter dated 8 February 1649.

28. Letter dated 15 February 1649.

29. Letter dated 26 June 1649.

30. Letter dated 12 October 1649.

31. Letter dated 22 November 1649.

32. Letter dated 6 March 1650.

33. Letter dated 17 July 1649.

34. Letter dated 19 December 1649.

GARETH ALBAN DAVIES

University of Leeds

WAS R.V. RICHARD VERSTEGAN?
The question of *Egluryn Ffraethineb* (1595)

Richard Rowland [Verstegan] is no longer a name to conjure with, but enigma he certainly remains. In the period from 1580 until 1620 and beyond he was recognized in England as a dangerous fellow, for did not his machinations with a view to restoring England to the Catholic faith threaten the Elizabethan settlement, and thereby undermine the very bedrock of the state?[1] Like Eliot's Macavity, the Mystery Cat, he was everywhere, yet nowhere to be found: the friend and confidant of the Rev. Robert Persons, he acted as go-between between English Catholics and those like himself who operated on the continent of Europe; like his associate Hugh Owen in Antwerp, he was *intelligencer* and spy; furthermore, as propagandist and translator of devotional texts into English, he contributed significantly to the work of the Catholic Mission in energizing and enlightening an uninstructed remnant keen to establish contact once more with their traditional faith. John Bossy aptly referred to Verstegan's "vital function" in that awesome task.[2]

The Antwerp recusant was a man of many parts. Catholic apologist and propagandist certainly, but he was also a businessman involved in the cloth trade of which Antwerp was an important centre, whilst at the same time he still pursued his scholarly interests. He had, whilst in England, been part already of the movement for the study and proper recognition of England's Anglo-Saxon past, an interest that was finally to bear fruit in his *A Restitution of Decayed Intelligence in Antiquities* (Antwerp, 1605), a milestone in the study of the Anglo-Saxon language and its associated institutions, but a testimony also to Verstegan's knowledge of tongues common and exotic, and his adumbrations of the notion that an *Ur-Sprache* underlay what would be later recognized as the Indo-European family of languages. During his years at Antwerp he also revealed his fine poetic instinct, in a volume entitled *Odes. In Imitation of the Seaven Penitential Psalmes, ...* (s.l., 1601), and in the English-language verses in one of the best-known emblem-books, Otto Vaenius's *Amorum Emblemata ... Emblemes of Loue with verses in Latin, English, and Italian* (Antuerpiae, 1608).

The focus of attention, however, in the present article is a short treatise in Welsh on the subject of rhetoric, from the pen of an Anglican cleric, Henry Perri. The volume was entitled *Eglvryn Phraethineb. sebh, Dosparth ar Retoreg, vn o'r saith gelbhyddyd, ...* (An Illustrator of Eloquence, that is, An Exposition of Rhetoric, one of the Seven Arts) [Lhundain, 1595].[3] The printer-publisher was John Danter, whose list from 1591 to 1596 reveals no predilection for any particular kind or genre of literature, and contains no other Welsh text or anything of Welsh interest – in other words, Perri's book was a straight commercial deal.

Egluryn Ffraethineb was Perri's only venture into print. In it he displayed considerable familiarity with the discipline of rhetoric, and with English handbooks on the subject, in particular Henry Peacham's *The Garden of Eloquence* [1577] in the corrected and augmented edition of 1593. He was also familiar with the method and classification of Petrus Ramus.[4] However, Perri's originality lay in the fact that – helped to some extent by an earlier treatise on rhetoric by the Biblical scholar William Salesbury – he sought his examples of rhetorical usage in Biblical text, and in medieval and contemporary Welsh poetry. In the latter case the book is an anthology of verse by both the better known and the more obscure of Welsh poets. The lexicographer John Davies of Mallwyd, in the introduction to his *Antiquae Linguae*

Britannicae ... Dictionarium Duplex (1632), was struck by Perri's knowledge of languages.[5] However, it is not so much the learning, be it of Latin or of modern languages, that marks out this treatise, but the application of current humanistic ideas to the Britannic language and its literature. As Perri tells his readers in the introduction, the language is not only worth the attention of scholars and patrons from among the nobility, but like other languages at this time it should be enriched through contact with the example of classical literature. His explicit aim through his lessons in rhetoric is to raise standards, and thereby the status of the language. Not only will men of letters or poets turn to it, but the gentry themselves are called upon to choose it as the medium of communication with each other.[6]

In one sense therefore, this is not so much a treatise on rhetoric, as a paean of praise for the Britannic tongue. We cannot be certain whether in searching for friends and associates to help advertise and celebrate the publication of his book Perri dropped a hint as to where the emphasis lay. Certainly, a number of them, among them the more distinguished, took the invitation in that spirit. For instance, John Dee's brief stanza dwells on the closeness of Welsh to the forms of Latin and Hebrew, and expresses his conviction that the language was not a minor one in comparison with Latin. Referring specifically to these commendatory verses, R.J. Roberts commented on John Dee's position among the Welsh intelligentsia as "a key figure in providing them with an identity and a role in Britain and Europe, because he was himself one of them, one who had absorbed, however uncritically, the whole range of renaissance learning."[7]

Perri's origins have not as yet been fully studied and taken into account, so that the significance of the *Egluryn*, and of the circle of scholars and friends that celebrated its arrival, has not been properly assessed.[8] Bishop Humphrey Humphreys, in the additions he submitted for Philip Bliss's prospective edition of

Anthony à Wood's *Athenae Oxonienses*, identified Perri as a member of a patrician family from Flintshire, and a descendant of Ednywain Bendew, progenitor of one of the fifteen royal tribes.[9] Gwilym Lleyn in his Welsh Bibliography asserted more precisely that Perri was a scion of Maes-glas (Greenfield).[10] If so, he was probably, judging by his patronymic, a son of Harri ap Thomas ap Harri. If he was legitimate, his mother belonged to one of the northern *advenae* families, long established on the Welsh Border, namely the Hanmer, she being Marged fch. Jenkin Hanmer. On the other hand, the pedigrees do not refer to a son Harri or Henry at the appropriate point, which may mean that his mother was a *gordderch* (mistress), a state of affairs not unusual in that society.[11] Henry Perri's presumed sister or half-sister married a son of one of the main branches of the great family of Mostyn. He was William Mostyn of Basingwerk, which took its name from the abbey there, whose lands the family had acquired at the Dissolution. He was made sheriff of Denbighshire in 1552.

The uncertainty about Perri's origins is reflected in the existence of a totally different descent given him by J.E. Griffith in his study of the pedigrees of Anglesey, an island with which Perri was certainly to become associated.[12] Here Perri appears as a descendant of the royal Tudur (Tudor) family of Penmynydd. Assuming that the pedigree is erroneous, we may still ask whether it has any connexion with that given above for Maes-glas. There is one detail of possible relevance: Perri's paternal great-grandmother is given as Rose fch. Huw Hanmer, *gordderch* of a priest Syr Robert Owen. Looking across to the Maes-glas line, we find a Rose fch. Gruffudd [Fychan] Hanmer.[13] The vague knowledge of a Hanmer connexion may have led Anglesey genealogists to confuse two lines of descent, and thus take Henry Perri for their own.

Again if the identification is correct, Perri matriculated from Balliol College, Oxford, on 20 March 1578/9 at the age of eighteen. He took his M.A. degree in March 1582/3. He did not take his B.D. until June 1597, after a gap for which there is no obvious explanation. Bishop Humphreys reported that Perri "travelled much abroad, and had bin marryed and setled in another country" before coming to the diocese of Bangor.

What little information we have about Perri has to be seen in a different light, once we take into account the religious affiliations of the Maes-glas family, and indeed of many others in that part of Wales at this time. The historian of Catholic recusancy in Wales commented that Flintshire was "one of the most Catholic ... of all the Welsh counties in this period". He notes also that there were as many as 1200 recusants there between 1582 and 1624.[14] Maes-glas was one of the gentry families that remained loyal to its Catholic faith over a long period, as witnessed by the appearance of its members – especially the women – in the recusancy records.[15] Furthermore, it became increasingly difficult for Catholic families to admit their true faith openly, with the result that open or declared recusancy offers us only the visible face of a much more widespread Catholic allegiance, to be practised only occasionally, in secret, and at considerable peril.

The profile of Perri's career becomes plainer and firmer if we make the assumption that he at some time returned to the Catholic faith. The fact that he took his B.A. and M.A. degrees in Oxford indicates that he had not at the time any religious scruple that forbade him to take the Oath of Supremacy, as required. However, we may surmise that presumably under the influence of the missionary priests he decided, in 1582 or later, to revert to Rome, and practise his religion openly by going into exile to certain Catholic countries. This would help explain his instinctive and idiomatic familiarity with French, Italian and Spanish, as revealed in the opening Letter to his fellow countrymen.[16] That he was not intent on the priesthood is suggested by the fact that he married. For reasons unknown, he finally decided to return home and begin his studies for the Anglican priesthood. If our interpretation is correct, his reconciliation with the Protestant faith, however genuine, certainly coincided with the period when Catholics were under the greatest pressure to conform, since otherwise their families faced financial ruin, and individuals were threatened with imprisonment, or even death. Their lives, indeed, became "a very nightmare of insecurity".[17]

Since it was only in 1597 that he took his B.D. degree, Perri's vocation for the priesthood was in its early stages in 1595. We may surmise that eventually, because of the influence locally of Richard Bulkeley of Beaumaris whom he served as chaplain, he acquired a number of Anglesey incumbencies, the earliest at Rhoscolyn with its two chapelries. Again one's suspicions are aroused. The Bulkeley family were regarded as closet Catholics, and had family ties both with the Puwiaid of Penrhyn Creuddyn, near Llandudno, and with the Lleweni family in Denbighshire, both notoriously 'malignant'.[18] Furthermore, Sir Richard was suspected of having had a hand in the Babington plot of 1586.[19] Was Perri, with his Catholic background, deemed by Bulkeley to be a useful instrument towards providing Catholic devotions for himself and others, at night in lonely chapelries? That Perri himself sought out Catholic connexions is certainly borne out by his choice of second wife. She was the daughter of Robert Vaughan of Beaumaris, the mother being Grace fch. William Coetmor.[20] Grace's father was a close kinsman of Maurice Griffin, a member of the Bangor Penrhyn family, who became bishop of Rochester under Mary (1554-58); kinsman also of the two brothers Glynn, Jeffrey and William. The first was an eminent canon lawyer in London, the second a Cambridge don, distinguished theologian and Catholic apologist, who served as bishop of Bangor under Mary. All three were involved in the founding of Friars School, Bangor, in 1557.[21]

Awareness of Perri's Catholic background, and the strong

possibility that he subsequently returned, half-heartedly or not, to the Protestant faith, bid fair to giving more attention both to the occasion of the publication of *Egluryn Ffraethineb*, and to the cloud of witnesses attending it. The book itself was dedicated to John Salisbury of Lleweni, in which he is given rather fulsome praise, among other things, for his staunch loyalty to Queen Elizabeth. The wish is also expressed that God will make of him a "perutile ... Ecclesiae membrum, contra religionis hostes fortissimus heros" (f.a1). The house of Lleweni had been noted, however, for a different loyalty, that to Rome. In one instance, indeed, that allegiance was deemed to override the subject's obeisance to the royal throne, for Thomas, John Salisbury's elder brother and heir to the estate, had been involved in Anthony Babington's plot in 1586 to kill Queen Elizabeth, and place Mary, Queen of Scots, on the the throne of England, an involvement for which he paid with his life.[22] John Salisbury's own religious position remains unclear, but his son Robert's widow was cited as a recusant, as were the wives of other Lleweni kinsmen.[23] In any case, what was at issue for John Salisbury in 1595 was not so much the exact nature of his religious propensity, but the cloud of suspicion that still lingered after the Babington plot. Perri's picture of him as the loyal subject, and the defender – presumably – of the established religion, would have been very welcome.

Of the various commendatory verses those of William Mathew, Esquire, are the only ones that hint, bafflingly to be sure, at the historical circumstance affecting Perri's treatise. It is well-nigh impossible to recognize the exact identity of this wellwisher: certainly a man of education, if not a graduate of either university, then someone trained at the Inns of Court, and, in either case, an accomplished poetaster. His name, given the nature of these verses, suggests he may have been a member of the celebrated Catholic family of the Matheuaid (Mathews) of Llandaf (Llandaff), Radur, and other places in south Glamorgan where they had taken root. A possible candidate is William Mathewe, from Glamorgan, *armiger*, who matriculated from Brasenose College in Oxford on 4 July 1579, aged 13. Significantly there is no sign that he took his degree.[24]

The poet addresses an unspecified *thou*, which the context suggests could be Perri's patron of Lleweni, or Perri himself.[25] In reality, William Mathew is apostrophizing the Welsh language, but along with it its learning and its literature. The poet declares that however difficult was the fate he and his companions had been obliged to suffer, their dedication to the Welsh language and to learning had remained constant:

> Thou sole companion of our oft chang'd State,
> Sprong from the bowels of this sea-wald Ile:
> Whom al-deuouring time could not exile,
> So haue we constant beene despite of fate.
> That how soeuer fortune tyrannizde,
> We euer thee with all affections prizde.

The nature of that fate emerges more clearly when the reader reflects on what is encoded in the word *exile* and in the reference to tyranny. The "oft-chang'd State" must refer to the religious changes that affected the country from the reign of Henry VIII forwards, and more particularly the return to Protestantism after the brief spell of Mary's reign. The exile tangentially alluded to is not that of the Protestants who went abroad during Mary's reign, but of those Catholics who, in more recent times, fled the tyranny and persecution that marked Elizabeth's. The very word *thou* in this second layer of meaning may encompass the Catholic faith to which they had also remained constant. Such a reading is apparently challenged and contradicted by the opening of the second stanza:

Now since the splendor of a blessed time
Hath raizd our fortune, wee will reare thy praise

If this is so, how can it also refer to Elizabeth's reign? The answer lies in the time of composition, the final years of that reign, when a sense of despair and dismay among recusants was giving way to the hope that with the coming of a new monarch the Catholic faith would be tolerated once more. At an official level, any mention of succession and successor was stamped upon, but behind the scenes attempts were being made and discussions held towards a reconciliation with Rome.[26] It should be emphasized, nevertheless, that at the primary level William Mathew is extolling a period in which Renaissance learning in Wales is now being given proper recognition.

If my reading is broadly accurate, then the key to the publication of *Egluryn Ffraethineb* lies in the word reconciliation. It is a bringing together of scholars of both Catholic and Protestant persuasion – a number of whom were from Flintshire and Denbighshire – who were united in their love of humanistic learning, and of the Welsh language, and the literature to which it gave voice. Protestantism is most clearly represented by Huw Lewys, who contributed a short Latin stanza encouraging Perri never to cease "linguam exornare Britannam". Lewys was the translator, via the English language, of Otho Werdmüller's *Ein Kleinot. Von Trost vnd Hilff in allerley Trübsalen* ...(1548). Werdmüller was a Zürich pastor, and Lewys's version of that treatise appeared in 1595 under a title that recalls that of Miles Coverdale's English translation, namely *Perl mewn Adfyd* (A Pearl in Time of Misfortune). Lewys dedicated his work to Richard Vaughan, at that time still Archdeacon of Middlesex, but soon to be translated to be bishop of Bangor.[27] Another Protestant, indeed a Calvinist, was Henry Holland, who contributed a rather creaking Latin panegyric of Henry Perri.[28] In contrast, we have a contribution by William Middleton, poet and privateer, who was certainly of Catholic persuasion, and wrote three *cywyddau* to "Y Ffydh Gatholi[c]" (The Catholic Faith).[29] Another got his place because of his friendship with John Salisbury of Lleweni: William Rankins would in 1598 dedicate his *Seaven Satyres* to Sir John.[30]

Whatever difference existed between the religious convictions of these well-wishers, they had in common their linguistic and literary enthusiasm: witness, for instance, Henry Salesbury (Salisbury), whose *Grammatica Britannica*, published in London in 1593, had already expressed unequivocally the view that the Welsh language, in its antiquity and its grammatical forms, was a match for all comers.[31] As for Henry Perri himself, his zeal matches that of the poets who celebrate him. In one respect, however, he does have an axe to grind. Understandably, given his background, he is most anxious after his return from abroad to demonstrate publicly his Protestant credentials. He thus shows his respect for the notion of having the word of God in one's own language, taking many instances of rhetorical device from a Welsh rendering of Holy Writ. He follows William Salesbury's translation of the New Testament (1567), but offers his own version of the Hebrew of the Old Testament rather than what was now available in Bishop William Morgan's Bible of 1588.[32] More pointedly, he refers to the Mass as defiling Christ's suffering (52-53), and argues that the expression "This is my body" is to be taken in a metaphorical sense (11). Certainly he wished to make it crystal-clear where he stood theologically, even at the risk of overegging the pudding.

We now reach the puzzle towards whose resolution the above discussion has been a prelude. Placed in the most prominent position at the head of the commendatory verses are poems by a certain R.V. and by John Dee. It is surely significant that Bishop Humphreys in his additions to the *Athenae*

Oxonienses omitted all reference to these two, though he does mention at least some of the other contributors. In the case of Dr John Dee, perhaps Humphreys thought that his reputation as astrologer and magus was sufficient to justify passing over him in prudent silence. But was it prudence also that caused Humphreys to omit R.V.? As to R.V.'s identity, it was W. Carew Hazlitt who suggested that behind those letters lurked Verstegan the recusant.[33] Petti acknowledges that for reasons of security Verstegan showed an aversion to signing his name, and that he frequently used these initials. However, in this particular instance Petti commented: "There is only the remotest possibility of his authorship" (p.100). We must presume that in Petti's view there was no reason for associating Verstegan with Wales and Welsh letters. Franklin B. Williams took a different view of the author's identity, tentatively attributing the verses, again with no reasons given, to a certain Robert Vaughan.[34] No obvious candidate presents himself. A much stronger contender is Richard Vaughan (1550-1607), future bishop of Bangor, who certainly was a scholar as well as a cleric, and had, in fact, written Latin verses in praise of Sir John Price (Prys)'s attempt to counter the views on Welsh history expressed by Polydore Vergil in his *Anglica Historia* (1534). This was the *Historiae Brytannicae Defensio, Ioanne Priseo equestris ordinis Brytanno Authore* (1573).[35] Two arguments against identifying Vaughan with R.V. are: firstly, that if Perri was anxious to have what could be his own future bishop on his side, he would not have been content to leave Vaughan's identity obscured by his initials, nor placed that contribution in proximity to a poem by John Dee; secondly, Humphrey Humphreys (1648-1712), a successor to the Bangor see, whose information had come from Perri's own son-in-law, is unlikely to have passed over Bishop Vaughan's identity in silence. Furthermore, Vaughan's *congé d'élire* in November 1595 sits uneasily with the fact that the book was published in that very same year – we must assume in such a case that Perri had prior notice of the prospective election. This is not impossible, if we consider that Perri had good London connexions, as is suggested by his success in persuading John Dee at Mortlake to compose a poetic trifle in his favour. In any case, such prior knowledge of Vaughan's election would seem a *sine qua non* for Perri's action in giving his R.V. such prominence, both in place and size of letter.

One way of testing whether R.V. was Vaughan is to compare the poem in *Egluryn Ffraethineb* with what was certainly a composition of Vaughan's (*Ri. Vaughani*) in John Price's *Defensio*.[36] Both are characteristic examples of the Latin versifying of that period, both are linguistically competent, both poets are versant in Latin scansion but reveal slight blemishes. Indeed at that level nothing differentiates them, and if R.V. is more adventurous in his use of alliteration ("Verbaque mirifice mollibus apta modis"), there is a touch of it also in Vaughan's "Tu patris & patriae famam per secula seruas". Looked at in this way, the poems suggest that R.V. might as well be Vaughan as Vaughan R.V.

These arguments notwithstanding, other considerations carry greater weight. In particular, as practisers of verse R.V. and Richard Vaughan are very different. Vaughan may be dutiful, but he is exceedingly dull. His verse limps from couplet to couplet, whereas R.V. develops his poem logically and limpidly from beginning to end. In order to vary the rhythm he uses enjambement to good effect, and he ends cleverly and unexpectedly with the word *suam*, thus lending final emphasis to Perri himself as the object of praise, doing so in the context of his abilities as a linguist. In other words, this is a poem written by an accomplished poet.[37] Some of its other subtleties will come to light when I look at this *Carmen Encomiastichon* in greater detail.

The evidence of the poems indicates, therefore, that Vaughan was not R.V. But this does not necessarily mean that R.V. must be Verstegan! Are there certain features of the verse that suggest his hand? Use of a more archaic Latin form *ast* (as distinct from *at*) is consistent with the Verstegan that was possibly friendly with Spenser, and who showed a preference for older words in his translation of *Lazarillo de Tormes* (1576) – if I have identified the translator correctly.[38] On the other hand, the argument should not be pressed too hard, since *ast* also conveniently solves a problem of scansion.[39] Again the use of alliteration referred to earlier is certainly a characteristic feature of Verstegan's English verse: for instance in a line from the beautiful lullaby to the Virgin, "My babe, my blis, my child, my choyce".[40] Nevertheless, fondness for alliteration is found in other contemporary poets too.

If we turn to the contents of R.V.'s poem of commendation, a little more evidence emerges. Firstly, it is a poem by a linguist, familiar with the arguments in favour of enriching the vernacular languages; familiar also with the claims currently made for the antiquity of the Welsh language, but aware that it is nevertheless held in contempt by certain people. In fact, R.V. was indebted for some of his remarks, even opinions, to the address to the reader ("Ad Lectorem") that served as introduction to Henry Salesbury's *Grammatica Britannica* of 1593.[41] R.V. is less strident than Salesbury in his condemnation of those that show contempt for the language, noting simply: [*lingua*] "contempta diu iacuit cum gente", but he has picked up the point about the antiquity of Welsh, and its right to stand comparison with any ancient tongue: claimed Salesbury, [*lingua*] "quae cum antiquissimis totius Europae linguis lepore, argumento & regularum certitudine certare possit". What brings R.V.s poem closer to Salesbury's address is the discussion in the latter of the phonic roughness attributed by some to Welsh, its "hiulcam & asperam literarum pronunciationem". In reply to these critics Salesbury remarks that similar things have been said by the ignorant about Latin, Greek and Hebrew. Furthermore, a mingling of the harsh and the smooth is what gives music its beauty. Later the author argues that this *asper* quality is a sign of the language's antiquity. R.V. has been taken by this argument about roughness of sound, indeed by implication accepts its existence in the case of Welsh, but then goes on to contrast it with the clarity of its structure ("Sit licet asperior sonus, at structura diserta"), the latter point bringing us back to the remark cited above concerning the "regularum certitudine". R.V. seems afterwards to have been struck by the smoothness of certain Welsh sounds also, a feature implicit in what Salesbury had said about mingling the soft and the hard: "Nam naturae nihil est convenientius, quam dura mollibus, lenibus aspera, & acutis gravia connectere". R.V. has introduced likewise the comparison with music, since the words of the language (its *verba*) are "mirifice mollibus apta modis", melodic indeed! The word *mirificus* may also have attracted R.V., for it is used by Salesbury at a later point.

Finally, it is worth noting that R.V. has brought together, in a context that is lyrical rather than technical, terms that belonged essentially to the rhetorical discipline: thus *structura* (a word that Dee uses too), *disertus* that was used of good clear expression, *asper* rugged of style, *sonus* tone or character, *nitor* for grace and elegance of style, *lumen* for stylistic ornaments, *decus* indicating grace or embellishment. Again *excolere, ornare, splendor,* and other technical terms find their echo here. Thus R.V., while noting how Perri has dedicated himself to the art of rhetoric, displays in a playful way his own knowledge of that same art. One other point. At the beginning R.V. remarks on the appropriateness of adding refinement (*excolere*) to Biblical text: he may have had in mind William Middleton's metrical version of Psalm 119, and Henry Salesbury's of Psalm 15, which appear in the *Egluryn*.

Interestingly, Richard Verstegan would soon produce his volume of *Odes* (1601), which included his metrical versions of the Seven Penitential Psalms.[42]

R.V. in his poem shows his awareness that grammatical studies of Welsh have been made by other scholars: Salesbury himself refers to Siôn Dafydd Rhys's [Dr John Davies] *Cambrobrytannicae Cymraecaeve Linguae Institutiones* (1592), but R.V. knows of the work of more than one ("alii"), so that he may be referring also to Gruffydd Robert's *Gramadeg Cymraeg* (Milan, 1567). Once more this indicates his interest in language, and reveals that his curiosity has extended to the British tongue. Significantly, R.V. also admires Perri's knowledge of several languages.

The above evidence offers no proof that R.V. was Verstegan, but it creates an identikit picture of a man very like him – a scholar with a particular interest in language, who shows admiration for another's comparable skill in the acquisition of foreign tongues; a poet of considerable ability, sensitive to the sound and rhythm of words, clever too in exploiting linguistic ambivalences; likewise a good Latinist, thoroughly versed in the terminology of rhetoric, and at ease in the composition of Latin verse – Verstegan's most important, indeed notorious, book to date had been in Latin, his *Theatrum Crudelitatum Haereticorum nostri Temporis* (1587). All this may be so, but what of R.V.'s acquaintance with the Welsh language, and his sympathy with the attempt made by Perri to cultivate and enrich it? This is a subject that requires more detailed attention.

I have argued elsewhere that Verstegan, or to give his name more accurately, Richard Rowland [Verstegan], was of Welsh origin.[43] If I am right, he was a son of the house of Rowland [Wynn] of Penhesgyn Isaf, in the parish of Llansadwrn, Anglesey. However, he may have been brought up in London, his contact with Wales appears to have been only occasional, and although he had some knowledge of the Welsh language, he was not fluent in it. In contrast, his *A Restitution of Decayed Intelligence* does reveal an interest in Wales, its history, its language, its pedigrees and its heraldry. Furthermore, Verstegan there shows incidentally some knowledge of the work of Welsh scholars, and his respect for them – a situation paralleled by what we find in R.V.'s poem, which bespeaks someone acquainted with Welsh scholarship at second hand, rather than being directly involved in it. Verstegan had been an exile on the continent since 1582, but this did not dim his interest in the political, religious, and scholarly affairs of his homeland. We may surmise that he was also in a position to maintain occasional contact by secret visits from Antwerp.

How might Henry Perri have come in contact with Verstegan? If the former had, in fact, been an exile for some years on account of his Catholic convictions, then it is quite feasible that he met Verstegan in Paris, or in Antwerp. Certainly that acquaintance would have had to be deep enough for Verstegan to respond to a request by Perri for a poem of commendation. The book's eventual publication would strengthen considerably the Catholic presence in *Egluryn Ffraethineb*. But why should Perri make such a request? The explanation must lie more in a shared tradition of learning than in any attempt to court controversy, although it is worth recalling that Verstegan had likewise shown a conciliatory spirit in the search after a *rapprochement* between Catholic and Protestant.[44] As for the very bold initials R.V., these might suggest to a few contemporary readers, especially those who were Catholic, the identity of the author of the *Theatrum Crudelitatum*, but Verstegan was as yet in the relatively early stages of his career, and had by 1595 only used those initials in one other work, so that this signature could hardly have been intended to have a great impact.[45]

Perri's relation with Verstegan may possibly have come about, or been reinforced, through a different circumstance. I have already mentioned Perri's second marriage, to the daughter of Robert Vaughan of Beaumaris, and his wife Grace Coetmor. The latter was a sister to Elin Coetmor, wife of the squire of Penhesgyn Isaf, Richard Rowland Wynn, who may have been – so I have argued – a brother or half-brother to Richard Rowland, the future Antwerp recusant. This would make Perri Verstegan's nephew. The family connexion that I have posited may – or equally may not – have a relevance in the context of *Egluryn Ffraethineb*, the reason being that we remain in the dark concerning the commencement of Perri's association with Sir Richard Bulkeley, and the date of his arrival in the Island of Anglesey. One thing is certain: the marriage of Robert Vaughan and his bride Grace took place in 1582,[46] so that it is not feasible for Perri to have married their daughter Elizabeth by 1595. On the other hand, Perri could well have been resident in Anglesey and in contact with the Vaughan family of Beaumaris – home also of Sir Richard Bulkeley – before that year, in which case the relation with Penhesgyn could of itself have helped establish or reinforce the contact with Verstegan.

Egluryn Ffraethineb is a remarkable testimony to the lively debate in Wales – and also in certain London circles – concerning the Welsh language, its present state of decay and neglect, and above all the need to apply to it that process of enrichment that had taken place in the case of French, Spanish, and Italian. In addition, Perri apparently believed that enthusiasm for the language, and for the literary heritage it expressed, should not be the exclusive preserve of any sectarian coterie, either Protestant or Catholic. Rather were they for everyone. The language too was a common inheritance, and the challenge was to use it, and write it. Such inclusiveness points also to the desire for a religious reconciliation which, alas, never came to fruition. Since there is no conclusive proof that R.V. was actually Verstegan, we cannot speculate as to whether he was part of, or party to, such a scheme.

In contrast, the evidence presented here does strengthen somewhat the view that the Antwerp recusant's roots were in Anglesey, in which case his graceful contribution to Perri's volume may have owed something to the passionate nostalgia felt by any *Monwysyn* in exile beyond the Menai Strait.

APPENDIX

CARMEN ENCOMIASTICHON
IN LAUDEM BRITANNICAE LINGUAE
& OPERIS

Gratia cuique sua est linguae, sed maxima sacris,
    Quas docti scriptis excoluere suis.
Ast reliquas aequat, superatque Britannica linguas,
    Qua magis antiqua est nulla, fluensque magis.
Sit licet asperior sonus, at structura diserta est,
    Verbaque mirifice mollibus apta modis.
Quae contempta diu iacuit cum gente, nitori
    Reddita nativo est, splendidiorque redit.
Grammatices rudimenta alii, sed lumina solus
    Rhetorices mira Perrius arte dedit.
Sic pergat decus esse suis, ornetque vicissim,
    Linguarum varia cognitione, suam.

R. V.

Ri. Vaughani in Authorem

Quid facis, O Camber? cessas antique Brytanne?
    Ardua quin Prisi respicis acta tui?
Priseus infesto Polydori vindicat ore,
    Res regni validas (Brute vetuste) tui.
Brenne, Brytanne pugil, tibi quis vincendo secundus?
    En Romanorum bis quia victor eras.
Tu cum fratre tuo sparsistis nomina latè,
    Italiae restant, quae, monumenta, probant.
Arthur & Heroum princeps, quem personat orbis,

Prisaei casta, perstrepis historia.
Prise perite vale, spectate domiq; forisq;
   Iura sciens, aequè dans ea, scriptor, Eques:
Tu quoq; succedis proles gratissima patri,
   Qui nobis patrium nobile tradis opus:
Tu patris & patriae famam per secula seruas,
   Et pius es patri tu, patriaeq; pius.

Thou sole companion of our oft chang'd State,
   Sprong from the bowels of this sea-wald Ile:
   Whom al-deuouring time could not exile,
So haue we constant beene despite of fate.
   That how soeuer fortune tyrannizde,
   We euer thee with all affections prizde.

Now since the splendor of a blessed time
   Hath raizd our fortune, wee will reare thy praise
   With Madregals, Sonnettos, Roundelaies;
And add (Art-graced) Prose to Art-like Rime.
   Thus *Perry* doth in his best graced vaine,
   Where first he breathd, imploying there his paine.

Praise cannot add more worth, but shewe affection,
   And vertue of it selfe, it selfe doth grace;
   Then cease my pen, lest more, thee more disgrace;
Since nought thou shew'st. but thy Arts imperfection:
   Let better wits his labours higher raise,
   Or let them cease, the worke it selfe will praise.

William Mathew, Esquire

NOTES

1. His persistence as a controversialist during the following reign is shown in A.F. Allison, "A Group of Political Tracts, 1621-1623, by Richard Verstegan", *Recusant History*, 18 (1986-1987), 128-42.
    I am very grateful to Professor R. Geraint Gruffydd for his helpful criticism and comments on an earlier draft of this article.

2. John Bossy, "The Character of Elizabethan Catholicism", in *Crisis in Europe 1560-1660: Essays from Past and Present*, edited by Trevor Aston (London, 1965), pp.223-46, quotation on p.238. For Verstegan's biography we must still largely depend on the article on him [Richard Rowlands] in *DNB*, Edward Rombauts, *Richard Verstegen: Een Polemist der Contra-Reformatie* (Brussels, 1933), and A.G. Petti, "A Study of the Life and Writings of Richard Verstegan" (University of London M.A. thesis, 1957). More recently, I have sought to demonstrate that his ultimate origins were in Anglesey, and that he may be identified with the translator of the Spanish picaresque novel *Lazarillo de Tormes* – see G.A. Davies,"The English *Lazarillo de Tormes* (1586) and its Translator: David Rowland of Anglesey or Richard Rowland Verstegan?", *Transactions of the Honourable Society of Cymmrodorion*, 1991, pp.99-128 (Part One) and 1992, pp.45-78 (Part Two); also "David Rowland's *Lazarillo de Tormes* (1576): The History of a Translation", *The National Library of Wales Journal*, XXVIII (1994), 349-87.

3. See facsimile edition by G.J. Williams (Caerdydd, Gwasg Prifysgol Cymru, 1930), and introduction. Also the sections on Perri in Bedwyr Lewis Jones, "Testunau Rhethreg Cymraeg y Dadeni", University of Wales M.A. thesis, 1961, pp.120-75 (BLJ subsequently here), and in W. Alun Mathias, "Llyfr Rhetoreg William Salesbury", *Llên Cymru*, II(1952-1953), 71-81, at pp.74-76.

4. See BLJ, p.123, p.125, p.139 and p.142. On Ramus, see ibid., p.148 and pp.154-55.

5. See the Welsh translation of Davies's Latin in Ceri Davies, *Rhagymadroddion a Chyflwyniadau Lladin 1551-1632: Cyfieithwyd, ynghyd â Rhagymadrodd a Nodiadau* (Caerdydd, Gwasg Prifysgol Cymru, 1980), p.127.

6. For the more general context of these ideas in Wales, see Ceri Davies, op. cit., pp.4-10.

7. See his reflections on ideas expressed by the late Gwyn A. Williams, in R.J. Roberts, "John Dee and the Matter of Britain", *Transactions of the Honourable Society of Cymmrodorion*, 1991, pp.129-43, quotation on p.143.

8. See the introduction by G.J. Williams, the *DNB* and *Y Bywgraffiadur Cymreig*. Also BLJ, especially pp.165-166.

9. *Athenae Oxonienses*, i, 666-7.

10. Gwilym Lleyn, *Llenyddiaeth y Cymry* (Llanidloes, 1865), p.71.

11. See P.C. Bartrum, *Welsh Genealogies A.D.1400-1500*, 18 vols. (National Library of Wales, 1983), *Ednywain Bendew*, 3(A1), the line of Maes-glas (Greenfield), Treffynnon, Tegeingl. Also his *Hanmer*, 1(B). Details also in J.Y.W.H., "Sheriffs of Denbighshire", *Arch. Camb.*, 3rd Series, XV (1869), 1-29, on p.11 and p.21.

12. J.E. Griffith, *Pedigrees of Anglesey and Carnarvonshire Families* (Hornchurch, 1914), p.106 (*PED* subsequently here).

13. Bartrum, *Hanmer*, 1(B).

14. Emyr Gwynne Jones, "Catholic Recusancy in the Counties of Denbigh, Flint and Montgomery, 1581-1625", *Transactions of the Honourable Society of Cymmrodorion*, 1945, 114-133, at p.120. See also his *Cymru a'r hen Ffydd* (Wales and the Old Faith) (Caerdydd, 1951), passim.

15. "Catholic Recusancy", pp.121, 131 and 133, *Cymru a'r hen Ffydd*, p.27.

16. *Egluryn Ffraethineb*, f.B1v.

17. See Philip Hughes, *The Reformation in England*, vol.III (*"True Religion now established"*) [London, 1954], ch.III ("Conflict"), pp.335-83, quotation on p.369. For the penalties during the eighties and early nineties, see "Catholic Recusancy", p.115.

18. *Cymru a'r hen Ffydd*, p.30.

19. See Emyr Gwynne Jones, "'History of the Bulkeley Family' (N.L.W. MS 908E)", *Transactions of the Anglesey Antiquarian Society and Field Club*, 1948, 1-99, at p.28. The querying of Perri's right in law to take a Beaumaris woman as his second wife may possibly reflect local anti-Catholic sentiment – see *Athenae*. The Bulkeley family may epitomize what John Bossy defined as a "withdrawal to the seigneurial household", in which the bonds of Catholic continuity have been residually maintained, but "withdrawn from the public order of the parish into the private order of the household" – see his "The Character of Elizabethan Catholicism", originally in *Past and Present*, 21 (April 1962), 39-59, at p.40; reprinted in *Crisis in Europe 1560-1660* (see note 2 above).

20. *PED*, p.84 and p.106.

21. See e.g. Henry Barber and Henry Lewis, *The History of Friars School* (Bangor, 1901), passim, and the Fourth Centenary Number: *The Dominican: Friars School, 1557-1957*, ed. E.W. Jones and J. Howarth, ch.II: "Friars School from its Foundation to the Year 1789", especially pp.27-31. See also my forthcoming study of Bishop Griffin.

22. For the background, see A.H. Dodd,"North Wales in the Essex Revolt of 1601", *English Historical Review*, LIX(1944), 348-70, who notes that Lleweni, as a result of the plot, had been put "under a cloud" (355). See also *Y Bywgraffiadur* under Thomas Salusbury (1564-86).

23. "Catholic Recusancy", pp.120-21.

24. On the Mathew family, see *Cymru a'r hen Ffydd*, p.34. Also J. Barry Davies, "The Mathew Family of Llandaff, Radyr and Castell-y-Mynach", *Glamorgan Historian*, vol.11, ed. Roy Denning (Barry, s.a.), pp.171-87.

25. Folio reference unclear. I have included the text of the poem in the Appendix.

26. See e.g. Philip Hughes, op. cit., III, 385-87. There were some Catholic priests in England who supported the succession of James VI of Scotland. My reading is given some confirmation by a Catholic poet, William Middleton, also represented here, in the address to the reader of his *Psalmae y Brenhinol Brophwyd Dafydd, ...* (Llunden, 1603). In it he includes what seems a prudent gloss on William Mathew's poem. We are reminded how "notable things in our language" have been "deuoured of time" (cf. Mathew's "al-deuouring time"). Referring to the Welsh language's miraculous survival, he extends the "many alterations and changes of Princes" back to the legendary Brutus, but like Mathew he celebrates the increase in learning "in this most blessed age wherein God hath giuen vs a King, indued with many heroicall vertues", who is also descended from the great Welsh forbear, Brutus. Cf. the praise given James I of England by Verstegan in his poem at the beginning of *A Restitution*.

27. On Lewys and his translation, see *Perl mewn Adfyd gan Huw Lewys yn ôl argraffiad 1595*, ed. W.J. Gruffydd (Caerdydd, 1929).

28. See *Y Bywgraffiadur*, under the Holland family of Conwy.

29. See *DNB*, and William Williams, "Three Fragments", *Journal of the Welsh Bibliographical Society*, IV(1932-1936), 257-65, section I (pp.257-62) on Middleton and the recently discovered *cywyddau* (259-60).

30. See *DNB* and BLJ, p.160. It is difficult to assess Rankins's religious position.

31. On Henry Salesbury, see *Y Bywgraffiadur*, and Ceri Davies, op. cit., in which a Welsh translation is given of Salesbury's dedicatory letter to the Earl of Pembroke, as well as of his eloquent address to his reader (pp.93-95 and 95-100). Salesbury took some of his contemporaries to task for their lack of knowledge of the Welsh language, and their contempt for it.

32. See G.J. Williams's introduction to his edition, p. vii and note.

33. See A.G. Petti, "A Bibliography of the Writings of Richard Verstegan (c.1550-1641)", *Recusant History*, 7(1963-64). Petti gives as his reference Hazlitt's *Second Series of Bibliographical Collections and Notes on Early English Literature 1474-1700* (London,1882), p.70. Unfortunately the reference is incorrect, though we do find Verstegan's name on that page as a printer of [Richard Broughton], *The First Part of the Resolvtion of Religion* (1603). In perusing the other volumes of Hazlitt's *Collections* I have failed to find the information to which Petti refers. *Egluryn Ffraethineb* itself is described in *Collections* [1893-1903] (London, 1903), p.298, with no reference to the commendatory verses. We must assume that Petti saw the attribution elsewhere in Hazlitt's writings.

34. See Franklin B. Williams, *Index of Dedications and Commendatory Verses in English Books before 1641* (London, The Bibliographical Society, 1962), p.188, with reference to *Egluryn* (STC 19775). Among those who attended the ancient universities, only Robert Vaughan, pleb. from Caernarfonshire, seems eligible. He matriculated from St Edmund Hall, Oxford, on 22 December 1576, at the age of 20. There is no sign that he took his degree.

35. I am grateful to Professor R. Geraint Gruffydd, University of Wales (Aberystwyth), for this suggestion. See also BLJ, p.161. On Richard Vaughan, see *Y Bywgraffiadur*. The *congé d'élire* of his election to Bangor is dated 6 November 1595, and he was consecrated on 25 January 1596 – see Browne Willis, *A Survey of the Cathedral Church of Bangor and the Edifices belonging to it* (London, 1721), list of bishops, no.49, on p.109.

36. I am grateful to the late Professor E.J. Wood (University of Leeds) and to Mr Ceri Davies (University of Wales, Swansea) for the benefit of their expert advice on these two examples of Renaissance Latin. The text of both poems is made available in the Appendix.

37. Mr Ceri Davies in a letter to me (26 July 1994) has emphasized R.V.'s technical mastery, citing some of the instances mentioned, and noting others.

38. See articles by me referred to in note 2.

39. I am grateful to Mr Ceri Davies for making the latter point.

40. See Louise Imogen Guiney, *Recusant Poets ... With a Selection from their Work* (London & New York, 1938), pp.211-15.

41. *Grammatica Britannica in usum ejus linguae studiorum ...* (Londini, Thomas Salesburius, 1593), ff.**2-**3v.

42. See BLJ, p. 157. I have already mentioned Middleton's metrical psalms (1603). Verstegan's versions of the Seven Penitential Psalms would first appear in his *The Primer, or Office of the Blessed Virgin Marie* in Antwerp in 1599, pp.174-81. He emphasizes (f.A2^v) that he has aimed at a close, rather than a pleasing, rendering.

43. See note 2.

44. See my "The History of a Translation", p. 351. A certain R.V. was also responsible for *Englands Joy* (London? 1601?). Certain features – e.g. the acrostic – suggest Verstegan, but the fawning display of loyalty to Elizabeth may seem rather extreme. In any case, what makes the attribution very unlikely is the anti-Papist sentiment: "Nor Pope, nor Spaniard now shall none preuaile". Petti is probably right in rejecting this as Verstegan's work.

45. See Petti, "Bibliography".

46. See *PED*, p.84 and p.106. The Conwy parish register gives 22 July 1582 as the date of their marriage. Robert Vaughan is described as being "de Villa".

MARGARET A. REES

Trinity and All Saints University College

THE GAZE OF GOD
DOÑA LUISA DE CARVAJAL Y MENDOZA AND THE
ENGLISH MISSION

'Understand ... the profound nature
of your soul ... It is a being
reached by the gaze of God'.

(Hadewijch of Antwerp)[1]

Anyone afoot in what were then the very outskirts of London, near the Flemish Embassy, before daylight on October 28, 1613, would have seen a blaze of lanterns bearing down on a small house. Sixty halbardiers, with both infantrymen and cavalry back-up troops, were escorting the Recorder and the Sheriff of London in a dawn raid, bearing with them King James I's written instructions. The house once surrounded, soldiers set up scaling ladders to give them entry to the garden and battered down the heavy double doors. Before long, alerted bv the hullabaloo, no less a person than the Flemish ambassador was on the scene, quickly followed from the Spanish Embassy by the Conde de Gondomar, Don Diego Sarmiento. A royal order, the king's horses and men, the capital's leading legal authorities, now joined by two Catholic ambassadors – surely what brought them all together on that Autumn morning must have been a massive threat to the security of the realm and international affairs.

In fact, the first soldiers past the doors found to their astonishment that their dangerous prey was a delicate foreign woman in her late forties, clearly living in the utmost poverty, her only companions four young girls, one of whom (ill already) is said to have died of shock the next day. So dumbfounded were the men that any order to search the property was forgotten, and they did not come across the incriminating sight of the oratory laid out for Mass. When the target of all this dawn activity was arrested – riding, at the Conde de Gondomar's insistence, in the ambassadorial coach – she was escorted all the way across London by a horde of armed men and officers of the law, as well as by protective Catholic Embassy officials. No sooner was she imprisoned, after questioning in Lambeth Palace, than the Spanish Ambassador's wife summoned her own carriage to drive to the prison, and sent a message to King James that she herself intended to remain there until he released his prisoner.

The storm centre of all this activity, Doña Luisa de Carvajal y Mendoza, was a long way from the peaceful surroundings of her girlhood home in Almazán. After donating all her inherited wealth to St Alban's College, the seminary in Valladolid where young men from Britain were trained as spiritual assault troops,[2] she had set off herself for the land from which stories constantly came of Catholic martyrdom. The longing to be martyred may have affected her later in life than it had one of her role models, Teresa of Avila – she had harboured it from the age of seventeen instead of seven – but the intention was just as strong, and there was no uncle, as in Teresa's case, to intercept her and return her to her home. After resting for a while with Jesuits and Discalced Carmelites in Paris, she landed on Dover beach on May 1, 1605.

The charges brought against her at Lambeth Palace by the Archbishop of Canterbury, on the instructions of King and Council, were twofold: (a) that she had set up a Catholic convent (or several) in the heart of London under the King's very nose, and (b) that her constant proselytizing work, together with her connections abroad, made her a worse threat than several priests to the political stability of the land.[3] Luisa refused to accept that the Archbishop had any jurisdiction over her (her letters always refer to him as 'el falso arzobispo'), but, had she defended her case, she would have certainly accepted the charges and seen them as a testimonial to a job well done. Her letters amply document her actions and her delight in them.

The house raided in 'Spetele' (Spitalfields?) at James I's order was indeed meant as a challenge to the 'new religion', as the home of an order to be called the 'Congregación de la Soberana Virgen María Nuestra Señora'. 'Estoy deseosa que en este erial, en esta selva de sierpes y bestias fieras, nuestra pobre casita le sea a Nuestro Señor apacible y delicioso jardín' or, in more military terms, 'ella es un castillo levantado en las barbas de los enemigos de la Santa Iglesia. Parece que está desafiando a todos juntos'.[4] One of the rare words of approval that she wrote about anything on English soil was to describe the four 'angelillos' who, after careful appraisal, she took as novices. Among them was Ann Garnet, 'prima hermana' of Fr Henry Garnet, Superior of the Jesuits in England, and a doughty fist fighter who did battle and snatched back a rosary grabbed from Luisa on her way out of Mass.[5]

The second charge levelled against 'esa española' was two-sided. Live Catholics she cherished and comforted with every ounce of the energy and the funds available, arranging for their sons and daughters to be educated abroad, visiting them at home and in prison and tending to their every need; dead Catholics – the bodies of martyred priests – were brought to her to be prepared for burial with the greatest reverence and tenderness. Protestant 'heretics' had the same effect on her as would a public house full of drunks on a twentieth-century Salvation Army officer. Babies were removed for christening, supposedly to save poor mothers the fee, and were whisked off to a priest. With a courage which fed rumours that this was in fact a dangerous priest in women's clothing, she preached not only to individuals but – in what must have been truly spectacular scenes – to large crowds drawn by anger or curiosity to the shop in Cheapside or the impromptu courtroom where she expounded the true faith. Nor can King James have been happy for letters to be sent abroad commenting on the weak state of British defences, both military and naval, and the easy prey which the country would present to any 'armada' coming to help the faithful in Ireland or on the mainland.[6] With truly Teresian determination she outwitted the eventual international agreement that she should return to Spain. Whilst alive she persisted in carrying on with her mission, and it was only death, not through martyrdom but through prison-induced illness, that finally loosened her grip on London. In 1615 her body set off in a ship named 'La Luisa de Londres' heading for San Sebastián and a burial place chosen by the King of Spain himself in the Real Monasterio de la Encarnación.

What drove her on? Some missionaries to New Spain found interest – delight even – in their mission's surroundings. Luisa's reactions to England never varied during her nine-year stay, and they read like a parody of the modern English Tourist Board's worst nightmares of foreign impressions. The beds, the food, the 'constant' rain and total dearth of sunshine, the 'catarro fuerte' which afflicted her, all contributed to her letters' refrain with variations: 'esta selva espesa de fieras' (no. 33. A Magdalena de San Jerónimo, 14 December 1605). The desire to carry out God's will is the sole force that keeps her in the front line, 'aunque sea muriendo cada momento, como puedo decir que muero, todos los que me acuerdo que estoy en esta Isla. Si El se sirviere que salga della, no habrá mejor vía para el amor propio...'(no. 183. A Magdalena de San Jerónimo, 24 July 1606).

On an earthly level, there is no question about the main factor that made possible her London campaign: that is her illustrious birth and connections, which served her as they had done Hildegard of Bingen. The document authorizing her monthly grant is signed 'Yo, el Rey', and her correspondents include – apart from British Jesuits and other religious – her uncle, Don Bernardo de Sandobal y Rojas (Cardinal of Toledo); her cousin, Doña Isabel de Velasco, wife of Luis Carrillo de Toledo, viceroy of Navarre; and the Duke of Lerma himself. Her family tree included some of the noblest names in the land,[7] and when she was orphaned at the age of six it seemed fitting for her to be brought up in the royal palace where her great-aunt was 'camarera' to the Infantas Isabel Clara Eugenia and Catalina, and nurse to the prince, Don Diego. On her great-aunt's death, it was an uncle, Don Francisco Hurtado de Mendoza, marqués de Almazán, one-time ambassador to the German court, who took her into his household. Even with every coin of her inheritance given to the Jesuits for the English mission, these royal and aristocratic connections formed a powerful network to support her venture, guaranteeing her the sanctuary and succour of the Spanish Embassy and active help from other Catholic ambassadors, even before dawn on an October morning. Ronald Cueto has shown how even working-class women of this period, such as Mauricia Pérez de Velasco, who had been dealt a 'strikingly meagre hand... in the game of life', could bc profitably aware of the functioning of interests and connections in the Catholic Monarchy.[8] Doña Luisa, born in comparison, with a handful of genetic aces, was superbly placed to give James I and his Council of State the occasional uneasy half-hour on behalf of the Catholic Church.

Birth and connections may have been part of the wherewithal, but what was the driving force that, from the age of seventeen, had made her focus on the English mission and spend the last nine years of her life in a country that was anathema to her? Clearly the real fuel came from the intense spiritual life that biographers note in her even as a small child wearing for preference a diminutive Franciscan habit and walking barefoot in her room to imitate the friars she admired, and so chaste that she repulsed a kiss proffered by any male, even her father, with cries and tears. All this was recorded of her tastes and instincts before she was six. From her early teens, her life with her pious and learned uncle was almost that of a seminarian, steeped in charitable works, extreme asceticism, and long hours of prayer, biblical and theological reading and discourse. As an adult in Madrid, rejecting marriage, she chose a life-style for herself and three or four companions which rivalled in bare poverty any reformed Carmel. This aristocrat wore the coarsest cloth, slept on a straw palliasse with a horse blanket over her, and painfully learned ordinary household chores.[9]

These are glimpses of her spiritual life from the outside, but there is a window which gives a far more intimate view into her mind: the window of her poetry. As far as is known, all her poems were composed in Spain.[10] The hurly-burly of the London campaign generated close on two hundred letters that have survived, some dealing with practical matters (even down to the refurbishing of the ambassadorial gloves[11]), others giving fascinating insights into the lives and deaths of beleaguered Catholics, but these years were scarcely conducive to the 'emotion reflected in tranquillity' which is poetry. There are several high evaluations of her verse. 'En poesía religiosa y en su siglo, nadie la sobrepasa en castellano'.[12] 'Doña Luisa de Carvajal es, indudablemente, la más ilustre poetisa religiosa de cuantas florecieron en España durante el siglo XVII'.[13] Perhaps, with the ever-increasing discovery of writings by women (including Sor Cecilia del Nacimiento, some of whose poetry was once thought to have been by San Juan de la Cruz), Luisa's rating might have fallen a little today, but such league tables would presumably have been a matter of supreme indifference to her. Certainly the poems – sonnets, 'romances', 'letrillas' and 'redondillas' – have all the technical expertise of someone who had been a very apt pupil of her uncle, Don Francisco Hurtado de Mendoza, author himself of a volume of verse. Again Luisa's cultured background benefited her, this time with an obvious familiarity with contemporary poetry. As a woman, her education may have been informal, but it could not have been more high-flying and throughout her teenage years must have resembled one-to-one Oxbridge tutorials with an expert in Latin, theology and religious writings. Her cousins might steal away from their father's evening readings and discussions after a decent interval, but she, the 'hija de su alma', apparently remained.

Her surviving poems are fired throughout with a passionate devotion to Christ which fully explains her heroic mission to London, and perhaps suggests a level of personal mystic experience. Her religious education has clearly borne fruit. These were days when, as Terence O'Reilly points out, devout laymen and women had access to treasures of monastic spirituality, in spite of Inquisitors' objection to, for instance, Fray Luis de Granada writing 'theology for carpenters' wives'.[14] Santa Teresa's writings were available and it is known that Luisa had access to San Juan de la Cruz's works in manuscript. Sometimes she lets us hear a clear echo of a well-known play on words. 'Soneto espiritual de Silva, de sentimientos de amor y ausencia profundísimos' (no. 15) begins '¿Cómo vives, sin quien vivir no puedes?' and the second stanza of no.17 ('Soneto de Silva al Santísimo Sacramento') 'Muerte eres, vida eterna, de mi muerte'. 'Que sólo el vivir muriendo / porque no mueres, te aplace', says the soul to the heart in 'Romance espiritual de interiores sentimientos. Habla el alma que los padecía, con su corazón' (no. 2). In her 'Versos nacidos del fuego del amor de Dios', Teresa de Jesús had written: 'Vivo sin vivir en mí, / y tan alta vida espero, / que muero porque no muero.' In the same vein, San Juan in stanza eight of 'El cántico espiritual' asks 'Mas, ¿cómo perseueras / O vida, no uiuiendo donde viues ...?'. Might there be another echo, fainter certainly, of 'El cántico espiritual' ('que adolezco, peno y muero') in the description that Luisa gives of an intensifying grief 'que me mata, y me lastima, / y me acaba, y me atormenta'? ('Quintillas espirituales de Silva', no. 5).

'Silva' herself and her shepherd lover belong well and truly in the pastoral tradition of the day, with its long history stretching back to the *Cantar de los Cantares*. Sometimes Luisa's verses fit Solomon's lines as closely as do Juan de la Cruz's. One sonnet of hers which later found its way into anthologies presents a biblical scene. 'En el siniestro brazo recostada / de su amado Pastor, Silva dormía, / y con la diestra mano la tenía / con un estrecho abrazo a sí allegada.'

In this ecstatic sleep '"El corazón del alma mía / vela, y yo duermo"'. She calls out to the 'ninfas del Paraíso soberanas' that she is 'enferma y muy herida / de unos abrasadísimos amores' and appeals to them to surround her with 'odoríferas manzanas' and 'amenas flores'. Perhaps during the evening readings at Almazán Luisa listened to Luis de León's translation of the 'Song of Solomon', which contributed to bringing the Inquisition's wrath down on his head. If so, she would have heard lines such as 'Esforzadme, rodeadme de vasos de vino, cercadme de manzanas, que enferma estoy de amor. / La izquierda suya debajo de mi cabeza, y su derecha me abrazará'.[15]

Among the vast range of potential subjects for religious verse it is Christ himself on whom Luisa focuses, drawing on imagery which is again familiar from Juan de la Cruz's poetry, sometimes from Teresa de Jesús's verse and prose, and is rooted firmly in the traditions of neoplatonism and courtly love. Fire dominates, as in her 'lira', 'En la profesión de alguna religiosa', with its refrain 'que el corazón de amor tiene abrasado' (no. 49), but we also find the wounds and pain of love; love's banner; captives taken in war; chains and arrows; the theft of the heart; the darkness of absence. A whole compendium of these images forms 'Letra espiritual de Silva. De afectos de amor de Dios' (no. 10), but perhaps the most significant of its verses for the whole tenor of her work is the fifth stanza:

> Si, con sólo mirar, queda
> hecho absoluto señor
> del alma, tomando en ella
> pacífica posesión,
> *¿qué serán veras de amor?*

Throughout her poetry it is the face of Christ, above all his gaze, that shines out.

It goes without saying that religious teachers had encouraged such devotion from the early days of the Church. Nicolas of Cusa (1401-1464) was just one theologian who recommended focusing attention on a picture of the holy face of Jesus as the initial step toward Christian contemplation.[16] Grace M. Jantzen points out that, nearer Luisa's own time, the radiant attractiveness of God so absorbed John of the Cross, 'whose prose writings are on the whole notable for their austerity', that he 'nearly trips over himself when it comes to describing the beauty ... of God'.[17] Speaking of his longing, he prays:

> que de tal manera esté yo transformada en tu hermosura,
> que siendo semejante en hermosura, nos ueamos entrambos
> en tu hermosura, teniendo ya tu misma hermosura; de
> manera que mirando el vno al otro, vea cada vno en el otro
> su hermosura, siendo la vna y la del otro tu hermosura sola,
> absorta yo en tu hermosura; y assí te veré yo á ti en tu
> hermosura y tú á mi en tu hermosura, y yo me veré en tí en
> tu hermosura y tú te verás en mí en tu hermosura; y assí
> parezca o tú en tu hermosura y parezcas tú yo en tu

hermosura y mi hermosura sea tu hermosura y tu hermosura mi hermosura; y assí seré yo tú en tu hermosura, y serás tú yo en tu hermosura; porque tu misma hermosura será mi hermosura; y assí nos ueremos el vno al otro en tu hermosura.'

('El Cántico espiritual', commentary on stanza 36)

San Juan's soul is left, as he put it in stanza seven of the 'Cántico', with 'un no sé qué que queda(n) balbuciendo'.

Teresa de Jesús too, in a passage that has notoriously attracted the attention of video-makers recently, urged her daughters about '¡...la ganancia que hay de arrojarnos en los brazos de este Señor Nuestro, y hacer un concierto con su Majestad, que mire yo a mi amado y mi amado a mí; y que mire El por mis cosas, y yo por las suyas! ¡No nos queramos tanto que nos saquemos los ojos, como dicen! Torno a decir, Dios mío, y a suplicaros, por la sangre de vuestro Hijo, que me hagáis esta merced: "béseme con beso de su boca"' (*Conceptos del Amor de Dios*, cap. IV). It is sometimes argued nowadays, in a time of increasing concentration on women's spirituality, that Teresa, like some medieval forerunners – Gertrude the Great of Helfta, Mechtild of Magdeburg, Catherine of Siena, Beatrice of Nazareth – illustrates a contrast with male mystical writers, even such an affective theologian as St Bernard. The claim is that for some women 'there is every indication that, far from the erotic being simply an allegory for the spiritual, it is precisely through actual eroticism that lessons of God are to be learned' (Jantzen, 133-34). One example is Hadewijch of Antwerp whose works appeared in the first half of the thirteenth century and who, at matins one Pentecost Sunday, saw Christ in the form of a man, 'looking like a human being and a man, wonderful, and beautiful, and with a glorious face . . . Then he gave himself to me in the shape of the sacrament'. 'The account is of an actual, though visionary encounter . . . It is spiritual love-making.' With such women writers 'there is a direct, highly charged, passionate encounter between Christ and the writer'.[18] Louis Bouyer too sees a male/female difference of concept when he compares Hadewijch to St Bernard. Hadewijch is 'opposed to Bernard in that she does not admit absolutely the distinction between a human love for Christ the man and a divine love for Christ the God: for her, not only does the second pass through the first, but the first would be going the wrong way if it did not imply the second from the beginning, since there are not two Christs but a single Person in two natures. So it will be the same with any authentic love for him: it cannot for a single instant make an abstraction of his divine, incarnate Person.'[19] On the other hand, it is difficult to imagine a more personal, erotic union than that described between Juan de la Cruz's soul and the 'esposo' in 'El Cántico espiritual'.

Luisa joins the paean of delight sounded out by the theology of beauty: 'mi rutilante alborada', 'mi Belleza', 'esa sacra vestidura /. . ./ que del amor fue tejida / en la Rosa inmaculada' (no. 8); 'el bello mozo / diestro en el flechar del arco' (no. 9); 'la rutilante luz de tu hermosura' (no. 12). One striking facet of Christ's appearance in her poetry is her unwavering concept of his looks: always with chestnut hair brighter than the sun, and dazzlingly blue eyes. He is 'aquel de los garzos ojos / y del cabello castaño' (no. 9). Was this perhaps how he appeared to her in some vision, or could some Flemish painting, regularly seen in her years in the royal palace with its connecting door to the convent of the Descalzas Reales, have left a lasting impression on her? David Davies points out to me that the National Gallery has Bosch's 'Christ being mocked and crowned with thorns' in which Christ has auburn or light brown hair, and that Philip II acquired a later copy for the Escorial where it was recorded in 1574. He has also drawn my attention to the fact that slightly earlier, in the fifteenth century, the figure of Christ was not open to the personal imagination because of a supposed eyewitness account of his appearance. The 'eyewitness', a fictitious Lentulus, Governor of Judea, was said to have described to the Roman Senate:

'A man of average or moderate height, and very distinguished. He has an impressive appearance, so that those who look on him love and fear him. His hair is the colour of a ripe hazel-nut. It falls straight almost to the level of his ears; from there down it curls thickly and is rather more luxuriant . . . His forehead is wide, smooth and serene, and his face is without wrinkles or any marks. It is graced by a slightly reddish tinge, a faint colour. His nose and mouth are faultless . . . His eyes are brilliant, mobile, clear, splendid . . ., his hands and arms are fine . . . He is the most beautiful among the children of men.'[20]

Might Luisa's scholarly uncle have read to her a translation of this Greek forgery, well known in the Renaissance world? In her 'Redondillas espirituales de Silva al buen empleo de su amor y frutos que de él sintió' (no. 1) she gives a full-length portrait, not only hair and eyes, but forehead, eyebrows, 'la nariz afilada / de notable perfección', mouth, lips, teeth, 'manos como la nieve / . . ./ en las cuales matizaban / las rubicundas heridas', the feet – 'entre cuantos hombres son / no se vió tal hermosura'.

Above all, it is 'la fuerza de su mirar' which radiates throughout the poetry; 'cuyo mirar, de amor mata, / que tiene un mirar extraño, / y tal que al más diamantino / pecho allana de un asalto' (no. 9). It is these 'garzos ojos serenos' which, as in 'El Cántico espiritual', transform the landscape with beauty. Flowers spring up, birds sing praise and the sky is golden while 'a él se volvían / los cristalinos espejos / en que los cielos se miran' (no. 7). Over the shepherdess this gaze has absolute power,

'. . . con sólo mirar, queda / hecho absoluto señor / del alma' (no. 10). 'Volvió a mí sus ojos, / y de ellos salió / fuego vivo, ardiente, / que a Silva abrasó ... / Y arcos imagino que sus ojos son / porque una saeta / de ellos despidió' (no. 31). The language is conventional, but it seems to me that it is fired by individual feeling, perhaps individual experience.

Not even the Higher Education Funding Council has devised a scale of points to assess the difference between verse and true poetry, and this leaves the field blissfully open for individual instinct. One section of 'Redondillas espirituales de Silva al buen empleo de su amor y frutos que de él sintió' shows the 'Pastor' seizing Silva by the hand and leading her into a garden. Biographers tell that, with her uncle's permission, Luisa often spent hours praying in the castle garden. Often too during family excursions into the countryside she would wander off to some quiet spot to meditate. There are striking landscapes, by day and by night, in her poems which reflect both her love of nature and her knowledge of neoplatonic/pastoral literature. Yet the garden scene in these lines of the 'Redondillas', adding colour and detail to Teresa de Jesús's allegory of the watered garden, has for me the mysterious quality that draws a reader to return to a poem over and over again, until the memory has it secure.

Responding to the Royal presence, the flowers pour out their scents, and all – lilies, jasmine, white rosebushes – become perfection. Sunflowers transmute into pure gold, anemones glow more brightly. Carnations, roses and violets intertwine. The greenery, fruit trees and south wind play their part in the idyll, and the spring 'manando a toda porfía; / por la tierra se vertía / hasta que a sus pies llegaba'.

It was this paradise of a spiritual garden with its ecstatic love, where the Beloved 'me mostró / la fuerza de su mirar' that Luisa was aiming to recreate in her London convent, before King James's soldiers stormed the walls. After seeing the rapturous intensity of the poems, we need look no further for the driving force that made Luisa donate all her inheritance to the service of her God, set sail for England, and spend the remaining years of life battling in surroundings that she detested, dying in effect a martyr through imprisonment. It is as though, years later in New Spain, Sor Juana Inés de la Cruz spoke for Luisa de Carvajal when she wrote: 'If we look at his [Christ's] presence, what jewel is more lovable than his divine beauty? If any human beauty has jurisdiction over the wills and knows how to subject them to itself..., what would this incomprehensible Beauty do, what would it move, what would it not do, what would it not move, through whose beautiful face as through smooth crystal the rays of the Divinity made themselves transparent?'[21]

NOTES

1. Letter 18. Quoted by Louis Bouyer, *Women Mystics*, trans. Anne Englund Nash (San Francisco: Ignatius Press, 1993), p. 29.

2. 'In February 1607 ... an English novitiate was opened at Louvain. Once again this was made possible by Spanish munificence. Doña Luisa de Carvajal left 14,000 ducats for the English mission in her will dated at Valladolid, 22 December 1604. She asked no more in return than that "some little place" be found for her body in one of the churches of the Order she admired so much. Richard Walpole, then at Valladolid, and Vice-Prefect of the English Mission, was her principal executor. She insisted her money should be "applied to the founding of a novitiate of English religious of the Society in whatever kingdom or part of the world shall seem to Father Persons to the greater glory of God". Not even Persons's worst enemies could accuse him of sluggishness. As soon as her last wishes became known, he acquired a property in Louvain which had once belonged to the Knights of Malta. It was on high ground commanding the whole city. Below it was a walled garden, and on the slope of the hill pleasant walks among the vine-terraces. Although it was within the city walls, it was completely quiet and tranquil—altogether suitable for its purpose.
    The first novices were six who were already priests, two scholastics, and potential lay-brothers. Thomas Garnet was the first novice there to take his vows. Thomas Talbot was the first novice-master. In 1614 St John's, as it was known from the connection with the knights, sprouted a college of philosophy and theology. At the end of the same year, the novices were transferred to Liège, where John Gerard had much to do with purchasing a house for them'. Francis Eduards, *The Jesuits in England: from 1580 to the present day* (Tunbridge Wells: Burns and Oates, 1985), pp. 44-49.

3. See Luisa's letter to the Carmelites in Brussels, dated 14 November 1613, in which she writes that the Spanish

Ambassador 'no traga esto de irme, si no le muestran por qué, y no tiene por suficiente la queja que le dan y se dió en el Consejo de Estado delante dél y más de veinte consejeros dellos, que fue que si soy monja y he fundado algunos monasterios dentro de Inglaterra, y que persuado a muchísimos a que dejen su religión y tomen la mía; y así, he pervertido gran número, trayéndolos a mi fe. Esto fue totalmente cuanto depusieron de mí.' This letter is no. 176 in Biblioteca de Autores Españoles *(BAE)*, vol. 179, ed. Jesús González Marañón and Camilo María Abad (Madrid, 1965, pp. 413-14. All references to Luisa's letters and poems are to this edition.

4. In letter no. 103, written to her cousin, the marquesa de Caracena, on 6 March 1609 *(BAE,* p. 284), and letter 151, also to her cousin, dated 19 October 1612 *(BAE,* p. 368).

5. No. 98. A Inés de la Asunción, 29 June 1608.

6. '¡Pobrecito Rey, que tanta desventura le cerca y le ocupa dentro y fuera del corazón! Si él quiebra la paz, poco debe haber discurrido en su negocio, porque no tiene ni dinero soldados..., ni navíos. Si alguna armada le viniera, en el estado en que está, cogiérasele como con las manos atadas.' No. 63. A Magdalena de San Jerónimo, 2 August 1606.

7. Her family tree, according to G. Marañón, appears on p. 16 of the *BAE* edition. Luisa's ancestry includes as many aristocratic names as would be expected from someone who was a playmate of the royal children. Her parents were Francisco de Carvajal y Vargas and María de Mendoza y Pacheco; her grandparents are listed as Gutierre de Carvajal, Magdalena de Mendoza, Luisa de Fajardo and Juan Hurtado de Mendoza.

8. Ronald Cueto, 'Connexions and Interests on the Path of Virtue: Mauricia Pérez de Velasco (c. 1598-1674) and the Expansion of the Augustinian Recollection in Spain', in *Recognitions: Essays Presented to Edmund Fryde,* ed. Colin Richmond and Isobel Harvey (Aberystwyth: National Library of Wales, 1996), pp. 351-74).

9. For a description by Inés de la Asunción, one of Luisa's companions, of the austere life in the 'casita' in the calle de Toledo, see *BAE*, pp. 26-27.

10. No. 32 is dated 1597, no. 46 about 1600. and Luisa herself records that nos. 4 and 5 were written in Madrid.

11. See no. 53, A Magdalena de San Jerónimo, June 1606.

12. Margarita Nelken, *Las escritoras españolas* (Barcelona: Labor, 1930), no. 232, pp. 74-76.

13. Serrano y Sanz, *Apuntes para una biblioteca de escritoras españolas, desde el 1401 al 1833.* Quoted in *BAE*, p. 424.

14. In his paper on 'Monastic Spirituality in the Age of Reform' given at the First International Cañada Blanch Conference, Manchester, 19-20 December 1996. The papers are to be published.

15. Luis de León's translation, made for a nun, Doña Isabel de Osorio, dates from before his imprisonment by the Inquisition in 1572 and was finally published in Salamanca in 1580. Luisa's sonnet, with its similar phrases, is no. 19.

16. See *The Victim of God* (New York: Ungar, 1960). pp. 1-6.

17. Grace M. Jantzen, *Power, Gender and Christian Mysticism*, Cambridge Studies in Ideology and Religion (Cambridge University Press, 1995), p. 288.

18. Jantzen, p.135. On the subject of the erotic and the mystical it is interesting to read Fr Noel O'Donoghue's view that 'the *eros* in question here is not a self-indulgent or possessive *eros*... It is rather a question of that basic and all-pervasive vital force in man and woman which is the energy of creation, whose truth is always creativity, whose joy is true to itself only when it is creative. This holy force is at the root of all reverence and all true religion' (*Mystics for Our Time. Carmelite Meditations for a New Age* (Edinburgh: T. and T. Clark , 1989), p.14).

19. Bouyer, pp. 23-24.

20. See Michael Baxandall, *Painting and Experience in Fifteenth-Century Italy. A Primer in the Social History of Pictorial Style* (Oxford: Clarendon Press, 1972), pp. 56-57. I am indebted for this reference to David Davies, Senior Lecturer in the History of Fine Art, University College, London.

21. *Primer Sueño*, quoted by George H. Tavard, *Juana Inés de la Cruz and the Theology of Beauty. The First Mexican Theology* (Notre Dame/London: University of Notre Dame Press, 1991), p. 30. For the Spanish original see Sor Juana Inés de la Cruz's *Obras completas*, ed. Francisco Monterde (Mexico City: Porrua, 1975), p. 836.

AUSTEN IVEREIGH

University of Leeds

THE SPANISH-AMERICAN 'REVOLUTIONS' (1808-23)
A Preliminary Burkean View

The fame of Edmund Burke (d. 1797), the greatest English parliamentarian of the eighteenth century, has rested largely on his prescient denunciation of the French Revolution.[1] In his articulation of both a doctrine and a policy that countered the historical forces arising from the turbulence of 1789, he is often thought of as the father of modern conservatism. To that first great experiment in totalitarian innovation, he offered the first great resistance; and it was in Burke that counter-revolutionaries of the nineteenth and cold-warriors of the twentieth centuries found their mentor. And yet, as Conor Cruise O'Brien passionately demonstrates, it is not easy to dress Burke as a conservative, then or now. He was a liberal – a sound Whig – who opposed the Protestant Ascendancy in Ireland, the introduction of new taxes in America, and slavery anywhere. He was formed by the Enlightenment of Montesquieu and Locke, and by the inheritance of England's Glorious Revolution. He was a liberal who opposed the French Revolution; or rather, he opposed the French Revolution *because* he was a liberal.[2]

Despite Burke's notorious opposition to the French Revolution, he was known to have sympathised a few years earlier with the colonial uprising in America. Such apparent inconsistency can be explained away, as in Namierite historiography, by portraying Burke as an unprincipled participant in the unprincipled politics of patronage; or, as Marx sought to, in a vicious footnote in *Capital,* as the lackey of rotating paymasters.[3]

Such attacks are discreditable for any number of reasons; the most important of them is that the inconsistency they seek to explain in Burkean thinking is not an inconsistency at all: the American and French Revolutions, although they share the term 'revolution', are *essentially* different. The Revolt of the Thirteen Colonies, like the Glorious Revolution to which it appealed, was a 'limited' revolution, designed to preserve the old constitution against an innovative concept of sovereignty imposed upon it by England. Burke 'supposed they were fighting, not to acquire absolute speculative liberty, but to keep what they had under the English Constitution.'[4] The Revolution in France, on the other hand, was 'limitless'. It introduced into the body politic of Europe an entirely new, and despotic, notion of sovereignty, which would cause France – and other countries that came into her orbit – to lurch from anarchy to tyranny, through 'transmigrations, fear and blood', to fall eventually into military despotism.[5] The shared term 'Revolution' obscures the sharp differences *in essence* between the American and French cases.

Burke died in 1797: eleven years before the Napoleonic invasion of the Iberian Peninsula triggered the formation of the first creole juntas in Spanish America, in the first stage of a lengthy, and often bloody, transition from Viceroyalties to independent republics. If Burke ever spoke or wrote about Spanish America, this is not recorded in popular compilations of his writings; and even if we were to uncover 'Burke on Spanish America', there is little reason to suppose Burke had any particular understanding – beyond, that is, his political perspicacity – of the region.[6] Yet in spite of – or perhaps *because* of – this lacuna, it is worth asking: how would Burke have viewed the Spanish-American Revolutions? – a defence of the liberties of the ancient constitution, or an aberrant innovation? – 'limitless' or 'limited'?

The first part of this essay will attempt a succinct distinction between the spirit and philosophy underpinning the American and

French revolutions, as Burke saw them. In turning to the Spanish-American example, we will look firstly at the 'Old Constitution' of the Hispanic world and how this manifested itself in America before 1750. We then consider the Bourbon violation of that constitution, and ways in which the philosophical matrix underlying the Reforms caused Spanish-Americans to consider the possibility of independence. We consider the 'Road to Independence', weighing up the relative impact of foreign revolutions against the 'internal' reaction in favour of the old constitution before, lastly, glancing at the Spanish-American revolutions and their development from a Burkean standpoint.

Burke on America, Burke on France

Burke did not advocate independence for America, but he opposed prosecution of a war against the colonial revolt:

> When any community is subordinately connected with another, the great danger of any connection is the extreme pride and self-complacency of the superior, which in all matters of controversy will probably decide in its favour ...
>
> They have been told that their dissent from violent measures is an encouragement to rebellion. Men of great presumption will hold a language which is contradicted by a whole course of history. *General* rebellions and revolts of an whole people were never *encouraged*, now or at any time. They are always *provoked*.[7]

The provocation was the new absolutist claim by the British Parliament to omnipotence and omnicompetence in its dealings with the colony. 'A new party', complained John Dickinson in 1774, had arisen in England, which sought to 'erect a new sovereignty over the colonies inconsistent with liberty or freedom.'[8] Or as Burke recognised: 'It affords no matter for very pleasing reflection to observe that our subjects diminish as our laws increase...'[9] The American Revolution was carried through on eminently conservative principles; the justification of the revolution was a legal justification, appealing to the traditional rights of Englishmen embedded in the English Constitution. London's authority was rejected, not because it competed with nascent political organs of representation, nor because it was unpopular, but because it sought to arrogate absolute power in defiance of England's own traditional Constitution. This defiance of absolutism was predicated on the assumption of the rule of law; at least rhetorically, therefore, the American Revolution did not counter one 'absolute will' (King or Parliament) by another 'absolute will' (that of the people), but rather appealed to the rule of law which opposes all absolutism. In this, the American Revolution therefore looked back to a sixteenth- and seventeenth-century conception of organic community. Nor was this an abstraction: eighteenth-century society was close-knit (the original Thirteen Colonies comprised an area smaller than Venezuela) and local county politics was vigorous.[10]

The American Revolution, then, was a 'limited' revolution: it did not seek a new notion of sovereignty, but rather appealed to an old notion (the English Constitution) violated by modern practice (late eighteenth-century absolutism). In Burkean terms, this was the procedure of all good government: sound reforms made with reference to the principle of antiquity. This was the principle of 1688 – 'The Revolution was made to preserve our *antient* indisputable laws and liberties, and that *antient* constitution of government which is our only security for law and liberty'[11] – that transferred with equal merit to America in 1776.

Indeed,

> ...on a supposition that the Americans had rebelled merely in order to enlarge their liberty, Mr Burke would have thought very differently of the American cause ... Mr Burke had several conversations with him about that time, in none of which ... did he discover any other wish in favour of America than for a security as to its antient condition ... he always firmly believed that they were purely on the defensive in that rebellion ... [for] under the system of policy which was then pursued, the Americans could have no sort of security for their laws or liberties, or for any part of them, – and that the very circumstances of *our* freedom would have augmented the weight of *their* slavery.[12]

The Revolution in France, conversely, did not contradict monarchical absolutism by an appeal to the rule of law, but to a counter-absolutism, that of the 'General Will'.[13] Sovereignty would no longer be divided, but invested wholly in the Executive power; the National Assembly would have 'every possible power, and no possible external control'; while the regional *Parlements –* which had kept alive the old constitution during the reigns of arbitrary princes – were reduced to agents of central authority. A new oligarchy of wealth, and the impoverishment of the working classes, flowed from the assertion of individualism in law. The real basis of power was the army; it would not take long for the army to cease to be the instrument of arbitrary power, and to assume direct control.[14] The logic of militarism was implicit in the introduction of a new metaphysical concept of sovereignty – in which the Will of Man, expressed in the state, becomes the ultimate sovereign, above and outside of which there is no higher authority; and which abolishes all distinction between public and private spheres, between governing and governed, or between authority and law. The logic of the French Revolution was a swing between individualism (the disaggregation of civil society) and despotism (the assertion of arbitrary authority resting on force).[15]

The Old Constitution of the Hispanic World

The thought of the sixteenth-century scholastics of Salamanca – which defended medieval contractarian views of sovereignty even as Hapsburg kings denied them in practice – expresses for the Hispanic world that which Burke describes as 'the old constitution': a set of assumptions, or criteria, of sovereignty, developed over time, and perceived as immanent in the polity. This is not the place to discuss the trend towards absolutism under the Hapsburgs in the sixteenth and seventeenth centuries, impelled by the extension of the Castilian model to other realms in the peninsula; it is only important to note, uncontroversially, that this extension encountered resistance in Aragon, Catalonia and Valencia, *because* the old constitution was assumed. Such assumptions halted the creation of a unified nation-state until at least the War of the Spanish Succession (1700-1714). The *monarquía* – only this term, and never 'Spain', as Ronald would forcefully remind students and colleagues, is legitimate – was a federation of kingdoms, bound together by a variety of contractual and consensual arrangements. The most vivid example of this inability of the central state to override traditional autonomies, the failure of Olivares's reforms in the first half of the seventeenth century, is incomprehensible without taking into account the force of the old constitution.

The old constitution can be summarised using Machlachlan's useful three headings: the nature of a monarch's moral and political subordination to divine authority; the ruler's relationship with his subjects; and the extent to which legislation conveyed actual authority.[16]

In Francisco Suárez (1458-1517)'s restatement of the medieval tradition, the community *(corpus mysticum)* precedes the existence of political institutions. Obedience is due to rulers to the extent they rule in accordance with pre-established law. Authority was simultaneously limited in two major respects: first, by its origin in consensus: the people, by agreeing to form a government, created an authority whose duty it is to promote the common good; the state was an expression of society, rather than the obverse, from which it followed that 'lesser' societies (guilds, fueros, municipalities) were pre-existent natural societies which delegated certain authority to the state in the interests of the common good. Secondly, authority was limited by deference to the higher law of God immanent in the Church and society.[17]

From this it followed that the ruler was bound to his subjects by a host of contractual obligations. However remote and revolting to monarchs, the Fuero Real (1255) and the *Siete Partidas* (1265) retained their force. This residual feudalism was defended by the Salamanca theorists in their distinction between civil power and authority – the right to administer the community's power; a king possessed only the latter. Violation of that limit resulted theoretically in forfeiture of authority. Francisco de Vitoria (1485-1546) extended the notion of the monarch's community obligation to the New World in his assertions that overlordship was established strictly for the benefit of the Indian, not to the profit of the European; and this obligation underlies the enactment of the New Laws of 1542, governing the obligations of Spanish overlords to their Indian subjects, to which Spanish Americans later appealed as a charter.[18] As in the peninsula, the history of colonial Spanish America is pockmarked with popular revolts protesting at extra levies imposed without the consent of the governed. The legitimacy of the protest derived from the claim of municipalities to the sovereignty of the original community that antedated the royal establishment. The investiture of a new viceroy in the New World was accompanied by a solemn oath to protect all the 'fueros, franquezas, libertades, preeminencias y mercedes' previously granted. The premise was that the monarch ruled separately over each kingdom: 'the association of Charles [V]'s various territories was ... similar in character to the association of territories that together formed the medieval federation of the Crown of Aragon.'[19]

What of the force of law? The Indies were heavily governed, but the Crown set its face against the emergence of a New World nobility by a diffuse, pluralistic structure of overlapping jurisdictions. The system, in Lynch's words, 'was all too successful in its almost obsessive determination to prevent the excessive concentration of power at any single point.'[20] The structure was imprecise and horizontal; this made for administration that was flexible – if unwieldy and disputatious. The notorious *obedezco pero no cumplo* device was a legitimate, and accepted, means by which the legal emanations from ill-informed Madrid could be disregarded by a colonial officer if they were perceived to contradict local realities. The very abstraction of the theological and legal matrix underlying authority provided a broad arena in which conflicts could be resolved through negotiation, without ever challenging the monarch's authority. The realities of power might determine the resolution of a conflict; in this sense, the lofty principles of the old constitution might belie realities on the ground. But rule did not rest on force; shared principles regulated the empire. There is no convincing alternative explanation for the astonishing absence of the coercive power of the state in administering a vast, and fissiparous, colony before 1750.[21]

The Hapsburg consensus state – as opposed to the subsequent Bourbon absolutist state – could be seen in four main areas. First, creoles increasingly participated in the colonial bureaucracy, initially by right but increasingly in the seventeenth century through sale of office and *beneficio*. The growing predominance of creole officials meant a dilution of royal authority, but also the creation of an intermediate layer between the fiscal demands of Madrid and the resistance of local taxpayers. Secondly, the *corregidor* – who bought his office in Spain – received his income through the exercise of the notorious *repartimiento de comercio*, an economic monopoly in Indian districts. Whatever its effect on the Indian economy, and its role in fostering native rebellion, the *repartimiento* embraced a network of local groups with vested interests, and was quasi-autonomous in respect of Spain. Thirdly, the advance of creoles in the *audiencias* – such that by the 1760s the majority of judges in the *audiencias* of Lima, Santiago and Mexico were creoles – was an important manifestation of creole autonomy and influence at the highest level. Lastly, the viceroys themselves, although *peninsulares*, were only able to profit from their office through collaboration with local interests, and in this way also became part of the consensus.[22]

The empire inherited by Charles III was therefore the product of a colonial compact predicated – in theory as well as in practice – on the assumptions of the old constitution, within whose framework America had developed a strong degree of autonomy. It would be superficial, however, to describe the indicators of vigour and independent development, which America manifested in so many ways in the eighteenth century, as 'incipient nationhood'. To describe it thus would be to accept uncritically the doctrine of a political nationalism, which has its roots in French-revolutionary notions of popular sovereignty, and the cult of individuality of Fichte and Herder.[23] The influence of such notions as proximate causes of Spanish-American independence are here being debated; to assume them would beg the question. It is enough to note that America in the eighteenth century required skilful handling by Spain: an acknowledgement, that is, of the realities of autonomy, and a perpetuation – or even enhancement – of the flexibility and pluralism implicit in the old constitution. Instead, the Bourbon response was to seek to counter manifestations of autonomy, to reassert imperial control, to harness American resources to the narrow requirements of the metropolis, and, as we shall argue, to violate the old constitution through the imposition of a philosophical matrix which undermined the scholastic premises which bound America to Madrid.

The Bourbon Violation of the Old Constitution

The attempt to override the old constitution by the eighteenth-century administrative revolutions globally termed the 'Bourbon Reforms' caused bitter reactions in Spanish America and stirred colonial sentiment to the possibility of independence. The Reforms failed in their ultimate objective of securing for Spain an escape from economic and military failure. While that failure had causes which remain the subject of historical dispute, it is important to note that failure was a possibility in a way that was inconceivable in the old constitution. The Bourbon Reforms presupposed an *ideology* – a rationalist construct born of Enlightenment materialism and faith in dispassionate pragmatism – which must either be accepted or resisted. In the Bourbon system, there was little room for compromise with local realities, little possibility of generating consensus: the traditional pluralities and diffusion of the old constitution were seen as corrupt and ineffective.

The Reforms took as the criterion of their own success the generation of material prosperity. When prosperity was created – through the liberalisation and simplification of intra-colonial trade, the streamlining of taxes, and the opening of ports – this was seen in Spanish America not as a demonstration of the validity of the Reforms, but as a long-awaited adjustment to economic realities. The failure of the Reforms, therefore, was not a failure in its own terms – increased revenues were collected, while exports from Spanish America to Spain quadrupled in 1778-96 – but in ways that were inconceivable within the closed Bourbon ideological framework.[24] Physiocratic economic doctrine (on which the Reforms were predicated) postulated a series of natural economic laws that could be uncovered by rational enquiry and then implemented. Social, political and moral factors were considered irrelevant to the objective operation of these laws. A failure of economic reform due to political conflict was, therefore, inconceivable; and yet this is precisely what occurred. In attempting to strip away from the colonial empire the gradually-accrued elements of consensus and sovereignty, in order to leave only a bare, 'rational', administrative structure, the reformers clashed with colonial habits and expectations. The Reforms ended by producing only endless conflict: enlightened officials versus obstinate creoles; arrogant reformers versus oppressed colonials. New fissures, inconceivable in earlier centuries, spread across Spanish America: between subject and object, between reformer and reactionary, between peninsular and creole. These divisions in the short term undermined the implementation of the Bourbon Reforms: 'When the goals of the reformers coincided with economic reality or the wishes of the colonial population, they succeeded; in other circumstances, they failed.'[25] In the long term, they lost America.

The colonial grievances are well known. The reform of colonial administration on vertical lines, the conscious policy of de-creolization of the upper echelons of Church and bureaucracy (so that judgeships in Mexico City, for example, went from having a ratio of creoles to peninsulares in 1750 of 8:3, to a ratio in 1800 of 4:10), the imposition of new taxes without consent, and the extension of state control over the Church – most dramatically, in the expulsion of the Jesuits – were all accompanied by an increase in coercive power to stifle dissent.[26] De-creolization, especially, contributed to fostering independence sentiment, by effectively imposing a separate identity on Americans. Benedict Anderson talks of the 'pilgrimages of creole functionaries', cramped both vertically (the upper levels of administration were closed) and laterally (they served only in the territories of colonial Mexico or Chile, such that these became the 'imagined communities' of the post-independence nation-states), in which bonds of commonality were formed.[27] The Reforms implied a fundamental adjustment in the constitution, such that Spanish America was increasingly seen no longer as the overseas kingdom of a universal *monarquía*, but rather as a dependent and subservient territory – a 'colony' which could be harnessed and subjugated for the benefit of the 'metropolis'.[28]

As ideologies are prone to do, this conception denied realities: of America's autonomous growth, and of America's strength relative to that of Spain. One of the Reform's prime agents, José de Gálvez, refused to acknowledge New Spain's transparent prosperity, claiming that the colonial administration had allowed the territory to degenerate; contrary advice was denounced as reactionary.[29] Reform, as expressed in the notorious advice given by the Count of Revillagigedo in 1794 to his successor as Viceroy of Mexico, sought the extinction of American manufacturing, because it threatened that of Spain: 'It should not be forgotten that this is a colony which must depend on its mother country, Spain, and must yield her some benefit because of the protection it receives ... dependence would cease once European manufactures and products were not needed here.'[30] Imposition of reform that denied local realities, harmed local interests and suffocated nascent autonomies, naturally provoked resistance; but Bourbon ideology was incapable of revising policies in the face of opposition. The abrogation of the old constitution had made accommodation impossible:

> The obstacles – including entrenched traditional officials, a powerful monopoly-linked merchant community, contraband trade, and the general desire of Spanish-Americans to manipulate or adjust their own internal situation – did not deter reform-minded innovators. While Hapsburg agents would have viewed the creation of such powerful opposition as both a policy failure and a crisis, eighteenth-century officials accepted it as part of the larger problem of administrative and economic rationalisation. As a consequence, conflict between reformers and those who adhered to the traditional political philosophy began immediately.[31]

The Reforms contained a logic of suppression. In New Spain, the establishment of the tobacco monopoly, the formation of the colonial militia (which entailed forcible recruitment), and the expulsion of the Jesuits, led to urban riots and popular revolt, which were suppressed with ferocity by veteran peninsular regiments. Resistance to innovation and abuse of power found expression in the revolts of 1780-81 in Peru (the Tupac Amaru uprising), New Granada (the Comuneros) and Venezuela, which were defused by a combination of coercion and negotiation. To the extent that these revolts were perceived to threaten creole supremacy – the revivalist Inca movement led by José Gabriel Condorcanqui, especially, posed a social challenge that could not be neglected by creoles – their suppression could count on creole involvement. These were not yet 'nationalist' revolts. But they were crucial to the development of national consciousness, not because they were revolts (these there had been under the Hapsburgs) but because they demonstrated that the old formula of 'long live the King, down with bad government' was obsolete. The distinction under the old constitution between Crown and government had been invalidated by Bourbon centralisation; the Crown was now directly responsible for the actions of its servants. Colonial protest was now *ipso facto* directed against the King; and the King *ipso facto* suppressed colonial revolt. Because the King furthered peninsular interests against that of the colonies, the rebels characterised the Spanish authorities as outsiders and the Americans as claimants to their own countries.[32] In this way, the Reforms sparked off a cycle of innovation, resistance, suppression and further conflict, which fortified Spanish-American nationality.

So it was not the grievances *per se*, but the incapacity to resolve grievances within a framework of consensus, which served to undermine Spanish rule in America. In this sense, Crown religious policy illustrates both the new matrix and its consequences. The campaign against ecclesiastical jurisdiction and property carried forward by the Reformers was at its most dramatic in the expulsion of the Jesuits, but was far wider than this significant event. The harnessing of Church to State was not new: the Conquest itself had been marked by the regalist policies of Ferdinand and Isabella. But regalism had been justified, as well as opposed, by scholastic theology; regalism had continued to uphold *fueros*. Scholasticism had provided the framework within which Hapsburg laws concerning the governance of the Indies had been framed. Charles III, conversely, 'waged a relentless campaign against the "subversive" theories of Suárez';[33] and it would be to his doctrines that many of the fathers of Independence looked for a justification of self-rule.[34] By substituting the old scholastic framework, with its dual societies of Church and State, for a monistic absolutism, the Bourbons eroded the traditional deference to the monarchy. The erosion of deference created the possibility not just of Spanish-American independence, but also for Spanish liberalism and republicanism: not because of any essential link between the Church and monarchy, but because the absorption of ecclesiastical jurisdiction and property by the State enables absolute power, and absolutism must sooner rather than later provoke a reaction in favour of vanquished liberties. This was the view of the Archbishop of Mexico (1802-11), Francisco Javier de Lizana y Beaumont, who complained bitterly about the abuse of royal power and the seizure of Church property in New Spain in 1804, and warned Madrid that, 'it was principally through the secular and regular clergy that the Americans have been and are loyal to God and the King ... he who has the priests has the Indies.'[35]

The Road to Independence

It was no accident, therefore, that the first to give cultural expression to 'Americanism', or *criollismo*, were the Jesuits exiled in Europe. Most of the 2,500-odd expelled were creoles, and among them were some of Spanish America's finest intellects; their nostalgia, and indignation at the 'foreign' assault by the Bourbons, were strongly to influence Independence leaders.[36] The incendiary writings of the Peruvian Jesuit, Juan Pablo Viscardo y Guzmán (1748-98), are an invaluable source of evidence that the Bourbon reconquest had alienated the creole élite and provoked independence: his *Carta Dirigida a los Españoles Americanos* of 1799 was copied and later turned up in the hands of leading independence warriors, among whom were Francisco de Miranda and Mariano Moreno. Viscardo harnessed Montesquieu and Adam Smith to his case, but not Rousseau: 'in effect', notes Brading, 'Viscardo's rejection of the Crown stemmed as much from the silent erosion of the political and cultural values once imparted by post-Tridentine Catholicism as from the direct influence of the Enlightenment.'[37] Miranda, the head of an aborted early attempt at an uprising in Venezuela in 1806, and later Simon Bolívar's lieutenant, was explicit in his abhorrence of the French Revolution, thinking it 'fatal to the peace and progress' of the Spanish-American peoples. Moreno, an early disciple of Viscardo, graduated to more radical texts, and published *The Social Contract* in Buenos Aires in 1810 'for the instruction of young Americans', but he considered Rousseau 'delirious in religious matters' and condemned the attempts by French rationalists 'to make God the author and accomplice of despotism', and so suppressed those chapters in *The Social Contract* which advocated a *religion civile*.[38] French ideas were influential; the Revolution was widely discussed; but the doctrines – which bore a superficial resemblance, after all, to early-modern scholastic anti-absolutist doctrines – were filtered through the Spanish-American philosophical matrix.

There were also regional variations: there were more *afrancesado* intellectuals in the River Plate (which experienced between 1796 and 1808 an influx of French privateers disseminating pamphlets) than, say, in Chile; and these variations may partly account for disagreements between historians on the relative significance of the impact of French doctrines.[39] The variation in French radical influence between Argentina and Chile also helps to account for the differing political developments between these two nations in the period after Independence (discussed below). It is also important to note that, while among small groups of educated urban creole professionals in the 1780s and 90s, gathered in masonic cliques and *Sociedades Patrióticas*, French and American revolutionary ideas were circulated, read and discussed in promiscuous fashion, these were limited circles.

The broader reception of revolutionary tracts is open to question: – a Frenchman in Cumuná in 1807 observed that pages from *The Social Contract* , the writings of Tom Paine, *The Rights of Man*, and Viscardo's *Carta*, were all being used to wrap up food from the shops.[40] The small, seditious conspiracies in major towns in Spanish America, such as that of La Guaira in Venezuela in 1797, demonstrated that among intellectual cliques these texts were discussed; but the conspiracies were unsuccessful because they ran up against the natural conservatism of the creole élite.

Creoles were caught between, on the one hand, an absolutist monarchy in Spain, and, on the other, the threat of revolt from below. The justified paranoia of the creole élite, delicately poised at the apex of a pyramid which embraced huge numbers of *gente de color*, had been fuelled by the slave revolt and massacre of planters in Saint-Domingue (Haiti) in 1791; *any* change in the status quo therefore implied the possibility of social ferment which could well threaten their lives and property. Creoles were at once underdogs *and* nobles, as Bolívar himself – radical creole patriot and social conservative – well exemplifies. But the conspiracies also failed because in terms of values they were without roots in wider society. They emerged in opposition to the values of the old constitution which were more broadly adhered to. The effects of this isolation would be reflected in the post-independence period, when the liberals, who had been formed in these cliques, emerged as leaders of radical or *exaltado* groups, and encountered resistance in wider society to their attempted reforms. In this way, paradoxically, liberalism in the early nineteenth century emulated the role of the Bourbons in the late eighteenth: the reforms (especially in regard to the Church and the disentailment of Church property) were often similar; and like the Bourbons, the liberals would later find themselves battling against a truculent, 'unenlightened' society.

After 1810, and the formation of creole juntas throughout

Spanish America, French and scholastic doctrines jostled together, often within the juntas, and often intermixed. An historian cannot readily separate them. One example of a reasonably authentic defence of the 'old constitution' was the creole rebellion in Cuzco of 1814, in which a ruling junta was elected with support from Indians and other Andean towns. The revolt spoke of the 'atrocious despotism' of Spain's governors, complained that the Jesuit college and church, 'once a house of prayer', had been turned into an irreverent barracks, and appealed to old scholastic arguments that unjust laws and despotic government did not command obedience.[41] But even in Buenos Aires, where a Portuguese spy had earlier observed that 'there exists an independence party, French in origin, and republican ... [this is] a plague which has infected the Río de la Plata to an inconceivable degree,'[42] when Saavedra, Moreno and other prominent creoles gathered in the junta of 25th May 1810, they referred to the compact of Suárez's *pactum translationis*, rather than that of Rousseau, and the debate abounded in scholastic notions of sovereignty. The oath of allegiance to Ferdinand VII may have been a 'mask' which concealed a genuine desire for independence, but the arguments in favour of self-rule appealed to the old constitution.[43]

The Spanish American Revolutions: a Burkean view

Possibly the most Burkean figure in Spanish-American Independence was a Mexican Dominican, Fray Servando Teresa de Mier (1763-1827), author of *Historia de la revolución de Nueva España antiguamente Anáhuac* (1813). A colourful figure, with a long and colourful life, he was the object of ecclesiastical censure for his bizarre theory that Quetzalcoátl was really St Thomas the Apostle, who had come to Mexico in the time of

Christ and converted the Indians, who had then apostatised (and conducted human sacrifices in confusion of the Eucharist) until re-converted by the appearance of the Virgin Mary to Juan Diego. Neither these elements of his life, nor his picaresque escapades, however, concern us as much as his role as chief theorist of Mexican independence. As Brading demonstrates, Mier was a confessional republican, a liberal Catholic, a Whig who in London 'studied in that old school of practical politics', reading 'its Burkes, its Paleys and its Benthams.'[44] As such, he was a vehement opponent of Jacobinism, as well as of monarchy. He was also a stalwart defender of the old constitution, noting that Catholicism and despotism were irreconcilable, and that implicit in French Revolutionary anticlerical doctrine was a demagoguery that could but end in tyranny. Like Burke, and applying Burke's analysis, Mier was a political prophet, foreseeing with remarkable accuracy Mexico's descent into anarchy and fanaticism and military despotism.

Mier looked back to the New Laws of 1542 as the ancient constitution of the New World. The American territories constituted true kingdoms, and thus possessed equal sovereign principality, as Italy, Flanders and Aragon. The Bourbons had eroded the old constitution, but it still endured as the political foundation of Mexico, such that, once the Bourbon dynasty had abdicated, sovereignty (according to scholastic premises) reverted to the people, with whom the Crown had celebrated the original pact. The Cortes of Cádiz, with its fundamental tract, the Constitution of 1812, created a new sort of state, a single state based on a fictitious Spanish nation, which reduced America to the status of a subject colony; this the Cortes lacked authority to do. The 1812 Constitution, the product of French Revolutionary ferment, was the work of doctrinaires; it had replaced the positive legislation of over two centuries by administrative chaos. For America to be free, America must now emancipate itself from

Spain, because Spain, not America, had changed. A republic was to be favoured, but a centralised republic, a moderate federation, buttressed with a strong executive, that could concede liberties gradually. In Europe only England had escaped anarchy, because it relied on a few fundamental laws which protected individual liberties and eschewed a written constitution; Mexico should follow this example.

When Congress reassembled after the overthrow of Iturbide, however, Mier was defeated by the radicals, who, prompted in large measure by instructions from state capitals, adopted a federalist constitution of sovereign states, rendering the executive subordinate to Congress. In December 1823, Mier delivered his Prophecy, noting that for Mexico to emulate the United States was fatal: the Anglo-Americans were a homogeneous, educated, compact people, with a tradition of political debate and virtual self-rule; they had formed their confederation to unite against the oppression by England. Mexico was heterogeneous, with a tradition of subjugation, and ethnic and social divisions. Mier then proceeded to attack the principles espoused by the radical deputies, warning that to take refuge in the 'will of the people' as a metaphysical notion was to replace the tyranny of the monarch with the tyranny of the mob. Sovereignty, he argued, resided in 'the legal will' of the constituted bodies of government and their elected representatives, not in 'the people' itself. He foresaw 'division, emulation, disorders': there would be a period of anarchic demagoguery, in which the State would be plundered for the benefit of narrow sectoral and provincial interests; to be followed by military despotism. As Brading observes: 'few prophets have been more accurate in their predictions than Padre Mier.'[45] The radicals introduced legislation expelling Spaniards from Mexico, so challenging the post-colonial settlement of Iturbide; this was a prelude to the radical legislation of the Reform, which was to plunge Mexico into anarchy and civil war for much of the nineteenth century.

Anglo-Americans to the north were the heirs of a tradition of politics stretching back to the seventeenth century, to Parliament's victory over the Crown; however radical the pronouncements of the American Revolution of 1776, theirs was a revolution predicated on minor adjustments to the charter inherited from Britain. The rule of law was upheld. The causes of alienation – a reaction to absolutism which violated the old constitution – were similar in both North and South, but the Spanish-American post-independence period was mostly marked by a swing, comparable to France, between anarchy and despotism, as Mier had predicted for Mexico. The revolutions in Spanish America, while predicated on a defence of the old constitution, were generally captured by the advocates of the new, because of the absence in the Spanish-American tradition of a developed local political culture capable of formulating and debating the tenets of the old constitution, as could be found in the Thirteen Colonies to the north. The revolutions tended to be captured by the radicals, although the opposition of conservatives, and the resistance of wider society to radical (especially anticlerical) reforms, would lead to a painful search for a framework of legitimacy that could reconcile liberty and order. The career of the radical creole patriot Simon Bolívar, forever writing constitutions and later abandoning them in favour of dictatorship, is emblematic of this trajectory.[46]

* * *

Nineteenth-century Spanish-American liberalism assumed many of the tenets of enlightened absolutism. Liberals had low expectations of the mass, seeking to reform 'from above' through classically Bourbon measures such as the abolition of Indian and communal lands, and secularisation. Liberals tended also to suspend democratic institutions faced with the 'unreadiness' of the people. Yet the conditions of Spanish-American independence had been created by the alienation from enlightened assumptions, and a defence of the old constitution. As a result, much of the conflict generated by radical reforms in post-independence Spanish America repeated the conflict generated by the Bourbon Reforms in the 1760s-90s. And just as the Bourbon matrix could not accommodate opposition without calling into question the self-justification of reform itself, so the liberal project engendered the same cycle of innovation, revolt and suppression – with the difference that the post-independence states were unable to rely on expanding trade receipts and military strength to enforce the reforms.

This pattern can be vividly seen in the River Plate, where the provinces rejected the absolutist powers assumed by the Buenos Aires junta under the radical triumvirate of Bernardino Rivadavia. In a mirror reflection of the declaration of the Junta of 1810, the provinces argued that Rivadavia's absolutism, demonstrated by his suppression of the provincial juntas, disentitled Buenos Aires to dominion over the other provinces; they had already been alienated by the views espoused by his 'oligarchy of intellectuals'. Following the collapse of the 1819 Constitution, therefore, the River Plate disintegrated into petty states under caudillo rule. After 1822, Rivadavia's reform programme in Buenos Aires Province, which embraced radical anticlerical measures autocratically enforced, plunged the province into civil war for two years; from this anarchy emerged Juan Manuel de Rosas's dictatorship from 1829 to 1852.[47]

It is interesting to note that the territories of the new republics broadly corresponded to the old Hapsburg units, which appears further to suggest that the impulse behind Independence was the preservation of the old constitution. The old seats of the *audiencias* became the national capitals; each of the new Spanish-

American republics had been an administrative unit from the sixteenth to the eighteenth century.[48] Disputes over national frontiers arose where the seventeenth-century jurisdictions had been overridden by the Bourbon Reforms. The new units did not last: New Granada did not endure as Gran Colombia (by 1830, Quito and Caracas had gone their separate ways), and Buenos Aires, after 1778 the viceregal seat of La Plata, lost Asunción and La Paz almost immediately after 1810.

This 'natural' gravitation to Hapsburg traditions was not, however, reflected in the constitution of the new states. The intromission of liberal constitutionalism undermined the attempt to construct the Habsburg patrimonial state, while proving ineffective as an alternative. The necessary synthesis – in which the traditional patrimonial state could be resurrected with the minimum of concessions to Anglo-French constitutionalism appropriate to a new nineteenth-century republic – generally eluded Spanish America.[49]

The grand exception was Chile, where a unified aristocracy under Diego Portales erected in 1831 a political system that proved durable and flexible. For most of the nineteenth century, order and peace in Chile contributed to, and was reinforced by, economic growth, military success, steady population growth and social mobility, under a government that married order and liberty. Unlike other Spanish-American republics, Chile's system allowed for a gradual liberalisation: the four 'Portalian decennials' – forty years of presidents peacefully succeeding each other through elections – gave way in 1871 to a liberal, reformist administration. The Chilean Code of 1833, 'a model of originality', was drafted by Mariano Egaña, who in Europe in the 1820s had absorbed Burkean ideas.[50] Chilean conservatives, along with relatively isolated figures such as Padre Mier, seemed to grasp the Burkean premise that 'the science of constructing a commonwealth ... is, like every other experimental science, not to be taught *a priori*'; and that the compact between government and governed is 'a partnership not only between those who are living, but between those who are living, those who are dead, and those who are still to be born.'[51] Reform, however worthy in abstract, therefore required careful negotiation through appeal to broad values and assumptions, lest the authority which is the safeguard of liberty be undermined. Or, as a Chilean newspaper expressed this in 1845:

> There are in nations certain habits, prejudices and facts to which there is much attachment, and only the slow and gradual action of civilisation can make them disappear. If one tries to uproot them by force, a perilous reaction can supervene ... The Conservative hand touches such circumstances with caution ... Thus it is that no abuse, no prejudice which seems to have played its part in the common well-being will disappear, or be destroyed, until the majority is ready for this.[52]

NOTES

1. Of his many writings on France, the most famous remains *Reflections on the Revolution in France and on the Proceedings in Certain Societies in London Relative to that Event* (1790); references here are taken from the Penguin edition 1968) ed. Conor Cruise O'Brien.

2. See C.C. O'Brien, *The Great Melody: A Thematic Biography and Commented Anthology of Edmund Burke*, Minerva 1992, pp. 595-604.

3. On the Namierite attack, *ibid.*, pp. xli *et seq.* Marx wrote: 'The sycophant – who in the pay of the English oligarchy played the romantic *laudator temporis acti* against the French Revolution just as, in the pay of the North-American colonies at the beginning of the American troubles, he had played the liberal against the English oligarchy – was an out-and-out vulgar bourgeois.' *Capital* I, Moscow 1954, p. 760, n. 2.

4. *Parliamentary History*, cit. in *Melody*, p. 427.

5. *Reflections* p.342. Much of Burke's credibility as a political analyst derives from his power of prophecy. Nine years after Burke's death in 1797, Napoleon Bonaparte seized power in precisely the manner, and after precisely the events, foreseen in *Reflections*.

6. This is a preliminary, and speculative, assertion, awaiting verification from the Burke ms in Sheffield.

7. *A Letter to the Sheriffs in Bristol*, cit. in *Melody*, p. 165.

8. Quoted by R.G. Adams, *Political Ideas of the American Revolution*, N. Carolina 1922, p.82n.

9. *Letter to the Sheriffs* in *Melody*, p. 165.

10. Political participation was restricted to white male Protestant property-holders (excluding, therefore, women, children, servants, slaves, Catholics, Jews, free blacks, native Americans and non-English Europeans) but this still meant that 75% of the adult male population of, say, New England, could vote in local elections. See P. Carroll & D. Noble, *The Free and the Unfree. A New History of the United States*, Penguin 1984, p. 96.

11. Burke, *Reflections*, p. 117.

12. *An Appeal from the New to the Old Whigs* [April-May 1791] in *Melody*, p. 445.

13. 'It is ... of infinite importance that [the people at large] should not be suffered to imagine that their will, any more than that of kings, is the standard of right and wrong.' *Reflections*, p. 191

14. *Reflections*, pp. 287, 307, 314, 325, 330-40.

15. For a discussion, see J. Talmon, *The Origins of Totalitarian Democracy*, 1961, ch. 2; & J. Marejko, *Rousseau et la dérive totalitaire,* Lausanne 1984, pp. 23-25.

16. C. Machlachlan, *Spain's Empire in the New World: the Role of Ideas in Institutional and Social Change*, California 1988, ch. I.

17. On Suárez: G. Franchesci, 'Francisco Suárez y el origen del poder civil', in A. Dell'Oro Maini *et al., Presencia y sugestión del filósofo Francisco Suárez*, Buenos Aires, 1959, pp. 53-74.

18. Machlachlan, p. 9. A later Spanish American might be Mier, discussed by D. Brading, *The First America. The Spanish Monarchy, Creole Patriots, and the Liberal State 1492-1867*, Cambridge 1991, p. 593.

19. J. Elliot, *Imperial Spain 1469-1716*, Penguin 1988, p.167.

20. J. Lynch, 'Spain and America before 1700', in L. Bethell (ed.), *Colonial Spanish America*, Cambridge 1987, p. 64.

21. Machlachlan, pp. 123-5.

22. Lynch, *Bourbon Spain*, pp. 332-6.

23. On nationalist doctrine there is a broad bibliography. See, eg, H. Seton-Watson, *Nations and States. An enquiry into the origins of nations and the politics of nationalism*, London 1977, p.6.

24. This interpretation differs from that of historians who do not consider the premises or nature of the Reforms as flawed *per se*, but rather their implementation: eg R.A. Humphreys – 'The Bourbon Reforms came too late, they did not go far enough, they were given insufficient time, to save the empire' – in *Tradition and Revolt in Latin America*, p. 82.

25. Machlachlan, p. 128.

26. For a summary, see D. Brading, 'Bourbon Spain and its American empire', in L.Bethell (ed.), *Colonial Spanish America*, pp. 122-62, and Lynch, *Bourbon Spain*, pp. 336 *et seq.*

27. B. Anderson, *Imagined Communities. Reflections on the Origin and Spread of Nationalism*, 5th ed. Verso 1989, pp. 58-9. Further reflections on the origin of Spanish-American nationalism by D.A. Brading, 'Nationalism and State-Building in Spanish-American History', in E. Posada-Carbó (ed.) *Wars, Parties and Nationalism: Essays on the Politics and Society of Nineteenth-Century Latin America*, ILAS 1995, pp. 89-107.

28. See D. Brading, 'Bourbon Spain and its American empire', in Bethell (ed.), *Colonial Spanish America*, p. 161. He describes the contemporary 'vogue in Madrid for the terms *metropolis* and *colonies*'.

29. Machlachlan, pp. 94-5.

30. Quoted in J. Lynch, *Bourbon Spain 1700-1808*, Blackwell, 2nd ed., 1993, p. 362.

31. Machlachlan, p. 96.

32. J. Lynch, *The Spanish-American Revolutions 1808-1826*, 2nd ed., New York 1986, p.24.

33. Carlos O. Stoetzer, *The Scholastic Roots of the Spanish-American Revolution*, New York 1979, p. 121.

34. G. Furlong, 'Francisco Suárez fué el filósofo de la Revolución Argentina de 1810', in Dell'Oro Maini *et al.*, *Suárez*, pp. 76-112. Charles C. Griffin questions the relative importance of *suarecismo* – 'The Enlightenment and Latin-American Independence', in R. Humphreys & J. Lynch (eds.), *The Origins of the Latin-American Revolutions*, New York 1965, p. 42. For a discussion of Suárez's contractual doctrines versus those of Rousseau, see A. Ivereigh, *Catholicism and Politics in Argentina 1810-1960*, Macmillan 1995, pp.10-15.

35. Brading, *The First America*, p. 513.

36. See M. Batllori sj, 'The role of the Jesuit exiles', in Humphreys & Lynch, *Origins*, ch. 4; and Brading, *The First America*, ch. 20.

37. Brading, *The First America*, p. 540.

38. See Ivereigh, *Catholicism*, p. 40.

39. See discussion between Caillet-Bois, an Argentine, and Encina, a Chilean, in Hunphreys & Lynch, *Origins*, chs 7 & 8.

40. Encina in Humphreys & Lynch, *Origins*, p. 107.

41. Brading, *The First America*, pp. 554-5.

42. Caillet-Bois in Humphreys & Lynch, *Origins*, p. 105.

43. On the influence of scholasticism in the Mayo pronouncements: cf. R. González op, *Las Ordenes Religiosas y la Revolución de Mayo*, Buenos Aires 1960, p. 8; and R. Carbia, *La Revolución de Mayo y la Iglesia*, Buenos Aires 1945, pp. 16-17.

44. Cit. in Brading, *The First America*, p. 600.

45. Brading, *The First America*, p. 600.

46. See V.A. Belaúnde, *Bolívar y el pensamiento político de la revolución hispanoamericana*, Caracas 1974; & D. Bushnell, 'The Last Dictatorship: Betrayal or Consummation?', *Hispanic American Historical Review*, 63:1 (Feb 1983), pp. 65-106.

47. Ivereigh, *Catholicism*, pp. 43-6.

48. Anderson, *Imagined Communities*, p. 54.

49. Richard Morse summarized by F. Safford, 'Politics, Ideology and Society', in L. Bethell (ed.), *Spanish America after Independence c.1820-c.1870*, Cambridge 1987, pp. 116-7.

50. C. Hale, 'Political Ideas and Ideologies in Latin America, 1870-1930', in L. Bethell (ed.), *Ideas and Ideologies in Twentieth-Century Latin America*, Cambridge 1996, pp. 140-1.

51. Burke, *Reflections*, pp. 152-3 & 194-5.

52. *El Orden*, October 26 1845, cit. in S. Collier & W. Sater, *A History of Chile 1808-1994*, Cambridge 1996, p. 59.

MANUEL BERMEJO MARCOS

University of Leeds

D. JUAN VALERA Y LAS MUJERES, O EL "DON JUANISMO" DE VALERA

El gran prosista que fué Valera, cuyo dominio de la lengua española y su inimitable estilo fueron reconocidos de inmediato por lo mejor de la crítica y los estudiosos de su tiempo y del presente como uno de nuestros más grandes escritores del siglo XIX, no alcanzó en vida, para sus males, la reputación de "escritor popular". Ni como novelista, ni como crítico, ni como él mismo pretendía, aunque en eso me parece que sin tanta razón, como poeta en verso, que en prosa muy pocos le igualan. Es decir, no llegó a ser nunca autor del gran público y no como sólo lo fué para una minoría culta de la sociedad española. Y no creo que fuesen "los laureles de gloria y fama", que tal título hubiese llevado consigo, lo que echaba de menos cuando se quejó de no alcanzarlo durante toda su vida, sino unas razones más prosaicas, más rastreras hubiera podido decir él: las puramente económicas.

El éxito inmediato de *Pepita Jiménez* no se tradujo en ediciones de miles de ejemplares, sino más bien de unos pocos centenares; e igual sucedería con el resto de sus admirables novelas. Con lo obtenido por la mejor pagada de ellas... "no habría ni para comprar un modelo de vestido para mi esposa", decía con más que una chispita irónico-andaluza de exageración hablando de esa "sindineritis crónica" que padeció toda su vida.[1]

En esta mala fortuna de no llegar "al gran público" hasta después de "muerto y bien muerto", como diría del teatro valleinclaniano un desafortunado crítico teatral en *A.B.C.* en los años sesenta, al ser tímidamente repuestas (¡y con enormes

145

tijeretazos de la ignorante y fanática censura franquista!) las *Comedias bárbaras* en Madrid, me hace pensar en lo que, por desgracia, le ocurrió también al creador de los *esperpentos*. D. Ramón, todavía más desafortunado que Valera, se debatió no sólo con la "sindeniritis" valerina sino que bordeó la peor pobreza gran parte de su vida. En cambio, y como para compensar, sus herederos siguen cobrando hoy los pingües derechos que tanta falta hicieron al autor, que murió casi en la miseria y sin conocer la gloria de que hoy goza con toda justicia.

Si como escritor, decía, no alcanzó "popularidad" entre el gran público como la alcanzaron Galdós o la Pardo Bazán, para no citar más que a los dos escritores coetáneos comparables, es evidente que como hombre de mundo, como ejemplo de caballero español fino, culto, elegante, excelente conversador y brillante en las más altas esferas sociales del país, y sin tardar mucho en el extranjero, don Juan Valera no tuvo rival, incluso antes de abandonar su Andalucía natal, para instalarse en la Corte, en cuyos salones adquirió muy pronto fama de cortejador dicharachero y galanteador afortunado; en otras palabras del "don Juan" que anunciaba su mismo nombre, por su buen tipo y belleza natural, su desenvoltura de ingenio, su gracia y su talento.[2]

Las damas se lo rifaban, a juzgar por lo que de esos tiempos nos cuentan el mismo escritor y sus biógrafos. (Valera en una cartas deliciosas a sus padres, que nos siguen causando asombro y sana envidia incluso hoy, siglo y medio después, por la saludable e inusitada franqueza en las que les cuenta, con pelos y señales, pero sobre todo con una gracia y un desenfado admirables en una sociedad tan puritana en apariencia como la de mediados del siglo pasado, sus peripecias erótico-amorosas más íntimas y atrevidas.) Muy pronto, repito, se ganó fama de don Juan, "conquistador de damiselas a la cosaca", como él mismo repetiría; amores y amoríos ligeros, coqueteos y aventurillas sin trascendencia entre la mejor sociedad española de su juventud. Y como "resistió" soltero hasta bien entrada la cuarentena, doblando en edad a la jovencita que le condujo al altar..., su "donjuanismo" parecía ratificarse, y su fama, en este sentido, seguiría creciendo, cuando la armonía conyugal, la felicidad, empezó a dar señales de no ir por tan buenos caminos, lo que no tardaría mucho en suceder.

Por otra parte, y con toda la razón, Valera ha sido considerado como el iniciador de la novela sicológica española moderna, el escritor que más acertadamente supo recrear a la mujer, porque las amaba, y bucear después en el alma femenina convirtiéndola en indudable protagonista principal de sus mejores ficciones, analizándola bajo el potente microscopio de su sensibilidad creadora como nadie antes que él lo hubiera hecho en nuestra novela.[3]

Evidentes son, pues, la atracción que sintió siempre por el bello sexo y la importancia que tuvo la mujer en la vida y en la obra de nuestro autor desde sus primeros pasos por el mundo. Tal vez la más duradera y visible influencia femenina sobre su formación y su futuro carácter, por ser la que ocupa el primer lugar en su vida, sea la figura de su madre, Doña María Dolores Alcalá-Galiano y Pareja, marquesa de la Paniega. A una clara inteligencia unía el refinado cultivo del espíritu que su hijo echaría de menos en el oficial de la Armada, D. José Valera y Viaña, que fué su padre. Era la madre mujer de claro talento, ambiciosa y de buen gusto natural, con la rara ventaja añadida de haber sido educada con el refinamiento del siglo XVIII francés llegado hasta ella por medio de un anciano abate, su preceptor, escapado de Francia durante la revolución de 1789.[4]

La marquesa puso todo su empeño en instruir delicadamente a sus hijos desde los primeros años, educación directa, amorosa y llevada a cabo con rigor. Sintió, desde siempre, una predilección especial por Juan; el instinto materno le anunciaba que, de entre todos su hijos, éste sería el que más fama y honores daría al nombre familiar y, sin menospreciar a los otros tres hijos, José el mayor y heredero del título, fruto de un primer matrimonio del que enviudó muy pronto, con el general suizo D. Santiago Freuller, y Sofía y Ramona, sus hermanas, Juan fué siempre para la marquesa su esperanza mejor. Algo así como la secreta ilusión de que alcanzara en la vida el triunfo que a ella misma, pese a su talento, ambición, fuerza de voluntad y cultura le estaba vedado sencillamente por haber nacido mujer en la sociedad española de su tiempo. Para ella su hijo nunca dejó de ser el niño grande, inteligente, sensible, guapo y bueno que tanto prometía: su Juanito.

De la mano de sus padres, ambos con más títulos y presunción de sangre noble que fortuna y obligados a vivir con relativas estrecheces toda su vida un poco por bajo de la clase social a la que pertenecían, y por tanto algo desengañados, a poco de soltarse a caminar, aprende las primeras letras. Y como la madre descubre pronto el claro ingenio de su hijo, volcará sobre él su propio caudal de conocimientos en esos años en que de más cuido necesita el alma humana y con menos trabajo absorbe cuanto se le enseña, la primera infancia.

Peligrosas, aunque fructíferas, enseñanzas de unos maestros cuya moral era más o menos el resentido desengaño; tales principios harán que el hijo nunca se desprenda en el futuro de una cierta capa de reservas, dudas e irónico escepticismo como se ve en casi toda su obra. Sin apartarle de los juegos propios de un muchacho de su edad le hacen notar la diferencia que existe entre el vivir como ganapán y el disfrute de los placeres del espíritu. Solamente así no nos extrañamos de que el mismo Valera nos cuente que "...a los seis años leía libros de poco amena historia y a los once o doce a Voltaire".[5]

Tal hecho, en una criatura normal, sin una madre que velase sabiamente por la formación de su hijo y que le hace aprender latín, francés e inglés, cuando otros a su edad se andan por las cartillas más elementales, resultaría poco menos que imposible.

D. Juan Valera y las mujeres

No en el caso de Valera, al que se intentaba, desde el comienzo, preparar para el mejor logro de una vida brillante. Tal proyección o influjo materno puede afirmarse que le dejó muy marcado, ya que no se agotaría hasta la muerte de la marquesa, ocurrida en Francia, en junio de 1872.[6]

Tras las primeras letras y humanidades, estudiadas en Cabra, cursa en el Seminario de Málaga Leyes y Filosofía, leyendo "sin orden ni concierto" cuanto cae en sus manos,[7] "contagiándose" de un pasajero y breve sarampión romántico, tras los entusiasmos de la adolescencia que le producen los versos de Byron y Espronceda, al que llegó a conocer personalmente e incluso leyéndole algunos de los suyos, aquellos osados primeros versos que publicaría en el semanario local *El Guadalhorce*. Por esos años -¡a los 13!, nos dice su mejor biógrafa- "...sentíase enamorado de una jovencita muy bella de 14 años, luego Condesa de Cabarrús...", precisamente cuando su hermano mayor le conduce a Granada para estudiar en el Colegio del Sacro Monte el primer curso de Leyes y donde, además, se aficionará para siempre a la lectura y traducción de los clásicos latinos con gran aprovechamiento.[8] El segundo curso lo sigue ya en la Universidad; publica más poemas en las revistas *La Alhambra* y *La Tarántula* y convence a sus padres para que le dejen irse a Madrid a estudiar el tercero, tantas son las prisas que tiene por triunfar y lucirse en la capital. Y sin duda triunfó en los salones más aristocráticos de la Corte, en los que no tardaría en hacerse popular y adquirir fama de "conquistador", enamorándose perdidamente,¡a sus 17 años!, de la bellísima poetisa española, nacida en Puerto Rico, y que por haber vivido varios años en Cuba pasa por cubana, Gertrudis Gómez de Avellaneda, "..a quien requerí de amores...", escribió en las notas a su poema "A Lelia", inspirado por ella. La cual, pasada ya la treintena y con muchas más experiencias amorosas que el entusiasta y precoz pretendiente, lo rechazaría delicada pero firmemente, lo que no impediría que mantuviesen después excelente amistad y admiración mutua, y cuando ella fallezca en el más triste olvido, muchos años después (1873), don Juan fuera una de "...las doce personas que asistan a su modestísimo entierro."[9] Este fué el primero de los varios enamoramientos de Valera con mujeres mayores que él, como veremos.

Las experiencias, devaneos y triunfos del irresistible galán en "la dolce vita" madrileña del curso académico 1842-43 no se correspondieron con idéntica fortuna en sus estudios: ¡suspendió el curso completo!

Sus padres le obligaron a regresar a Granada, en cuya Universidad, a fines de 1844, obtuvo el grado de Bachiller en Jurisprudencia.

Para celebrarlo su padre le costeó la edición de su primer libro, *Ensayos poéticos*, un tomito de versos, Ed. Benavides, Granada, que vió la luz el mes de abril. Con las impaciencias de todo escritor novel pasó a los pocos días por la tienda del editor para informarse de cómo iban las ventas y descubre con horror que no se había vendido ni un solo ejemplar. (Él eleva la cifra: nos dice "ni tres se habían vendido".[10]) La malherida vanidad, el juvenil orgullo y la amarga desilusión que le produjo la indiferencia del público lector, le llevan a recoger la edición íntegra, 300 ejemplares, y "enterrarla" en el desván de su casa familiar, en Doña Mencía. Solamente su madre lo consuela sin perder la fe en él: "Esto no marchita tu gloria ni tu talento...", y termina alentándolo con malicioso humor: "¿Pensabas tú que los españoles son gente para gastarse diez o doce reales en un libro?"[11]

Termina, dos años después, la Licenciatura en Derecho y a fines de 1846 vuelve a Madrid dispuesto esta vez a brillar con luces propias, labrarse una profesión que le permita no tener que depender de sus padres. Pero encerrarse en un despacho y trabajar como "pasante" o aprendiz de abogado no era lo suyo, y como la

D. Juan Valera y las mujeres

familia tiene muy buenas relaciones en "las alturas de la mejor sociedad" prefiere volver a divertirse, tomar parte en bailes y fiestas y, de paso, aprovechar cuantas aventurillas erótico-sentimentales se presenten como, en carta de 14-1-1847, les cuenta a sus padres con gracejo inimitable sus aventurillas, ya sea con una antigua amada que tuvo en la adolescencia, Paulina, ahora casada y "Condesa de C..."[que parece prometer mucho y que pudiera ser la condesa de Cabarrús de que nos habla su biógrafa cuando lo llevaban a estudiar a Granada, seis años antes] o con la que más a mano tiene..."la joven viuda, mi compañera de habitación...sigo con ella muy amigo, pillo lo que puedo y, vea lo que vea, entienda lo que entienda, no me quejo ni me doy por ofendido, que al fin el ofenderme cuando no hay derecho ninguno es una necedad."[12]

Valera, que como muy bien afirma uno de sus mejores estudiosos, M. Azaña, "..no se había asimilado noción alguna capaz de hacerle sentir en el comercio amatorio falsa vergüenza ni el rubor de lo pecaminoso", parece consagrarse principalmente al divertido devaneo, o lo que hoy se llamaría el ligue más desenfadado, que a nada compromete pero satisface y calma las urgencias eróticas de la pareja. Frecuenta las reuniones, fiestas y bailes en los más refinados salones aristocráticos, del Duque de Rivas, del Duque de Frías, Heredia, Cabarrús y, especialmente, el de la Condesa de Montijo, en el que "Se agolpaban...los rancios y advenedizos, "pollos" aristocráticos, literatos, políticos, abogados que empezaban a ganar millones con los pleitos surgidos de la desvinculación. Era el foco más brillante de la sociedad de Madrid, el mejor campo de maniobras para un joven ambicioso."[13] Valera no pareció aprovechar las oportunidades de ese "joven ambicioso" de que nos habla Azaña para ascender en la cucaña profesional sencillamente porque no se conformaba con llegar a ser otro leguleyo millonario más, ni un nuevo rico de las finanzas, ocupaciones que no acaban de parecerle dignas de un

151

hombre de su clase y condición. Brilla en dichos salones, sobre todo entre las damas, el elegante señorito andaluz, ambicioso, sí, pero con una ambición de glorias más altas e imperecederas, las del arte literario.

Se ha repetido con razón que en el capítulo "Para qué sirve", de su novela *Las ilusiones del Doctor Faustino,* nos deja ver casi un trasunto autobiográfico de su misma situación, a los 23 años, con una carrera que no le satisface y en un mundo cuyas posibilidades no le ofrecen salida digna de sus inclinaciones más sinceras. Vemos en esas páginas sus propias dudas, sus perplejidades y angustias ante los caminos -las oportunidades- que la vida le presenta. Incapaz de proseguir con sus planes originales de trabajar con un abogado de fama, primero, y abrir bufete propio y luchar en Madrid cuando adquiera la experiencia y el oficio necesarios para triunfar en la carrera, terminó por seguir otro camino mucho menos incómodo: "Como mi fuerte no es el trabajo, y menos de esta clase, ahorqué la toga, quemé la golilla, y, aprovechándome de una buena coyuntura, me metí de patitas en la diplomacia, donde con bailar bien la polca y comer pastel de *foie-gras* está todo hecho",[14] le cuenta, burla-burlando, a un amigo.

Ha sido nombrado agregado sin sueldo, es decir "meritorio", en la Embajada de España en Nápoles, de la que es titular el Duque de Rivas, viejo amigo de la familia. Allí permanecerá dos años y medio, iniciando una carrera de diplomático que, aunque nunca le satisfizo, le permitirá vivir con esa cierta holgura que da el dinero...sin tenerlo, pues se quejó siempre de padecer "sindineritis crónica", acostumbrado a vivir a lo gran señor y derrochando generosamente más de lo que el sueldo le permitía, "alegrías" que únicamente con su pluma no hubiera podido costearse. Pero fué muy provechoso el tiempo transcurrido en la "corte poético amorosa" del duque-poeta, como la llamó M. Azaña. La formación clásica iniciada en su adolescencia va a echar ahora raíces más profundas, gozando "al vivo" de aquella vieja cultura latina evolucionada, familiarizándose con la lengua italiana, mejorando su latín y estudiando el griego bajo la férula del profesor Constantino Eutiquiades...y los valiosos alientos de una dama muy atractiva de la que no tardó en enamorarse perdidamente. De la mano del Duque, y alentado por él, irá el juvenil Valera progresando tanto en el oficio poético como en la vida (¡y hasta rivalizando con su jefe en enredillos amorosos!). En aquella "...breve corte...más agitada por los lances amorosos que por los negocios de Estado y los ejercicios poéticos, Valera desempeñó un papel brillante."[15]

Su afición a gozar de "amistades íntimas" con las damas mejoraría con las prácticas napolitanas, en donde maduró rápidamente, con experiencias propias o ajenas, su técnica amatoria ya que antes era, a todas luces, "un galán más ardoroso que experto".[16]

La llegada a Nápoles de "...la muy alegre marquesa de Villagarcía, corazón no menos gozoso que experto",[17] seis años mayor que Valera, señalemos, alborotaría el cotarro de la Embajada. Todos, jefe incluído, pretenden llevarse el más que tentador gato al agua.

A la chita callando, y aún antes de que llegara la alegre marquesa a Nápoles, pues se encontraron en Roma, parece ser que el agraciado había sido el joven aprendiz de diplomático, aunque dé a entender que los enredos con "la Saladita" -como con humor un tanto pueril se llamaban entre sí- eran "puro juego y coqueteo inofensivo". Eso fué lo que por discreción (virtud que hasta entonces no se había molestado en lucir) quiso hacer pensar en las cartas de aquellos días, e incluso después, como se ve en una de sus chistosísimas cartas desde Brasil -Rio de Janeiro, 4 de agosto de 1853- a su admirado D. Serafín Estébanez Calderón. (A quien también conocería en Nápoles, siendo desde entonces hasta su muerte -fines de 1867- su mentor y consejero literario, animándole a escribir y vaticinándole acertadamente una brillante carrera como escritor.) Cuenta a su amigo con desenfadado humor cómo "poéticamente" había puesto fin a la amorosa contienda el Duque de Rivas: "Ya en Roma había yo tratado a esta misma Villagarcía, y ganado su corazón hasta el extremo de que me confiase el atrevidísimo y endiablado proyecto de seducir al Padre Santo; pero nunca imaginé que ya jamona y *más catada que colmena*, pusiese a la Legación de España ... en ocasión de hacer mil desatinos. Ello es que Embajador, Secretarios y Agregados, todos la querían gozar y la cortejaban a porfía. Una noche al fin el Embajador ofendido nos dijo que la dama corría de su cuenta: y tomándonos por los doce pares, y convirtiéndose él en Carlo-Magno, aunque en apariencia de burlas, se levantó de su asiento, y con voz llena de cólera mal disimulada, nos habló de este modo:

> Merecida ha de ser, no arrebatada
> Angélica en mi tierra, paladines
> Que aún no es del todo báculo mi espada
> Ni estoy sordo al rumor de los clarines."[18]

Varios estudiosos que se ocuparon de estos temas, incluídos M. Azaña y C. Bravo Villasante, se inclinaron a pensar que el devaneo fué cortado de raíz por el Duque de Rivas y "la cosa" no llegó a mayores. Pero una carta, del 7 de julio de 1850, ya mencionada por Azaña, de la muy "liberada" Saladita a Valera (cuando éste, vuelto de Nápoles a Madrid, acababa de ser nombrado agregado de número en Lisboa) en la que le invita a pasarse un mes de vacaciones con ella en Villagarcía, deja bien claro el grado de "intimidad" a que habían llegado. O sea, empleando una típica expresión valerina: "que el negocio había llegado a lo vivo" y que los juegos amorosos de Nápoles entre los

"Saladitos" no fueron tan inocente pasatiempo como Valera quiso hacer creer.[19]

Nos parece, por otra parte, natural que Valera tuviese interés en aparentar discreción cuando descubrimos -por otra carta de "la Saladita" del 26 de julio[20]- que el tal "divertimento" o ligue erótico, sin mayores consecuencias para los felices "pecadores", había coincidido en comprometedor paralelismo con la que se ha llamado "la pasión amorosa más profunda" de cuantas vivió este enamoradizo cuanto cerebral don Juan...Valera. (Aunque a ojos del enamorado galán totalmente insatisfactoria, por no haber llegado a "la consumación").

Que la marquesa de Villagarcía estuviese al tanto de dicho enamoramiento le añade a mi juicio sal y gracia al "affaire" de los "Saladitos", ya que el cinismo era compartido.

Pero estos amores -correspondidos sólo en lo espiritual, que no a gusto del enamorado- por "la Muerta", o la Dama Griega, como la llama Valera en sus cartas, eran otra cosa más seria. Había llegado a Nápoles, mediada ya la primavera de 1848, Lucía Palhadile y Callimachi, Princesa viuda de Cantacuzeno, por su primer matrimonio, y Marquesa de Bedmar por su segundo, del que había tenido un hijo.[21] Como nunca se acostumbrara a la sociedad y el ambiente madrileños y había sido prácticamente abandonada por el marido, que ejercía en la Corte madrileña, desde hacía tiempo, de "cortesano favorito" de la Reina Isabel II, decidió cambiar de aires y establecerse en un clima social y físico más atractivo para su delicada persona como lo era el napolitano. Y desde que se conocieron en la tertulia de los Duques de Bivona, sus cuñados, parece que se estableció entre los dos una corriente de fuerte simpatía, que pronto se transformó en admiración y más tarde en atracción ardiente y mutua. Ella, aunque de salud delicadísima, enferma casi permanente (su extremada palidez, lo demacrado de sus facciones, hicieron que de inmediato el Embajador y Valera la apodaran, con humor bastante carpetovetónico "La Muerta") conservaba todavía físicamente cierta belleza, un delicado atractivo, pese a estar ya muy lejana su juventud, pues le sacaba al galán más de 20 años.[22]

Dama de una gran personalidad, sólida y amplia cultura, exquisita educación y refinada sensibilidad artística y literaria fueron atractivos irresistibles para el joven diplomático, que se enamoró perdidamente de ella, pues por fin parecía tener ante sí aquella mujer ideal -su "ideal de mujer"- con que tantas veces había soñado el juvenil poeta. De la admiración sin límites pasó a la pasión más sublime e irrefrenable. Y aunque espiritualmente ella le correspondiera casi con la misma fuerza, idéntico amor, jamás consintió en entregársele, en hacerlo feliz del todo. Y como Valera nunca creyó en el puro "amor platónico" (pensaba que eso era pura "sofistería", hipocresía, un fallo de la naturaleza o simple aberración, porque jamás logró separar el cuerpo del espíritu) sufrió lo indecible por sentirse sinceramente defraudado, a pesar de los besos y caricias más dulces que se intercambiaban. No podía conformarse, como le suplicaba que la aceptase su bien amada, con el amor purísimo que ella le ofrecía, porque "...yo podría ser tu madre...-le dice Lucía-...No, no, amante", replica colérico el fogosísimo enamorado.[23] De nada sirvieron los enfados, rabietas con lágrimas y escenas melodramáticas del decepcionado Romeo. Lucía, que está en espíritu tan enamorada de su joven pretendiente como él lo está en cuerpo y alma de ella, no cederá a sus embates; porque ceder, en sus condiciones de enferma crónica y sobre todo por la diferencia de edad, le parece a la dama una forma indigna de manchar, casi prostituir, una relación de amorosa pureza que desea conservar para siempre, aunque tenga que hacer un esfuerzo más doloroso todavía que el de su impaciente amado. Y no es puritanismo, ni retraimiento en su vida sentimental: "Al huir de Nápoles y del dolor de la pasión de Valera, ella, recién llegada a París, no tiene inconveniente en caer en brazos de varios amantes consecutivos. Pero es porque a ellos no les quiere...son sólo la satisfacción de una necesidad para ella."[24]

Regresa Valera a Madrid a fines de 1849, entristecido y deseando olvidar de una vez y para siempre el que, a sus ojos, por no haber alcanzado lo que tanto ansiaba, fué su gran fracaso sentimental. El primero y tal vez el más fuerte trauma amoroso de su vida, del que no estoy muy seguro lograra liberarse del todo nunca, ese amarguísimo final de su ardiente y sincerísima pasión - viva siempre en su corazón sensible- por "la Muerta": "La persona a quien he querido yo más en el Mundo...que viene a Madrid el 15 del corriente [le escribe a su amigo S. Estébanez Calderón en 1854, cinco años después de haberse separado de ella]..y a quien deseo con ansia volver a ver. Siempre, a pesar de la larguísima ausencia he tenido por aquella dama de Oriente una singular devoción y un acendradísimo cariño, y aunque ahora vuelva fea como el diablo, y vieja y estropeada, temo que la voy a querer de nuevo con el ahinco antiguo."[25] ¿Será que durante esos años su amor por "la Muerta" se ha ido decantando...? Es decir, ¿ ya no tiene las exigencias físicas de los días napolitanos ? Tal vez empieza a reconocer la deuda que con Lucía tiene pues fué mucho lo que le ayudó en su camino de escritor animándole con sus positivos e inteligentes consejos a que trabajase de firme, a estudiar la lengua griega, que llegó a dominar, y especialmente a mejorar su autoestima, sentimiento que le flojeaba mucho, así como en tantas cosas más que sirvieron para depurar su sensibilidad natural y artística.

También busca, al regresar a Madrid, no tener -a sus 25 años- que depender económicamente de sus padres, hacerse una carrera de "pretendiente" en la Corte: "Mi amor propio está comprometido y debo ser algo o reventar", le confiesa a su padre. Pero sus muchos miedos, su orgullo de sangre y su claro raciocinio le advierten que no tiene madera de vividor y cucañero, de cínico buscavidas. Lo que, unido a sus serias aspiraciones de artista, su aparente pereza para organizarse mejor...y su afición a la vida fácil que no puede costearse con sus escasos recursos, le hacen caer en un constante desánimo pesimista, en sentirse a disgusto en un país que le resulta insufrible por su vulgaridad chabacana: "Este país es un presidio rebelado. Hay poca instrucción y menos moralidad; pero no falta ingenio natural y sobra desvergüenza y audacia". Incluso le fastidian "..su aridez y el tristísimo aspecto de estos campos, que no dan sino desconsuelo al corazón".[26]

Se consuela, cómo no, acudiendo a las elegantes fiestas y salones favoritos de la aristocracia, volviendo a los fáciles triunfos de enredos y amoríos superficiales, como el que tuvo con la hija de su primer jefe, Malvina Rivas, que lo veía con muy buenos ojos, con el beneplácito familiar. Pero Valera, que para nobleza pobre ya tenía bastante con la propia ve que no es un buen partido para solucionar sus problemas financieros de por vida, y chicolea sin comprometerse a nada, a pesar de que la joven le gusta, conservando su amistad y simpatía, llamándola siempre "la Culebrosa" y llegando hasta comentar con su padre (detalle sólo mencionado una vez en sus cartas, que me parece se le ha escapado a los biógrafos que hablan del "enredo") que Malvinita, la hija del Duque de Rivas, además de "culebrosa" y sin fortuna, ¡era bizca![27]

Valera, en esos meses de impaciente espera, a pesar de sus ocasionales diversiones galantes, no halla consuelo ni con los eruditos, que le parecen "mal educados, sucios y pedantes" y ni siquiera las féminas logran quitarle el mal humor..."mientras las mujeres estén mal educadas y sean tan ignorantes y vulgares en nuestro país."..."Mucho echo de menos también a *la Muerta*". ¿Cómo encontrar algo que se parezca a *la Muerta*?", se pregunta con sincerísimo dolor en esas instructivas y graciosas confesiones que son las cartas que escribe a sus padres. Además, las exigencias del sexo aprietan: "...tengo que apelar a todo mi estoicismo para no andar por ahí en busca de querida o con ella, dado caso que la hallase a mi gusto. Esta afición mía a las faldas es terrible y si no fuera por lo caro que es Madrid y lo escaso que estoy de dinero para estar aquí en los círculos elegantes, andaría yo de reunión en reunión haciendo la corte a las damas..."[28]

No parece haber mejorado mucho de fortuna, en esa búsqueda de aventuras más o menos "espirituales" cuando, por fín, es nombrado agregado con sueldo (¡12.000 reales de sueldo al año!) a la Embajada de España en Lisboa, en donde empieza por encontrar que "...Las mujeres se visten aquí de un modo bestial. Llevan capas como los hombres y un pañuelo blanco en la cabeza, tan puntiagudo y almidonado, que dan ganas de reir al verlas", dice en carta de 28-8-1850, y dos meses después le cuenta a su padre: "...no he visto en mi vida mujeres más feas que las damas de Lisboa, salvo raras excepciones".[29]

Pronto debió de hallar por lo menos una excepción, a la que no parece hacerle muchos ascos el empedernido "faldero", Julia Pacheco, acaudalada mocita de padre portugués y madre española: "Esta señora [le cuenta a la Marquesa de la Paniega] que ha sido bastante alegrita, es de muy noble familia extremeña, tiene un hermano senador en Madrid, viejo, rico y sin hijos..." y le dice que es ahora viuda de un portugués que les dejó cierta fortuna, lo que sin duda, unido a los encantos personales de la joven, atrae vivamente al galanteador no ocultándosele que, entre bromas y veras, la damita en cuestión, con la bendición de su mamá, anda muy enamorada del apuesto buen mozo y diplomático cordobés. Consideró muy seriamente el matrimonio pese a que había empezado por broma haciendo de ella, y por chiste, un "esperpento" al llamarla "semijorobada". Conviene recordar, de pasada, que J. Corominas documentó el término "esperpento" en un texto de Valera, y que en toda su obra, y especialmente en sus miles de cartas, en donde escribe con más libertad, se pueden espigar docenas de ejemplos de la técnica que tan magistralmente emplearía más tarde Valle-Inclán, llegando a convertirla en originalísimo género literario. Desde Brasil le dirá a Estébanez Calderón: "En todas las cosas, hasta en las más serias, veo yo algo de ridículo y me aflijo sobremanera", y más adelante explica: "Lo que me mueve a risa es lo que asímismo me mueve a piedad".[30] Valera, fino humorista andaluz tampoco puede mirar la realidad sin encontrarle el ángulo ridículo, degradante y desmitificador, aunque sin la ferocidad del gallego, a cada cual el honor debido.

Aclara de inmediato que "...su joroba es una burla mía, fundada sólo en que la muchacha no se tiene bastante derecha"...y que "...la semijorobada es, además de rica, bien criada, bien presentable y, con joroba y todo, asaz apetitosa, para que yo no le tenga ascos a solas, ni en público me avergüence de llevarla por compañera. Yo, si fuese fea, no me hubiese enredado con ella", aclara por si las dudas. Y si la fortuna de la luso-extremeña hubiera sido mayor, me temo que don Juan Valera hubiese sucumbido a la tentación matrimonial pues parecía dar por sentado que un matrimonio "de conveniencia", con sus talentos personales y su "palmito", estaba más que justificado. Pero casarse por los 80.000 duros que confiesa tiene de dote la novia... no acabó de convencerle, aunque anduvo muy cerca del compromiso matrimonial. Al final y tras "...madurísimas reflexiones y de los cálculos más exactos y detenidos..."[teniendo en cuenta] "...mi horror al matrimonio y mi deseo de pindonguearme por ahí solterito aún y de andar en el Brasil en bromas y fiestas, entre blancos, negros y mulatos...Yo le doy mil vueltas y al fin sospecho que me he de quedar soltero." [31]

Como para cumplir tal propósito pidió un destino en Brasil, a donde llega a fines de 1851 recién ascendido a Secretario de Legación con un sueldo anual de 18.000 reales. Se instala en casa de su jefe, D. José Delavat, un español tan afable como atrabiliario, afincado en aquel país desde hacía 35 años y del cual se burlará, no sin cierta afección, en sus cartas. En los casi dos años que pasó en Río mantuvo regular correspondencia con familiares y amigos, en especial con su mentor y admirador literario D. Serafín Estébanez Calderón que le acuciaba a escribirle más y más, tanto era lo que disfrutaba con la belleza de las cartas y el originalísimo humor de su discípulo y amigo. Cartas divertidísimas y escritas en un estilo tan familiar y archiatrevido que incluso en nuestros días algunos de sus más íntimos detalles han sido tachados de "crudezas excesivas" por alguno de sus estudiosos. El salpimentado humor con que las adereza y el arte con que las escribe me parecen suficientes como para justificar tales "libertades", que salen de su pluma convertidas en joyas literarias de superior calidad.

Pero el primitivismo de la vida en Río de Janeiro, tras las refinadas elegancias europeas, le resulta francamente insoportable. Reconoce y admira la grandiosidad del paisaje, demostrando el asombro sincero de todo europeo sensible al descubrir la impresionante belleza e inimaginable feracidad de aquella exuberante Naturaleza americana que tiene ante los ojos, casi una selva virgen todavía hoy, siglo y medio después, apenas sin salir de la bahía de Guanabara, en cuyas orillas se asienta la capital carioca. Las incomodidades del diario vivir le impedirán el disfrute, y un conocimiento algo más profundo, de tanta hermosura a este "civilizado" señorito andaluz. Le abruman las contrariedades: "...el calor me mata, y un dolor de estómago casi continuo me quita el gusto para todo. Las calles...mal empedradas, los coches son caros y detestables, las distancias enormes, la comida nauseabunda, los negros que la sirven descalzos de pie y pierna y apestando a lo chotuno y las habitaciones mal alhalajadas, y llenas de arañas, curianas, lagartijas, mosquitos, salamanquesas, alacranes y otros monstruos horribles y asquerosos". Mas no escapa a su agudeza que "...La fecundidad de esta tierra se comunica también al hombre, y si no pare, se empreña muy a menudo...La sífilis es aquí más variada y esquisita [sic] que en Europa, y así mismo todo género de fiebres y enfermedades cutáneas". Tampoco la sociedad brasileña le atrae mucho: "...las mujeres están bozales, y los hombres ocupados en los negocios políticos o mercantiles..."[y aunque] "...los brasileños son muy amigos de la música y de la poesía..." desconocen las otras bellas artes "...y me parece que no hay un edificio bueno, ni un cuadro, ni una estatua en toda la ciudad".[32]

La vida en casa de su jefe tampoco le resulta ideal: "La suegra de mi jefe es una serpiente que si hubiera sido como ésta la del Paraíso, ni hubiera seducido a Eva, ni Eva nos hubiera traído al mísero estado en que nos vemos" [y su marido] "...es flaco como un espárrago, largo y estirado, feo de veras, muy chupado de carrillos, con gafas verdes, y una nariz afilada y mayúscula verde así mismo por la punta, y en lo más colorada como un tomate. Con tan fea catadura aduna el señor Arêas, que así se llama, el más emberrinchinado carácter del mundo y una formalidad más profunda que la sima de Cabra". La esposa del jefe "...es casi tan santa como fea..." y, además de un niño de diez años, el matrimonio tiene una hija "...de ocho o nueve primaveras, que siempre está llorando y dando gritos...y acaricia a su hermanito a cozes [sic] y bocados", el padre la llama "su curiana", dudando Valera de su éxito en la vida "...pues la muchacha es fea como el pecado". Cuando el apacible D. José pierde la paciencia ante el endiablado geniecillo de la criatura vaticina: "Si sigue así cuando se case, aviado está su marido". ¡Lejos estaba Valera de pensar, cuando le cuenta la escena a su amigo Estébanez Calderón, en que trece años después "el aviado" iba a ser él!

Tampoco parece haberle sonreído mucho la fortuna erótico-amorosa en tan fértiles como propicios campos cariocas, pues se queja casi constantemente de tener que recurrir a los "amores mercenarios", como le había dicho a su amigo desde Lisboa.[33]

Ahora le dirá: "Me consuelo, pues, con lo que hallo para el consumo público, que no es cosa buena ni segura; negras y mulatas sobre todo".

De la única dama de la que se encaprichó, una "Armida-Mariquiña" que concedía sus favores a precios fuera del alcance de sus menguados recursos, nada logró y bien que lo lamenta: "Las siete u ocho cartas que escribí a Armida pidiéndoselo eran cosa de gusto, y siento no guardar copia, y hasta me dan intenciones de pedírselas para copiarlas". Tendrá que seguir los consejos de su jefe para que le haga caso a una "...cotorrona sabrosa, ex prima donna, francesa de nación, y casada hoy con el Alfio de Río de Janeiro, usurero riquísimo. Yo la había siempre desdeñado..." D. José le dice sabiamente: "Harto sé que la tal señora está ya algo madura, mas no está podrida, como acaso lo estén las putas con que Vd. anda. Y como no tiene nada mejor debe tomar sin melindres lo que le dan de regalo, y aun si quiere con dinero encima..., la gallina vieja hace buen caldo". Y cuenta luego, con gracia insuperable sus peripecias amatorias con Jeannette, dando detalles tan íntimos como regocijantes y con tanto arte y humor que me parece difícil que alguien haya podido superar después, ni en las más osadas piezas de la literatura erótica de su tiempo, en la "novela galante" posterior, ni en la más atrevida de las "sonrisas verticales" de la actualidad.[34]

Algo menos de dos años pasó Valera en Brasil, al cabo de los cuales, aduciendo fastidios estomacales, logra una oportuna licencia que le permite regresar a Lisboa en setiembre, a fin de terminar su medio compromiso matrimonial con la "semijorobada" y luego a Madrid para reanudar sus "chicoleos sociales" y publicar sus primeros artículos de crítica literaria. Casi dos años pasó en la Corte que le sirvieron para ascender en su carrera diplomática y para obtener un pasajero destino de menos de un año en la Legación de España en Dresde, donde, aparte de mejorar algo su más que elemental conocimiento del alemán, pasó frío y se aburrió un poco, aunque descubre y empieza a apreciar la música sinfónica ("páseme Vd. la palabreja", le dice a su amigo Estébanez con frase que me parece sintomática del desconocimiento que hasta entonces había de ella en nuestro país) de compositores como "Handel, Bethowen [sic], Mozart, etc.", prácticamente desconocidos en España. En Dresde, y a pesar del éxito que tienen entre el elemento femenino que frecuentan, tanto su jefe, Pizarro, como él mismo, por ser tomados como "...dos bichos raros y que las damas se admiran de nuestros ojos árabes. Yo paso por el más árabe de todos los españoles aquí residentes...Pero esta extraña admiración que Pizarro y yo inspiramos no pasa de ser meramente platónica: y admirados y todo, nos tenemos que resignar a ir a putas: las cuales son en Dresde poco agradables, si bien calientes..."[35]

En el otoño de 1854 Valera fué nombrado Secretario de la Misión Extraordinaria, encabezada por el Gran Duque de Osuna, que España envió a la Corte del Zar Alejandro II de Rusia. Dicho viaje, de fines de octubre a primeros de julio, sería importantísimo para él por muchas y varias razones. La primera, tal vez la más importante, porque en los primeros meses, especialmente, disfrutó como únicamente un ser de su extraordinaria sensibilidad -y pareja sensualidad- puede hacerlo. No sólo con las bellezas naturales o artísticas que le ofrecen ciudades y lugares famosos visitados, palacios, iglesias, castillos, catedrales, museos de arte, etc., sino por el boato brillante de ese fabuloso mundo de la vieja nobleza europea que recibe a estos "grandes de España" con los brazos abiertos. Los banquetes y comilonas, bailes y fiestas de todo tipo, funciones de teatro, conciertos, prostíbulos y demás lugares de jolgorio y diversión a los que acude, o le llevan, y en donde el sensual Juanito Valera se siente vivir con alegría pagana y nueva. La vida, soñada siempre por él como una fiesta maravillosa, le resulta ahora exactamente así, y la disfruta a más no poder. Mas como no sabe vivirla sin compartir su alegría vital con los demás por ser de natural generoso, va escribiendo una serie de más de medio centenar largo de extensas y bellas cartas a su familia y amigos (especialmente a su jefe en Madrid, D. Leopoldo Augusto de Cueto, al que irrespetuosamente apodará "Leopardo Angosto de Cuello" y al que había prometido dar cuenta epistolar de sus andanzas. Sentía comezón imperiosa de escribir y no hay género más apropiado para desarrollar la espontaneidad y sencillez de estilo que el epistolar. Hombre extrovertido al que divertía al máximo el espectáculo de la vida contemplado con su penetrante y burlesca mirada, sirviéndose ahora de una técnica y un donaire aprendidos en su autor favorito, el del inmortal *Quijote*, pero asimilados como se debe y actualizados, traza una divertidísima crónica de la Pomposa Misión española, ideal para las bromas más "valerescas" y jocosas, por lo que de grandilocuente petulancia tenía. Nunca antes su espíritu crítico se había manifestado con más gracia que en esta acertadísima caricatura que son sus cartas desde Rusia. Con mano maestra va trazando la crónica semi-secreta de las peripecias de estos personajes españoles en la Corte del Zar Ruso, marionetas de "grand guignol" en sus manos. Y lo extraordinario es que no se contenta con narrar las andanzas de los demás sino que llega, en el colmo del desenfado y atrevimiento, a pintar su autocaricatura más perfecta contándole a los lectores su fracasada aventura "joco-erótico-amorosa" con la famosísima "cocotte" y actriz francesa Magdalena Brohan. El españolísimo grito de queja machista -"¡Y encima, no me la pude tirar...!"- resuena entre líneas (que es como Valera dice siempre lo más sabroso, sibilino o importante del asunto) de manera tan patéticamente cómica que nos hace pensar en escenas de lo mejor de nuestra "novela picaresca", auto-caricaturizándose el autor como sólo aquellos genios supieron hacerlo.

Su estilo, en estas cartas, alcanza una sencillez, una elegancia y jugosidad muy pocas veces superadas en su obra novelística posterior. No sin razón dijo M. Azaña de ellas: "En posesión plena del estilo, escribe su obra maestra del género epistolar".[36]

Que su prosa es más ligera, espontánea e incluso más bella en sus cartas que cuando novela tiene fácil comprobación. Al comienzo de tan deliciosas "confesiones" le cuenta a su jefe: "No tengo más remedio que hacer de todo esto una novela". Y disfrazando cuanto conviene, salió de su pluma, cuatro años después, *Mariquita y Antonio*. Compárese lo que de las primitivas cartas aprovecha el novelista y se verá que más que imitación es copia; en ambas habla el protagonista en primera persona; en las cartas escribe a un amigo, en la novela el protagonista cuenta a su inexpugnable amada las penas de su corazón, la decisión de matarse tras el rotundo fracaso amoroso. Los cambios efectuados son ligerísimos, salvo el uso de las personas verbales no hay gran diferencia pero...qué distinto el resultado.

En las cartas Valera "revive" sus experiencias, se autocontempla en la fracasada aventura con el preciso distanciamiento burlón acertando plenamente en la diana artística y produce una deliciosa pequeña obra maestra, lo cual no sucede, por desgracia en la versión novelesca. Lo que en las cartas era espontáneo y auténtico, en la novela, que es casi transcripción literal, toda la aventura nos suena a falsa, a pura invención literaria, a cosa muerta. Lo que en la carta al amigo nos conmovía y hacía reir a la vez, por su oportuna verosimilitud, en la inacabada novela nos deja fríos, huele a "esfuerzo consciente por hacer arte", como de pié forzado.

La experiencia rusa, que tan maravillosamente había comenzado, acabaría terminando amargamente para Valera. La publicación de las cartas, aunque convenientemente expurgadas por su jefe en Madrid, produjo la natural irritación en el Duque de Osuna, el cual, en adelante le mostró una desacostumbrada frialdad que Valera, alma cándida pese a su espíritu zumbón, no entiende y de la que incluso se asombra, echándole la culpa de "su desgracia" a los "chismosos" que "...al dar el soplo pusieron en ellas más hiel de la que tengo yo en todo mi corazón".[37]

En su viaje de vuelta a España (efectuado antes que el resto de la Misión) se detendrá en París para llevar a cabo dos visitas. Una a la Brohan, la causante de sus "dolores" físicos y penas sentimentales en Rusia y con la que, pese a todo, había concertado al despedirse, una entrevista en la ciudad del Sena, pues ella regresó cuando él, pero en coche, que Valera no tomó por no enojar aún más al ofendido Duque de Osuna, su rival en la aventura, menos afortunado todavía, al parecer, que su Secretario. Del resultado de esta visita no hay noticia, solamente unos "billetitos" y promesas de amistad. Y la segunda para ver a Lucía, "la Muerta", a la que halló, a casi diez años de su primer encuentro napolitano, muy cerca de serlo de veras.

Desde su retorno de Rusia, verano del 57, hasta su reingreso en la Diplomacia, en el verano de 1865, cuando fué nombrado Ministro Plenipotenciario en Francfort, lleva una vida muy activa en Madrid: como periodista, ayuda a fundar y escribe en los periódicos satíricos *La Malva* y *El Cócora,* primero, y luego como redactor principal del diario *El Contemporáneo,* así como tomando parte activa en la vida política, saliendo elegido Diputado por Archidona y después por Priego. Fué elegido, a los 37 años, miembro de número de la R.A.E. y la editorial Rivadeneira le publica un volumen de *Poesías,* Madrid 1858, dando a luz luego otro, su primero en prosa, *Estudios críticos sobre literatura, política y costumbres,* Madrid, 1864. Durante estos activos años, nos dice su biógrafa, no le faltaron al elegante hombre de mundo "aventuras galantes".[38]

Mas no tardando mucho da las primeras muestras de que le empiezan a cansar tales diversiones. Pasa ya de los cuarenta y su razonadora mente le recuerda que se va haciendo tarde para crearse su propia familia. Al cesar de su puesto diplomático en

Francfort, setiembre de 1866, pasa unos días de vacaciones con
sus hermanas en Biarritz y se encuentra con la viuda de su antiguo
jefe en Río, y el resto de la familia Delavat, y se sorprende de
encontrar que aquella criaturita aborrecible, de la que dijo en una
de sus cartas ..."es fea como el pecado", 13 años después es una
jovencita llena de encantos y que le atrae muy favorablemente,
aunque por discreción o timidez se lo calle hasta cerca de un año
más tarde. Cuando llevado de las prisas y dejando que su
cerebro, no el corazón, razone, la pide en matrimonio a la Señora
Delavat, que acepta encantada la petición, con la natural sorpresa
por parte de la joven, que ni se había enterado del "repentino"
enamoramiento de aquel elegante señor andaluz de 43 años -¡ella
tiene 20!- que las acompañaba y obsequiaba en los paseos
setembrinos de Biarritz.

Una boda más o menos"apañada" por dos personas
maduras, para una jovencita con poca o ninguna experiencia
sentimental, sólo por milagro podía salir bien. Y el milagro no se
produjo. La boda tuvo lugar en París, el 5 de diciembre de 1867.

Cuesta trabajo entender la decisión, tan rápida como
inesperada, del apresurado novio para casarse con tantas prisas en
un hombre con su experiencia erótico-sentimental. Haciendo un
somero recuento de sus relaciones amorosas anteriores al
"flechazo" de Biarritz, dejando de lado los frecuentes encuentros
puramente eróticos y olvidándonos púdicamente de los
"mercenarios", como él llamaba a las socorridas "peripatéticas",
cualquier lector de sus biografías puede encontrarse nada menos
que con una docena de nombres de "amadas" anteriores a
Dolorcitas Delavat.[39]

Y lo que sorprende, todavía más que el número, es la
variedad de carácter y sensibilidad entre ellas, que van desde la
más espiritual a gusto de este peculiar don Juan (pero al mismo
tiempo la más insatisfactoria, porque no se le entregó físicamente
como él hubiera deseado) a las más puramente "carnales", como

la Brohan y la Armida brasileña; o entre la poetisa Gertrudis G. de Avellaneda, ardiente y sensual belleza de los trópicos con la "semijorobada" y poco menos que insignificante pequeño-burguesa Julia Pacheco, de Lisboa.

Se diría que no le preocuparon las diferencias, que amaba con los sentidos, que obedecen al cerebro, más que con el corazón, aun cuando en el caso de "la Muerta" pareció totalmente incapaz de separarlos, sufriendo mucho por ello. ¿Será que, como el prototípico Don Juan, desde el original de Tirso hasta el de Zorrilla, este Don Juan también prefiere la cantidad a la calidad...? ¿Es que no habíamos hablado de que tenía un "ideal de mujer", al referirnos a sus relaciones con "la Muerta"...? Verdad es que lo apuesto de su figura y el encanto y la gracia de su ingenio fueron armas poderosísimas que le hacían irresistible siéndole facilísimo "derribar cuantas fortalezas" femeninas le apetecieron, y no fueron pocas, como ya se dijo, excepto en los tres casos citados.

Pero nuestro D. Juan Valera, aunque muy sensual y activo en sus enredos amorosos está muy lejos de ser el "vendaval erótico" de que nos habló Américo Castro al estudiar al primero de ellos. Al contrario que aquel, D. Juan Valera no se conforma con gozar de la mujer, entendida simplemente como"la hembra del hombre", ni mucho menos, aunque sea fácil llegar a esa conclusión, como lo hicieron quienes, sin matizar, de ello le tildaron en su juventud. Y es que el concepto que tiene Valera de "la Mujer" es muy diferente al que la realidad le iba brindando, salvo en muy contadas ocasiones. Una realidad que no casaba con su "ideal" descrito en varios textos suyos. (Y mucho más pormenorizadamente en sus mejores novelas, pero analizarlas aquí me llevaría un espacio del que ya no dispongo.) Uno de los más claros lo hallamos en un cuento, "El bermejino prehistórico". Dice allí uno de sus personajes, D. Juan Fresco, muchas veces portavoz del autor: "...la mujer...no se cría naturalmente. Lo único que se cría es la hembra del hombre. La verdadera mujer es producto artificial, que resulta de grande esmero y cuidado y de exquisito y alambicado cultivo".[40]

El recuerdo siempre latente de la mujer que más influyó en su formación y personalidad posterior, su madre, le empuja a buscar ese "colmo de perfecciones", esa "perla cultivada" a la que tanto se acercaba "la Muerta". Para Valera, como para Unamuno,[41] el amor de mujer tiene mucho de maternal. Quizá en Valera sea menos fácil verlo, tan llenos de escarceos puramente físicos se nos dan sus juegos sentimentales lo que le diferencia radicalmente de D. Miguel, monógamo declarado que se realizó amorosamente en Concha, su mujer. Pero recordando, siquiera sea superficialmente, los personajes femeninos de Valera, desde Pepita a Rafaela la Generosa, Doña Luz o Juanita la Larga, encontramos en todas ellas un deseo, un ansia maternal que se manifiesta en querer conformar a su antagonista masculino, dominándole -¡y hasta recrearlo!- adornándole con las mejores virtudes propias. En su ensayo "Meditaciones sobre la educación humana", volvió a exponernos su "ideal": la mujer como educadora futura "...debe recibir una educación más cuidadosa y esmerada que la que el hombre recibe..." [puesto que] ..."la mujer forma, cría y modela al hombre, no sólo materialmente, concibiéndole y llevándole en sus entrañas, sino también moral e intelectualmente, influyendo en su espíritu."[42] Nuestro "don Juan" hubiera sido muy diferente de haber encontrado una mujer similar a "la Muerta", con mejor salud y unos años menos, la cual, como su madre había hecho con él, le hubiera comprendido, consolado y alentado, "moldeándole" en lo posible, es decir, una compañera espiritual y físicamente apasionada, además de una madre perfecta para sus hijos... y un poquito también para él.

Para su desgracia, y resulta incomprensible que Valera no lo viese claramente así antes de prendarse de ella, Dolorcitas Delavat de ningún modo podía satisfacer sus esperanzas. Señorita de buena familia, clase media acomodada, con esmerada educación "colonial" y muy de esa típica mentalidad europea del siglo XIX (¡en España hasta mediados del XX!) en donde las mujeres eran poco menos que inútiles para otras cosas que fuesen las llamadas "labores propias de su sexo", tocar el piano, pintar y cantar como distracciones artísticas, además de hacer bordados primorosos, alternando y brillando en sociedad al lado del hombre que la había escogido como compañera y madre de sus hijos. Dolores Delavat, con su formación burguesa con pretensiones, ni siquiera entendió lo que de ella esperaba el hombre que la llevó al altar. Incomprensión que muy pronto la empujaría a buscar refugio en la educación y cuidados de sus hijos, brillando en las ocasiones en que está junto a él, en recepciones y fiestas en los salones a que los cargos políticos y diplomáticos del marido les obligan a concurrir. Aunque no tardando mucho cada vez con menos frecuencia, ya que muy pronto empezaron a vivir largas temporadas de separación, decididas casi siempre por ella, a lo largo de su vida matrimonial. Consciente, o puede que inconscientemente, muy pronto se fué alejando no sólo del "ideal" de mujer que buscaba el marido, sino también, lo que es más triste, de él. Aquel vaticinio medio en broma de su jefe en Río se va convirtiendo en amarga realidad. La Dolorcitas de los primeros años se convierte no tardando mucho en fuente de dolores profundos para su marido, que por todos los medios se muestra paciente y más que benévolo con ella, tratando siempre de complacerla.

Parece evidente que si no hubo ese enamoramiento sólido y verdadero por parte de ninguno de los dos (ella al parecer se quedó muy sorprendida cuando la madre le comunicó que Valera le había escrito pidiéndola en matrimonio), al menos el novio tenía mucha ilusión y grandes esperanzas de felicidad compartida. Tres semanas antes de la boda escribe desde París a su amigo P. A. de Alarcón, que le había aconsejado el matrimonio:

"Voy a seguir su consejo de Vd; voy a casarme si Dios no lo impide o si no lo estorba el diablo. La novia...es graciosa, chiquita, muy buena y tiene 20 Abriles". La juventud y los encantos personales de la Sta. Delavat y su relativamente buena posición económica, además de la firme decisión de terminar con sus devaneos amorosos, debieron decidirle a dar el importante paso.

Pero las dificultades económicas (aficionadísimos ambos a la gran vida e incapaces de una rigurosa administración y de vivir con arreglo a sus posibilidades, siempre gastaron más de lo debido) serán un motivo más, casi de inmediato, para ásperas discusiones, tozudas desavenencias y disgustos, que por parte de su mujer, caprichosa y antojadiza, no hicieron sino aumentar toda su vida. Pese a la tolerante paciencia del marido la distancia entre ellos va agrandándose más cada día. Dolorcitas muy pronto se convierte en insoportable, como se puede ver, a pesar de la prudencia del gran señor que siempre fué Valera y el tacto con que le da sus quejas, en la colecciónes de cartas a su mujer de que hoy disponemos. Especialmente esclarecedoras y patéticas son las escritas sin tantas "pleguerías" y velos púdicos a su hermana Sofía, su paño de lágrimas en tantos años de infelicidad conyugal. A principios de 1877 le dice: "Mi mujer hace más de cinco años que no es mi mujer, sino mi enconada enemiga. Dice que me odia o me desprecia, y no obstante sigue viviendo en mi compañía para achicharrarme la sangre. Las peloteras que tenemos son espantosas...y razones hay para que yo me ahorque. Cualquiera que no tuviese mi calma, ha tiempo, se hubiera ahorcado: pero yo no quiero dar ese gusto a Dolorcitas...En suma, esto es vivir con una loca furiosa...estoy aviado." Y a fines del año siguiente vuelve a decirle: "¡Qué horrible pesadilla y qué desgracia tan enorme fué mi matrimonio con esta muchacha tontiloca!"[43]

Pero ya mucho antes, a los cuatro años y medio de casados le confesaba Valera a su madre: "Mi mujer es el mismo demonio.

Ayer me ha dado un día espantoso, y hoy, durante el almuerzo, me ha armado otra camorra no menos horrible. Esto no se puede sufrir, y sin embargo no hay más recurso que sufrirlo. Sería ridículo, odioso, bestial, que tuviese yo que pegar a esta muchacha, y me temo que las cosas puedan llegar hasta el extremo de tener que pegarle." Explica luego los amargos detalles y termina confesándole con gran dolor: "Me he engañado por completo. Crea Vd. que no hay criatura de más perversa índole que mi mujer. Yo creo que hubiera sido un marido excelente con otra mujer cualquiera".[44]

También a su amigo Menéndez Pelayo le confiesa desde Lisboa: "Yo, a más de viejo, estoy desengañado, estéril, triste como la muerte. Mi casa es el rigor de las desdichas. No me ha valido la posición que aquí tengo, [está de Ministro Plenipotenciario] los dineros, tal vez más de lo conveniente, que gasto, ni nada, para que mi mujer esté alegre y satisfecha y no me muela." Y termina aconsejándole: "No se case usted nunca." Consejo que le repetirá seis años depués, cínicamente matizado: "No se case usted o cásese con dos o tres millones de pesetas, o con mujer casera que no sueñe jamás en entrar en la *high life*".[45]

Cuando por falta de malicia política, en julio de 1883, Valera se vió obligado a poner la dimisión de su cargo en Lisboa, por lo que se confiesa contrito y desalentado y su mujer le escribe una carta al parecer comprensiva y conciliatoria, don Juan le contesta de inmediato haciéndole una completa y sincera confesión del amor que todavía siente por ella y la necesidad de una correspondencia: "Tú lo puedes aún todo conmigo, como quieras y como me quieras...Yo necesito que me animes, que me estimes, que me quieras.Tu desdén me mata. Cuando te pones algo bondadosa conmigo, me siento revivir...Búrlate de mí; despréciame; pero he de confesarte aquí que tienes singular dominio sobre mi alma. Todas mis iras, todas mis rabietas contra tí son de enojo porque no me quieres...Hago mil tonterías y sandeces desesperadas porque no me quieres; deseo a veces morirme porque no me quieres...Aquí me tienes, pues, humillado, convicto y confeso. Quiéreme por amor de Dios".[46]

De poco le sirvieron tan humildes y sincerísimas declaraciones que tienen más verdad, aunque más dolor, que las que le hizo, por carta, trece años antes, cuando le declaró su amor. Su Dolorcitas -a estas alturas ya solamente dolores, con minúscula, de todo género para Valera- no se conmueve por mucho que su marido le recuerde que él necesita su cariño muy de veras, sus alientos y su comprensión. Ella prefiere ignorarle, en esto como en muchas cosas más, y hacerse la sorda para continuar amargándole la vida.

Empeñado de nuevo en tener paz a toda costa decide, a sus 60 años, poner tierra por medio, añadiéndole esta vez el Atlántico, y logra que le nombren Ministro Plenipotenciario en los Estados Unidos. Desde Washington, hacia donde viajó en Enero de 1884, sintiéndose más solo de lo que imaginaba, no tardará mucho en echar de menos la compañía de la familia e intenta sutilmente que su mujer cambie de opinión -se negó a salir de Europa- pero no tuvo mucho éxito. En las cartas a su hermana Sofía D. Juan, que empieza a sentir la edad que tiene, se queja amargamente de lo mal que lo ha tratado siempre su esposa. Los adjetivos con que la califica son muy duros, lo que hace suponer, en hombre tan comedido, lo mucho que ha sufrido por su culpa. Y aunque el sueldo que tiene el cargo le permita hacer algunos ahorros para ir pagando las deudas a que las manías de grandeza de su mujer le llevaron, y el que los Estados Unidos no acabara nunca de satisfacerle como país, pese a su modernidad y su progreso evidentes, maldice más de una vez la debilidad de carácter que le empujó a pedir aquel puesto. Eso, unido a un sobrino impertinente y medio loco que se llevó como Agregado, y que le amarga la existencia a diario con sus desafinados "cantos nasales" y su pésima crianza, parecen ser penitencia cruel por sus pecados.

Incluso las cartas a su mujer, escritas con toda cautela para no enojarla aún más, revelan lo patético y triste de su situación. Para animarla a ir a verle con sus hijos le habla del importante papel que tienen en Washington las esposas de los "Ministros": "Para mí es evidente que te llevarían en andas; que [con tus talentos y conocimiento de lenguas] serías el centro de la sociedad culta y de la *high life* de aquí, y que me valdrías de mucho, si aparentabas (al menos) quererme y considerarme".[47] Cuánta amargura en esta confesión de su infelicidad, en la última frase.

Pero la difícil esposa no le hace caso: "Se pasa meses sin escribirme; y cuando me escribe, llena la carta de insultos, quejas y desvergüenzas. Eso me entristece". Otras llegan... "llenas de duras e injustas recriminaciones contra mí", por lo que el más que paciente esposo terminará por cansarse, y tratar de olvidar sus penas del mejor modo posible. Le había llamado la atención, al llegar a Washington, la facilidad con que las norteamericanas jóvenes se dedicaban a flirtear, cuando veía cómo lo hacían con su sobrino, el concertista desgañitado, que tanto le irritaba. Y por otra parte nada más fácil que brillar en sociedad, para un ser tan encantador y tan acostumbrado a ello, como lo era don Juan, a pesar de sus sesenta años bien llevados. Precisamente a poco de contarle a su hermana las tristezas y desengaños de su vida matrimonial, es cuando empieza a hablarle de la facilidad que tienen las yankees, como él escribe, para "el flirteo". Pese a sentirse viejo... "Sin embargo, tal es la manía de flirtation de las Señoritas americanas, tan románticas son algunas, y tan aficionadas a lo que [sic] brilla por algo, que siempre hay unas cuantas que flirtean conmigo, lo cual a mi edad, no pasa de ser una extravagancia absurda, sobre todo para ellas. Las peores, sigue diciendo, son las que han llegado "solteritas" a los 25 -30 años: "Las Misses de aquí, con tal de *flirtear*, flirtearán con un macaco". Y en otra: "Por dicha o por desgracia, según quiera considerarse, tengo ya 60 años. Si no, correría gran peligro mi virtud...siempre tengo damas que gustan de flirtear: y dicho sea en sigilo, Misses también, que no reparan en que estoy casado, ni ven en ello obstáculo a sus inocentadas", le cuenta en febrero del 85, cuando lleva algo más de un año en Washington y va tomándole más gusto al "autodestierro" norteamericano. Le habla de cómo "reciben" y las fiestas que organizan, los lunes por la noche, en la Legación de España, lo bien que lo pasan con las gentes del Cuerpo Diplomático y la que le armaría Dolores, si se enterase de "...estas diversiones; sólo por la mera sospecha, está hecha una leona: no me escribe y su aborrecimiento sube de punto cada día...[ni siquiera se contenta con las 2.000 pesetas mensuales que le manda] pero necesita, más aún, tenerme consigo a fin de vejarme, molerme y atormentarme sin cesar..Si hubiera sido medio tratable, hubiera yo sido el mejor de los maridos...pero creo que ni hecha de encargo, hubiera podido buscarse para mí mujer más enemiga, más aborrecedora, más dura censora de mis faltas y más sorda y ciega...y cerrada...a toda impresión favorable y amistosa hacia mí...En lo profundo de mi alma estoy herido de su odio, de su desdén, de sus malos tratos...Y a veces añado: pues no soy tan feo, ni tan despreciable, porque todavía, con más de sesenta años, tengo quien guste de mí". Quince días más tarde, el 17-3-1885, a las puertas de la primavera, le repite que las damas son "...en extremo aficionadas al flirteo, cuyos límites son harto difíciles de marcar. Resulta de todo que me olvido con frecuencia de que tengo 60 años...Hace doce años Dolores no quiere *ser mi mujer*: pero siempre se pone furiosa contra otra que me desdeñe menos y que no me halla tan viejo, tan feo ni tan averiado. Todo esto es muy triste: y no porque yo haya tenido jamás una pasión viva por Dolores, hasta el punto de que me matasen sus desdenes: sino porque, hasta con ella, si no me hubiera desdeñado, hubiera sido yo, y sería el más dulce, fiel y afectuoso de los maridos. Menester ha sido que Dios o el Diablo me haya proporcionado en mi mujer a mi más cruel enemiga..." Seis días después, como el chiquillo que ha hecho una travesura y busca el perdón de sus mayores, Valera confiesa a Sofía: "Además aquí he caido mejor que en parte alguna, y casi me rifan, casado, con hijos y con 60 años.Verdad es que el decidido afán de flirteo es cosa pasmosa entre estas Misses. La hija del nuevo Ministro de Negocios Extranjeros, Miss Catherine Bayard, tiene cierto platónico entusiasmo por mí, y nos vemos y nos escribimos con frecuencia las mayores finuras, tiquismiquis y sutilezas afectuosas...Ya ves si estoy bien. ¿Qué conseguirá otro que yo no consiga? Yo sí que puedo decir ahora que tengo el padre alcalde. Si Dolores llegase a saber de este y otros flirteos, se echaba a la mar y se venía aquí nadando a hacer escenas...He recibido además varios lunes: hoy será el último porque ya no me cabe la gente en casa.Viene la flor y nata de las damas de aquí y claro está que no falta la Señorita Catalina".[48]

Una semana después le dice: "Las mujeres de la sociedad son aquí más desatinadas que en parte alguna y tienen la culpa de todo. Ejemplo para inter-nos. Una solterita me hizo ir a Nueva York para estar con ella cuatro o cinco días." (¡ Nada de extraño, para los que sabemos que Valera no creía en los amores "platónicos"!) Y hasta algo de jactancia hay cuando le dice, dos semanas más tarde: "porque sigo siendo el compañerito muy amado, a pesar de mis sesenta años, de la hija mayor del Secretario de Estado, la cual es de lo más extravagante, independiente y extraordinaria en todo, que puede imaginarse." En la carta siguiente le dice alegremente: "Yo por aquí no lo paso mal. Yo no sé si es extravagancia de Miss Bayard o si estoy aún verde y lozano; pero ella se ha enredado conmigo con la mayor decisión. Aquí, las solteras que pasan de los 25 años, echan a rodar todo respeto, atropellan por todo y hacen cuanto se les antoja.Yo estoy curado de espanto, pero me pasma y me quedo boqui-abierto con los atrevimientos y locuras de estas Señoritas. Cierto es que Miss Bayard es la más loca y extravagante de todas; pero te aseguro que hay otras muchas que no le van en zaga." En las cartas siguientes, como llevado de un remordimiento súbito, añade que "echa muy de menos la paz, el calor y el dulce reposo del hogar doméstico, de que nunca he gozado". Para decirle doce días después: "Aquí sigo en las más extrañas relaciones con la Señorita Bayard. Todo esto es absurdo a los 60 años, pero no tengo yo la culpa. Si hubiera dado con una mujer medianamente cariñosa y razonable, yo hubiera sido casero, juicioso, tranquilo y excelente marido y padre de familia." Vuelve a culpar a su mujer... "que me pone siempre de viejo, yo me demuestro que no lo soy: y como ella me desdeña tanto, me doy el gusto de demostrarme que no todas las mujeres son del mismo parecer."

El terrible golpe de la muerte súbita de su hijo predilecto, Carlos, víctima del tifus, le afectará gravemente y sin duda lamenta muy de veras el que su mujer no le hubiera hecho caso, trayéndole a sus hijos y evitado la tragedia. Que Catherine Bayard le ayudará a sobrellevar, rodeándole de la ternura de que tan necesitado andaba: "Es singularísimo el afecto que le ha entrado por mí a esta Señorita Bayard", que cuida al poco a su madre agonizante en su tierra. Don Juan empieza a pensar en volverse a España y le afligen muchas cosas al hacerlo. Una de ellas, y no la menor, cortar su romántico enredo con "esta extravagantísima ternura de Miss Bayard, a quien al cabo tendré que plantar para ir a recibir puntapiés en el trasero, o por lo menos sofiones y bufidos de mi Penélope, después de imitar yo a Ulises, huyendo de mi Circe o de mi Calipso"..."Esa Miss, y casi me alegro, está ausente ahora y me deja libre de ternuras...Difícil va ser romper este lazo", dice temeroso, a mediados de julio, aclarando aún más en la siguiente: "Todos los días nos escribimos largas cartas...[le recuerda que hubiera preferido vivir] "con mi legítima mujer: pero no es mía la culpa, si esto no sucede; durante 14 años, he sido desdeñado, pisoteado, vejado, y tratado peor que un perro sarnoso".

Cuando el 13 de enero, de 1886, sin aviso previo, por los periódicos se entera de su "traslado" a Bruselas, va a desencadenarse la segunda y última gran "tragedia" de las que Valera sufrió en Washington. Ante su negativa a ignorar dicho traslado como le implora su amiga, tres días más tarde, y en el mismo lugar en el que tan feliz había sido, Miss Bayard..." abrumada por el dolor que siente por el traslado de don Juan, se suicida en la antesala de la Embajada."[49] "Imagina mi dolor y la situación horrible, insostenible, en que aquí me veo.[le dice a su hermana]. Tranquilízate. Yo espero resistir este golpe, y sobrevivir para mis hijos. Miss Catalina Bayard, llena de talento, de chispa, de gracia y de saber, tenía las ideas más espantosas de pesimismo: amaba, deseaba la muerte: era su preocupación: su idea constante. Lo que es yo, por esta mujer, me hubiera quedado aquí, y aún hubiera renegado de la patria y me hubiera hecho yankee. Ha sido una cosa tremenda." Para terminar, en la última que escribe a su hermana desde Washington: "De nada, absolutamente de nada me remuerde la conciencia. Yo ni he engañado, ni he seducido, ni he prometido lo que no podía cumplir. Yo no tengo la culpa de desesperaciones, de locuras, de pesimismos, de horrores. Para curarlos y evitarlos hasta me hubiera yo quedado aquí de cualquier modo. Y en cuanto a mi *flaqueza* en dejarme querer, me parece que no es tan fácil hacer del Hipólito o del Joseph, cuando tiene uno todavía su alma en su almario". Y aún le cuenta que "las Misses aquí son violentas y desaforadas" y que una de ellas le ha escrito una carta "donde se insinúa fieramente" mas él ha tenido que negarse: "Mira, pués, si soy desventurado y dichoso a la vez. Malditas sean mis dichas".

¿Dónde se ha visto un "don Juan" semejante, llorando con el más sincero y amargo dolor, tanto por haberse dejado seducir como por el trágico final de la seductora, y maldiciendo desde lo más hondo de su alma sus "triunfos amorosos"...?

Su sorpresivo traslado como embajador de España a Bruselas, anunciado en un telegrama de prensa en enero de 1896 (se habló de una "maniobra secreta" del Secretario de Estado norteamericano, con la aquiescencia del Ministro de Estado español, para "sofocar" el "affaire" de su hija con Valera, y que provocó tres días después el sorprendente suicidio de la apasionada Miss Bayard) tuvo lugar a mediados de mayo, pasando en la capital belga algo más de dos años, a trechos acompañado por su familia, lo que no sucedía en mucho tiempo. Que con los dos años y medio que pasó en Viena con el mismo cargo -enero de 1893 a julio del 95- fueron prácticamente su despedida del mundo de la diplomacia, mundo y oficio de los que nunca se mostró enteramente satisfecho, reduciendo mucho su vida pública también, puesto que hasta su muerte, diez años después, y con su claridad mental intacta, siguió disfrutando del vivir y escribiendo con ayuda de un amanuense ya que su ceguera progresaba irremediablemente, recluído los últimos años en su casa. Pero recibiendo en tertulias literarias famosas tanto a sus viejos amigos escritores como a los más jóvenes de aquellos años de finales y principio de siglo.

Y trabajando en el final de un hermoso discurso (que le había encargado la Real Academia para celebrar el tercer centenario de su publicación) sobre la obra literaria que más estimaba, el *Quijote*, abandonó este mundo el 18 de abril de 1905.

Quienes todavía se empeñen en seguir considerando al creador de *Pepita Jiménez* como un "don Juan", aunque todo lo refinado que se quiera, tendrán que reconocer que, como en tantas parcelas literarias, Valera no fué otro "don Juan" más, sino un Don Juan único.

Leeds, Navidades de 1996.

NOTES

1.   "...un vestido bueno de Worth para baile. No es menester que el vestido tenga encajes riquísimos para que cueste 8.000 reales. Ahora bien, yo he tenido la dicha de escribir una novela titulada *Pepita Jiménez*, que ha sido celebrada, que ha tenido gran éxito. ¿Podré comprar el vestido con el producto total de *P.J.*? En manera alguna. *Pepita Jiménez no ha llegado a valerme 8.000 reales*". Apud Bernardino de Pantorba, *Juan Valera*, Ed. Cia. Bibliográfica Española, Madrid, 1969, pag. 146. Y a su amigo Menéndez Pelayo le escribirá en 1887 que la edición "Yankee" de la más famosa de sus novelas le produjo 4.000 reales, aunque se habían tirado muchos miles de ejemplares: "A mi ver está probado que todo editor yankee es cien veces más bandido que el más bandido de los editores españoles", *Epistolario Valera-Menéndez Pelayo*, Ed. Espasa Calpe, Madrid, 1946, pag. 381.

2.   "En Doña Mencía se afirma que nuestro autor heredó el talento de su madre, más bien fea, a juzgar por los retratos que de ella se conservan, y la belleza de su padre, que pasaba por ser el hombre más guapo de toda Andalucía", P. Romero Mendoza, *D. Juan Valera .(Estudio biográfico-crítico con notas)*, Eds. Españolas, Madrid, 1940, pags. 17/18.

3.   "En *Mariquita y Antonio* (1861), asoma un tipo de novela harto distinto del que solía gustar el público. No la concluyó, por indolencia... Es lástima... Valera, acabándola, se habría adelantando en la renovación literaria del género; ventaja que de todos modos le pertenece, mediante *Pepita Jiménez*, en la novela psicológica", M. Azaña, *Ensayos sobre Valera*, Alianza Editorial, Madrid, 1971, pag. 206. El propio autor había escrito años antes a este respecto: "Hay otra clase de novela en las cuales, examinadas superficialmente, nada sucede que de contar sea. En ellas apenas hay aventuras ni argumento. Sus personajes se enamoran, se mueren...como los demás del mundo. Considerados aislada y exteriormente...sus lances...suelen ser todo lo contrario de memorables y dignos de escritura; pero en lo más íntimo del

alma de los personajes hay un caudal infinito de poesía que el autor desentraña y muestra, y que transforma la ficción de vulgar y prosaica, en poética y nueva...Suelen ser novelas de las que buscan lo ideal dentro del alma y que podemos llamar psicológicas". J. Valera, "De la naturaleza y carácter de la novela" (1860), en *Obras completas,* Vol. II, Ed. Aguilar, Madrid, 1949, pag. 195.

4. Vid. E. Jiménez Caballero, "Conmemoración de D, Juan Valera", en *Revista de Occidente,* Madrid,Vol. VII, 1924, pags. 140 y siguientes. Valera en *Las Ilusiones del Doctor Faustino,* al pintar a la madre del protagonista, hace un delicado trasunto de los rasgos más destacados de la suya.

5. Vid. "Noticia autobiográfica" en el *Boletín de la Real Academia Española,* Vol. I, Madrid, 1914, pag. 130.

6. Como consecuencia de un accidente ferroviario en Juvisy, según se afirma en Juan Valera – *Cartas a su mujer*, Editadas por Matilde Galera y C. de Coster, Publicaciones Excma. Diputación, Córdoba, 1989, pag. 14.

7. "Porque, a decir verdad, nada aprendí nunca en la escuela, ni en el estudio, ni en la Universidad; todo lo que sé, que es bien poco lo he aprendido conmigo mismo, sin orden, sin maestro y sin un fin determinado". Notas de Valera a la edición definitiva de sus *Poesías*, y que recogió en sus *O.C.,* Vol.1, Ed. Aguilar, Madrid, 1947, pag. 1511.

8. Vid. C. Bravo Villasante, *Vida de Juan Valera,* Ed. Magisterio Español, Madrid, 1974, pag. 20.

9. Idem., pags. 25-26.

10. "Noticia autobiográfica" citada, pag. 132.

11. Carta inédita de la Marquesa de la Paniega a su hijo, 15 de mayo 1844, Apud. M. Azaña, *Ensayos sobre Valera,* Alianza Editorial, Madrid, 1971 pag. 24.

12. J. Valera, *Obras Completas,*Vol. III, Ed. Aguilar, Madrid, 2a. edición, l947, pags. l2-l3.

13. Manuel Azaña, *Ensayos sobre Valera,* pags. 24-26.

14. J. Valera, *O.C.,* Vol.III, ed. cit. pags. 15-16.

15. M. Azaña, "Valera en Italia", en *Ensayos sobre Valera,* pags. 27, 69-83.

16. Idem, pag. 72.

17. Idem, pag. 73.

18. Vid. *Juan Valera-Serafín Estébanez Calderón (1850-l858).* Edición de C. Sáenz de Tejada, Editorial Moneda y Crédito, Madrid, 1971, pag. 216.

19. Idem, pags. 51-52.

20. Vid. M. Azaña, obra citada, Nota 41 pag. 257.

21. "El Marqués [de Bedmar] descollaba entre los galanes más apuestos de la Corte, y fué, sin duda, uno de los más favorecidos. Gentilhombre de cámara de S.M. la Reina, obtuvo en la cámara regia la privanza a que podía aspirar su personal gentileza...", cuenta, no sin malicia M. Azaña, obra citada, pag. 79.

22. Vid. *J. Valera-Serafín Estébanez Calderón (1850-1858)* [Editado por C.Sáenz de Tejada], Editorial Moneda y Crédito, Madrid, 1971, pag. 53.

23. Vid. C. Bravo Villasante, ob. cit., pags. 43-44 y 46.

24. Vid. *J. Valera-Serafín Estébanez Calderón (1850-1858),* pag. 54.

25. Idem, pag. 268.

26. J. Valera, *O.C.* Vol.III, ed. cit., pag. 27, 28 y 29.

27. Idem, pag. 38. [Dice de pasada, bromeando acerca de los adelantos de la ciencia: "Montemayor, el día menos pensado, saldrá volando en su *Dédalo,* y todo el mundo se quedará bizco, como la *Culebrosa".*]

28. J. Valera, *O.C.,* III, ed. cit., pgs. 34-36.

29. Idem, pags. 39 y 41 respectivamente.

30. *J. Valera-S.Estébanez Calderón (1850-1858),* ed.cit., *pags.* 209-210.

31. J. Valera, *O.C.,* III, pags. 50, 51 y 52 y *Cartas íntimas (1853-1897)* [Editadas por C. Sáenz de Tejada], Editorial Taurus, Madrid, 1974, pag. 41.

32. *J. Valera-S.Estébanez Calderón,* pags. 164-165. Respecto a la fecundidad de la naturaleza brasileña alguien, siglo y medio después en la hermosa ciudad de Río, me pondría en chistosa actualidad la aguda observación valerina: "El verdadero deporte nacional brasileño no es el practicado por Pelé, el fútbol, como se cree en Europa, sino el fornicio, para el que se entrenan con envidiable entusiasmo desde muy jóvenes los brasileiros."

33. Las portuguesas como tengo dicho a Vd. son feísimas; lo que si no excusa, explica por qué algunos ricos fidalgos, por ejemplo el marqués de Balada y el de Viana, more graecorum adolescentulis delectantur. Yo no tengo amores, si no son los que se venden baratos, y paso una vida bien sosegqda, asaz desabrida y prosaica". Idem, pag. 113.

34. Idem, pags. 219-220. Sirva como ejemplo de lo que M. Azaña calificó de "nimia crudeza" la desopilante estampa de los ejercicios ecuestre-amatorios que exigen las inmensidades disparatadas del "chomino" de su pareja. Nos la remata con otra perla: "Ma Jeanette está empeñada en que le haga yo un

chiquillo para que herede al viejo ladrón de su esposo. Yo lo procuro: pero en vano. Ni Hércules lo conseguiría. ¿Quién ha de llenar aquel pozo sin fondo...?"

35. Idem, pags. 281 y 284.

36. Vid. J. Valera, *O.C.*, Vol. III, ed.cit., pags. 72 a 209 y en especial las cartas del 13 y 23 de abril de 1857, pags. 162 y ss.; y M. Azaña, *Ensayos sobre Valera,* ed. cit., pag. 162.

37. J. Valera, *Correspondencia,* en *O.C.* III, pags. 110 y ss. Y se pregunta después "¿Qué pueden ellos comprender de mis teorías sobre la broma y la risa en que está basada y, por tanto, disculpada mi conducta?" Para terminar: "A mí no me remuerde nada de lo que digo del Duque; peores cosas digo de mí mismo." (Idem., pags. 186-187).

38. "Incorregible galanteador, de sobra conocida es su afición a las faldas, halla acogida excelente entre muchas desenfadadas señoras que rinden culto a la aventura galante. Más de una antigua amada sigue mirándole con buenos ojos. Cuando no, Valera es el primero en buscar la aventura hacia la que su inclinación le arrastra", C. Bravo Valera, ob. cit., p. 156.

39. La Condesa de Cabarrús, su primer amor de adolescente y aventura posterior, siendo ya ella casada y no muy satisfecha de su matrimonio; la poetisa G. G. de Avellaneda, que rechazó su declaración amorosa; la Condesa de Villagarcía; Lucía Palhadile, "la Muerta; Malvinita Rivas; Paulina, la joven viuda, vecina de cuarto; la Stolz, famosa cómica de sus días lisboetas; Julia Pacheco, Laura Blanco, la Armida brasileira, "ma Jeannette", la del sexo descomunal, Magdalena Brohan...y Dolorcitas, que hace la número 13.

40. J. Valera, "El bermejino prehistórico", *O.C.*, Vol. 1, ed. cit., pag. 1072.

41. Vid. Luis Sánchez Granjel, *Retrato de Unamuno*, Ed. Guadarrama, Madrid, 1957, p. l28.

42.   J. Valera, *O.C.,* Vol. III, pag. 1410.

43.   J. Valera, *Cartas íntimas. 1853-1897,* Editorial Taurus, Madrid, 1974, pags. 118-120.

44.   Idem., pag. 105.

45.   Vid. *Epistolario de Valera y Menéndez-Pelayo, 1877-1905,* Ed. Espasa Calpe, Madrid, 1946, pags. 109-110 y 420.

46.   J. Valera, *Cartas a su mujer,* ed. cit., pag. 97.

47.   Idem., p. 135. Eso le decía el 21 de mayo de 1884. Ocho meses después vuelve a la carga y aprovechando que ella le ha contado que está "...más joven *y menos fea que antes*; lo cual entendido por mí, que *antes* y siempre te hallé bonita, distinguida, elegante y graciosa; significa que has de estar muy guapa, y yo lo creo y me complazco en esperar que te conserves así , y que te vuelva yo a ver y a contemplar con mi pobre cariño, desde hace tantos años, pagado sólo con desaires, sofiones y desdenes", pag. l49 de la misma obra.

48.   J. Valera, *Cartas íntimas,* pags. 252-259.

49.   C. Bravo-Villasante, *Vida de Juan Valera,* pag. 247.

MICHAEL E. WILLIAMS

Trinity and all Saints University College

THE PRESIDENT OF THE SEMINARY: THE WILL OF THE PRINCESS AND THE FAVOUR OF THE APOSTOLIC SEE. LISBON 1876

Ronald Cueto's interest in Iberian affairs is by no means confined to Spain. On many occasions he has shown his appreciation of Portugal and things Portuguese. In 1968 he was fortunate in being able to pay a visit to the English College, Lisbon, a few years before it closed its doors for ever. I remember one particular occasion on that visit when in the presence of Fr. Hilary Griffin O.P. the after-dinner conversation turned to the Civil War in Nigeria and the presence in Lisbon of a strong pro-Biafra lobby located in one of the more expensive hotels. The complexity of the issues and the intermingling of secular and religious values engaged us long into the night. As a reminder of that evening and as a tribute to a friend and colleague in the early days of Trinity and All Saints, I hope the following story of Lisbon a century before his visit might interest him as a keen researcher into local archives and ecclesiastical history. At least it should remind him that when visiting Portugal it is so often a case of "Toujours la même histoire".

———————

On May 5, 1865 the Infanta Isabel Maria drew up a will and made three priests at the English College, Peter Baines, Lawrence Richmond and Richard Duckett, her executors and heirs. Isabel, the daughter of João VI, had been President of the Regency Council during her father's last illness and was Regent during the

187

troubled years 1826-1828 when the supporters of her brothers Dom Miguel and Dom Pedro disputed the throne. After the succession of Miguel in 1828 she retired from public life and spent her last years at her quinta at São Domingos de Benfica. She spent much of her life in charitable works and her attempts to establish the Sisters of Charity of St. Vincent de Paul in Lisbon were assisted by the then President of the English College, Joseph Ilsley.[1] The nomination of three professors at the College as executors came to the knowledge of the English bishops. At their Low Week meeting of 1866, presided over by the newly appointed but not yet consecrated Archbishop Manning, they expressed anxiety lest this arrangement might have political implications and involve not only the bishops of England but also the Holy See. Accordingly, Peter Baines who was President of the College and one of the executors, called on the Infanta at Benfica and she assured him that she had taken legal advice and that there was nothing in her will that contravened the laws of Portugal, nor was there any danger of the College being compromised. Moreover she had the approval of the Holy Father of all that she had done.[2]

There the matter rested and it was only on the death of the Infanta on April 22, 1876 that the arrangement became public knowledge. On Monday April 24 *The Times* of London, with the dateline Lisbon April 22, announced the death of the Princess and with another report dated April 23 stated: "The late Princess Isabella has left all her property to the directors of the English College of St. Peter and St. Paul, Lisbon: Monsignor Baines, Dr Duckett and Father Richmond." The *Diario Ilustrado* of Lisbon on April 26 carried a picture and a warm tribute to the late Princess by Fernando Costa together with a copy of the will. Other newspapers also printed copies of the will. In it the Princess declared herself to be unmarried and stated that she had not amassed a fortune since she considered it her duty to share her wealth with the poor. She had no outstanding debts and then went on to give a list of bequests. She left money for masses to be said for herself and her family and was especially anxious that these should be entrusted to priests of exemplary life and piety. She left small gifts to members of her household and to various named charitable institutions.[3] There was one item of a more political nature whereby she laid claim to a sum of £50,000 sterling which was part of her inheritance from her father, the late King João VI, which the government had not yet handed over to her.[4] Finally, she named the three English priests executors and sole and universal heirs to all her property that had not been included in the foregoing bequests. This included lands, jewels, silver plate and various rights, bonds and shares. She expressed her trust in their ability, religious sentiments, and sound conscience to act without offence to God. To assist them in their work she designated Francisco Manuel de Faria e Mello.

The will created a sensation. In its account of the funeral of the Princess at the church of São Vicente the *Diario Ilustrado* noted that despite the official ceremonial and solemnity of the obsequies with a salute of guns from the Castel São Jorge every quarter of an hour, the shops remained open and there was no manifestation of grief apart from what had been ordered in the official programme. Public feeling did not reflect the official court mourning.[5] The bequests she had made to her servants and household were considered mean and niggardly. On the day of the funeral there were adverse comments about the three foreign priests inheriting her wealth. There was a certain amount of surprise, as the 'Inglesinhos' were well known in the city and had up till now never been considered as legacy hunters. Public criticism continued for some months and Baines reported that in its "Revista do Ano 1876" the Condes Theatre had a comic sketch in which three clerics were portrayed as leaving for England, each with a suitcase full of money they had been given by a certain member of the nobility.[6]

But Baines had other things on his mind apart from the legacy. The death of the Infanta coincided with the publication of Bishop Vaughan's report of his visitation to the overseas seminaries.[7] Among the recommendations was that Lisbon should cease to accept senior students and only take boys to study the humanities. The seniors, philosophers and theologians, would go to the College at Valladolid and in return Valladolid would send its students of humanities to Lisbon. Neither of the two Iberian Colleges was pleased by this suggestion and the two rectors rejected it outright.[8] It was thought that the Archbishop of Westminster, Manning, and some of the other bishops were showing a rather unhealthy interest in the affairs of the colleges abroad.[9] There was a suspicion that some members of the hierarchy wanted Lisbon to be closed and these suspicions were strengthened by the attempts of the Bishops of Liverpool and Beverley to withdraw two of their diocesans from the teaching staff at Lisbon. Both of the priests concerned, Cawley of Beverley and Singleton of Liverpool, held key posts, professor of dogmatic theology and procurator. As we shall see, this threat to the continued existence of the College was eventually to draw Baines to seek support from Rome.

However, Rome was already aware of the recent happenings in Lisbon. The Princess had been a frequent visitor and had been present in St Peter's in 1870 when papal infallibility was defined. Her near neighbours at São Domingos de Benfica were the Fronteira family; members of that family had been for many years benefactors of the English College and some were ardent papalists.[10] During her last illness the newly appointed Papal Nuncio, Domenico Sanguini, had written to Cardinal Antonelli, the secretary of State, requesting the Apostolic Blessing for the dying princess.[11]

He was assured of the Holy Father's prayers and on her death he was asked to convey the sympathy of the Pope to her family and friends. The Nuncio replied in a long letter to the Secretary of State.[12] He gave an account of her last moments and edifying death and how, as well as the Nuncio himself, the King and Queen and other members of the Royal Family had paid their visits to the dying woman. He then went on to describe to Antonelli the scandal that had been caused by the publication of the will in the newspapers. In her last testament the names of the reigning King and Queen were not even mentioned and servants who had attended her for many years were left but a pittance. The sense of shock was aggravated by the fact that the main beneficiaries were foreign priests. There was an opinion that the English priests were simply fiduciary heirs who had the obligation of selling goods and devolving the moneys on others, the heirs of Dom Miguel. The Nuncio said he did not wish to intervene in the affair. He did not know the value of the jewels and silver plate but there was the large sum of £50,000 sterling owed to her and her heirs by the government. He enclosed in his letter a cutting from a newspaper which referred somewhat scathingly to Isabel Maria's observance of old-fashioned procedures in her palace such as her doctor always kneeling when he took her pulse and how no one was allowed to present her with anything unless it was handed to her on a silver plate and the donor making a genuflection.

The tone of the Nuncio's letter to Antonelli shared the critical note of the press reports. This is hardly surprising as it was written the day after her death. But two months later Sanguini wrote to Rome again, this time to Cardinal Franchi, the Prefect of Propaganda Fide.[13] He repeated the information already communicated to Antonelli concerning the will and the reaction of the Portuguese press, but there had now been another development. Father Richmond had died several years ago, so in effect there were two executors and heirs, Baines the President and Duckett the Vice-President. On June 16 last (1876) there was a reception at the Nunciature to celebrate the thirtieth anniversary of the election of Pope Pius IX. The superiors of the various religious houses in the city were invited, but Dr Baines was unable to attend on account of illness and he sent his Vice-President, Dr Duckett, in his place. While Duckett was at the Nunciature the superiors of the College were summoned by Baines to a meeting in Council.[14] It was decided to send Duckett back to England and appoint Thomas Cawley as Vice-President in his place. Duckett was no longer considered a suitable person to continue as professor of theology and Vice-President. When he returned from the reception at the Nunciature Duckett was informed of his dismissal. In his letter to Rome the Nuncio says that he is just reporting the facts as he knows them. Although aware of what had happened, the Nuncio was still waiting to be informed officially by the President of Duckett's dismissal when a certain distinguished gentleman and personal friend came to him and enquired if the news were true that the President had had an altercation with Duckett concerning the Princess's will and that as a result of this the Vice-President had been expelled from the College. The Nuncio denied the suggestion but he saw the problems that could arise in connection with the will of the Infanta and so he wrote immediately to the President inviting him to the Nunciature to talk things over. At this meeting Baines told him how he and the other professors considered that Duckett was unsatisfactory in his teaching of theology and did not treat the students with sufficient care and consideration. Moreover he was distracted by other occupations. The Nuncio pointed out to Franchi that his position as Protector of the College was only nominal and as he had only recently arrived in Lisbon there was little he could do beyond reporting the matter. But as Bishop Vaughan had recently made a visitation, he would be the one to consult for further information. The Nuncio asked whether the authorisation of Propaganda Fide and the consent of the bishops of England and the Protector were required before the expulsion of a Vice-President and professor of theology. Baines had told him that if the superiors and the President decided unanimously on a matter in Council then they had the authority to take action. In view of the publicity that the will of the Infanta had received and the death of the third executor and heir there was a danger that it might be thought that the President was trying to get rid of Duckett in order to retain to himself all that had accrued from the will. In the light of this, the decision taken in the College Council seemed to be inopportune and he was trying to persuade the President to postpone Duckett's departure. However, the Nuncio did not want these events to harm the reputation of the College and in order that Rome might not draw false conclusions about the general condition of the College, he concluded his letter with an eulogy of the College's contribution to Catholic life in Portugal.[15]

The advice to consult Vaughan was evidently taken since on July 29 Vaughan wrote in Italian from Salford to Rome about the Duckett affair.[16] He said that some years ago the superiors of the College were nominated as executors of the Infanta. The English bishops were anxious to avoid any possible difficulties that might arise that could be harmful to the College, but they had been assured that the Princess had taken legal advice and obtained the approval of the Holy Father. When he made his visitation to the College the Princess was still alive. As to Dr Duckett, any reports that he had received concerning him had been through the students and so he had no comment to make since he did not know the superiors' opinion. But he could say that Duckett was a different sort of person from the President and his "mutabile carattere" was not likely to be appreciated by the students. He was a man of many talents and great energy, and was the only one on the College who preached well in Portuguese, so that he exercised considerable influence outside the College. He was a pious, zealous and cultured priest although sometimes lacking in prudence. As to the opportuneness or not of his dismissal, that was a matter for the Nuncio. In the event, Duckett's return to England was deferred but only for a few weeks. After this he continued to carry out his responsibilities as executor and heir and letters passed between him in England and Baines in Lisbon. In December the President tried to persuade him to return to Lisbon and stay as a guest in the College so as to assist more easily in some business transactions, but he pleaded that his parish duties prevented this. Baines had to rely for assistance on Francisco Manuel Faria e Mello, the man nominated by the Infanta in her will.

Baines played his cards close to his chest. When friends wrote congratulating him and the College on their good fortune, he assured them that he had received strict and secret instructions on how the money was to be disposed of. "I will carry out to the letter the wishes of the good lady who has such confidence in me as not to hesitate to place her entire property in the keeping of my conscience. Congratulate me then, if you will, on the honour done me by the royal princess but not on my becoming a rich man".[17] He never seems to have disclosed these secret instructions in their entirety. In his letter book there are extracts but he was afraid to trust a complete copy of them to the post.[18] The fullest account that we possess is however explicit enough.[19] The heirs were instructed to sell all her rural and urban property except for the Convent of São Domingos, which was to be given to the Sisters of Charity of St Vincent de Paul of Paris.[20] There were detailed orders as to where the money raised by the sale of property, jewellery, silver plate, shares and other rights was to go. It was to be divided into three parts: two of these were to go to a certain person for the education of her children. Baines leaves a blank space for the name but it was quite obviously the Infanta's sister-in-law, the widow of Dom Miguel, who was living in exile.[21] The remaining third part was again to be divided into three. Two of these three parts were to go to the College of São José at Torres Vedras whose superior was Fr Sebastião Pedro Martins Ribeiro. Should this enterprise of which she had great hopes fail, then this portion would be given to the English fathers of the College of St Peter and St Paul. This would be for Portuguese boys who were aspiring to the priesthood so that they could study either at the English College in Lisbon or at another English college in England. In either case, in the college that benefited from this clause (either at Torres Vedras or Lisbon), each year on the anniversary of her death all the priests would say mass for the repose of her soul, assisted by the prayers of all the students. The remaining third portion was to go to the executors themselves as a token of gratitude for fulfilling their duties as executors and heirs.

There followed a long list of personal bequests to those who had been in her service, to friends and relations, including the gift of a painting by Perugino to Dom Fernando, the husband of the late Queen Dona Maria II.[22] This secret document is dated February 12, 1873 and its contents answer some of the objections that were raised about her meanness and neglect of family in the published will. A codicil dated October 25, 1874 says that Baines and Duckett had asked that the donation to the College of São José should not pass to the English College, instead it would go to the fathers of St Vincent de Paul. This change was no doubt due to the superiors of the College foreseeing a difficulty in accepting Portuguese boys in a College that was specifically founded for those who were to serve the mission in England. In place of this the English College was left the Quinta d'Amara with all its lands and the transfer taxes would be paid from her own estate. It is recorded that this property was sold and the money raised was devoted to improvements to the country house at Luz and the property at the Quinta da Pera. From the documentation preserved in the Lisbon Collection at Ushaw it is not easy to calculate the exact sum raised by the sale or what the executors received. But in October 1877 Baines paid Duckett as a first instalment £400 due to him as one of the executors and calculated that each of the heirs would in the end receive about 10,000 *reis*, the equivalent of about £2,000 in money of the time.[23]

Some details of the sale are recorded. A collection of her jewels was taken to London and realised £4,283. 10s. 2d. which was banked in the New London and Brazilian Bank and transferred to the Lisbon branch.[24] Various offers were made for other items. The King, Dom Luis, wished to purchase a collection of 38 snuff-boxes.[25] Baines was granted a special audience of Dom Fernando to tell him about the Perugino painting.[26] In his letters Baines shows evidence of enjoying his work. In a letter to Duckett [27] he remarked: "The Infanta's Confessor brought me a few days ago a bag full of articles which I suppose he pulled through the grate of the confessional". Members of the teaching staff at the College had their own comments. One of them observed in a letter of January 5, 1878: "I believe he (Baines) is going to call us together about some more construction at the Quinta da Pera. We shall soon get through the Infanta's bequest at this rate. I think it would not have been amiss to have applied a little of it to the raising of our salaries".[28]

One outstanding item that could not be resolved immediately was the £50,000 sterling owed to the Infanta by the government. "Her Majesty's Minister here whom I consulted advised me not to be the first to move in the matter and to go *pari passu* with the other claimants. In accordance with this advice I spoke to the Conde d'Azambuja who agreed to feel his way by advising with his lawyers first and then along with us to induce the other claimants to join in a common effort to obtain our due in case the lawyers approve of this move". So wrote Baines to Duckett in May 1878.[29] He expressed much the same opinion to his lawyers, Arnold & Co., London, in March 1872. The Count of Azambuja, one of the grandchildren of João VI and so a nephew of the Infanta was pursuing the claim. Baines foresaw that it would be a long and costly business and was concerned about what would become of Duckett and himself if the claim failed.[30] But by 1880 Azambuja had given up the claim.[31]

Baines and Duckett remained friends. Baines was anxious that his former Vice-President should be given a suitable appointment in England.[32] Duckett went to the mission at Norwich and thanks to the generosity of the Duke of Norfolk the parish acquired the site for a new church on the edge of the town. The large church of St John the Baptist stands today as the Cathedral of the Catholic diocese of East Anglia and is a monument to Duckett's days as parish priest. But long before that church was built, in 1880 Duckett received a visit from Baines who was on holiday in England. The parish priest received the President with lavish hospitality. The Staffords were an old Catholic family and they resided at nearby Costessey. Duckett and Baines were invited to dine with Lord Stafford and later in the week Baines officiated at the Corpus Christi procession in the grounds of Costessey Park. What is more, the Mayor of Norwich entertained the two clerics to lunch at the Guildhall and he gave them the loan of his steam launch for a cruise to Yarmouth, accompanying them for part of the journey. After five very full days Baines departed with invitations to all and sundry to visit him whenever they were in Lisbon.[33]

Three years after the Norwich visit Baines died in Lisbon and it was then that one of the possible reasons for the dismissal of Duckett came to light. The Nuncio at Lisbon was now Gaetano Aloisi Majella, and he wrote to Cardinal Simeone, the Prefect of Propaganda Fide.[34] Duckett's name had been put forward as a possible successor to Baines as President of the English College. In his report to Rome the Nuncio said that there was one circumstance that made the proposal of Duckett somewhat unsuitable and dangerous. This related to the legacy. The affair was now over but Duckett had insisted that the Portuguese government should be held to its obligation to pay the outstanding £50,000 that was owed to the Princess and her heirs. The Papal Secretary of State had advised Baines not to insist on this for the good of the College. So Duckett never became President but spent the rest of his life in Norwich.[35]

In conclusion: It would be a mistake to judge these events solely in material terms. It is true that the College benefited financially from the will and so was able to carry out improvements to the property at Luz and Quinta da Pera. But this was not the only outcome, nor the most important. The choice of English College priests as executors and heirs was a pragmatic decision of the Infanta Isabel Maria. It was a way of circumventing the law so that her sister-in-law, the widow of Dom Miguel, would inherit the family fortune. Her knowledge of the College and its superiors led her to put full confidence in them to carry out her wishes and she saw this decision as a tangible way of showing her appreciation of their work for the Church. The Nunciature soon realised that the link between the English College and the Infanta's circle of Catholic friends was of special significance in these years immediately following the loss of the Papal States. There was a rallying to the Papacy among many traditional Catholics and this was to be encouraged. At this time not all the English Bishops were in favour of keeping the College open, but the Holy See stood firmly by Baines, its President, and realised that the College must continue in existence – as much for the sake of the Church in Portugal as for the needs of English Catholics. This strengthened the hand of the President who was able not only to overrule the suggestion made by Bishop Vaughan's visitation but also to override the desire of the Bishops of Liverpool and Beverley to recall their priests teaching in

Lisbon. On February 2, 1877 the Nuncio wrote to Cardinal Franchi at Propaganda Fide concerning the future of Cawley the professor of dogma and Singleton the procurator. He pointed out that the duties of the priests at the College included the pastoral care of sailors of the Royal Navy when they visited the Tagus, hearing confessions, instructing in the faith and often receiving people into the Catholic Church. Moreover the greater part of the nobility of Lisbon confessed to priests of the College and frequented the College chapel for the sacred functions, especially during Holy Week. There were sermons in Portuguese as well as English and the plain chant was executed to perfection.[36] Franchi replied on March 20 promising that he would contact Archbishop Manning and on July 31 he was able to say that as he had received no reply from Manning it was clear that he adhered to the request to allow Cawley and Singleton to continue at Lisbon.[37]

The final word can be left to a later Nuncio. Gaetano Aloisi Majella, writing in 1883 to the Cardinal Prefect of Propaganda Fide, said this about the College: "The universal respect for the priests, both superiors and professors...and for the students, is such that I have been able to put forward the College to the Portuguese bishops as a model for their own seminaries, which for the most part are far from being houses of ecclesiastical education...the divine offices are celebrated in the College church with such regularity and edification as are only equalled in the ecclesiastical colleges in Rome...the closure of the College would be blameworthy and harmful for Portugal and in particular for the capital city where the most urgent need is for edifying priests, but no less a need to see the sacred rites performed with proper reverence and decorum." [38]

NOTES

The sources for this article are mainly to be found in the Lisbon Collection (henceforth L.C.) at Ushaw College, Durham. These are the archives of the English College of Saints Peter and Paul, Lisbon. Founded in 1622 by Dom Pedro Coutinho, it closed in 1971. I have also consulted the archives of Propaganda Fide in Rome (P.F.) and the Archivio Segreto Vaticano (A.S.V.).

1. Fortunato de Almeida, *Historia de Portugal* (Coimbra,1929), Livro X, Tomo 6, pp. 342-62.

2. L.C. *Wills.* Memorandum of P. Baines, July 6,1866.

3. One of these bequests was of 6000 reis a month to "poor blind Daniel O'Faril widower of Brigida Handeley and father of two girls, Margaret and Mary, who were servants in my house".

4. For details of this unpaid legacy see Fortunato de Almeida, *Historia de Portugal*, Livro X, Tomo 6, pp. 68-9, note.

5. To many residents of Lisbon the Infanta was a figure from the distant past and associated with an unhappy period in the history of the country and the absolutist rule of Dom Miguel.

6. L.C. *Baines Letter Book.* Baines to Fr Smythe, January 15, 1877.

7. Bishop Herbert Vaughan of Salford had been commissioned by the English hierarchy to visit the overseas seminaries. His *Report of the Conditions of the English Catholic Colleges in Italy, Spain and Portugal* was published in April 1876.

8. L.C. *Baines Letter Book.* Baines to Guest, Rector at Valladolid, May 9,1876.

9. L.C. *Correspondence.* Manning to Baines, May 19,1876. In his reply to Manning, August14,1876, Baines states that he is not prepared to take any steps to alter the present arrangement. If the real intention is to close the College then let the matter be laid

before the Pope at once. There is no danger of the Portuguese government interfering with the College. If there were, the British government would protect British property. He is sorry but he and his colleagues have to oppose the bishops and doubtless the 72 Lisbonian priests in England would too. See also *Baines Letter Book,* 259-64.

10. Fortunato de Almeida, op. cit., p. 391, refers to Isabel Maria's presence at the definition of papal infallibility. The seventh Marquis of Fronteira, D. José Trasimundo, acted as witness to a codicil to the Infanta's will in May 1875. D. José's mother was an Oeynhausen, and a certain D. Joanna d'Araujo Carneiro d'Oeynhausen not only paid for an extension to the College church in 1856 but also carried letters to Rome on behalf of the then President, Joseph Ilsley. A covering letter of the President referred to her as "benefactrix huius collegii et Sancta Sede adictissima". P.F. *S.C. (Congressi),*17, ff. 83-86.

11. A.S.V. *Nunziatura di Lisbona*, 289. Fascículo 3, f.405.

12. A.S.V. op. cit., f.411.

13. Letter of June 30, 1876. P.F. *S.C. Congressi)*, 17, f.98. A.S.V. *Nunziatura di Lisbona*, 289.

14. Decisions about the conduct of College affairs were taken by the Council of Superiors which consisted of the President and other chosen members of staff.

15. P.F. *S.C. (Congressi)*, 7, f.107. Sanguini to Franchi. "Il rifugio di quasi tutta la nobiltà di Lisbona per le confessioni e per l'assistenza alle varie funzioni di chiesa. Le feste si celebrano con dignitoso apparato. Le cerimonie sacre si aseguono con essatezza ed il canto Gregoriano va alla perfezione."

16. P. F. *S.C. (Congressi)*, 17, f.102.

17. L.C. *Baines Letter Book*. Baines to Miss O'Cleary, April 30, 1876.

18. L.C. *Baines Letter Book*. Baines to Duckett, January 13, 1877.

19. L.C. *Baines Letter Book*. Extractos das Instrucções, p. 449.

20. Fortunato de Almeida, op. cit., Livro X, Tomo 6, pp. 342- 62. The Infanta was involved in helping the Sisters of Charity to establish themselves in Portugal. One of the obstacles was whether their obedience would be to the local bishop or to Rome. On March 1, 1857, a ship taking 25 sisters to Brazil called in at Lisbon and the sisters attended mass and received communion at the English College before going to pay their respects to the Infanta.

21. Sophia Adelaida von Löwenstein-Wertheim, the widow of Dom Miguel, was living abroad and supporting seven children, one son and six daughters, all born between 1852 and 1862.

22. Dom Fernando was the widowed Consort of Dona Maria II. He had married again morganatically and was living in Portugal. He belonged to the Saxe-Coburg-Gotha family and was a cousin of Prince Albert, Consort of Queen Victoria.

23. L.C. *Baines Letter Book*. Baines to Duckett, October 9,1877.

24. L.C. *Baines Letter Book*. Baines to Duckett, October 4,1876.

25. L.C. *Baines Letter Book* Baines to Duckett, March 7, 1877.

26. L.C. *Baines Letter Book*. Baines to Dom Fernando's secretary, January 30, 1877.

27. L.C. *Baines Letter Book*. Baines to Duckett, December 16, 1876.

28. L.C. *Correspondence*. Eden to Cawley, January 5, 1878.

29. L.C. *Baines Letter Book*. Baines to Duckett, May 11, 1878.

30. L.C. *Baines Letter Book*. Baines to Arnold and Co, March 14, 1879.

31. L.C. *Baines Letter Book.* Baines to Duckett, March 5, 1880.

32. L.C. *Baines Letter Book.* Baines to Mgr Fisher, July 6, 1876.

33. Archives of St John's Cathedral, Norwich. *Dr Duckett's Rough Diary.*

34. P.F. *S.C. (Congressi)*, 17, f. 127. Gaetano Aloisi Majella to Cardinal Simeone, Prefect of Propaganda Fide, April 3, 1883.

35. Dr Duckett died July 7, 1910. In none of the tributes paid to him at his funeral, in the diocesan magazine, or in the Lisbon College magazine, is there any mention of the Princess's will. However, the college magazine informs us that it was decided that the College Literary Society should henceforth be known as 'The Duckett Society', I am indebted to Mrs M. Osborne, the Northampton Diocesan Archivist, for information about Duckett's later career.

36. A.S.V. *Nunziatura di Lisbona*, 289, f.19.

37. A.S.V. *Nunziatura di Lisbona* , 289, f.26.

38. P.F. *S.C. (Congressi)*, 17, f.127.

J.A. DRINKWATER

University of Leeds

CONSUMING DESIRES IN GALDOS'S
LA DESHEREDADA

Central to Galdós's literary vision of late nineteenth-century society in *La desheredada* (1881) is his investigation of a modern urban consumer culture and the way in which this intersects not only with issues of power and class, of production and fiction, but also with the construction of the female protagonist as consumer and consumer item, consumed with and by her deep-rooted obsessions.[1] Just as importantly, the novel deals with the conventional topos of the consuming of desire and beauty by time, old age and illness which forms the background to the unfolding of the plot, and underlines the way in which even the modern forms of social life in Madrid are subject to the dictates of the natural environment within which they occur.

The multiple layers of meaning which arise from the treatment of the different forms of production and consumption in the text are captured in the ostensibly natural image of the spider and its web which recur in the text. This image carries within it a series of possible meanings: the suggestion of the artifice necessary to produce such a complex structure as the web or the society it represents, the idea of the blind instinct which drives the spider to weave its web, and at the same time hints at the insidious threat presented to the naive individual who may be trapped and swallowed up by the moral and economic freedoms apparently offered in modern city life. On a springtime outing with Miquis at the opening of the novel, 'Isidora vio un araña que se descolgaba de un hilo, un pájaro que llevaba pajas en el pico, una pareja de

205

mariposas blancas' (67). When Sánchez Botín first attracts her attention at Mass, Isidora reflects upon the glances cast by the men there at the women present and figures that 'si tanto flechazo de ojos dejase una raya en el espacio, el interior de la iglesia parecería una gran tela de araña' (277), prefiguring the way in which she will be caught up in his concupiscent designs. By the time she is installed as Sánchez Botín's mistress, the insect has wrought its silent work, and when Botín discovers her liaison with Joaquín Pez, '[Isidora] [p]ensó en las prenderas, en las peinadoras, en los chismes y enredos que forman invisible tela de araña en torno a toda existencia equívoca e inmoral' (321). The web is, of course, an extension of the metaphor of the labyrinth or whirlpool of the city, the 'voraginoso laberinto de las calles' (480) in which Isidora is swallowed up at the end of the text, which has been related on the macrolevel to the 'endless, repetitive historical cycles' experienced by modern Spain in crisis, and on the microlevel to the 'whirlpool of status, money and goods in which the modern social subject is caught up'.[2] Both sets of images relate metonymically to other motifs in the text, notably Miquis's views on the 'la armonía y el admirable plan del Cosmos [...] evolución tras evolución, enlazados el nacer y el morir' (67); Isidora's tangled thoughts, which Miquis promises to help her to put straight: 'poniendo las cosas en su verdadero lugar, te las hará ver claras y sin telarañas' (430), or the minds of the mad patients in Leganés, whose ideas 'son nuestras ideas, pero desengarzadas, sueltas, sacadas de la misteriosa hebra que gallardamente las enfila' (16); and the endless, patient sewing of Emilia Relimpio who labours to construct a stable existence for herself within the limitations of her social station.

Critical interpretations of the society of *La desheredada* differ quite markedly. On the one hand it may be seen as characterised by the loss of individual identity in chaos, proliferation and endless (re)production,[3] whilst on the other it is, under the influence of Naturalism, considered as 'an organic whole, a network of relationships of mutual dependence and mutual influence'.[4] By means of an examination of the spider and web image, these two conflicting – but nonetheless valid – formulations of nineteenth-century society may be brought together in order to tie in at the same time with the commentary on the work of the novelist which is implicit in *La desheredada*, and thus produce a broader understanding of Galdós's conception of the workings of society and of his role in it. In the same way as the spider constantly (re)produces its environment, the intricate, delicate web, so social interaction and the language of the text are initiated or elaborated endlessly in recurring patterns defined (in late nineteenth-century terms) by natural or given laws. Whatever the fate of the individual, the web, the fabric of society, and language will be regenerated and the cycle of production and consumption will continue. Similarly, as the complex structure which sustains the spider is constructed ultimately for the purposes of entrapping and consuming, so the social world ensnares and feeds off the subject, just as the text generated by the writer/narrator deceives and envelops the reader in its fictions. Thus the spider, modern society and the omniscient narrator/author all occupy a comparable place as designers of the structures which serve to draw in – or sometimes to exclude – the fly, the subject or the literary character; and like the spider, the social world and the author are also capable of the endless reproduction of their societal or literary structures.

The primary level on which Galdós deals with issues of production and consumption in *La desheredada* is in his analysis of emergent capitalism and social divisions seen from the different perspectives of Miquis, Bou and Mariano. This provides a vital backdrop for an understanding both of Isidora's social pretensions and of the ambiguous status which she has in the novel as both consumer and consumed. The increasing industrialisation suggested by the urban setting and the depiction of the workplace throws into relief the divisions of – for want of a better term – class which rest upon the lower status conferred by active participation in production, and the passive or parasitical lifestyle of those who consider themselves to belong to the upper echelons of society and who are epitomised in the person of Joaquín Pez, (despite, or perhaps because of, the fact that his aristocratic connections are held by virtue only of marriage and are therefore a sham). This lifestyle is also aspired to or emulated by the self-seeking representatives of the mercantile or lower orders (Sánchez Botín, Gaitica, even Mariano) who feed (or wish to feed) off those who are foolish enough to stray into their trap. Miquis comments acerbically on such behaviour: 'No habrá algún día leyes para enfrenar la alta vagancia [...]. Puesto que tanto se ha hablado del derecho a la vida, ¿existirá también el derecho al lujo? Si el populacho nos pide los talleres nacionales, la alta vagancia nos pedirá algún día los casinos costeados por el Estado' (247). The honest toil of the worker Juan Bou is thus pitted against the speculation of the social parasite in search of gain and luxury: yet in both cases the immediate object of their endeavours are the consumer goods which are the sign of social value, for, notwithstanding his strong views, Juan Bou, the great defender of the people is, paradoxically, implicated in the processes of capitalism which forge the life of the working classes, a point which cannot have been lost on Galdós in his role as producer of novels which, while critically analytical of contemporary society, were also bound up in the development of the bourgeois economy: 'Sus primeros años de trabajo en Madrid fueron muy felices, y ganó bastante dinero. Entonces había algo de renacimiento industrial, y empezaba a desarrollarse el gusto por presentar los objetos mercantiles con primor, halagando los ojos del que compra' (283). He and Mariano are, however, diametrically opposed in their views on money and production:

'En el fondo de su alma, Pecado anhelaba ser también sanguijuela y chupar lo que pudiera, dejando al pueblo en los puros huesos; se desvivía por satisfacer todos los apetitos de la concupiscencia humana y por tener mucho dinero [...] En esto se distinguía radicalmente de su maestro, amantísimo del trabajo. Bou no quería galas, ni lujo, ni vicios caros, ni palacios; lo que quería era que todos fuesemos pueblo [...] que cada cual no fuera propietario nada más que de la cuchara con que había de comer la sopa nacional' (287). Bou's own ideas on the subject are firm, and reintroduce the use of insect imagery to suggest the natural workings of society: 'Todo lo demás es superfluidad y lujo, es explotar al obrero, chupar su sangre [...]. Ved esos que andan por ahí, toda esa chusma de esos señores y holgazanes ¿De qué viven? De nuestro trabajo. [...]. Nosotros somos las abejas; ellos, los zánganos; nosotros hacemos la miel; vienen ellos y se la comen' (289).

Isidora, as previously mentioned, is presented in all her facets both as the archetypical consuming subject of modern society and the object of male consumption. The fact that she moves constantly between the two positions points to the shifting identities conferred by the commodification of social life, and also to the uneasy status of women whose social standing is largely defined by the men with whom they are connected (hence Laura Relimpio's unrealistic hopes for her daughters' marriage). Just as Juan Bou is a worker with radical anti-capitalist views, yet implicated in the processes of capitalism, so Isidora can be seen alternately as the victim of the consumer economy and its firmest ally. It is a generally accepted view that the emergence of the nineteenth-century novel is related to the rise of capitalism and the bourgeois classes, and that the realist novel defends and enshrines the values of a bourgeois society (social order, domestic virtue, religious morality), or at least provides 'knowledge of the hidden underlying structures of capitalist social relations' which permits an analysis of these structures.[5] This bourgeois society is divided into the spheres of the public and private, in the latter of which women are relegated to a strictly circumscribed role outside the realms of production and enterprise, in such a way that their value is as objects of exchange rather than producers of wealth. At the same time, the nineteenth-century novel is, as never before, a consumer commodity, the product of enterprise, a status which coexists ambiguously with its role as a purveyor of lasting and universal values. The later decades of the century in Spain saw a proliferation of mass-produced novels for a reading public which consisted chiefly of women who, therefore, whilst seemingly controlled by the values enshrined in these works, also came to occupy an important social space as the readers of such texts. What consumer commodities like these offer to their public is romantic fantasy and wish-fulfilment: by making of repressed desires the stuff of the text, and by providing momentary satisfaction of those desires, they stimulate the need in the reader to return for more, thus creating an addiction which ensures the continuing success of the genre. But the frustrations of this merely temporary satisfaction of desire lead not to the maintenance of the bourgeois order, but, as is clearly the case of Isidora (and other characters in the novel), to a disruption of it as the consumer seeks new fulfilments.[6] Not only Isidora, but many other characters in the novel – her father, Mariano, the Peces, not to mention don Santiago Quijano, and José and Laura Relimpio – 'feed on fictions', both creating and disrupting the social (dis)order of Madrid.[7]

Isidora is characterised from the outset as a desiring subject, beset by 'múltiples deseos' (21), which cause her the simultaneous pain and pleasure of insatiable desire, 'ardiente gozo y punzante martirio' (117), and her aspirations are indicated by her metaphorical hunger, thirst and eating or consuming: 'una sed de su espíritu' (59), 'vivísimos apetitos que conmovían su alma [...] devoraba con sus ojos' (117), 'aquel apetito de comprar todo, de probar diversos manjares, de conocer las infinitas variedades del sabor fisiológico' (229). In Chapter 7, 'Tomando posesión de Madrid', the levels of Isidora's involvement in the consumer process are outlined. On the one hand she exists as a reader or consumer of romantic fiction, feeding her fantasies on the sentimental *folletín*: 'Yo he leído mi propia historia tantas veces' (116). This constant re-reading of her life at the same time generates in her mind a continuous narrative, elsewhere referred to as a 'fabricación mental' (60), in which she contemplates the satisfaction of her desires in an imagined time when she will have unlimited power of choice and spending. The reader of *La desheredada* is, then, constantly subject to the production of Isidora's own level of mental narrative which is a symptom of her obsessive desire and also serves to draw attention to Galdós's own process of writing of the text. This mental perspective is paralleled in Isidora's constant passage through the streets in the orgy of spending and window-shopping which is the physical manifestation of her attempts to fulfil her desire. The abundance of adjectives used in the descriptions, the luxury of the goods on display, and their superfluity and triviality – 'Cuántas invenciones del capricho [...] o superfluidades llamativas' (117) – suggest how Isidora's real hunger, her real needs, are supplanted by greed and a perversion of appetite, a 'desordenado apetito' (127). Here, as in other novels by Galdós, food occupies a central position in the narrative, and there is constant slippage beween its literal and metaphorical significance.[8] In *La desheredada*, the chief role of food is that of the great divider of classes, to which the description of the Christmas fare of the wealthy and that of the lower classes attests in Chapter 14, 'Navidad'. The reference to 'la sopa nacional' (287) reinforces the awareness of the unfair distribution of wealth and food in contemporary Spain, and the spectre of the hunger contingent on extreme povery lingers constantly in the background. For this reason, food becomes a signifier of social status, and thus by extension of social aspiration as well. Isidora's attention is drawn to luxury foods, to the 'comestibles finos, el jabalí colmilludo, la chocha y el faisán asados [...] con otras mil y mil cosas aperitivas' (118) in the shop window in Chapter 7. Here, as at other points in the narrative, she rejects plain (and sometimes nourishing) food, in favour of fancy dishes which provide too rich a diet. Her association of plain food with the common people presents a threat to her aspirations and causes Isidora to lose her apetite. Thus, when Miquis takes her to eat at the *ventorrillo*, she cannot eat the food, and when she visits her aunt and Mariano '[Isidora] ni hablaba ni hacía más que probar la comida' (51). Similarly, when the Relimpio family refuse to sit down to Christmas dinner with the criminal Mariano, Isidora at first rejects the plates of food which are to be sent up to them, and offers Mariano some insubstantial *turrón* instead. Later, in dire financial circumstances, Isidora insists on purchasing luxury food, both when Sánchez Botín dispenses with her services, and later when she takes up again with Joaquín Pez, who uses her to obtain money to pay off his debts.

Isidora, of course, also becomes a commodity in the marketplace, in a process which has been analysed by different critics. Luis Fernández Cifuentes examines the way in which through the workings of language the beautiful woman and the shop-window luxuries become gradually identified with each other, until Isidora recognises her place as a consumer item and acts accordingly: 'she will finally become aware of the fetishism of the mechandise, and the extent to which it is not only her beauty, namely, her beauty as a sign, that makes her most valuable in the arcades of the city. She is no ordinary commodity, she is a luxury commodity, a fetish. The only way to preserve the nobility of her beauty, to make it publicly recognised, is to put it up for sale'.[9] Stephanie Sieburth also comments on the way in which people become commodities as commodities take on the human characteristic of arousing desire, which culminates in Isidora's decision to turn to prostitution.[10] Sieburth interprets this as a positive choice for Isidora, which liberates her from the restrictions of bourgeois marriage or the life of slave-labour in a factory which would otherwise have been the only options open to her. As Sieburth explains: 'Isidora owns the means of production [...] she will create and sell herself as a commodity [...] as a fetishized luxury item [...] as she does this she will be free'.[11] However, what such commentators fail to highlight is that Isidora's trajectory, although it does indeed involve her commodification, also traces her movement away from the paradise – the natural world before the fall – described in the Retiro in Chapter 4, 'El célebre Miquis', and her degeneration as a desirable commodity in the course of the novel. The emphasis is not so much on the fact that Isidora sells herself as a luxury, as that this apparent luxury is illusory, or subject to decay. Prominent in the text are the warnings that beauty, youth and money, the cornerstones of Isidora's commodity status, will themselves be consumed by time, age and infirmity. There are the references already alluded to in the springtime Eden in Chapter 4 from which Isidora will be expelled, as is indicated by her eating of an orange 'como Eva la manzana' (76) offered to her by Miquis. The eating of the orange transforms Isidora into a sexualized being and into a commodity, precious jewels, before the eyes of the infatuated Miquis: 'Sus labios, empapados en el ácido de la fruta, tenían un carmín intensísimo, hasta el punto de que allí podían ser verdad los rubíes montados en versos de que tanto han abusado los poetas' (75). At the same time it warns of Isidora's imminent fall from innocence, of the ephemerality of her beauty which will wither with the passing of spring and youth, and of her mortality. It is through Miquis, with his fascination for evolutionary processes, that we are reminded of the nature of living things as the product of transformation: 'la planta de flores hermosas y aromáticas es simplemente una transformación de las sustancias vulgares o repugnantes contenidas en la tierra y en el estiércol' (73). In Chapter 28, Isidora shudders at the *memento mori* which confronts her in Miquis's lodgings: '- De quién serán esos pobres huesos?... – Son de mujer. Quizá una tan hermosa como tú. Mírate en ese espejo' (362).

The chief way in which Galdós signals Isidora's own fate is through his concentration on the decay of objects, and the parallel of Isidora's life with that of other unfortunate women. One of the extended warnings takes the form of the account of the sombre Aransís palace, and the story of Virginia de Aransís, which together form an ironic corrective to Isidora's yearnings for a sophisticated aristocratic life. Virginia de Aransís, who Isidora has been led to believe is her mother, is in fact a victim of the honour code and, having borne two illegitimate children, is effectively walled up, 'emparedada' (150) by her mother by way of punishment, until she goes mad and dies of a fever; her circumstances are certainly not ones to be aspired to by Isidora. Similarly, Virginia's room is described in terms of decay and death, prefiguring the rooms in which Isidora will later live: 'Sobre la chimenea permanecía un jarrón con flores que fueron naturales y frescas nueve años antes. Eran ya un indescriptible harapo cárdeno, que al ser tocado, caía en particulas secas y sonantes, como los despojos de cien otoños. En los muebles finísimos, de caprichosa construcción, los dorados se habían vuelto negros [...] todo de tal manera invadido por la muerte, que parecía próximo a caer' (147). The conventional motif of the blooms of youth which wilt and wither are echoed elsewhere in the text where the flowers with which Isidora comes into contact are destroyed either inadvertently or wilfully and predict her own end: 'Con tanto paquete entre las manos, se le ajaron las rosas' (120); she strips the petals from the flowers which Juan Bou sends her in prison, and tramples on them. This decay is picked up again in the description of Isidora's home in the calle de Hortaleza, with its second-hand, second-rate furniture and decorations made of fragile, disposable fabrics, which are the spoils of other people's failures:

> Había mucho [mueble] procedente de liquidaciones [...]. Caso todo lo restante procedía de esas almonedas apócrifas, verdaderos baratillos de muebles chapeados, falsos, chapuceros y de corta duración. La sala lucía [...] un centro o tarjetero [...] de piezas tan frágiles y de tan poco peso que era preciso pasar junto a él con cuidado, porque al menor roce daba consigo en el suelo. El mármol [de la consola] se escondía bajo una instalación abigarrada de cajas de dulces, hechas con cromos, seda, papel cañamazo y todo lo más deleznable, vano y frágil que imaginarse puede. (248)

In a recent study on Victorian narrative in England, Andrew Miller investigates the effects of commodification on and in the novel, and points to the parallel between the constant circulation of goods in the Victorian novel which 'powerfully describes the sexual circulation of diminished, commodified women'.[12] In particular he considers the significance of goods sold in auction sales: 'these goods, the opulent detritus of economic failure, retain the traces of the misfortunes they have witnessed and announce the approaching misfortune of those who [...] decide to buy'.[13] Similarly, in *La desheredada*, Isidora's identity is inscribed in the objects which surround her, which, like her, are destined to pass from owner to owner in a process of constant circulation until they lose their veneer of beauty and are no longer viable currency. At the end of the novel, Isidora, ravaged by illness and hunger, exclaims: 'Valgo mucho, y valdré muchísimo más' (475), but her claims to worth by this stage are empty ones.

Like the furniture which is used in the process of passing from owner to owner, so Isidora's descent into the streets and into common prostitution marks the bottom point in her decline in value, and her social – and eventually literal – death. All of this she has already foreseen in her vivid nightmares in prison, in which the motifs of her consuming desires – and the desires which consume her – are resumed in a grotesque and terrifying charade: 'Otras veces era gran señora, y estaba en su palacio, cuando de repente veía aparecer un esqueleto de niño, con la cabeza muy abultada, y los huesos todos muy finos y limpios, cual si fueran de marfil. [..] Luego se borraba el niño del campo de los sueños, y aparecía Joaquín en mitad de una orgía, ebrio de felicidad y de champaña. Por delante de la mesa se paseaba una sombra andrajosa: era ella, Isidora. Todos la miraban y prorrumpían en carcajadas. Ella se reía también; pero, ¡cosa rara! se reía de hambre' (409).

NOTES

1. All quotations are from Benito Pérez Galdós, *La desheredada*, Madrid: Alianza, 1967, and will henceforth be cited in the text.

2. Marsha S. Collins, 'Sliding into the Vortex: Patterns of Ascent and Descent in *La desheredada*', *Anales galdosianos*, XXV (1990), 13-23, p. 18, p. 19.

3. Stephanie Sieburth, 'Enlightenment, Mass Culture and Madness: The Dialectic of Modernity in *La desheredada*', in *A Sesquicentennial Tribute to Galdós (1843-1993)*, ed. Linda M. Willem, Newark, Delaware: Juan de la Cuesta: 1993, 27-40, p. 27.

4. Eamonn Rodgers, *From Enlightenment to Realism. The Novels of Galdós, 1870-1877*, Dublin: Trinity College, 1987, p. 70.

5. The quotation is a paraphrase of Lukacs in Terry Lovell, *Consuming Fiction*, London: Verso, 1987, p. 14.

6. see Lovell, p. 154.

7. see Beth Wietelmann Bauer, 'Isidora's Agnorisis: Reading, Plot and Identity in *La desheredada*', *Anales galdosianos*, XXIV (1989), 43-52, p. 46.

8. see, for example, Sarah E. King, 'Food Imagery in *Fortunata y Jacinta*', *Anales galdosianos*, XVIII (1983), 79-88, which considers the male characters as consumers of the female, and hunger as a metaphor for sexual appetite or unsatisfied (maternal) desire.

9. Luis Fernández Cifuentes, 'Signs for City in the City of Galdós', *MLN*, 103 (1988), 289-311, p. 310.

10. Sieburth, p. 33.

11. Sieburth, p. 39.

12. Andrew Miller, *Novels behind glass. Commodity culture and Victorian narrative*, Cambridge: Cambridge University Press, 1995, p. 31.

13. Miller, p. 21.

JOHN MACKLIN

University of Leeds

SOCIETY, RELIGION AND THE MODERNITY
OF GALDOS'S *MISERICORDIA*

One not very surprising feature of the approach of a new century is the increased interest in the previous *fin de siècle*. It is not necessary to agree with Elaine Showalter that 'the last decades of the twentieth century seem to be repeating the problems, themes, and metaphors of the *fin de siècle*'[1] to at least concede that many of the preoccupations of the twentieth century have their roots in that period of intellectual and social turmoil around the year 1900. The key word for defining the whole era was 'transitional', as Holbrook Jackson, writing in 1913, insists: 'People said it was a period of transition, and they were convinced that they were passing not only from one social system to another, but from one morality to another, from one culture to another, and from one religion to a dozen or more'.[2] The conventional wisdom, of course, is that in the case of Spain the transition to modernity was slow, painful and delayed and indeed the preoccupation of writers and intellectuals with the problem of Spain, whose final relegation from its once powerful position as imperial power is marked by its defeat by the United States as the nineteenth century neared its end, has been amply documented and studied. Some interpretations which identify this problem entirely with the mindset created by an all-pervasive Counter-Reformation Catholicism stress the fact that modernism in the Church, so influential elsewhere, was virtually non-existent in Spain. While theological modernism has been identified by many critics, most notably in Spain by Juan Ramón Jiménez, with the wider phenomenon of artistic modernism, Spain seems to present a curious case of the one emerging without the other.[3]

In general the dominant literary mode for the tentative expression of the new, modern vision has been deemed to be poetry, in the form of symbolism and its consequences, while prose writing appears to remain more conventional until the full flowering of modernism after the First World War. Spain is arguably atypical again since, despite the importance of *modernismo*, for twentieth-century Spanish fiction, the *annus mirabilis*, comparable in significance if not in prestige to Modernism's 1922, has been considered to be 1902, the year in which the Spanish novel finally appeared to shed the constraints of Realism and emerge as the new novel of the twentieth century, with the publication of *Amor y pedagogía*, *Sonata de otoño*, *La voluntad* and *Camino de perfección*. Exactly one hundred years ago, however, in 1897, there were published in Spain two major novels, Galdós's *Misericordia* and Unamuno's *Paz en la guerra*, both of which could be termed transitional on the road from realism to modernism. *Misericordia* in particular, for all its naturalist appearance, has often been studied in terms of its alleged modernity, though it is inevitable that each new age reads the works of the past through eyes that are its own. An early example of this approach to Galdós's fiction in general is Ricardo Gullón's *Galdós, novelista moderno*.[4] More recently, a special issue of *Insula* in September 1993 was dedicated to Galdós, 'un clásico moderno'.[5] John Varey, in an essay on charity in *Misericordia* wrote emphatically that '[t]his is no longer the world of the determinist novel, the so-called scientist endeavouring to work out a formula. This is the new novel, the novel of the turn of the century, the novel of will'.[6] There is, moreover, a widespread consensus among critics that Galdós's realism is *sui generis*, and within an indigenous tradition that has frequently been labelled Cervantine. The author himself, in the

Prologue to Clarín's *La Regenta* (1901), lends validity to this view in his comments on realism: 'En resumidas cuentas: Francia, con su poder incontrastable, nos imponía una reforma de nuestra propia obra, sin saber que era nuestra; aceptémosla nosotros restaurando el naturalismo y devolviéndole lo que le habían quitado, el humorismo, y empleando éste en las formas narrativa y descriptiva conforme a la tradición cervantesca'.[7] It is a commonplace of Galdós criticism to insist on the limitations which the epithet 'realist' places on his creative talents. In any case, Galdós, particularly in the later phase of his career, became deeply interested in out-of-the-way religious questions and in the existence of hidden, mysterious worlds, an interest which sits uneasily with any notion of simple or naive realism.

That said, we need to be cautious about the uncritical application of the term 'modernism' to Galdós's later works, and to be aware that modernism and modernity are not exact equivalents, though their meanings often overlap and interrelate in complex ways that have to do with both formal considerations and thematic concerns. Nevertheless, although considerable imprecision surrounds the word 'modernity' in the sense that it can be applied specifically to the new and unprecedented conditions of our century or cover all post-Enlightenment thought up to the postmodern challenge, we all broadly know what we mean by modern literature, if only in terms of some commonly accepted features such as transcendence of realism, formal experimentation, problematising of character and identity, a new treatment of time, artistic self-consciousness. In the specific case of the novel, any consideration of literary change would seem to involve realism, modernism and postmodernism, conceived either in terms of radical breaks or as successive phases in thinking about and engagement with the aesthetics of representation. In this essay, rather than attempt a historical classification in order to demonstrate that *Misericordia* is either another manifestation of the 'turn of the novel' or a work still essentially in the realist mode, as Nicholas G. Round argues so persuasively,[8] I want to consider it in the context of some of the issues linking fiction and modernity in Spain, and to ask what kind of modernity Galdós's novel can be said to embody. While inevitably this will involve allusions to the role of the imagination, narrative-making, radical fictionality, autonomy, it will also involve a recognition of Galdós's engagement with contemporary concerns. This is important since modernism is often construed, following its construction by the New Criticism in terms of the verbal icon, as a flight from history and society into the orders or consolations of form. Some critics have endeavoured to depict the novel in precisely this way. Germán Gullón, for example, seems to link *Misericordia* to the kind of novel in which it is necessary to seek 'un nuevo orden', which will arise when 'el ímpetu representacional mimeticista sea sustituido por el interés en lo formal, cuando las novelas adopten estructuras independientes de los sistemas de valores externos, y vayan convirtiéndose en textos autosuficientes'.[9] Here we find *Misericordia* inscribed within a particular construction of Modernist autonomy. Scott Lash's definition is characteristic: 'Aesthetic modernity ... constitutes a break with representation, hence a certain self-referentiality, and above all a set of formalisms'.[10] We may find useful a model of modernism which aligns itself with the view expressed here, stressing by implication at least a retreat from history into myth, a divorce between artistic structures and the orders of the world, a movement from temporal to spatial form, the notion of the text as linguistically self-generating. There can be another view of autonomy, however, which need not be so radically and fundamentally non-referential, but which does involve a movement from the conceptual to the aesthetic or, more appropriately in Galdós's case, from the rational to the imaginative in the artist's engagement with the world. Thus rather then locate *Misericordia* in terms of a movement away from representation to autonomy, conceived in terms of oppositions, it is instructive to see its modernity in the context of a wider concern with the imagination, or with different modes of knowing and understanding, pervading all post-Enlightenment thought from the Romantics to postmodernism. At the same time, it is important not to uproot the novel from its very specific, Spanish, cultural and historical context. Galdós's concern with the very real, and unpalatable, social conditions of Madrid in the 1880s is all too evident in the text and is underlined in the author's own 1913 preface to the Nelson edition of the novel.[11] He was aware of the historical circumstances which led to those conditions and also of the religious underpinning of social attitudes to poverty, principally through the practice of charity. Religion, moreover, with its otherworldly preoccupations, was perceived as very much part of reality and inseparable from the individual's moral engagement with his world and also from his interpretation of it. Fiction, it hardly needs stating, offered an ideal form for an exploration of these questions. Therefore, while we may discern in the period of modernity an increasing suspicion of scientific and rational systems, of plot and plotting, and a scepticism about the validity of grand narratives, narrative continues to be a prominent mode of understanding so that, although *Misericordia* might problematise representation, it is not anti-representational. Galdós is concerned in *Misericordia* with both the nature of society and the nature of narrative, which becomes a particular form of knowing.

When it was first published, *Misericordia* attracted remarkably little comment, even from those who might have been expected to review it, such as Clarín and Emilia Pardo Bazán, and it does not begin to receive attention until the 1940s, with the work of Joaquín Casalduero and Angel del Río[12], and this attention then increases in the 1960s and intensifies in the 1970s, especially in North America, stimulated by the fiftieth anniversary of the author's death. Approaches to the novel have largely fallen into two categories, those dealing with the socio-religious dimension, in particular charity, and a later, smaller group, concerned above all with the mysterious appearance of Don Romualdo and the workings of the creative imagination.[13] For Joaquín Casalduero, who recognises, like other critics, that the spiritual dimension of *Misericordia* offsets the sordid and depressing features of Naturalism, the general structure of the novel proceeds from the confrontation between reality and imagination to their fusion and finally to the creation of reality by imagination.[14] For Gustavo Correa,[15] the act of imagining is also an act of creation, while for Leon Livingstone, the presence of don Romualdo represents Galdós's refusal to accept a unilateral, purely materialistic conception of reality.[16] Mariano López Sanz neatly encapsulates the consensus view that 'Galdós realiza en *Misericordia* la síntesis armónica del mundo de la materia y del mundo del espíritu, de la realidad observada y de la imaginación creadora'.[17] Otherwise, for those who concentrate on the religious aspects, the appearance of don Romualdo is explained by being given the status of a miracle, the direct intervention of God through the agency of Benina in human affairs. This view is given added weight by virtue of the fact that his appearance occurs at a point when she questions most her own ability to carry on: 'Faltábale ya la energía, y sus grandes ánimos flaqueaban; perdía la fe en la Providencia [....] no había más remedio que sucumbir y caer diciendo: "Llegué hasta donde pude: lo demás hágalo Dios, si quiere"'.[18] It is of course a curious sort of miracle, for what he brings is material comfort which is shown to have negative effects on the characters: Juliana becomes domineering, indeed is virtually unhinged. Paca is subdued and barely alive, being described in the 'Final' thus: 'la cabeza gacha, los ojos caídos, el mirar vago, perdido en los dibujos de la estera, el cuerpo apoltronado, encariñándose cada día más con la indolencia, el apetito decadente, el humor taciturno y desabrido, las ideas negras'(235-36). Frasquito loses his life, and Benina and Almudena are cast out from the respectable world of bourgeois society. The miracle is no solution for them, certainly not on the material level, and for the others it is not life-giving. If Benina is to be portrayed as a God-like figure, it is not because she works miracles. For several critics, not only Russell[19], she is likened to Christ, in her humility and in her practice of true charity, anticipatory of post-Vatican Council theology, but the real parallel is with the suffering Christ, whose Passion leads to Redemption. As she views the world around her, at her lowest point, the narrator says of her: 'Había alcanzado glorioso triunfo; sentíase victoriosa, después de haber perdido la batalla en el terreno material'(227). This is not just military imagery, as Peter Bly suggests[20], but the language of Christ defeated but triumphant, whose loving sacrifice brings fulfilment and victory and brings it, moreover, in this world and not the next. Inevitably, this implies a rejection of modernity as embodied in the social world of Galdós's Spain, of inequality and facile, institutionalised and ineffective solutions, in favour of a different kind of human relationships, based on self-sacrifice and community. Benina's acceptance of her own reality implies too an acceptance of the supernatural, a belief in mystery. This at times is synonymous with superstition, with belief in dreams and prophecies, in the *Samdai* and hidden treasures, but is still not easily dismissed. Romualdo, or the two Romualdos, one real, one invented, acts as a narrative device to create a bridge between the natural and the supernatural.

If this is one kind of explanation, it is not to deny that the appearance of Don Romualdo is the most perplexing aspect of the work. Those who wish to integrate it into a broadly mimetic framework, that is, without reference to the supernatural, do so by pointing either to coincidence or to a subliminal awareness on the part of Benina of the existence of a priest of that name in Madrid. From another perspective, that of modernist introversion, it can be construed as a metaphor for fiction-writing, and provide the basis of a fairly consistent interpretation of the novel. In the cases of the interesting articles of John W. Kronik and Nicole Malaret, Don Romualdo's appearance is a facet of the novel's metafictional dimension, a valid, if partial, approach to a rich and complex novel. This kind of reading enables tensions and contradictions within the text to be resolved by an appeal to the self-contained nature of the literary artefact. Kronik observes that 'Benina's purported creation of Romualdo is Galdós's metaphorical representation of the process and significance of fiction'.[21] Benina invents a story to satisfy her mistress. To add plausibility to this story, she provides a name, a place of work, a set of family relationships, a set of physical characteristics and, when necessary, irons out any inconsistencies in her narrative. She does of course appear as a character in the narrative of which she is narrator. Moreover, the narrative is reader-directed in that doña Paca stimulates the narrative and indeed at times appears to compete with Benina for control of it. At all events, Paca fully epitomises that 'willing suspension of disbelief' which is a prerequisite of novel-reading, since for her don Romualdo is real, if for Benina he is invented. Benina is in practice a Realist writer and in this she contrasts with Galdós's transgressive, non-mimetic mode. Where Benina, through necessity, seeks verisimilitude in her narrative, Galdós, in his, creates uncertainty.

Benina and Galdós are not the only fiction-makers in the text, for *Misericordia* contains a proliferation of narratives, construed as the imposition of plots upon the face of reality. All the characters weave narratives. Even Don Carlos's accounts are precisely that, accounts of the world in terms of financial transactions. At the beginning of the novel, the beggars have a narrative about *la caporala*, to which some subscribe and some do not, that she is really well off. At the end, Juliana, despite the evidence of the good health of her twins, is convinced they are going to die and links this, in characteristic plot or pattern making fashion, to her treatment of Benina. Similarly, there are a number of embedded narratives in the text. Almudena recounts his own autobiography, and his accounts of the *Samdai* are a fantastic narrative-making. Frasquito Ponte and Obdulia, in keeping with Frasquito's use of the imagination as 'la facultad preciosa de desprenderse de la realidad' (88), invent a fantastic world which acts as an escape from the miserable conditions of the world they are required to inhabit. As Rupert Allen has shown, this pattern is characteristic of the behaviour of all the characters and is a manifestation of different kinds of compensatory neuroses.[22] In these cases, as in earlier novels by Galdós, imaginative fictions corroborate rather than deny the existence of the real world. The condition of fictionality confirms a sense of the real by pointing up their difference. On the level of the workings of the imagination, Benina's narrative is of a different order to that of the other narratives in the text, to which it nonetheless bears a relation. Although Allen goes so far as to implicate Benina in the general process of self-delusion and sees her grip on reality progressively weaken, most notably when she forgives Juliana at the end with the words of Christ, the fact is that there is a correspondence between her constructions and the orders of the world. She invents a character called Romualdo and he, or someone very like him, eventually materialises. This fact quite naturally surprises her, and in the latter part of the novel she wrestles with the contradictions inherent in material realisation of her own fiction. Not only does she invent a character but, as Kronik suggests, she also creates a future that comes to pass. It is this future-directed aspect of *Misericordia* which is really radical.

An acceptance that language and signs can construct the real is not difficult in relation to the past. It is equivalent to accepting that the human imagination has the capacity to reshape the past, the world of history, to impose different orders on fragmentariness and contingency. This is the basis, after all, of historiographic metafiction, which takes the past to be ideologically and discursively constructed and is thus inherently critical of all representations. In *Misericordia*, it would appear that the materialisation of Don Romualdo is different, but is part of the novel's religious significance. His coming into being is the imposition of the illusion, or of the power of illusion, its realisation in the mind of the reader, and creator. As we have seen, illusion in *Misericordia* is of essentially two different kinds: illusion as escape, which Galdós generalises from private to public, showing how it applies to a whole society, and illusion as a strength with which to confront the harshness of the material world. The difference between them is fine, characteristic of a novel which functions above all at margins and boundaries. But in the context of our consideration of the modernity of *Misericordia*, the Romantic notion of imagination as a non-conceptualisable power is made to stand in opposition to reason as an instrument of individual self-determination. It is perhaps surprising that so much time has been spent on explaining Don Romualdo, when what really matters is his inexplicability, except in the terms I have just described. Narrative of course imposes on events an order, or induces the reader to impose an order upon them, and in this case forges links between two events which are not logically related. The compulsion to establish the nature of the link between them is a metaphor for our sense-making impulses. For all the critical claims about the power of imagination to create reality, Benina herself does not fully believe that she has achieved this. If, on the one hand, she imagines herself asking Romualdo's forgiveness for having invented him, and can wonder 'si por milagro de Dios, habría tomado cuerpo y alma de persona verídica, el ser creado en su fantasía por un mentir inocente' (173), she can also say unequivocally: 'Ya estoy segura, después de mucho cavilar, que no es el don Romualdo que yo inventé, sino otro que se parece a él como se parecen dos gotas de agua' (237-38). Galdós does not remove the intriguing aspect of the anticipatory nature of Benina's invented story, but he introduces enough differences between the two Romualdos so as not to destroy the realist illusion completely. The importance of the don Romualdo episode is precisely that it creates uncertainty pointing to a loss of faith in the possibility of a complete, reliable or transparent representation of what is true. While, for some, don Romualdo may be an expression of a frustration at the finite limits of the material world, he can also be seen, in his ambiguous textual status, as showing the limits circumscribing the certainty of human knowledge, a refusal of dogmatic assertions of the truth. Both epistemologically and ontologically he is an enigma.

The novel at least implicitly, then, explores the creative process of fiction-making in defiance of verisimilitude and, moreover, is at pains to negate any purely material conception of the world, and any belief in the possibility of arriving at the truth about the world, by probing the boundaries of the physical and the non-physical, the real and the fantastic. In *Misericordia*, moreover, the creative capacities of the protagonist, Benina, and her doubts about them, are bound up with the social and religious implications of the work, themselves conceived in terms of the inseparability of the spiritual and the material that underpins Galdós's peculiar version of naturalism. Benina consistently professes her faith in at least the possibility of miracles, and her belief that all originates in God: 'y aunque no había visto ningún milagro, esperaba verlo el mejor día' (69), or 'los sueños, los sueños, digan lo que quieran, son también de Dios' (127). Quotations abound, particularly in the latter half of the novel, which underscore the impossibility of determining what is real and true: 'esta vaga fluctuación entre lo real y lo imaginativo' (139), 'la extraña confusión y mezcolanza de lo real y lo imaginado' (171), '¿cuántas cosas se tuvieron por mentira y luego salieron verdades?' (73). In most of these cases, the emphasis is not upon the creative capacities of the imagination, but on the uncertainties of knowing or arriving at the truth. The presence of this concern implies rather than denies a link with the world of history. We have become accustomed to versions of modernism which divorce art and literature from social and ethical concerns, and this is precisely the basis of the postmodernist critique of modernist autonomy and of those versions of postmodernism which postulate a new engagement with politics, for exmple, through theories of desire, of the bodily. Social concerns are not absent, however, from allegedly modernist writing, and the combination of non-realist features with social engagement imparts to much of it its Janus-like, transitional quality. Moreover, since the religious question, so central to everything in late nineteenth-century Spain, is so obviously woven into the fabric of the novel, and the theme of religious tolerance, in opposition to dogma, is worked out in different ways, one might ask whether the whole issue of truth and falsehood, however much it is conceived in artistic terms, is not also of vital political and social relevance. In *Misericordia*, the exploration of imagination seems integrated into Galdós's analysis of contemporary society.

As is well known, *Misericordia* engages with familiar Galdosian themes: illusion and self-delusion, the ambiguities of the conflict between moral behaviour and survival and self-interest, the hollowness of Restoration society, the pernicious effects of formulistic religiosity, the vitality of the *pueblo*, the decline into decadence of the middle classes described in this novel, with the customary vocabulary of neurosis, illness and morbidity, especially from Chapters VI to XIX. Even if it is not so explicit as in other novels, there is in *Misericordia* a sustained parallel between private and public. Historical events are mentioned at specific points, though often as a one-line reference, such as the marriage of the Queen, the death of Zorrilla, the African Wars, changes of ministries, and so forth. The fundamental historical thread is the relationship between religion and society manifest in the alliance between the Church and the conservative and commercial bourgeoisie. The interdependence of the two in economic terms, with the consequent underside of the economic system they sustain, the marginalised poor, is suggested metonymically not only in the locations of the novel, churches, lower middle class homes, but in the frequently telling detail. For example, Almudena and Benina sit under the statue of Mendizábal, unaware of who he is, in an unmistakable allusion to the first, ecclesiastical, *desamortización*, with its economic consequences, in particular the consolidation of the large estates and the worsening of the conditions of the rural poor. It is difficult to accept Peter Bly's conclusion that this reflects both Benina's 'dissociation from the flow of contemporary history' and Galdós's 'almost total antihistoricism'.[23] On the contrary, this episode, apparently incidental, establishes a link between the Church, the middle classes and wealth, and the condition of the poor, unaware perhaps of the economic laws governing their state. Galdós, at this stage of his career, may be at his most despairing about the state of Spanish society, but history is not absent. The theme returns with the invention, or appearance of don Romualdo, for it is the Church, in the form of this cleric, which is the instrument by which Paca's family is restored to some kind of economic security, although, as we have seen, the effects are not entirely beneficial, and more importantly, the *pueblo*, in the persons of Benina and Almudena, on whom the middle class, in the person of Paca relied, are excluded from this new prosperity. There is a particular irony in having the real don Romualdo bring news of the family's inheritance, since it was the invented Romualdo who provided the cover for Benina's charity and support for Paca and her family.

In his treatment of this theme, Galdós explores the social question through the prism of charity, and in the context of the religious debates of the late nineteenth century in Spain. For the conservatives of the Catholic revival, the social question, in the words of Raymond Carr, 'derived from the increased secularisation of society which had produced a godless working class'.[24] Ronald Cueto has commented forcefully on the dangers consequent upon the failure to draw a distinction between secularisation and secularism in a country like Spain.[25] In *Misericordia*, the practice of charity, predicated upon a belief that authority is being undermined through increased secularisation, reflects the state's reliance on Catholic charitable organisations to alleviate poverty in the context of soothing homilies, as in Trujillo's 'sermoncillo gangoso'(11), a policy which is both paternalistic and patronising. The presence of Guillermina Pacheco is a reminder of the role of Catholic middle-class ladies whose charity is linked to their proselytising among the traditionally non-practising poor. References to hospices like La Misericordia, and grimmer institutions like El Pardo, are reminders of the Church's role in welfare, or charity. The opening pages of the novel are of course a good illustration of the connection between bourgeois materialism and conventional devotional practice. Don Carlos uses holy water and then goes to the chapel of Nuestra Señora de la Blanca. Whether such a Virgin exists or not, the irony of the pun is unmistakable. Moreover, in his devotion to San Lesmes, a saint who according to tradition died through the effort of distributing wheat to the poor, Don Carlos reveals the degree of his self-delusion, and the fact that his journey ends in the chapel of the Cristo de la Fe links faith and materialism, the Church and capital.[26] The brutalising effects of the charity he practises are evident throughout the novel, as the poor are inspired with the values of selfishness, dishonesty, and greed. In Benina's words, 'en dondequiera que vivan los hombres, o verbigracia, mujeres, habrá ingratitud, egoísmo, y unos que manden a los otros y les cojan la voluntad' (230). The myth of a lower class reformed through a policy of recatholicisation is exposed. It marks a failure of the rational and the utilitarian. The kind of spirituality found in Benina and Almudena is devoid of rational support, just as Almudena's religious tolerance stands in contrast to the dogmatic adherence to the notion of the one, true religion as promulgated in the Catholic catechism of the time, and since. Moreover, in his depiction of the Jew Almudena's faith, Galdós emphasises its simple, sensuous, and folkloric nature, in contrast, for example, to the more intellectual Judaism of Daniel Morton in *Gloria*. The religious syncretism embodied in Almudena, and the non-rational foundations of his behaviour, however eccentric, are somehow more appealing than the existing economic and ideological bases of Spanish society. It is difficult then to separate the wider concerns of *Misericordia* from contemporary social and religious concerns, and rather than see the work as either realist or meta-fictional, it seems more appropriate to see its hybrid character as growing out of a number of related but differentiated ideas.

Given that *Misericordia* shuns a full-blooded naturalism, it might be expected to appeal to the adherents of idealism in literature. Nineteenth-century debates about realism and idealism were of course inseparable from religious controversies, as Marta M. Campomar demonstrates.[27] If realism was attacked by traditionalists for its concentration on the ugly and sordid and consequent neglect of man's spiritual needs and unseen realities, equally any stress on the unbridled imagination could lead to fantasy, which was dangerous and potentially sinful. In

Catholicism, aesthetics, especially Thomist aesthetics, was associated with the intellect, with reason, and in thinking through some of the dangers of idealism for a Catholic realism, some thinkers rejected a 'falso idealismo' in favour of some notion of 'lo verosímil'. Such a realism would naturally be quite different from an immoral and secular naturalism, but it would be real in the sense that anything fantastic, which could not be grasped by reason, would be banished from art, since God's creation was by definition rational and orderly. But Benina openly questions this, and especially the rational basis of truth, when she says: 'Inventa una cosas que luego salen verdad, o las verdades, antes de ser verdades, un suponer, han sido mentiras muy gordas' (238). Although Benina's examples of this are odd, it is at least an unorthodox formulation of the relationship between truth and error. However much *Misericordia* may seem to transcend the cold, clinical dissection of the material world associated with naturalism in its insistence on the spiritual dimension of human experience, its methods also stand in distinction to the principles of aesthetic orthodoxy promulgated in the nineteenth century in which creativity is inseparable from religion. In Galdós's novel, an imaginative, life-giving creativity which goes beyond the conventional, and not traditional religion, is the site of redemption.

The modernity of *Misericordia*, then, on one level, is its engagement with the religious questions of the day and its opposition to traditional values and, on another, its engagement with conventional representation. Its proper location in terms of literary history, however, is not on an axis between representation and autonomy, but in terms of its attitude to the fictional as a mode of engagement with the world. Galdós's text may be said to articulate the modern conviction that with the collapse of the redemptive framework of Christianity and of the rationalist Enlightenment belief in the possibility of human progress, literature, in its imaginative transactions with the finite limits of the material world, can fill the void at the centre of our systems of sense-making, can provide the 'imaginative expansion of human sympathy and empathy as a basis for that social and political solidarity no longer available in the philosophical, historical or religious grand narratives of the past', in the words of Patricia Waugh, written from a quite different perspective, but which seem applicable to this work.[28] From the Enlightenment, the three pillars of modernity have been reason, individual freedom and the notion of change towards progress. Galdós's view of history as purposeful progress in *Misericordia* betrays at least a degree of scepticism, with the failure of the politics of the Restoration, the decadence of the bourgeoisie, their alliance with a resurgent, if defensive, traditionalist Catholicism. But this is not the same as the antihistoricism we have come to identify with Modernism and which Frederic Jameson refers to as 'the disappearance of a sense of history'.[29] This is not the creation of artistic structures outside of time and space, a recourse to models of synchronicity and spatial form, the divergence between art and world, which lead to the extremes of formalism in which content is only a pretext for form. If Galdós does not deny or discredit history, his approach to reason is at least ambivalent. Similarly, while the excesses of the imagination may be exposed as fantasy, areas of man's creativity beyond reason are proclaimed as a kind of liberation and as containing the seeds of a more compassionate human community. The imaginative is not divorced from the existential. While Galdós's treatment of these concerns is, as I have indicated, rooted in the debates of the nineteenth century, they also connect with our most pressing postmodern concerns about knowability and decidability.

Even a superficial reading of *Misericordia* will reveal that Galdós repudiates any dogmatic view of what is true. Critics have often commented on the shifting nature of the mode of narration, a frequent occurrence in Galdós, as distinct from the classic omniscient mode which holds all other voices in any narrative together from the authority of its own standpoint. The construction of the novel involves a displacement of its authority from the centre to the margins. The narrator, on occasion, sacrifices omniscience, claims ignorance, comments on his linguistic inadequacies, and on others, calls attention to his structuring role ('atando ahora el cabo de esta narración'), to his status as 'historiador' and the text as a 'puntual historia' or a 'verídica historia'. This injection of uncertainty about representation of course extends to the replacement of the narrator by other narrators who compete for control of the material. Paca disputes Benina's authorial control over the narrative of don Romualdo and, on one possible interpretation at least, Benina seems to create the character who completes Galdós's novel. While the text reminds us that it is the imposition of an order by an author, we also detect a decentring of the author as the source of his discourse through the creation, and also appropriation, within the text of other texts in pursuit of a complex intertextuality. Among others, these texts are those of naturalist discourse, the picaresque and the Bible. In highlighting the provisional nature of their constructions of the real, *Misericordia* exhibits a distrust of the authority of the act of narration which many have identified as one of the hallmarks not only of modernity, but also of postmodernity.

Misericordia undoubtedly needs to be placed within the tradition of post-realist writing, the adversary of naive mimesis, committed to the belief that the real is a pre-existing situation which can be faithfully described in language, as distinct from an effect of rhetoric. If, in its movement away from the premises of nineteenth-century realism, the novel suggests that there are no limits to the domain of the imagination and its representations, it does not claim any empirically demonstrable validity for these.

But it does suggest that the worlds of the imagination have a kind of truth, even if this truth cannot be verified, and that Benina's imaginings, and the purposeful action which follows from them, have a value. If this involves an assertion of transcendence, then this is to say that *Misericordia* does not share the cultural pessimism of some versions of modernism and postmodernism. It might share with the latter an awareness of the power of discourses of domination, and recognise their fictionality, but its own imagined discourse can assert a freedom from them, even if it is fictional. On this kind of reading, *Misericordia* is being made to look, anachronistically, like a postmodern text. That is not what is intended, but in considering the modernity of Galdós's novel, it is difficult to avoid reading modernism through postmodernism. One is reminded of Lyotard's famous remark that the postmodern 'is undoubtedly part of the modern....a work can become modern only if it is first postmodern. Postmodernism thus understood is not modernism at its end but in the nascent state, and this state is constant'.[30] While its publication in 1897 points the literary critic to constructing a novel like *Misericordia* through the paradigm of Modernism, the nature of the text suggests that a chronological or periodising account will be inadequate. Moreover, the version of modernism, which has come into dominant use through Anglo-American criticism, and against which postmodernism is said to react, emphasises a retreat from history, elitism and, above all, artistic autonomy. The creation of don Romualdo, and the degree of self-referentiality in the novel, have led some critics to resolve its contradictions in terms of the self-sufficiency of the artistic work. Galdós, one imagines, would have agreed that while art is not the world, it is still in the world. To my mind, the imaginative concerns and non-realist aspects of *Misericordia*, which mark it out as a modern text, are not divorced from its worldly preoccupations which are bound up with profoundly religious questions raised by the age of modernity. While we would not wish to claim that *Misericordia* is a modernist text, it does, in various ways and in its own unmistakably Spanish context, engage imaginatively with the pressing problems of modernity and, for this reason alone, has serious claims to our attention in our own *fin-de-siglo*.

NOTES

1. Elaine Showalter, *Sexual Anarchy: Gender and Culture at the Fin de Siècle*, London: Bloomsbury, 1991, p.1.

2. Holbrook Johnson, *The Eighteen Nineties*, Brighton: Harvester, 1976, p.31.

3. For the importance of religious modernism in the wider intellectual context of Spain in the early century, see *Religión y Literatura en el Modernismo Español 1902-1914*, Co-ordinated by Luis de Llera, Madrid: Editorial Actas, 1994.

4. Ricardo Gullón, *Galdós, novelista moderno*, Madrid: Taurus, 1963.

5. *Insula. Revista de Letras y Ciencias Humanas*, Madrid, No.561, September 1993.

6. J. E. Varey, 'Charity in Misericordia', *Galdós Studies*, Ed. J. E. Varey, London: Tamesis, 1970.

7. Galdós's critical writings can be most easily consulted in. *Galdós. Ensayos de crítica literaria*, Ed. L. Bonet, Barcelona: Península, 1972.

8. Nicholas G. Round, 'Misericordia: Galdosian Realism's "Last Word"', in *A Sesquicentennial Tribute to Galdós 1843-1993*, Ed. Linda M. Willem, Newark Delaware: Juan de la Cuesta, 1993, pp. 155-72. Professor Round states unambiguously that the appearance of don Romualdo 'requires – and has – no metafictional status. The realistic assumption remains intact.' (p.170).

9. Germán Gullón, 'Misericordia: un milagro "realista"', *Letras de Deusto*, 8 (1974), 171-85.

10. Scott Lash, 'Postmodernity and Desire', *Theory and Society*, 14 (1985), 3.

11.   *Misericordia. Por B. Pérez Galdós. Con un prefacio del Autor escrito especialmente para esta edición.* Paris: Thomas Nelson & Sons, undated. Galdós's Preface is dated February, 1913.

12.   Joaquín Casalduero, 'Significado y forma en Misericordia', *PMLA*, 59 (1944), 1104-1110 (Reprinted in *Vida y obra de Galdós: 1843-1920.* Madrid: Gredos, 1951); Angel del Río, 'Aspectos del pensamiento moral de Galdós", *Cuadernos Americanos*, 6 (1943), 147-68.

13.   Among this latter group, the most prominent are, in addition to Gullón above, Nicole Malaret, 'Misericordia, una reflexión sobre la creación literaria', *Anales galdosianos*, 17 (1982), 89-95 and John W. Kronik, 'Misericordia as Metafiction', *Homenaje a Antonio Sánchez Barbudo: Ensayos de literatura española moderna*, Ed. Benito Brancaforte, Edward R. Mulvihill and Roberto G. Sánchez. Madison: University of Wisconsin, 1981, pp. 37-49.

14.   Casalduero, 'Significado y forma en Misericordia'.

15.   Gustavo Correa, *El simbolismo religioso en las novelas de Pérez Galdós*, Bogotá: Instituto Caro y Cuervo, 1967.

16.   Leon Livingstone, 'Interior Duplication and the Problem of Form in the Modern Spanish Novel', *PMLA*, 73 (1958), 398-99.

17.   Mariano López-Sanz, *Naturalismo y espiritualismo en la novelística de Galdós y Pardo Bazán*, Madrid: Pliegos, 1985.

18.   *Misericordia.* Buenos Aires: Espasa-Calpe, 1968, p.176. All references are to this edition and will henceforth be incorporated in the text.

19.   R. H. Russell, 'The Christ Figure in Misericordia', *Anales galdosianos* (1967), 103-30.

20. Peter A. Bly, *Galdós' Novel of the Historical Imagination: A Study of the Contemporary Novels*. Liverpool: Francis Cairns, 1983, p.172.

21. Kronik, 42.

22. Rupert C. Allen, 'Pobreza y neurosis en Misericordia de Pérez Galdós', *Hispanófila*, 33 (1968), 35-47.

23. Bly, p. 173.

24. Raymond Carr, *Spain 1808-1898*, Oxford: Oxford University Press, 1966.

25. Ronald Cueto, 'Our Lady, the French Revolution and Don Benito Pérez Galdós', in *A Face Not Turned to the Wall. Essays on Hispanic Themes for Gareth Alban Davies*. Edited by C. A. Longhurst, Leeds: The University of Leeds, 1987, p.167. See also his important work on Lorca's theatre, *Souls in Anguish: Religion and Spirituality in Lorca's Theatre*, Leeds: Leeds Iberian Papers, Trinity & All Saints, 1994, p.18.

26. The importance of religious references in this work hardly needs to be stated, but Ronald Cueto is surely right to remind us that in dealing with a writer such as Galdós, 'unavoidably Catholic imagery and iconography need to be decoded, if works of art that are the products of a once preponderantly Catholic culture are to be properly understood' in 'Our Lady, the French Revolution and Don Benito Pérez Galdós', in *A Face Not Turned to the Wall. Essays on Hispanic Themes for Gareth Alban Davies*. Edited by C. A. Longhurst, Leeds: The University of Leeds, 1987, p.167.

27. See Marta M. Campomar, 'Menéndez Pelayo and Neo-Catholic Aesthetics in the Nineteenth Century', in *A Face Not Turned to the Wall. Essays on Hispanic Themes for Gareth Alban Davies*. Edited by C. A. Longhurst, Leeds: The University of Leeds, 1987, p.171-92.

28.   Patricia Waugh, *Practising Postmodernism/Reading Modernism*. London: Edward Arnold, 1992, p.6.

29.   Frederic Jameson, 'Postmodernism and the Consumer Society', in E. Ann Kaplan, ed., *Postmodernism and its Discontents*, London: Verso, 1988, p. 28.

30.   Jean-François Lyotard, *The Postmodern Condition: a Report on Knowledge*. Manchester: Manchester University Press, 1984, p. 79.

J. ANTONIO RUIZ HERNANDO

E.T.S. Arquitectura de Madrid

LOS SEGOVIANOS Y SU PATRIMONIO MONUMENTAL EN LA SEGUNDA MITAD DEL SIGLO XIX

Las desamortizaciones del siglo XIX significaron un grave atentado contra el patrimonio histórico artístico de España, uno de los más ricos de Europa, pero fueron al tiempo el inicio de una tarea de estudio y recuperación del mismo. Las siguientes líneas intentan acercarnos a la realidad de una pequeña capital de provincia, de un esplendoroso pasado, pero sumida por entonces en una profunda decadencia, que ha merecido en nuestros días la consideración de Patrimonio de la Humanidad.

El 11 de octubre de 1844, se declaraba Monumento Nacional el acueducto de Segovia (1). Días antes, el 2 del mismo mes, el Director General de Obras Públicas se lo había comunicado al Gobernador Civil, quien a su vez lo había hecho al Ayuntamiento: *"Gratitud profunda abriga la Corporacion Municipal por la proyectada declaracion de Monumento Artistico á favor del Acueducto de esta Capital, que por su galanura y magnificencia de su construccion viene siendo desde hace siglos la admiracion de cuantos acuden á visitarle, merced á la fama europea que ha alcanzado. Asi es que el Ayuntamiento á quien el coloso Acueducto Segoviano sirve de timbre, no cumpliria como bueno si no se apresurase á manifestar su inmenso agradecimiento al Gobierno de S.M. (q.D.g.) por el proyecto de declarar monumento Artistico al que lo es sin rival desde el momento de su atrevida construccion"* (2).

Sin embargo, la Academia de la Historia iba a echar un jarro de agua fria sobre el municipio, pues a la Real Orden de declaración se acompañaba el siguiente informe, cuyo texto aún desconocían los ediles: *"Ninguna persona medianamente culta hubiera podido figurarse jamás que para mantener libre de vandálicos atentados el célebre Acueducto romano de Segovia, fuera menester ampararlo con declaraciones oficiales; pero es lo cierto que ha llegado en nuestros días á tal extremo el vergonzoso desconocimiento de su importancia arqueológica y de su arrogante belleza artística, que con razón se teme verlo barbaramente afeado con construcciones adosadas á su veneranda mole, si no se dicta una medida que lo salve de tales profanaciones.*

Circula por Segovia el rumor de que aquel Ayuntamiento, que ya en época no lejana había dado motivo de reclamaciones de la Real Academia de San Fernando, por ciertas obras de mal llamada <u>restauración</u> *que permitió ejecutar en el famoso acueducto, va á consentir que se haga alguna edificación arrimada á sus pilares; y considerando esta Academia lo grave de semejante proyecto, la triste idea que con su realización se daría á la Europa civilizada del actual estado de nuestra cultura, y la necesidad de precaver para lo sucesivo actos de igual índole, en sesión de 3 del corriente acordó dirigirse respetuosamente a V.E., como tenemos la honra de verificarlo, rogándole que se sirva inclinar el ánimo de S.M., á que sea declarado monumento nacional histórico el mencionado* <u>Acueducto de Segovia</u>*, poniéndolo de esta manera bajo la custodia ó inspección de la Comision de Monumentos de la provincia, sin que tenga aquel Ayuntamiento acción para dictar a cerca de él medidas que puedan afectar á su integridad y belleza artística"* (3). *En la sesión municipal de 22 de octubre el alcalde lo pone en conocimiento de la corporación, y añade "que el citado informe es agresivo para el Ayuntamiento actual y sus antecesores y aun para los Segovianos, porque se funda en inexactitudes é inconveniencias de tanto bulto que atacan la dignidad y decoro* *del Ayuntamiento y de Segovia, siendo asi que si precisamente hoy que el Acueducto existe es debido al venerando respeto que de siempre se tiene á tan grandioso portento arqueologico, por el que nada ha hecho la academia de la historia ni otra alguna mas que la primera en la actualidad ofender gravemente á Segovia y sus Corporaciones populares"*. Al ayuntamiento se le había herido en lo más profundo.

No sólo el Ayuntamiento, que cuatro años antes había elaborado un proyecto para que apareciera, *"en toda su magestuosa grandeza un monumento importante en el mundo, rarísimo en España y bien conservado como ninguno que se llama el Acueducto de Segovia"*, se sentía vejado; también la prensa local lo sintió como algo propio y "El Adelantado", "El Pardillo", y "La Tempestad" -que llegará a decir que los segovianos hubieran *"preferido se omitiera la declaración"*- saldrán en defensa de la dignidad ofendida de los conciudadanos. Pero fue sobre todo la Sociedad Económica Segoviana de Amigos del País la que, en su revista de 11 de noviembre de 1844, publicó un encendido alegato, firmado por Ezequiel González, que comienza parodiando las primeras palabras del informe de la Academia: *"Ninguna persona medianamente culta hubiera podido figurarse jamás que una Corporación de sabios, que una Corporación tan respetabilísima como lo es la Academia de la Historia, fuera capaz de estampar en un informe suyo, en un documento que había de publicarse en el periódico oficial del Gobierno y ser leido en todo el mundo culto, unas palabras tan incultas como las que dirige contra el Ayuntamiento de Segovia, y por consiguiente contra los segovianos todos. Aunque fuera cierto y exactisimo cuanto supone la Academia en su informe, nunca hubiera estado bien visto que usara de expresiones y frases impropias de la sabiduría y respetabilidad de sus ilustres miembros, y muy propias para lastimar, como han lastimado, la susceptibilidad de un pueblo y de su ilustre Ayuntamiento. ¡Y si*

245

siendo cierto los fundamentos de su informe no debía la Academia de la Historia usar semejante lenguaje, calcule el efecto que habrá producido en todos los segovianos, cuando nada hay más distante de la verdad, ni nada más injusto que lo expuesto en él!"

El asunto había trascendido más allá de la provincia y en ciudad tan lejana como Sevilla, un periódico local, La Unión Mercantil e Industrial, salía en pública defensa de Segovia. *"¡Ya quisiera la Corporacíon* sapiente *y* conservante *que sus monumentos* [se refiera a los declarados nacionales, que estaban bajo su amparo] *se parecieran al Acueducto segoviano, por lo bien conservados y atendidos!"* Es más, el 18 de noviembre, no duda en atacarla de manera bastante fuerte: *"¿Pero en qué ha dado señales de vida esa Academia?. ¿Qué obras de historia, de monumentos ó de descripciones de las preciadas joyas artísticas ha publicado?."* Y prosigue, que son justamente las personas cultas las que han de comprender y respetar a las ignorantes, *"Pero nos hemos equivocado: para hablar sin escrúpulos ni miramientos, no hay como ser académico. Es un título que vale tanto como una bula".*

La piedra había sido arrojada y el Ayuntamiento acordó acudir ante el Sr. Ministro de Fomento, pidiendo se reparase el agravio, de lo contrario, y pasado un plazo prudencial sin recibir disculpas, se entablaría contra la Academia de la Historia una demanda judicial por difamación, en los términos legales procedentes. Se daba como plazo el día 27 de noviembre. La enérgica respuesta de la corporación municipal puede entenderse mejor si tenemos en cuenta que no hacía todavía un año había sido duramente criticada, esta vez con toda razón, por Ezequiel González -quien paradojicamente ahora la defendía- por el derribo de la Puerta de San Martín.

El Ministro de Fomento hizo llegar a la Academia la protesta del Ayuntamiento y entonces ésta contestó con un escrito en que, a su pesar, se ve obligada a reconocer que cometió un error. Sin embargo, y sin duda muy pagada de si misma, desliza otras dos acusaciones. La primera referida al monumento en cuestión; la segunda a las puertas de la muralla. En 1880, dice, se habían efectuado trabajos inadecuados, e incluso *"en los pasados tiempos se consintió restaurar ese Acueducto Romano con una serie no pequeña de <u>arcos apuntados</u>"*. Por eso, aunque fuera un rumor infundado lo de adosar construcciones a los pilares del acueducto, no había que fiarse del Ayuntamiento, ¿acaso su apatía no había dejado arruinar las puertas de San Juan y de San Andrés *"que ya no existen"*?. Bien es verdad, continúa, que estas obras incorrectas partían de *"un celo generoso, pero poco ilustrado"*. Una de cal y otra de arena. No obstante la Academia, con su arrogante condescendencia, volvía a caer en el error y una vez más la revista de la Sociedad Económica Segoviana de Amigos del País, con fecha 14 de enero de 1885, arremetería contra el escrito. Aunque la cita es larga bien merece ser reproducida.

> *"Si la docta Corporación está tan enterada en toda España del estado de los edificios antiguos y de las construcciones dignas de ser conservadas por su mérito artístico, arqueológico é histórico, como da muestras de estarlo respecto á los de Segovia, entonces que dedique sus estudios y desvelos hacia otros trabajos, porque en este ramo ha entrado en una decadencia asombrosa, por falta de noticias exactas.*

> *"Pero, vamos adelante: no contenta con estas inconcebibles inexactitudes, y queriendo rebatir al Ayuntamiento el haber asegurado en su reclamación que el <u>Acueducto se conserva en toda su integridad,</u> le increpa duramente diciéndole que los arcos apuntados construidos en tiempo de la Reina Isabel la Católica, dan testimonio de lo contrario, considerando implícitamente como una profanación el haber sido restituidos en esa forma, y echando de ello la culpa, también implícitamente, al*

Municipio. Es necesario haber perdido los estribos, como se dice vulgarmente, para discurrir según lo hace en este asunto la sesuda y docta Corporación. ¿Qué culpa tiene el actual Ayuntamiento de que en vez de construirse los arcos en aquella época lejana siguiendo el estilo greco-romano del Acueducto, se reedificasen de figura apuntada?. ¿Qué culpa tiene el actual Ayuntamiento de que Isabel I concediese el permiso para reedificar los arcos con la precisa condición de intervenir en todo lo referente á este asunto el Prior del Convento del Parral, Fray Pedro de Mesa?. ¿Qué culpa tiene el actual Ayuntamiento de que en vez de nombrar un Arquitecto para dirigir aquella obra, se nombrase á un fraile, como se nombró á Fray Juan de Escobedo?. ¿Qué culpa tiene el actual Ayuntamiento, que aquel fraile no tuviese el gusto arquitectónico necesario para reedificar los arcos al igual de todos los demás del Acueducto, siguiendo é imitando su estilo y forma en todo?. Pues esas culpas, esas faltas y esos defectos, se las arroja al rostro la Academia de la Historia con la misma injusticia con que la increpó antes por haber derribado el Arco de San Juan y la Puerta de San Andrés, que estan de pié [por poco tiempo el primero] y lanzando una carcajada homérica contra las inexactitudes de la científica Corporación.

"Por lo demás, dada la época azarosa en que se reedificaron aquellos arcos y las circunstancias de su construcción, parecería natural que la Academia no sacase ahora á relucir los defectos de ésta, y menos que echase la culpa de ello al actual Ayuntamiento...

"No está menos ligera al sacar de todo ésto la consecuencia de que el Acueducto no se conserva en toda su integridad, motejando al Ayuntamiento por haberlo afirmado así, cuando los arcos apuntados dicen lo contrario. Pues diga lo que quiera la Academia, discurre con muy poca lógica, toda vez que el actual Municipio y sus antecesores desde Isabel la Católica, no tuvieron culpa de que el Rey de Toledo, Ali-Maamum, destruyera

los treinta y seis arcos que dicha Reina reconstruyó después en forma apuntada...

"Y si tan feos le parecen esos arcos á la Academia, y si su forma apuntada rompe la armonía y la belleza artística de tan majestuosa fábrica, como así es la verdad, en vez de echar la culpa de ello al actual Ayuntamiento, muy injusta é ilogicamente, ha debido hace muchísimos años proponer al Gobierno reparar ese gran defecto, pidiendo que dichos treinta y seis arcos apuntados se fueran reemplazando por otros de estilo greco-romano, lo cual se hubiera conseguido insensiblemente en treinta y seis años, haciendo un arco en cada uno de ellos. De este modo hubiera procedido con lógica la docta corporación, habría dado muestras de interesarse verdaderamente por la antigua integridad del Acueducto, y no hubiera cometido la gran injusticia de achacar al actual Ayuntamiento culpas que no ha cometido.

"Aunque es un poco tarde, y no tendría el mérito de la iniciativa, todavía es tiempo de proponerlo. Hágalo así, desde luego; ejerza su poderosa influencia cerca del Gobierno; consiga la reforma de los arcos apuntados, y habrá dado una prueba práctica de su buen gusto artístico y de verdadero interés por la belleza de esta magnífica y veneranda mole, la cual hasta ahora nada tiene que agradecer á la científica Corporación.

"Hágalo, pues, así, pronto, muy pronto, y se lo agradeceremos los segovianos y habrá imitado el celo de éstos, los cuales, sin ser Academia de la Historia, reedificaron diez arcos en 1867, desde el convento de la Concepción hasta cerca del Instituto, cuya redificación la hizo su Ayuntamiento con dinero propio, y no de figura apuntada, sino guardando el orden greco-romano del incomparable Acueducto".

En fecha tan temprana como 1844, el mismo año precisamente en que se declaraba el primer Monumento Nacional, que fue la catedral de León, ya comienza una cierta preocupación gubernamental por el acueducto. Efectivamente, la Academia de Bellas Artes de San Fernando se dirige a la recién creada Comisión de Monumentos Histórico Artísticos de la Provincia (de Segovia), pidiéndola que destapen dos arcos que se encontraban tapiados a la altura del convento de La Concepción. Dos años despues, ordena la reina que no se hagan obras en el acueducto hasta que no haya dinero para restaurarle integramente.

El acueducto era un edificio conocido desde siempre y su celebridad hacía que muchos viajeros extranjeros se acercaran a Segovia con el exclusivo fin de admirarle. En su *De rebus hispaniae,* el arzobispo Jiménez de Rada (s.XIII) escribe: *"Edificó [Hispán] una ciudad ...[que] se llama Segovia, donde construyó un acueducto que, sirviendose de una admirable fábrica, surte a la ciudad de caudales de agua".* Desde entonces hasta nuestros días, no ha habido historiador o viajero que no le haya dedicado unas líneas.

Jamás el Ayuntamiento había dejado de prestar particular atención al edificio y gracias a ello aún está en pie, no hay sino que leer los libros de acuerdos del Ayuntamiento desde el siglo XVI hasta nuestros días. Le había movido, en tiempos pasados, el concepto de utilidad, pues de él dependía la existencia de Segovia, pero no le eran ajenas la gracilidad y magestuosidad que derrocha; de hecho había sido elegido como escudo de la ciudad.

De las obras llevadas a cabo en el edificio nos vamos a detener sólo en aquellas inmediatas a la declaración monumental, obras que podrían haber provocado la susceptibilidad de la Academia, sobre todo las de 1856 y 1868. La primera, cuyo proyecto se debía a Miguel Arévalo, arquitecto municipal, habría consistido en reedificar cuatro arcos macizados, incluidos entre los que había reedificado Juan de Escobedo entre 1484 y 1489, arcos que se disponía a volver a levantar de medio punto y no apuntados como había hecho Escobedo. También eliminaba las cerbatanas que tanto daño causaban. La restauración de 1868, debida al arquitecto Nicomedes Perier se centraba en construir "*tres arcos de nuevo*" y desmontar y volver a montar "*dos arcos que se hallaban desplomados para unirlos a la nueva construcción*" (son los cinco arcos frente al antiguo convento de La Concepción, que llevan la fecha incisa en uno de los sillares).

No deja de ser un tanto extraño que la Academia de la Historia protestara por unas reformas que habían contado con la aquiescencia oficial. La proyectada por Arévalo lo había sido a instancias de la Comisión Central y la de Perier había sido aprobada por la propia Academia y por la de Bellas Artes de San Fernando (4). Dos años antes, Ramón Depret, secretario de la Comisión Provincial, había redactado un detallado informe en el que, entre otras cosas, pedía la supresión del tráfico rodado, excepto en dos arcos protegidos por guardacantones – "*a fin de evitar lo que solo esta Comisión pudo comprender cuando colocándose en la parte más elevada del puente sentía alli el ballesteo deque al paso de los carruajes sufría todo ese respetable e imponente monumento*", previsión que se adelanta en cien años a las medidas adoptadas recientemente por el Ayuntamiento. Pero sobre todo extraña la acusación vertida por San Fernando al decir "*que en las obras de restauracion que se han emprendido en el celebre acueducto de esta ciudad se había empezado a emplear el arco de ojiva*", lo que es inexacto. Los arcos que volvieron a levantarse no se hicieron apuntados, como en una teoría actual de restauración hubiera sido lo correcto, para respetar la obra del XV, sino de medio punto, tal y como entonces se entendía debía de hacerse (5). Error en que persistía increiblemente la Academia de la Historia en 1884, al momento de evacuar el famoso informe.

Estos hechos no tendrían mayor importancia, y no pasarían de ser una mera anécdota local, si no reflejaran la situación, cuando menos ambigua, por la que atravesaba España en todo lo concerniente al patrimonio artístico (6). Por aquellas fechas, Segovia contaba con un patrimonio arquitectónico sorprendente, pero eran años en que aún se desconocía buena parte de la historia de la arquitectura española y la atención de las comisiones provinciales, y en este caso la de Segovia, se centraba especialmente en el aspecto arqueológico, pues el peso de la Ilustración, y consecuente amor por el mundo clásico, había condicionado las primeras actuaciones de salvaguardia del patrimonio artístico y cultural español, hasta el punto de tener que dictarse órdenes prohibiendo a las comisiones que unicamente se preocuparan por la investigación arqueológica, en sentido estricto, olvidado o menospreciando el resto de los monumentos (7).

Curiosamente, en Segovia esta tendencia en favor de la clásico encontraba plena justificación en el acueducto, uno de los monumentos señeros de la arqueología romana en Europa. Para la Comisión provincial era el *"objeto privilegiado"*, el primero y más importante de sus monumentos -sin duda lo es- y en el volcaba su atención, no obstante ¿qué opinión le merecían los otros monumentos y la ciudad en sí?.

Cuando Isidoro Bosarte publica su obra Viaje Artístico a varios pueblos de España (1804), de las 96 páginas dedicadas a Segovia, treinta y siete lo son al acueducto y a los verracos celtibéricos; veinte a objetos muebles, once al monasterio del Parral y otras once a la catedral. Tan sólo menciona el resto de los templos, de los que dice ser góticas las iglesias románicas. La arqueología sigue predominando. Un cambio muy sustancial se produce con la obra de José Amador de los Rios, "Estudios artísticos. Monumentos anteriores al siglo XIII. Periodo Bizantino. Iglesias de Segovia", El Siglo Pintoresco (1847, t. III) en que escribe: *"El poco aprecio que han merecido á nuestros artistas y escritores cuantas producciones no se han acomodado estrictamente á los principios proclamados como absolutos, falseando la historia de las artes y hundiendo en el desdén común multitud de obras de grande estima, ha sido causa de que se* *hayan estas visto con el mayor abandono ... Conforme á aquellas preocupaciones que más que nunca se dejaron conocer a fines del último siglo por efecto de la reaccion verificada contra el Churrerismo [Churrigueresco], todos los viajeros que han escrito de Segovia, han desdeñado, cuando no despreciado enteramente, multitud de obras dignas en verdad del mayor estudio y que formando, por decirlo así, un bello conjunto, dan á la antigua capital de la **Estremadura Castellana,** un carácter peculiar que la hace distinguir entre la mayor parte de las ciudades españolas".* Y si bien Amador de los Rios comete un error, del todo punto disculpable, al decir que las iglesias de Segovia guardan una gran semejanza con las asturianas y de que San Millán es *"tal vez la más suntuosa y bella producción de las artes españolas en el siglo X",* su apreciación de que el conjunto de las mismas es lo que singulariza a la ciudad es de la mayor importancia, aunque reduzca su estudio a las notables. Años después José María Quadrado recogerá en su célebre libro noticias sobre todas.

La atención de la Comisión se centraba en el Acueducto, pero, a sugerencias de la Comisión Central, también habría de velar por la Vera Cruz (S.XIII) y por los monasterios de Santa María del Parral, Santa Cruz y San Francisco, todos del siglo XV, es decir aquellos edificios que citaron Ponz (1787) y Bosarte, pero no de aquellos otros que como San Agustín, La Merced y los Huertos no había llamado la atención de los viajeros, en especial los dos últimos. No quedaban bajo su amparo ni la catedral ni el Alcázar, por estar en servicio y no haber sido desamortizados.

La reorganización parroquial de Segovia, a principios de la década de los cuarenta, había suprimido el culto de algunas iglesias cuya feligresía había sido reagrupada. Esta medida administrativa había supuesto el cierre de San Nicolás, San Quirce, San Facundo, San Román, San Sebastián, San Pablo y San Juan, todas románicas y situadas en el recinto amurallado.

Los años de abandono las había ido deteriorando, por lo que, en 1859 y a propuesta de la comisión de Policía Urbana y Ornato Público del Ayuntamiento, se pedía la demolición de San Quirce, San Román, San Pablo y San Facundo, iglesia esta última que servía de Museo -más bien de almacén- de las pinturas y otros objetos procedentes de la desamortización. Con sus piedras podría restaurarse la portada de San Juan, a lo que se opuso la Comisión Central, no por evitar el derribo sino porque no correspondían al mismo estilo.

En verdad, y aunque se alegara su mal estado de conservación para acometer tal atentado, las iglesias debían de gozar de relativa salud, pues San Quirce, salvada de la demolición, es hoy en día sede de la Academia de Historia y Arte de Segovia. No era pues, como tantas veces se dice en los informes, el estado de ruina, y consiguiente peligro público, lo que movía a derribarlas. El problema ha de verse desde otro prisma: el de la modernidad.

En 1870 era elegido arquitecto municipal Joaquín de Odriozola y Grimaud. A este arquitecto, formado en la Escuela de Arquitectura de Madrid, se le debe, en gran medida, todo lo que de decimonónico hay en la ciudad. Hombre muy de su momento, opinaba que la salida de aquella decadencia en que se encontraba postrada Segovia iba unida a la de su reforma urbana y ésta al ferrocarril. A una ciudad sin recursos economicos -la espléndida industria de paños era un recuerdo- y aislada en el centro de España le era necesaria la rápida comunicación con el exterior. Odriozola emprendió una serie de obras destinadas a la mejor fluidez del tráfico rodado y unir el centro de la ciudad con la estación de ferrocarril, muy apartada del mismo. Además, el empleo de numerosa mano de obra suponía evitar el hambre, aunque fuera por unos meses, a numerosas familias obreras.

En 1883 había proyectado la nueva alineación de la Plaza Mayor al Azoguejo por San Facundo *"y establecimiento de un travía entre ambos puntos y la Estación del camino de hierro"*. Había dado un golpe de gracia al vetusto templo. Cierto es que resistirá algunos años, habida cuenta de su condición de museo, pero en 1894 será demolida, habiendo pervivido todo este tiempo a la ruina anunciada cuarenta años antes. Es posible, que de alguna forma, también estuviera involucrado el proyecto del tranvía en el derribo de San Pablo. En 1880, año en que Odriozola proyectaba una nueva alineación para la calle de San Juan, el propietario de la iglesia solicitaba licencia de obras. El Ayuntamiento se la denegó alegando que se la vendiera a la Diputación, porque *"podría interesar su derribo al ornato y comodidad del Palacio de la Diputación Provincial"*. En 1881 se procede a derruirla, empleándose su piedra en el muro de la calle de San Juan. El tercer templo derrocado por aquellos años fue San Román, éste sin ninguna justificación, al quedar al margen de la línea del tranvia. Ya en 1858, un año antes de que se dijera que estaba en ruinas, la Dirección General de Bienes de la Nación había pedido un informe a la Comisión Provincial, que le emitió en los siguientes términos: *"No encuentra, ni artistica ni historicamente méritos suficientes para repararla y conservarla; pues uniendo su opinión a la espresada por los Sres. Arquitectos que certifican en el expediente, resulta un templo de malas formas y pequeñas dimensiones; pues aunque su origen procede de un templete bizantino* [leáse románico] *se advierte acrecentado con varias adiciones del renacimiento, que sin temor pueden clasificarse como vulgaridades de aldea, por lo que no merece fijar la atención en aquellas informes masas. Sin embargo la Comisión se hace cargo de ciertos detalles arquitectónicos, que obstenta una portada de la fachada norte, macizada por ruinosa... igual reclamación debera hacerse de los detalles de dos sarcófagos o sepulcros platerescos que contiene la predicha Yglesia y conservan cenizas de personajes ilustres del siglo XVI al XVII"*. Ya Quadrado lo había anunciado: *"No tiene tan asegurada su decrépita existencia San Román, en cuyo pequeño ábside llaman la atención los capiteles de las tres ventanas, no menos que las bellas labores en el doble arco de su entrada lateral; y mucho será que no perezcan dentro de breve plazo con la vetusta torre y con la ruinosa iglesia de que forman parte".*

El informe de la Comisión Provincial es muy elocuente, -también de San Pablo se habían salvado los sepulcros-, porque nos dice cuales eran los factores que movían a la conservación de un edificio: la arqueología (clásica); la historia, y la belleza de las formas. Habrían de pasar algunos años para que comprendiera que las partes no valen en sí y que todas las iglesias configuraban un conjunto, a modo casi de escuela local, como había dicho mucho antes Amador de los Rios. Es posible que el derribo de la puerta de San Martín y el mal estado de la torre de San Esteban, hiciera cambiar de rumbo la opinión de la Comisión.

El día 6 de julio de 1894 caía un rayo en la torre de San Esteban, calificada por Quadrado como la más bella de España en su género, aumentando el daño que había causado el mal estado de su chapitel. Carlos de Lecea, vicepresidente por entonces de la Comisión, al solicitar ayuda para reparar el daño y evitar que aumente, redacta un escrito, lleno de interés, en que por vez primera se entiende la arquitectura religiosa de la ciudad como un todo al que no puede cercenarse: *"Proverbial es entre cuantos cultivan las bellas artes, lo mismo que entre los eruditos y los aficionados á los primores arquitectonicos de la antiguedad, emblema siempre de glorias y de grandezas que pasaron, la abundancia en Segovia de obras acabadas del estilo romanico, pricipalmente en atrios, portadas, cornisas, absides, canecillos y torres de nuestros vetustos templos, que son el encanto y la admiracion de viajeros instruidos, de artistas propiamente dichos y de todo aquel que siente en su alma apasionadas inspiraciones esteticas y el grato estimulo del buen gusto.*

Poco a poco hemos visto desaparecer con dolorosa pena, la yglesia de San Roman, que se distinguia por los bellos capiteles y labores de sus ventanas y las de la puerta tapiada al lado del evangelio; la de San Pablo, notable por la linda portada; la de San Pedro de los Picos, de la que apenas queda como signo de lo que fué el arco romanico, muy bien labrado en uno de sus costados, y algun templo mas, todos ellos ornados de historicos recuerdos al par que servian de panteon de los segovianos que ennoblecieron el nombre de su patria en los siglos medios. San Quirce, San Nicolas y San Juan de los Caballeros, mas o menos antiguos que los anteriores, no tardaran en correr su misma suerte, convirtiendose en ruinas las columnas y capiteles de sus arcos, las molduras y labrados de sus cornisas, las piedras esculpidas de sus porticos y todos los caprichos, alegorias y figuras que en unas y otras se distinguen.

Ruinosa tambien la de San Facundo, analoga en la cornisa y columnas de las ventanas de su abside á alguna de las anteriores, muy en breve habra de ser derribada como medida de politica urbana, sin que de tanto desastre, de tanta destruccion y tan continuo deterioro, se libren los templos ojivales de San Francisco, cerrado al culto, y el santuario del Parral, ni el mas moderno y robusto de San Agustin, ni los cubos y torres principales de las murallas, ni siquiera la serena puerta de San Andrés..." (8).

Lecea ve con horror como la piqueta se está cebando sobre la ciudad. Cuando la Academia de la Historia criticó, erróneamente, la actuación sobre el acueducto, añadía que así mismo se habían derribado las puertas de San Juan y de San Andrés. Tampoco era cierto esto último y en la enardecida contestación formulada por la S.E.S.A.P. se aclara, con cierta ironia, que están en pie. Sin embargo poco tiempo había de resistir la primera.

La defensa del Acueducto, asumida por toda la ciudad, se apoyaba en dos valores; el de la utilidad y el de la belleza, pero sobre todo en el primero, porque si aquel se hundía, la ciudad estaba condenada. Y así lo reconocía explicitamente el Ayuntamiento. De otra manera nadie podría explicarse, cómo, ya a principios de siglo, derribó el arco que, junto al Seminario, daba paso al "castellum aquae". Y si con el Acueducto tenía cierta prevención, debido a ser mundialmente famoso, el resto de los edificios de la ciudad, salvo el Alcázar y la Catedral, le eran por completo ajenos. La puerta de San Juan fue demolida en 1887, no sin el informe favorable de Lecea, de la Comisión y de la Academia de S. Fernando. Para ésta era suficiente con salvar los escudos, pues no encontraba "*belleza ni caracter suficiente para poder caracterizarle de Monumento artistico por su conjunto ni por sus detalles... y que pertenece a la mala época de la transicion del renacimiento al estilo llamado de Churriguera*". Más paradójica resulta aún la postura del Ayuntamiento con respecto a la puerta de San Martín. En 1873, había solicitado al Ejército la cesión de dicha puerta, y de la de San Andrés, para evitar que cayeran en manos de un particular; "*quien pudiera si no destruirlas, alterarlas en tales terminos que las privara del interés que las recomienda*". Pero diez años después procedía a su derribo, con la aquiescencia de la Comisión, que ante la enérgica protesta de Ezequiel González (S.E.S.A.P.), le tilda poco menos que de necio, pues el edificio carece de todo valor y así lo ha entendido el Gobierno.

¿Cómo explicar posturas tan contradictorias?. ¿Cómo navegar por este turbulento mar del patrimonio artístico?. En julio de 1844 se había constituido la Comisión de Monumentos Histórico Artísticos de la Provincia, integrada por: José Balsera (Jefe Político), Felix Sagau (Superintendente de la fábrica de moneda); Felix Pardo Garcia (canónigo); Antolín García (deán); Marco Antonio Cabrero (diputado provincial) y Mariano

Quintanilla (profesor de dibujo en la Escuela de Nobles Artes). La Comisión se dividía en tres secciones: Arquitectura y Arqueología -cuya finalidad era hacer excavaciones-; Bibliotecas y Archivos y Escultura y Pintura. Sus miembros eran elegidos por el Jefe Político, que a su vez la presidía, y por la Diputación. En noviembre de 1844 la Comisión Central, de la que dependían las provinciales, pide que se agregue Ildefonso Vázquez de Zúñiga, arquitecto y profesor de la Escuela de Nobles Artes. En 1885, eran miembros de la Comisión: Juan Rivas Orozco, Tomás Baeza, Mariano Llovet, Joaquín de Odriozola (Arquitecto Municipal), Ildefonso Rebollo, Luis de Bustamante y Antonio Bermejo (Arquitecto Provincial).

Es cierto que a lo largo de su singladura la Comisión contó con miembros muy cultos -Depret, Somorrostro, Lecea, Baeza, etc.- pero no lo es menos que su elección era una cuestión política y que la presencia del arquitecto municipal era inquietante. Efectivamente, y como quedó de manifiesto con ocasión del derribo de la puerta de San Martín, el juicio del arquitecto municipal, guiado casi siempre por la idea de transformar y adecuar la vieja trama urbana a la vida moderna, estaba en clara oposición con la salvaguardia de los valores culturales. Y su juicio, el de una persona "culta", era asumido, salvo raras excepciones, por todos los miembros de la corporación municipal. El derribo de la puerta de San Martín se hizo con el informe favorable del Ayuntamiento, cuyo arquitecto, Joaquín de Odriozola, que era a su vez miembro de la Comisión, había proyectado una nueva alineación para la calle de Juan Bravo, con la finalidad de unir la estación de ferrocarril con el centro mediante el consabido tranvía. El proyecto fue duramente criticado por la S.E.S.A.P. y por algunos miembros de la Comisión, entre otros, Bermejo, Baeza y Llovet, pero salió adelante. Si al poder que desde el Ayuntamiento podía ejercer el arquitecto municipal, añadimos que los criterios de valoración de un edificio o de intervención sobre el mismo estaban gestándose, tendremos una idea aproximada de la forma de actuar la Comisión (9). Ahora bien, no podemos juzgarla, habida cuenta de la precariedad con que se desenvolvía en todos los órdenes. Desde luego si el monasterio de El Parral está en pie es gracias a sus desvelos.

Para concluir, ¿se llegó a intuir que tal vez la ciudad entera era digna de ser considerada Monumento Histórico?. En 1858, el Gobernador se quejaba del estado de abandono en que se hallaba Segovia y que era necesario remozarla. Un año después, sugería S.M., a raíz de una visita girada a la ciudad, la conveniencia de revocar todos los edificios, excepto *"aquellos que construidos todos de sillería caractericen un estilo de Arquitectura"*. No es momento de entrar a analizar lo que esto significa, y que es del mayor interés, sí la respuesta que los propietarios elevaron al Ministro de la Gobernación, negándose en rotundo: *"Los que abajo suscriben propietarios en la Ciudad de Segovia á V.E. con la debida consideración exponen: que el Ayuntamiento de aquella Capital llevado sin duda del buen deseo de mejorar el aspecto de la población, pero traslimitando evidentemente sus facultades con gravisimo perjuicio de la propiedad urbana, ha dispuesto que en un breve plazo y bajo las mas severas penas se revoquen y pinten las fachadas de todas las casas enluciendolas de cal y dandolas del color previamente designado por la municipalidad... Segovia, Excmo. Sr. es una de las poblaciones mas antiguas del Reyno, las construcciones tienenn alli un sello especial, que les imprime caracter, de tal modo que donde quiera que se ve un edificio con las maderas de los entramados al descubierto, formando caprichosas convinaciones y con los pisos volados, unos sobre otros avanzando sobre la calle se dice **este edificio es de construccion Segoviana**."* ¿Quienes firman la carta?: el Conde de los Villares, la Condesa viuda de Torre Velarde y de Mansilla, Joaquín de Ezpeleta, el

Marqués de Castellanos, el Conde de San Rafael, Agustina Tortosa de Gilman, Joaquín Ceballos Escalera, el Conde de Santibañez, el Marqués de San Felix, Cristobal Fernndez de Vallejo, el Conde de Superunda y la Condesa viuda de Superunda. De doce firmas, ocho son de la nobleza, que ha abandonado hace años la ciudad y sólo retorna a ella de vez en cuando. No les mueve ciertamente el gusto por la arquitectura vernácula y popular, no adoptan una postura altruista con respecto a la ciudad de sus antepasados. Pero en este alegato, al negarse a revocar las fachadas de "*construcción Segoviana*", se estaba abriendo, inconscientemente, una nueva forma de apreciación: que el "Monumento", en una población como Segovia, es la ciudad en su integridad.

NOTAS

1.   *"Real orden, declarando monumento nacional el acueducto de Segovia.*

    Excmo. Sr.: S.M. el Rey (Q.D.G.), de conformidad con lo propuesto por la Real Academia de la Historia, y teniendo en cuenta la importancia histórica y artística del acueducto de Segovia, ha tenido á bien disponer sea declarado monumento nacional encomendando su custodia é inspección á la Comisión de Monumentos de aquella provincia.

    De Real orden lo digo á V.E. para su conocimiento y efectos oportunos. Dios guarde á V.E. muchos años. Madrid, 11 de Octubre de 1884. Pidal."

Para una mejor comprensión de la presente exposición, hemos de señalar que la declaración de un edificio como Monumento Nacional, por la que éste quedaba bajo la tutela y protección del Estado, es consecuencia de las desamortizaciones que, desde la primera, promulgada el 19 de septiembre de 1798, hasta la de 1 de Mayo de 1855, pasando por la muy famosa de 1835, habían hecho peligrar seriamente el patrimonio artístico de España. La venta a particulares, y consiguiente destrucción, de monasterios y otros edificios, había alertado a las personas más cultas del país. En 1836, la Academia de Bellas Artes de San Fernando había expresado a las Cortes su preocupación sobre el tema, pidiendo se evitara *"la demolición y ruina de algunos edificios de los antiguos conventos que por sus bellas formas, su perfección artística, su grande efecto y su interés para las artes ... deben conservarse a toda costa"* (B.O.E. 7-VI-1837). A tal fin se disponía (B.O.E. 2-IV-1844) que los Jefes Políticos (Gobernadores Civiles) de cada provincia remitieran al Ministerio de la Gobernación una relación de los edificios de interés de su zona. Es obvio que, dada la incultura del momento y la dejadez de los gobernantes, la orden no pasó del papel, por eso, en el mes de Junio se dictaba una real orden en cuyo artículo primero se decía: *"Habrá en cada provincia una comisión de **Monumentos*** *históricos y artísticos, compuesta de cinco personas inteligentes y celosas por la conservación de nuestras antigüedades*", comisión que a partir de 1854 pasó a depender de la Comisión Central de Madrid, que a su vez fue suprimida e incorporada en la Real Academia de Bellas Artes de San Fernando en 1857. A ellas les estaba encomendada la catalogación, estudio y defensa de todos los edificios históricos "*que habiendo correspondido a las Ordenes religiosas y demás corporaciones suprimidas, son hoy de la pertenencia del Estado*". Para evitar la destrucción de un inmueble de interés se llegó a la solución de declararlo "Monumento Nacional", recayendo tal condición por vez primera en la catedral de León (agosto de 1844), cuyas obras de restauración correrían a cargo del erario público, dada la falta de medios de su cabildo.

El nombramiento de los miembros de las comisiones, que era privilegio de los jefes políticos -cuya presidencia ostentaban- y de las diputaciones, así como la precariedad económica en que se desenvolvían y la presión local, son un reflejo de la turbulenta historia política de la España del pasado siglo y por ende su labor fue, en ocasiones, inoperante y aún negativa.

2. Aº. Municipal. CH.822.

3. Aº. Municipal. Libro de Acuerdos de 1884, sesión de 22 de octubre.

4. Museo de Segovia. C. M. 411.

5. Con motivo de este asunto la Comisón Provincial envió un escrito al Gobernador Civil, fechado el 15 de Julio de 1868, en el que, entre otras cosas, dice, "*existe una serie compuesta de catorce arcos ojivales y en el resto cinco del mismo genero intercalados entre los circulares, por lo que no puede decirse ni esta comision admitir que en las obras de restauracion se ha empezado a emplear el arco de ojiva, cuando ya existia hace trescientos ochenta ó mas años. El anacronismo pues, creemos no equivocarnos al decir, existe*

desde aquella epoca, sin que por esto haya dejado de comentarse y dar gran importancia por muchos autores a dicha restauracion. Sin embargo esta Comision, no obstante de que las obras de restauracion actuales se estan haciendo precisamente en el trayecto donde existen los catorce arcos ojivales; comprendiendo ese mismo anacronismo ha adoptado la forma circular ó de medio punto aun a riesgo de disentir de las formas que quedan existentes a uno y otro lado de la restauracion. En su consecuencia esta Comision no comprende como se haya informado tan equivocadamente a esa Academia...". Museo de Segovia. C.M. 531.

6.   Ordieres Díez, Isabel. Historia de la restauración monumental en España, 1835-1936. Madrid, 1995.

7.   Real Orden de 27-X-1852, corrigiendo *"el abuso introducido en algunas provincias, en las que se invierten las cantidades destinadas al principal objeto de aquel instituto en hacer excavaciones, las más veces inútiles, con el deseo de descubrir mosaicos y antigüedades".*

8.   Museo de Segovia. C.M. 894. San Agustín y San Francisco fueron demolidas a principios del XX.

9.   Poco ha variado en nuestros días la forma de constituir la Comisión de Defensa del Patrimonio, por lo que persisten algunos males de raíz.

ERICA SEGRE

University of Leeds

CUTURAL NATIONALISM AND BUÑUEL IN MEXICO, 1946-1955

'No crean [...] que sólo propugno por un cine
dedicado exclusivamente a la expresión de lo
fantástico [...] por un cine escapista [...]
desdeñoso de nuestra realidad cotidiana'[1]

The commemorative exhibition entitled with panoptic hyperbole
'¿Buñuel!: La mirada del siglo', held in the Palacio de Bellas
Artes in Mexico City in 1996, provides a point of departure for
the reception and contextualization of the filmmaker's lesser
known work. 'Vine de paso' he reminded Elena Poniatowska in
1977 in an elliptical interview in his Mexico City home.
'Nosotros nos nacionalizamos mexicanos [...] no somos
refugiados'[2]. A naturalized Mexican citizen three years after
crossing the border in 1946, Luis Buñuel directed twenty films in
Mexico – a long, idiosyncratic apprenticeship in would-be
commercial genres – which contributed through elision and astute
gaffes to the fracturing of the monolithic nationalist iconography
of the Mexican screen.

Buñuel's heresies had a more direct and immediate
resonance in the post-revolutionary irreverence of literary circles
dominated by Octavio Paz and Carlos Fuentes than on his
contemporaries in the Mexican film industry. Both writers were
personal friends and advocates of his provocative misreadings
and deviations from overarching nationalist rhetoric. The

265

incisiveness of these faux-naïf misreadings depended on the subterfuge of expatriate blunders, harnessed to the telling detail afforded by close collaboration with Mexican writers on the scripts (especially vernacularized dialogue), and with Mexican cinematographers and scenographers. They included Juan de la Cabada, Gabriel Figueroa, Mauricio Magdaleno, Manuel Alvarez Bravo. Not a few of these collaborators had contributed to the iconic physiognomies of nationalist exaltation and cultural narcissism of the Mexican screen in the 40s, working with the demagogic Emilio Fernández, the populist Ismael Rodríguez and the *costumbrista* Fernando de Fuentes. But if some of the collaborators' formation dated back to the halcyon days of La liga de Escritores y Artistas Revolucionarios (LEAR) founded in 1934 and the politicized Taller de Gráfica Popular, others like the playwright Rodolfo Usigli, the novelist José Revueltas and the abstract painter and scenographer Gunther Gerszo represented an artistic departure from the epic narratives of social realism, and a movement towards a committed aesthetic which favoured interior monologues, stream of consciousness and synthetic expression. In his most realized films in Mexico, Buñuel managed to hold both the background and the foreground in focus. This equilibrium between poetic penetration and 'la realidad tangente' owed a good deal to his interaction with practitioners of a pictorially-dominated film-making culture inspired by the physiognomic precision and totemic generalities of civic-minded graphic art in the 30s and 40s[3].

The exhibition's location was as emblematically significant as the purported centrality of Buñuel's visual legacy: subsuming the combined cultural nationalism of late Porfirian and post-Revolutionary Mexico. The Palace of Fine Arts, with its architectural accretions from art nouveau to artdeco in the service of autochthony, is a mausoleum of revolutionary mural art and the sacralized space of socially redemptive notions of culture.

Centrally located between the residual topography of the colonial city and the faded signs of the 19th century modernity which revised it, Bellas Artes is the embodiment of a particular tradition of hegemonic cultural practise pursued by successive revolutionary and post-revolutionary Mexican governments. In a recent retrospective article on a century of 'Difusión cultural' in Mexico, Carlos Monsiváis highlighted the quasi-utopian aspirations of the Departamento de Bellas Artes – divulgatory and integrative – whose inspirational matrix was the Palacio itself with its golden, renaissance dome. In the post-revolutionary decades it genuinely was 'el centro de la vida cultural, la zona iniciática', a position it currently occupies only notionally in the virtual reality of nationalist rhetoric[4].

1946, the year of Buñuel's arrival, marks the systematization of decades of obligatory polemic and foundational initiatives concerning *la mexicanidad* and its cultural prerogatives. With the establishment of the Instituto Nacional de Bellas Artes, official patronage is rationalized with a view to: 'custodiar, fomentar, auspiciar, vigilar y fortalecer todas las formas artísticas en que se expresa y se define el espíritu de México'[5]. Buñuel himself was invited to Mexico by one of the key cultural activists, a visionary of inclusive and redemptive cultural practice, the writer and ethnographer Fernando Benítez[6]. Chief editor of the major daily *El Nacional* and personal secretary to the Minister of State at the time of his encounter with the *cinéaste*, he contributed to the increased visibility and popularization of the arts, the renewal of debate on the relation between culture and society in Mexico, and supported a line of investigative national scrutiny as well as a generation of schismatic writers in the successful cultural supplements he founded for *El Nacional* and *Novedades* (including Paz and Fuentes). Buñuel arrives at the tail-end of the 'sexenio avilacamachista' (1940-1946), when the government's demagogic manipulation and consolidation of national stereotypes – the *tipicismo* inherent in the notion of *mexicanidad* – 'habían minado la base popular de esa introspección, convirtiéndola en un discurso político hueco y con fuertes visos de agotamiento'[7]. Significantly for a prospector of the margins, Buñuel's oblique entry into Mexico as a self-professed apostate of nationalist paradigms coincides with the gradual fracturing of dogmatic certainties concerning national identity and its legitimate cultural manifestations. He inserts himself into a period of transition and crisis which, as Juan Rulfo recalled, nourished the questing *desencanto* of a generation of writers: 'en la época que no se sabía hacia dónde iba el país, dominado por una crisis social económica, y donde el subdesarrollo era algo tremendo'[8].

Staging the exhibition in Bellas Artes was a provocative way of articulating an homage to Buñuel's dissident visions. That said, at least in one stylistic respect the interior of Bellas Artes was an apt setting. Buñuel's posthumous approval might be surmised from his comments on the set design in *El*: 'la escenografía es de un estilo que me gusta, porque mi padre [...] se hizo una casa en estilo 1900, un poco *art nouveau*. Yo tengo amor por esa época'[9]. In the context of identity politics and Transatlantic diplomacy it undoubtedly signalled an intention to reclaim Buñuel's 'lost years' for the canon. But also to defend not only the centrality of the films 'made in Mexico' and instigate a reassessment of their value, but to argue much more radically for the distinctive responsiveness to a Mexican cultural context which impinged on their manufacture and subject matter. The interpretative shift would ground what Buñuel called 'trabajos alimenticios' in the acknowledgement of historicity and cultural specificity sampled in *Las Hurdes/Tierra sin pan* (1932) , foregrounding the topicality of his subjects and his role as spectator/*cronista*[10].

In one of the catalogues which prefaced the exhibition, the film historian José de la Colina (a personal friend, persistent interlocutor and chronicler of the director) alluded to the underlying discursive scope of the title '¿Buñuel!: la mirada del siglo'[11]. He speaks of the need to revise the view that would denigrate the 'Mexican' films as exercises in expedient styles, products of Buñuel in the guise of 'un mero artesano camaleónico que filmara cualquier cosa que le ofrecieran'[12]. De la Colina argues against such a perception of an impoverished exile engaged in prosaic aesthetic negotiations. Buñuel in Mexico did not frivolously renounce 'la unicidad de una mirada de autor', did not suffer artistic amnesia or schizophrenia. His output there should be regarded as integrated, although diverse, and of undiminished aesthetic integrity[13].

An attentive review of his output suggests that Buñuel did not fly a flag of convenience when he adopted Mexican citizenship. Even his earliest films manifest a genuine receptivity to the realities of his adopted home, rather than a merely passive reproduction of established Mexican genres. Buñuel himself, when interviewed in later life, seemed to have tacit sympathy with this revisionary approach. Despite being a director with a well-documented penchant for trangressive disguises, Buñuel claimed that the films he directed in Mexico, many of them cast in popular genres – from the anthemic musical *Gran Casino* (1946) to the diptych *Simón del desierto* (1964) – eschewed the authorial condescension of 'hacer guiños de complicidad con el espectador' and denied intending to incite ridicule through a subtly parodic treatment of Mexican cinematic conventions[14]. A degree of opportunism does surface in the eclecticism of his projects in Mexico, with genre elements on occasion seeming fortuitous acquisitions rather than cultural incisions. In *La hija del engaño* (1951), Buñuel is characteristically oblivious to nationalist protocol and cultural purism in both Spain and Mexico. He readily decanted the Hispanicized melodrama of *Don Quintín el amargao* (1935) from his stint as a producer of commercial cinema in Madrid into the Mexican vehicle *La hija del engaño*. As he recalled in the mid 70s in a revealing conversation with José de la Colina, Luis and Janet Alcoriza 'mexicanizaron el argumento', in a vain attempt to retain some of the original's flavour which from the vantage point of exile had acquired a certain nostalgic appeal – 'tenía mucha chulería y mucho gracejo madrileños'[15]. The literal translation of the protagonist from 'un "echao pá delante" madrileño' into a stereotypical Mexican *macho* did not convince at the box office. Conversely, the success of the whimsical comedy *El gran calavera* (1949), which featured the popular Mexican actor Fernando Soler in one of his iconic roles as the endearingly dissolute patriarch with a heart of gold, shows Buñuel at his most astutely assimilative. This improbable tale of a dysfunctional, entrepreneurial family which is rehabilitated after a temporary immersion into a life of poverty and unremunerated but honourable toil in the inner city, demonstrated Buñuel's precocious command of the parabolic language of Mexican family melodrama coined by Juan Bustillo de Oro in the 30s in his nostalgia-inflected Porfirian sagas, and the epidemic populism of the *comedia arrabalera* of Ismael Rodríguez in the 40s. A director with a long-standing interest in oneiric rituals, and an abortive volvement in propagandist films in Hollywood, Buñuel was understandably receptive to the way in which the Mexican screen refracted and inculcated national mythologies.

As regards the reception of Buñuel's forgotten oeuvre, de la Colina vindicates the underlying integrity and interpretative independence of these *Mexican* films which place them on a par with his early and later European productions. Despite the overtones of a familiar polemic between metropolitan loci and post-colonial satellites, de la Colina's contention that Buñuel's was a universality grounded mordant specificity is suggestive. His years in Mexico were not parenthetical. Nor should the fact that the studios in question were Tepeyac, Churubusco and Clasa, and that the locations ranged from the outskirts of semi-tropical Cuatla, Morelos, and proletarian Iztapalapa, colonial Coyoacán and Chapultepec in Mexico City – to coastal Manzanillo, the villages of Guerrero and the vicinity of monastic Ixmiquilpan in the parched Valle del Mezquital, condemn these diverse films to the periphery of regionalist narrative and 'pintoresquismo delirante'[16].

The notion of an all-encompassing, totalizing, vision advanced by the title of the exhibition is undoubtedly a contentious gloss when applied to Buñuel – evoking a process of systematization and retrospective rationalization hardly in keeping with the director's signature surrealist debut with its ritually sliced eyeball. This strategy of radical ocular displacement was re-enacted in various on-screen gestures and conceits: the egg thrown against the camera lens in *Los olvidados* (1950), the knitting needle perforating the key-hole to castigate a suspected voyeur in *El* (1952); the cinematic plane in closeup registering the shattering impact of a point-blank discharge from a shot-gun in *Abismos de pasión* (1953). Against schematic linearity the point of view is exposed and complicated, disrupting placid consumption of the image in an attempt to disarm its hypnotic mystifications. In 1953 the usually evasive Buñuel explained his reservations about the reception of film and its abuses in relation to the purported retentive transparency of neo-realist celluloid, and the manipulation implicit in the omniscient point of view. In a contribution to a round table talk which was recorded, transcribed and later published in 1958 by poet-essayist Jose García Terres (editor of the premier cultural review *Universidad de México*), Buñuel acknowledged the insidious power of cinema on the viewer's 'habitad psíquico' – an unparalleled potential which however 'como ninguna otra [expresión humana] es capaz de embrutecerlo'[17]. In the same talk

271

he lamented – in the year of *Abismos de pasión* and *La ilusión viaja en tranvía*, a year after *El bruto*, *Robinson Crusoe* and *El* – that 'la luz cinematográfica está convenientemente dosificada y encadenada'[18]. Buñuel constructed his observations around a quotation from his friend and advocate of surrealism, Octavio Paz. They reveal the extent to which Bunuel's aesthetic affinities responded to the ongoing critique of monolothic ideologies forged by a new generation of Mexican artists. There is a tacit reciprocity in Buñuel's homage to Paz, for the younger man's seminal essay on the national imaginary, *El laberinto de la soledad* (1950), subsumed the bifocal vision and ocular conceits of the dissident Spaniard. 'Ha dicho Octavio Paz: "Baste que un hombre encadenado cierre sus ojos para que pueda hacer estallar el mundo", y, yo parafraseando agrego: bastaría que el párpado blanco de la pantalla pudiera reflejar la luz que le es propia para que hiciera saltar el Universo'[19]. In the appendix to the fourth edition, Paz alluded figuratively – in the wake of the Mexican Revolution and two World Wars – to the deadly mystifications engendered by Enlightenment reason, and the horrifying consequences of enforcing totalizing ideological schemata. He posits a disabused perspective, an emerging aperture in Mexican society in terms of a return to individual subjectivity, the internalization of experience and the rejection of official filters: 'Al salir, acaso, descubriremos que habíamos soñado con los ojos abiertos y que los sueños de la razón son atroces. Quizá entonces, empezaremos a soñar con los ojos cerrados'[20]. This goes some way towards what Carlos Fuentes identified in 1955 as a generational rerouting away from a static notion of representing national abstractions – the conventionally conceived realism of collective identity in print, canvas, murals, celluloid – towards expressing 'las tonalidades del paisaje del México interior'[21]. The humanist prescience of Alfonso Reyes – surrogate father of the new sceptics – had already signalled in 1944 the fracturing of the consensus on the veracity of nationalist aperçus concerning contemporary society and its ancestry. He alerts his readers to the developing fissure between the previously seamless amalgam of rhetoric and fact in 'Reflexiones sobre el mexicano': 'La apariencia nunca es desdeñable. Hasta cuando engaña da un indicio. [...] Dejarse guiar por los ojos no es un mal método, a condición de andar sobre aviso'[22]. One of the first to welcome Buñuel to Mexico, Reyes had by then influentially adopted the revision of the methodology of 'mexicanismo'. He questioned the exalted metaphysics of Samuel Ramos' classic *El perfil del hombre mexicano* and the populism of José Vasconcelos' education manifestos ('Alfabeto y jabón') in the 20s. The triumphalism of an institutionalized revolution struck increasingly implausible notes in a country where 'la lucha es elemental y áspera' for the voiceless majority[23]. He diagnosed for the benefit of a receptive generation of Mexican writers the origins of the national malaise: 'Nosotros mismos traemos cara de mala conciencia. Sabemos que hay cadáver en la bodega. Cuando pensamos en el país, vagamente nuestra subconsciencia nos representa inmensos reductos de poblaciones que arrastran una existencia infrahumana'[24]. According to Reyes, the proven defining trait of Mexican character was 'esta necesidad constante de la duda'. This natural predisposition in 'cartesianos nativos' should be cultivated as an emancipatory strategy, and as a lucidity of perception[25]. It is not coincidental that Fuentes' study of Mexican middle class hypocrisy , his second novel *Las buenas conciencias* (1959) acknowledges a debt to the demystifying trend encouraged by Reyes, suggesting a complementarity with Buñuel's dissociative lens in the dedication to the book: 'A Luis Buñuel, gran artista de nuestro tiempo, gran destructor de las conciencias tranquilas, gran creador de la esperanza humana'. The blighted landscape of Buñuel's initially controversial *Los olvidados* (1950), in which according to Paz' introductory presentation for Cannes 'la puerta del sueño parece cerrada para siempre', resonates with the dissonant voices of the debate in Mexico concerning nation and ideology, illusory social justice, political legitimacy and individual freedom[26]. For its detractors it was a travesty and a slur on national dignity, an act of base treachery on the part of an ill-informed *gachupín*. For its supporters, its implacable plot made the 'realidad espesa' of the marginalized urban population – divested of compensatory sentimentality and *pintoresquismo* – literally and intentionally 'insoportable'. Breton inadvertently captured the incisiveness of Buñuel's example in Mexico when in 1951 he defended the film against Stalinist critics and provincial piety: 'Para mí lo esencial es que de la desesperación y la furia que tan bien representan *Los olvidados* y *La edad de oro*, el ser humano sale fortalecido y más dispuesto a rechazar el yugo'[27].

As is well known, Buñuel's first feature film in Mexico *Gran Casino (o El viejo Tampico*, 1946) was atypical and a box-office flop. A contemporary Mexican reviewer speaks for generations of subsequent critics when he described the director whom he had apparently seen on location 'Perdido, titubeante, sin personalidad, naufragaba estéticamente'[28]. However, an interest in being false to type seems a distinguishing characteristic of Buñuel's sensibility, something he fully exploited in the heterogeneous films directed in Mexico. What has yet to be explained is why a supposedly conventional musical drama which reworked the stock elements which had made Mexican films so marketable, both at home and in Spanish America, did not make more of an impression at the box office. Set on the threshold of the heady, nationalistic days of the expropriation of foreign oil companies, it featured Jorge Negrete – (the original singing *charro*, the idol of the ever popular *comedia ranchera*) – and the Argentinian Libertad Lamarque (the doyenne of salon melodrama), with lively set pieces from cabaret *tropical* and burlesque, and the ubiquitous accompaniment of the celebrated *mariachi* trio, *Los calaveras*. The novelist Mauricio Magdaleno, who had worked on the scripts of most of Emilio Fernández' memorable proselytising rural dramas (from *Flor Silvestre* (1943), and the internationally acclaimed *María Candelaria* (1943) to *Maclovia* (1948) and *Pueblerina* (1948)) worked closely with Buñuel on the adaptation of Michel Weber's novel. Magdaleno's was a comprehensive expertise: although seldom mentioned as such he was active as a director in his own right with two films in 1944 (*El intruso* and *Su gran ilusión*), and two others in 1946 which apparently preceded his collaboration with Buñuel (*La fuerza de la sangre* and *La herencia de la llorona*). His script for Fernando de Fuentes' disenchanted satire of middle-class opportunism during the revolution, *El compadre Mendoza* (1933), was more indicative of his heterodox temperament than the folkloric simplifications he later regretted in his projects with Fernández. Jack Draper, who had been the cinematographer in both Carlos Navarro's *indigenista* drama *Janitzio* (1934) and Fernando de Fuentes dystopian *¡Vámonos con Pancho Villa!* (1935), provided some of the visual flair that ensured that the notoriously spendthrift memory of Buñuel should in old age preserve one scene from oblivion: 'el baile de Meche Barba en la sala del casino, entre la gente y las mesas. La cámara la sigue en una larga toma, ajustándose al movimiento de la danza, sin cortes'[29]

Whilst the film sought to tap the residual traces of the anti-imperialist, nationalist euphoria of the 30s, its 'feel good factor' for the crisis-riven forties was predicated on a number of questionable premises. By attempting the splicing of cinematic genres in a collage of visual and musical references, Buñuel side-stepped the class-specific nature of their audience appeal. Despite depriving Negrete of his *charro* emblems and folkloric props, the *macho* mannerisms of the *jinete* dogged his attempt to reinvent himself as a modern engineer, whilst Lamarque sought gamely to disguise her impeccable upper-class credentials and succumb to the call of the vernacular male. Both characters seem haunted by previous celluloid incarnations. At a rare recent viewing of the film, it became clear that the protagonists were unaware of their true roles as cyphers in Buñuel's often hilariously precise adherence to Mexican cinematic conventions of the period. The stilted diligence of their acting is reminiscent of the effects achieved by Buñuel's enigmatic directorial instructions in *Un chien andalou*, which made Pierre Batcheff and Simone Mareuil's a truly discontinuous affair. The attempt to respond to accelerating urbanization through a cross-over between rural nostalgia and industrial drama – redrawing the parameters of contemporary film by adapting existing conventions – proved a fantastic, ultimately unconvincing, hybrid mechanism. To what extent Mauricio Magdaleno made Buñuel aware of this growing trend in Mexican cinema – of picturing the drama of the province in the confines of the sprawling city – is unclear. *Gran Casino*'s ostentatious artifice seems to want to discredit such an initiative on both aesthetic and ethical grounds. Magdaleno returned to collaborating with Fernández – then undergoing a change of perspective from ruined pastoral and the blighted countryside, to the painted capital city as a site of inauthenticity and failed utopias. This thematic conversion was to culminate in *Salón México* (1948; released 1949) and other films set in a murky Mexico City of nightclubs, migrants and broken families, where the *cabaretera* and/or prostitute became the people's heroine to be pitied, desired and finally edified. The purported actuality of these scenarios in fact recycled a number of Porfirian tropes for modernity's moral crisis, strongly influenced by Zola. This amounted to a reworking of Federico Gamboa's best-selling novel *Santa* (1903) screen adaptations of which in 1918 and 1931 marked the inception of the Mexican film industry on the back of popular melodrama. The promise of such a development in *Gran Casino* remains as tantalizing and contrived as the kiss that was never consummated between Negrete's *charro* and Lamarque's middle-class lady – for Buñuel refused to conceive it visually, preferring instead a close-up of the lover's hand stirring a stick in oily sludge: 'para limpiarla de cursilería'[30]. This characteristic *gag* or *broma* – the apparently inconsequential sequence – a measure of his 'inconformismo y rebeldía', introduces the grain of critical reserve that underlies his relation with the Mexican film establishment at its most complacent. In 1953 he had occasion to reiterate his resistance to the false symmetries of bourgeois melodrama, criticizing 'el cine que se limita a imitar la novela', with its dated formulas '[que] repiten hasta el infinito las mismas historias que se cansó de contar el siglo diecinueve y que aún se siguen repitiendo en la novela contemporánea'[31]. Conversely, it was film – through the example of Buñuel's undeceived practice – that provided the source of inspiration for the renewal of narrative in Mexico.

The entertaining comedy *El gran calavera* opens with an off-centre scene set in a prison which prefigures the disjunct family order of the story-line. It also introduces Buñuel's skewed take on this familiar parable of the self-regenerative capacities of the middle classes. A close-up of a confusion of shod feet behind bars from which the protagonist's well-heeled pair separates, provides a metaphor for the social inequalities that underpin the plot. As well, perhaps, as suggesting an ironic pun on the pedestrian nature of the subject matter. The foundational emphasis on costume is appropriate in a comedy of manners in which the domestic order is temporarily subverted by the dereliction of a hedonistic father: social anarchy is incipient with servants smoking their master's cigars, offspring who drop out of university and are voracious consumers, wives who are ineffectual hypochondriacs, disloyal *compadres*, office employees who blithely ignore the boss sleeping and joking on the job. The collapse of central authority and ensuing dislocation of social hierarchy are savoured by Buñuel in Addisonian details, such as don Ramiro's meeting with his agitated business caretaker Alfonso. The sterling employee shifts between 'tú' and 'usted' forms of address schizophrenically confused as to his role – that of confidant or deferential subordinate.

The startling opening sequence bears a marked resemblance to an iconic photograph by Lola Alvarez Bravo, whose work continued the pungent social focus of Tina Modotti's distilled realism. Entitled 'El sueño de los pobres' and shot from above, it shows 'un niño dormido entre pilas de huaraches'[32]. The photograph was based on an earlier denunciatory photomontage with the same title which was shown as part of the exhibition of revolutionary posters by women held in 1935. The original composition included a strange mechanical contraption for the manufacture of coins descending on rails onto a child in rags asleep on a canvas sack. Although the photographic version toned down the explicit anti-capitalist polemic of the photomontage, it retained the disturbing equivalence between the Indian child and market commodities (an equivalence that Buñuel exploits in *Los olvidados*). Despite *El gran calavera's* up-beat humour, there are a number of vignettes which bear a family resemblance to both non-conformist graphics of 30s protest in Mexico, and the disjunctions of surrealist montage and collage in Europe. These vignettes break the complacent depiction of proletarian poverty – the quaint hive populism of the *casas de vecindad*, the false piety of 'honour and solidarity amongst the poor' – which the affluent family experiences as a kind of pantomimic fancy-dress (overalls, aprons, *rebozos*).

The most effective of these vignettes incorporates a montage counterpoint – a satiric device which became famous in the Angelus sequence in *Viridiana*. In the concluding acts of the film, the family has been restored to its residence in balmy Las Lomas, its members morally regenerated after their sojourn amongst *el pueblo*. The son has returned to university; the apathetic brother has discovered carpentry, and busies himself repairing the patriarchal mansion; his wife makes herself useful baking cakes; Don Ramiro is back in charge of the family business. The (happy) outcome of the film hinges on whether Don Ramiro's beautiful daughter, Virginia, marries the self-interested snob Alfredo or Pablo, the honest, industrious, working-class lad whom she met whilst temporarily bankrupt. At the wedding ceremony in which Virginia is to be married to Alfredo, the officiating priest's reading of St Paul's epistle is intermittently drowned by the advertising jingles being relayed by Pablo from loudspeakers mounted on his car. The jilted Pablo has adapted the commercial apothegms to suit the occasion, and like a latter-day preacher and pedlar combined, inveighs against the frailty of women, alternating between the threat of divine judgement and the promise of salvation that, absurdly, only the right brand of stockings can guarantee. In this sequence Buñuel smuggles in touches of desecratory humour based on some incidentally precise observations of contemporary consumer culture and its uninhibited mixing of sacred and profane registers. The 'moral consuetudinaria', which he later condemned escapist cinema for reaffirming, is exposed here in a competitive exchange of platitudes between Catholic homily and seductive advertisement:

> Sacerdote: A nadie, después de Dios, ha de amar más, ni estimar más que a su marido ... ni el marido...
> Pablo: La mujer es cobarde y traicionera como pueden ustedes comprobarlo en la Biblia. Acuérdense de la manzana. No se fíen de sus promesas ni de sus ruegos, únicamente las que usan medias Suspiro de Venus merecen ser amadas, y aun así con toda clase de reservas.

Sacerdote: ni el marido más que a su mujer, y así en todas las cosas que no contradicen a la piedad cristiana procurad agradaos...

Pablo: Medias Suspiro de Venus para mujeres decentes y económicas. Para mujeres que su amor no dependa de que suban o bajen las acciones de la bolsa. Compren medias Suspiro de Venus, si quiere evitar que la mujer que usted adora lo abandone por algún rico tonto. Juegue a la lotería nacional, la lotería nacional garantiza la fidelidad de la mujer amada.

Sacerdote: La mujer obedezca a su marido...

Pablo: Jamón del diablo, cómprelo en La Perfecta[33].

Unlike Bernardin de Saint-Pierre's eponymous tragic couple, Pablo and Virginia's improbable union is consecrated by the mythologies of the national screen intent on 'hacernos olvidar las penosas horas del trabajo cotidiano'[34]. As in *Gran Casino*, however, Buñuel prevents closure by again foregrounding the references to a complicit commercialism in the film's final scenes. The microphone in Pablo's car is still on and the couple's amorous reconciliation is publicized through loudspeakers to the expectant neighbourhood. The *cursilería* of the sentiments expressed is perhaps period-specific, and the endorsement of the family and the neighbourhood in the film (and by the imagined cinema audience) suggests a communal gratification that is a measure of *El gran calavera's* successful negotiation of collective desire. This supervised, courtly love bears little resemblance to the necrophiliac lengths to which wild passion would transport the anarchic male protagonist of *Abismos de pasión* – Buñuel's adaptation of Emily Brönte's novel *Wuthering Heights* – a personal favourite which was also popular with the surrealists. The satiric disjunction between the reality of daily struggle and images of the promised land – the perceived affinity between the myths of political rhetoric and commercial propaganda – was a recurrent motif in debates about the social effects of urban centralization in the 40s and 50s. In the concluding scenes in which requited love resembles 'esos relámpagos de erotismo adquisitivos que son los comerciales', Buñuel seems to recognize the role of cinema in Mexico in sublimating collective aspirations[35]. The closing shot is of Don Ramiro's archetypal family walking arm in arm in the middle of the street with broad, self-congratulatory smiles. Its sunny optimism – almost reminiscent of Dorothy and friends on the Yellow Brick Road – is so disproportionately fulsome as to be suspected of irony. Akin to the cosmetic retouching of a glossy publicity poster, it pays tongue-in-cheek homage to the trend amongst some of the most successful Mexican directors to disregard 'autenticidad extracinematográfica' in favour of a 'mitología populachera'[36]. The grim realities of life on the streets were being recorded by a new generation of Mexican photo-journalists like Nacho López and Hector García (as well as more obliquely by Juan Rulfo in his capacity as gifted amateur) who viewed the camera as 'el instrumento más apropriado para tratar de entender dialécticamente el mundo de las contradicciones, para exhibir la lucha de clases y comprender el hombre como individuo'[37]. Buñuel's next film, *Los olvidados,* shares an affinity with the scepticism and ethical rigour of such investigative photographers, who rejected 'Estos fotógrafos-turistas [que] retratan al zoológico humano sin considerarse como parte integrante del mismo zoológico. Y cuando muestran sus fotos llenas de "colorido local" y pintoresquismo folclórico, el comentario es inmediato: "¡ Qué bonito! ¡Qué interesante!"'[38].

One of the achievements of Buñuel in *Los olvidados* was to subvert the rigid formulas of two powerful currents in Mexican cinema. On the one hand, the *costumbrista* sentimentality and ingratiating humour of standard approaches to the subject of the urban under-class in such films as Ismael Rodríguez' *Nosotros los pobres* (1947), which made a virtue of their pitch for the populist common-denominator. On the other, the aestheticized view of tragic autochthony which elevated poverty to a kind of national martyrdom (as in Emilio Fernández' *Río Escondido,* (1947)) – films which readily assumed the moral and ideological highground.

Buñuel turned his back on the simulacras of screen poverty, camouflaged himself with appropriately ragged clothing and, sometimes armed with a camera, undertook to 'recorrer las "ciudades perdidas", es decir, los arrabales improvisados, muy pobres, que rodean México, D. F.'[39]. One of the most tenacious myths about the labouring classes in the capital, as projected by the national screen, was the notion of the uncomplicated persistence in the city of traditions governing communal life imported from the provinces: the idea of an unproblematic cultural transcription, admittedly requiring some adjustments but ultimately reassuringly continuous and unifying. In *Los olvidados* the corrosive effect of rural depopulation and massive immigration to the cities (especially to the capital) is captured in the dusty wastelands, the skeletal armatures of unfinished construction, the labyrinthine compression of settlements on a nameless periphery. The film was shot on location in Mexico City – especially the marginal, proletarian Nonoalco – and in Tepeyac studios. There is a significant affinity between Rulfo's oneiric vision of a country haunted by its unassimilated past, and Buñuel's delving in the subconscious of delinquent adolescents living on the detritus of modernity. It's an affinity based on a shared 'inconformidad con la estrecha sociedad que nos rodea', which had led both men to a repudiation of conventional realism in narrative and cinema[40]. Admiration for such a heteroclite sensibility, so at odds with what Buñuel cited as 'el optimismo del mundo burgués', apparently informed his intention to adapt *Pedro Páramo* for the screen – a project that was never realized[41].

Buñuel's research for *Los olvidados* coincides with a growing trend in cultural discourse to fix on the incommensurable expansion of the capital as a paradigm of a nation and national identity in crisis. Juan Rulfo's photographs of the Capital in the 40s and 50s capture the multiplying city in gestation, and the crisis of values of its displaced inhabitants – the visual and thematic context of *Los olvidados*. Photographs of passengers and pedestrians in silhouette show them caught in the web-like interstices of rail and tram lines criss-crossing a dusty plain, as phantasmal and ill-defined as their transitory passage, shrouded in the anonymity of the *rebozo* and *sombrero*. Of these secular pilgrims he writes in 1947: 'Ellos no pueden ver el cielo. Viven sumidos en la sombra, hecha más oscura por el humo. Viven ennegrecidos [...] como si no existiera el sol ni nubes en el cielo para que ellos las vean, ni aire limpio para que ellos lo sientan'[42]. The austerity of a landscape uninscribed by memory, whose inhabitants move between confinement and emptiness, provides the stage on which Pedro, El Jaibo, Ojitos and Meche's tragedy unfolds. It is from margins such as these that Buñuel begins to destabilize if not wholly dismantle a nationalist iconography which concealed its obsolescence behind an adherence to a deified Revolution.

According to the Mexican cinematographer Gabriel Figueroa, who was to make seven films with Buñuel, including *Los olvidados,* the director 'odiaba la fotografía' in films[43]. By the time of his collaboration with Buñuel, Figueroa had already worked with all the significant directors in Mexico (Fernando de Fuentes, Chano Urueta, Alejandro Galindo) as well as with John Ford (*The Fugitive* 1947) and had won many international awards (three at the Venice film festival in 1938,1948 and 1949; one at Cannes for *María Candelaria* in 1946; and others in Brussels, Madrid, Los Angeles and Czechoslovakia). Through his collaboration with Emilio Fernández in the 40s, he had had a decisive input in the development of an aesthetic of the Mexican sublime, which at its best made visible for the first time a transfigured 'México profundo'. Figueroa had spent his formative years in the Academia de San Carlos, and practised as a photographer before embarking on a career which took him from an apprenticeship with Gregg Toland in Hollywood, through stills photography to cinematography proper. He readily admitted his pictorial influences 'La pintura [...] a la que me siento entrañablemente ligado'[44]. Those influences ran from the high resolution luminosity of Flemish painters and the dramatic contrasts of Goya's *Caprichos*, to the monumental visions of his Mexican contemporaries José Clemente Orozco, David Alfaro Siqueiros and the mordant graphic work of Leopoldo Méndez, leader of the collective Taller de Gráfica Popular. By the time of *Los olvidados*, Figueroa was in his prime – with a distinctive artistic identity of his own. He was associated with a range of visual effects and perspectives that were not only celebrated, easily identifiable signatures but well on the way to providing emblems for some future archive of national traits. Figueroa's iconography in its concern with distilling the imperishable essence of autochthonous culture revisited the images coined by Edward Weston, Sergei Eisenstein and Paul Strand in their celebration of Mexico's primitive ethnicity in the 20s and 30s. This group of pioneers 'en donde se finca y se desdobla la mirada de Figueroa', suggested the outline of his highly stylized and selective aesthetic, with its emphasis on 'la fisonomía popular inexplorada' magnified in lingering close-ups, the lapidary contrasts between luminous sky and shadow-clad figures, the marked symmetries of nature and collective ritual[45].

On the set of *Los olvidados*, Buñuel's interventions prevented Figueroa from overlaying the unpalatable violence and cruelty with an aestheticized polish. The 'encuadre antiestético' which Figueroa sought to correct resisted the redeployment of a conventional visual currency and disorientated audience expectations[46]. The monolithic elegance of Figueroa's pictorial language was in danger of fetishizing precisely those aspects of reality that Buñuel hoped to expose raw. The jagged discontinuity of the scenes and imagistic associations enhanced the syncopated rhythms of the adolescents' lives. Buñuel's contrariness when offered the perfect composition became a feature of his unique collaboration with Figueroa.

There are ample grounds for agreeing with a recent judgement of Figueroa which praised his 'vocación nacionalista no afectada por chovinismo alguno'[47]. He sought to safeguard his professional independence by founding – with Jorge Negrete and Mario Moreno Cantinflas – an alternative Union to the corrupt and dogmatic *Sindicato Trabajadores de la Industria Cinematográfica* (STIC), whose abuses he denounced publicly in 1945. He refused to work in Nationalist Spain, explaining in a telegram to Dolores del Río: 'Para los buenos amigos y las buenas historias no tengo condiciones especiales, pero a Madrid iré si quitas a Francisco Franco del reparto'[48]. His lack of bigotry allowed him to cooperate with what amounted to Buñuel's revision of the *mexicanisms* of the Mexican canon, with a degree of equanimity unmatched by either the producer, Oscar Dancigers, or the technicians in the making of the film. In later life, the Spaniard claimed that the experience on the set exemplified 'uno de los grandes problemas de México, hoy como ayer [...] un nacionalismo llevado hasta el extremo'[49].

According to Buñuel, Oscar Dancingers reined in a number of startling surrealist disjunctions 'que rompieran con el realismo convencional' in a more decisive fashion[50]. The nature of the conventionalism at stake was much more specific than is usually admitted. In one instance, when El Jaibo accompanied by Pedro confronts Julian whom he blames for his stint in borstal, they meet on waste ground with the skeleton of an unfinished multi-storey building – a public hospital – in the background. Buñuel proposed the inclusion of a hundred piece symphony orchestra in the metal infrastructure in a scene which culminates in the cowardly murder of Julian. The mocking reference to the operatic gestures of bourgeois melodrama, its contrived pathos and gratuitous sentiment, is as resonant as its satire of the Mexican conventions of the genre. 'Cuando hice *Los olvidados* todas las películas Mexicanas debían llevar música, aunque no fuera más que por razones sindicales'[51]. Gustavo Pittaluga, the composer of the score (whose name didn't figure in the credits because he was not a Mexican national nor belonged to the official union), devised a musical counterpoint with abrupt dissonances reminiscent of Prokofiev which often undercut the prescribed pathos of climactic scenes. When the blind don Carmelo – manipulative and Fagin-like in his dealing with children, reactionary in his politics, a bigot with a vindictive streak – is stoned by the children after pleading for mercy, the mellifluous notes of compassion turn into a screech of derision.

In *Los olvidados* Buñuel provocatively rewrites the *comedia populachera* . The degree to which he departed from the established text is made clear by the reaction of the Mexican technicians on the set who were well-versed in the genre. The evidence is anecdotal but, given the hysterical reception the film received when it was first released (various Unions called for Buñuel's expulsion, members of the avantgarde denounced him and boycotted the film, the ultra-patriotic Jorge Negrete accosted him, etc), more than a little compelling. He was asked disarmingly by a member of his crew: 'Pero, ¿por qué no hace usted una verdadera película mexicana, en lugar de una película miserable como esa?'[52].

Buñuel's dystopian irreverence played precisely on the tension between popular expectations and the scandal of preconceptions shattered. *Los olvidados* plays provocatively with generic elements which had become enshrined as cinematic clichés in nationalist iconography. *Nosotros los pobres* by Ismael Rodríguez would certainly have qualified as an outstanding example of what *authentic* Mexican cinema of the period entailed. It provides the germ of *Los olvidados*'s ironic and quasi-parodic counterpoint. The execrable title for *Los olvidados*'s French release, *Pitié pour eux*, exposed the knee-jerk sentimentality of approaches to the subject-matter – endemic to melodrama rather than merely culture-specific – which Buñuel sought to undermine. Rodríguez's triumphant populist fantasy featured the screen legend Pedro Infante and the sultry Katy Jurado (both of whom were to star in Buñuel's uncompromising *El Bruto* (1952)), principals in a gallery of *costumbrista* stereotypes marked by distinguishing emblems of costume and props:

> 'Entran los cargadores con sus sombreros sin forma, sus pantalones raídos y sus mecapales al hombro; el voceador de periódicos en camisa playera, overol y cachucha cortada en picos y con adorno de corcholatas; las vagabundas harapientas en estado de ebriedad perpetua; la coqueta del barrio con mirada sensual, pestañas pintadas y humilde vestido entallado'[53].

The film celebrates a resilient, picturesque underclass, whose life is set to music, where traditional sacredness of family and home prevail, and whose unfailing good humour and stoicism wins the day. The inhabitants of this celluloid *inframundo*, true guardians of a vernacular tradition, speak in either musical refrains or proverbs, and view themselves as actors in a divinely-scripted national parable. It presents the *casa de vecindad* as *costumbrista* theatre where squalor, indigence and violence are sublimated in the epic marginality of *la saga arrabalera*. In the impregnable solidarity of *Nosotros los pobres* there is nothing to arouse the

indignation of even the most punctilious patriot. *Los olvidados,*
on the other hand, managed to alienate members of the film crew
even before its release. During filming the hairdresser was
famously seized by *amor patrio* and resigned, indignant at the
deviant portrayal of Mexican motherhood, in the scene in which
Pedro pleads for food and is repeatedly rejected ('Eso, en México,
ninguna madre se lo dice a su hijo. Es denigrante.')[54]. Against the
reassuring falsehoods of *Nosotros los pobres*, in which everyone
is redeemed through suffering, Buñuel's *Los olvidados* uses the
familiar mangy, scavenging dogs of Mexico City to symbolize a
less than edifying conclusion to the precarious survival of
abandoned children.

In *Los olvidados*, Buñuel fleshes out the stock ingredients of
the often sensationalist *crónica* of contemporary broadsheets (of
which he was a life-long, bemused consumer) – as he explained to
his Mexican critics. The scenarios are suggested by extant
cinema, journalistic cuttings, transcripts from the archive of the
Tribunal de Menores, and documentary photography. Whilst
Nosotros los pobres's opening analogy is to an illustrated book
found in a rubbish bin by two children, *Los olvidados*'s disturbing
ending in which the murdered Pedro's corpse is dumped 'en una
barranca llena de basura' is a deconstruction of such pictorial
abstractions. In the final sequences of the film, Figueroa
collaborated in the fracturing of his own preferred aesthetic. An
aesthetic in which a harsh reality transfigured through beautiful
plasticity could be conceived as a redemptive act in itself. Art
does not so much redeem in *Los olvidados* as indict.

El Jaibo, who has scuppered Pedro's chance of social
rehabilitation, murders his one-time associate in cold blood – and
is in turn gunned down by the police. Pedro's body is found by
Meche in her grandfather's stable – a refuge for the children
associated with a prelapsarian rurality. Together they conceal his
body beneath sacks on the back of a donkey. On the way to

dispose of the body which they fear will incriminate them, they cross paths with Pedro's distracted parent looking for her son in a scene which has the staged poignancy of Verdi's *Rigoletto*. Head bowed beneath a hieratic *rebozo* in the guise of repentant 'mater dolorosa', Marta's figure alludes to Figueroa's visual style inmortalized by close-ups of Dolores del Río in Emilio Fernández' rural tragedies and John Ford's *The Fugitive*. The shot of the clandestine cortege seen in profile against a cloud-filled sky resonates with Eisensteinian lyricism in the Maguey section of *Qué Viva México,* where the persecuted *campesino* couple acquires quasi-Biblical status in a similar composition. The elements of a primordial ethnicity – including the totemic Maguey – are shot from below on a rise which in Figueroa and Eisenstein have transcendent possibilities, and which in Buñuel is poised over a steep incline where human detritus is unceremonially dumped. The power of Buñuel's direction to disconcert originates in the denial of the kind of redemptive conclusion associated with Figueroa's iconography.

Buñuel's suspicion of the ideological appropriation of folklore – the mystique of officially consecrated popular traditions – had already impinged on the characterization of the reactionary Don Carmelo (played brilliantly by Miguel Inclán). This character's bi-cultural, polemically *mestizo* origins are attested to by his resemblance both to a Lazarillo in the picaresque tradition and a photograph taken by the director of a blind beggar on the streets of Mexico City. According to Buñuel the original script opened with a scene of street children who whilst scavenging in a pile of rubbish, find the portrait 'de una especie de "hidalgo", de caballero español , un tipo magnífico que había degenerado en mendigo de los arrabales mexicanos'[55]. The Mexican Pedro de Urdimalas, who was collaborating on the script, refused to subscribe to images which denigrated traditional Spain and its legacy in Mexico – and requested that his name did not appear in the film's credits. Don Carmelo emerges with his one-man band, singing nostalgic *corridos* for a living in markets and public spaces, whilst revering the memory and example of the autocratic Don Porfirio Díaz (or rather his reincarnation in Don Francisco Franco?), and harbouring not so latent paedophile tendencies. It is he who passes the most chilling sentence on the rebellious youngsters who have preyed on him and whom he habitually exploits: 'Así irán cayendo todos. ¡Ojalá los mataran a todos antes de nacer!'[56]. This link between a certain kind of nostalgic national folklore and authoritarianism had been affirmed positively by films such as *En tiempos de don Porfirio* (1939) and *México de mis recuerdos* (1943) by Juan Bustillo Oro, or the *comedia ranchera Allá en el Rancho Grande* (1936) by Fernando de Fuentes, which expressed a similar desire for the restoration of feudal values with images of philanthropic *hacendados* and loyal, colourful dependents. Buñuel discredits the mystifications of local colour, and resists the seduction of the picturesque with this disquieting portrait of the prototypical street-dweller and Everyman as a populist reactionary.

An alternative ending, apparently filmed by Luis Buñuel himself, has recently come to light in the the Filmoteca in Mexico City. Iván Trujillo, who made the find, suggests that the shorter ending was made to quell the anxieties of the film's producer. This version is openly conformist: '*light*, el clásico sentimental donde el bien triunfa sobre el mal y Pedro es redimido, regresa a la escuela y el Jaibo desaparece'[57]. It helps to establish the degree to which the director was conversant with the interplay of genre conventions and nationalist sensibilities in the depiction of vernacular culture. The exhumation of this discarded Manichean appendix to *Los olvidados* exposes the context of the film's production. It confirms that Buñuel's Mexico, in all its ambiguity, was indeed a revelation which ruptured nationalist façades for an emerging generation of Mexican sceptics.

When Rulfo, one such sceptic, rejected the essentialist presuppositions of 'lo mexicano', he made explicit what his writing had already enacted through the plurality of its voices and its shrouded, complex human identities:

> 'no representa ninguna característica lo mexicano, en absoluto. Lo mexicano son muchos Méxicos. No hay una cosa determinada que pueda permitirnos decir: Ahí es México. No, no es México. Ninguna de las cosas es México. Es una parte de México. Es uno de tantos Méxicos'[58].

From 1946 to 1956 Buñuel's films were not only incidentally produced in Mexico but more often than not *about* Mexico's synchretic society and its screen mythologies. They punctuate the trend for dislocating nationalist aperçus amongst a generation of Mexican artists and intellectuals. Buñuel aided this process by conjuring 'la súbita aparición de una verdad oculta y enterrada, pero viva': not only disturbing iconographic and genre conventions, but also making the medium of film more self-reflexive and less complacent, exposing both the machinery of its deceptions and its sometimes liberating artifice[59]. Buñuel was being modest when he expressed the hope to Jean-Claude Carrière that his recollections: 'ayuden a conocer a México de un modo bastante diferente, desde el lado del cine'[60]. His films had already achieveda disconcerting plurality of vision.

In the unfairly neglected *Abismos de pasión* (1953), Buñuel's genuine as well as strategic cultural bilocation underwrites the splendid hybridities of the adaptation. The film captures the insularity of an incestuous rural gentry. The arid *páramos* and the hot-house luxuriance of the tropical vegetation encircle the dilapidated fortress-like *haciendas*. Panoramic shots of a compressed habitation in the crevices of a mountainous terrain echo the quasi cubist views of the forgotten villages of Las Hurdes. The emphasis on a rugged land sustaining a primitive agricultural community and its often bloody rituals, is as informed by the violence and poverty of rural Mexico as it is rooted in the feudalism of ancestral Spain. The anarchic passion of El Jaibo returns to haunt the complacent in the savagery of Alejandro/ Heathcliff – whose rejection of *cursilería* makes for a peculiarly Mexican anti-Christ. According to his rival in the film (or as in *Un chien andalou* his bourgeois 'better self'): 'Es una bestia. Para él no existe nada respetable. Atropella con todo hasta con lo más sagrado para seguir sus instintos'. If Alejandro is ultimately a tragic rebel, he finds his cinematic vindication in *Viridiana* (1961), in which Francisco Rabal's libertine and free-thinker takes possession of the ancestral estate despite his illegitimacy. And, of course, just as Buñuel's Mexican films *are* Mexican, as I have argued, in more than the literal sense, they can also be made to resonate in a Spanish context.

NOTES

1. Luis Buñuel, 'El cine, instrumento de poesía', *Universidad de México*, 13 (1958), 1-2, 15 (p. 15).

2. Elena Poniatowska, *Todo México*, 2 vols (Mexico City: Diana, 1990), I, pp. 85 -86.

3. 'El cine, instrumento de poesía', p. 15.

4. Carlos Monsiváis, 'Un siglo de difusión cultural', *Universidad de México*, 554-555 (1997), 14-21 (p. 17).

5. Cited by Monsiváis, 'Un siglo de difusión cultural', p. 18.

6. See Luis Buñuel, *Mi último suspiro*, trans. by Ana María de la Fuente, 3rd edn (Barcelona: Plaza y Janes, 1983), p. 192.

7. Ricardo Pérez Montfort, 'Indigenismo, hispanismo y panamericanismo en la cultura popular mexicana de 1920 a 1940', in *Cultura e identidad nacional,* ed. by Roberto Blancarte (Mexico City: Fondo de Cultura Económica, 1994), pp. 343-83 (pp. 343-44).

8. Juan Rulfo cited by Yvette Jiménez de Báez in *Juan Rulfo: del páramo a la esperanza: una lectura crítica de su obra* (Mexico City: Fondo de Cultura Económica, 1990), p. 21.

9. Cited by José de la Colina and Tomás Pérez Turrent in *Luis Buñuel: prohibido asomarse al interior* (Mexico City: Joaquín Mortiz/Planeta, 1986), p. 95.

10. See José de la Colina and Tomás Pérez Turrent, *Luis Buñuel: prohibido asomarse al interior* (Mexico City: Joaquín Mortiz/Planeta, 1986), p. 71.

11. See *¿Buñuel!La mirada del siglo*, ed. by Yasha David (Mexico City: Museo del Palacio de Bellas Artes, 1996/97).

293

12. José de la Colina, ' El cine mexicano de Luis Buñuel', in *El ojo:Buñuel, México y el Surrealismo*, ed. by Tomás Pérez Turrent (Mexico City: Consejo Nacional para la Cultura y las Artes, 1996), pp. 63-68 (p. 64).

13. Ibid., p. 64.

14. *Luis Buñuel: prohibido asomarse al interior*, p. 107.

15. Ibid., pp. 70-71.

16. Coined by Jorge Ayala Blanco in *La aventura del cine mexicano: en la época de oro y después* (Mexico City: Grijalbo, 1993), p. 97.

17. 'El cine instrumento de poesía', p. 2.

18. Ibid., p. 1.

19. Ibid., p. 1.

20. See Octavio Paz,'La dialectica de la soledad' in *El laberinto de la soledad*, fourth edn (Mexico City: Fondo de Cultura Económica, 1964), p. 176.

21. Cited in *Juan Rulfo: del páramo a la esperanza*, p. 53.

22. Alfonso Reyes, *La x en la frente* (Mexico City: Porrua y Obregón, 1952), p. 75.

23. Ibid., p. 76.

24. Ibid..

25. Ibid., p. 79.

26. Octavio Paz, 'El poeta Buñuel', in *El ojo:Buñuel, México y el Surrealismo*, pp.29-33 (p. 30).

27.   From André Breton's previously unpublished 'Desesperada y apasionada', in *¿ Buñuel! La mirada del siglo*, pp. 35-37 (p. 37).

28.   Miguel Angel Mendoza cited by Tomás Pérez Turrent , 'Buñuel: pro y contra', in *¿Buñuel! La mirada del siglo*, pp. 51-57 (p. 52).

29.   See *Luis Buñuel: prohibido asomarse al interior*, p. 51.

30.   Luis Buñuel cited by de la Colina and Pérez Turrent, p. 50.

31.   Buñuel, 'El cine, instrumento de poesía', p. 2.

32.   See Olivier Debroise, 'Los fotomontajes de Lola Alvarez Bravo', in *Lola Alvarez Bravo: Reencuentros* (Mexico City: Consejo Nacional para la Cultura y las Artes/Instituto Nacional de Bellas Artes, 1989), pp. 9-16 (p. 11).

33.   Iván Humberto and Avila Dueñas, *El cine mexicano de Luis Buñuel: estudio analítico de los argumentos y personajes* (Mexico City: IMCINE/Consejo Nacional para la Cultura y las Artes, 1994), p. 27.

34.   Buñuel, 'El cine, instrumento de poesía', p. 2.

35.   Carlos Monsiváis, *Los mil y un velorios: crónica de la nota roja* (Mexico City: Alianza/Consejo Nacional para la Cultura y las Artes, 1994), p. 52.

36.   Jorge Ayala Blanco, *La aventura del cine mexicano*, p. 98.

37.   Nacho López, 'Mi punto de partida', *Generación*, 9 (1996), 13. The issue was devoted to *fotoperiodismo* in Mexico.

38.   Nacho López, 'Mi punto de partida', p. 13.

39.   Buñuel, *Mi último suspiro*, p. 194.

40. 'El cine, instrumento de poesía',p. 1.

41. Buñuel, 'El cine, instrumento de poesía', p. 15.

42. Juan Rulfo cited in the exhibition catalogue *La ciudad de Juan Rulfo: fotografías*, ed. by Américo Sánchez and María Inés Roqué (Mexico City: Museo Mural Diego Rivera, 1996), p. 11.

43. Cited by Cristina Pacheco, 'El seductor de la luz', *La Jornada*, 24 April 1994, pp. 4-6 (p. 6).

44. 'El seductor de la luz', p. 5.

45. José Antonio Rodríguez, 'La génesis de una mirada', *La Jornada*, 24 April 1994, pp. 9-10 (p. 10). Carlos Monsiváis, 'Una mirada sobre el siglo', *La Jornada*, 29 April 1997, p. 25.

46. Figueroa recounts a number of suggestive anecdotes in Elena Poniatowska's *Gabriel Figueroa: la mirada que limpia* (Mexico City: Diana, 1996). See pp. 103-04 for *Los olvidados*.

47. Monsiváis, 'Una mirada sobre el siglo', p. 25.

48. Cited by Raquel Peguero, 'La cámara de un melómano tremebundo', *La Jornada*, 24 April 1994, pp. 2-3 (p. 3).

49. *Mi último suspiro*, p. 195.

50. *Luis Buñuel: prohibido asomarse al interior*, p. 63.

51. Ibid., p. 57.

52. *Mi último suspiro*, p. 195.

53. *La aventura del cine mexicano*, p. 97.

54. *Luis Buñuel: prohibido asomarse al interior*, p. 60.

55. Ibid., p. 63.

56. *El cine mexicano de Luis Buñuel: estudio analítico de los argumentos y personajes*, p. 53.

57. Raquel Peguero, 'El otro final de *Los olvidados*, novedad en el ciclo de Buñuel', *La Jornada*, 29 November 1996, p. 27.

58. Cited in *Juan Rulfo: del páramo a la esperanza*, pp. 62-63.

59. Octavio Paz, 'Los olvidados', in *El ojo: Buñuel, México y el Surrealismo*, pp. 29-31 (p. 29).

60. *Mi último suspiro*, p. 193.

RUTH CHRISTIE

University of Leeds

JULIO LLAMAZARES: A RURAL POET IN AN URBAN AGE

'Para cada animal distribuían pasto diferente ...'

Julio Llamazares (born 1955) has published two books of poetry, *La lentitud de los bueyes* (1978) and *Memoria de la nieve* (1981)[1] both of which, in common with his novels and the majority of his articles and essays, have rural themes. This small poetic output has been well received by the critics, who have tended to read it as neo-romantic, emphasising the emotional content of the poems and interpreting them primarily as works of memory, mist and myth.[2] We may ask how rural poetry could be anything other than nostalgic or escapist in a rapidly changing urban age. Llamazares himself apparently sees his own writing as lyrical and romantic: he identifies in an Unamunian way with the *paisaje*, and regards literature as primarily a redemptory struggle with time.[3] In spite of this self-assessment, I believe there is a closer affinity between his work and that of his contemporaries and immediate predecessors than has hitherto been recognised. Furthermore, aspects of his poetry owe at least as much to the conceits and imagery of Góngora as to Machado and Unamuno. Llamazares is not a postmodern poet, except in the sense that anyone writing in a postmodern age must be so, but to read his work as essentially nostalgic and conservative is, I suggest, to misjudge his position as a rural poet in an urban age.

Llamazares has been included in the *postnovísimos* generation[4]. This is a thematically and stylistically fragmented group of poets who, after the metapoetic approach of many of the *Novísimos*, have felt free to find new own voices for themselves, often revisiting and re-using whatever traditional themes and styles they have been drawn towards. The tone of much of the poetry of this generation is distanced and ironical, born of the scepticism of the earlier group. But Llamazares does not approach his subject matter ironically. Furthermore, speaking of his work in general, he says he feels called upon to provide a justification for writing about a rural world, something to which he rightly objects. He blames the view of rural writing as somehow retrograde on an over-rapid post-modernisation of Spanish literature,[5] seeing his contemporaries as turning their backs on the rural, which he considers to be central to the Spanish consciousness: ' ... soy un escritor profundamente español. Ésta es una sociedad urbana con una memoria rural, como yo'.[6] But in defending the legitimacy of rural Spain as a the central theme of his writing he also denies some interesting aspects of his poetry. It may show no trace of irony or parody, but this does not mean that it is free of scepticism, or that because his subject matter is rural he can loop back to connect naively with an earlier discourse, as if the postmodern turn had not happened. Surely it is largely *because* he writes post-*Novísimos,* because of the rigorous questioning of the relationship between word and world, the ground-clearing achievement of their work, that he can enjoy the freedom to write unashamedly rural poetry.

Llamazares directly attributes the success of his work in general to its romanticism, which he sees as connected to the lot of his generation: ' ... a nuestra generación le ha tocado dar el salto entre la proximidad y el alejamiento respecto de la naturaleza. Alejamiento, y conciencia de la escisión, que son, por otra parte, una de las bases del romanticismo. Por eso lo que yo escribo es literatura romántica'.[7] But an essential feature of this romantic 'escisión' is the belief that living close to nature means living closer to one's authentic self; the break is not only between lifestyles, but also between a state of division and a state of oneness; the loss of an innocent unity with nature. This is not a loss which is mourned in Llamazares' poetry. The absence of this romantic attitude forms a further link between Llamazares and his predecessors. He shares with the *Novísimos* a strong sense of reality not as unity, but as differentiation. His poetry *is* nostalgic, but for difference rather than unity or oneness.

The same kind of argument can be made to counter any suspicion that to write about the rural in this day and age is somehow escapist. The social commitment of Llamazares' poetry saves him from this accusation. But this does not automatically indicate a return to a more humanistic poetry. Around 1980, when Llamazares' poetry was published, still almost half of the Spanish people lived in the countryside, facing a set of problems apparently unrelated to the concerns of contemporary poets, who were writing on the whole from individualistic or urban perspectives, and rarely as inhabitants of rural communities. The isolated mountainous regions of north-west Spain that Llamazares writes about are changing. They have come to be seen as potential tourist centres, or as nature reserves, and some communities, like Llamazares' own natal village, Vegamián, in the region of León, have been flooded to provide reservoirs for urban areas. But Llamazares never allows his concern for these dying communities to override his commitment to poetry. What is more, the social dimension to his poetry, in common with that of the *novísimos* generation, is born of an appreciation of the sophistication of man's adaptive capabilities, not an idealistic simplicity or an ideological conviction. But whereas the *Novísimos* were confronting the onrush of the new and the urban, Llamazares is coming to terms with the slow disappearance of an ancient rural way of life. Social change has happened at a slower pace in rural Spain, and there is a sense of inevitability and resignation in his poetry, which makes for an enigmatic tone, as it is not clear whether nature or man is reclaiming the land and destroying the community.

Both volumes are set in the same northern landscape and share many images and sentiments. The poems are not titled, but numbered, which enhances the reading of books as one, but there are important differences. *La lentitud de los bueyes* dwells heavily on abandonment, whereas *Memoria de la nieve* presents an imaginative repopulation in the shape of the Ibero-Celtic mountain people. So the poetry of both books is in a sense haunted by past inhabitants, but the ghosts of *La lentitud* are more recent, wandering the landscape with the poet, their voices mingling with his while those in *Memoria* are Ibero-Celtic phantoms: the tough, ancient and gnarled roots of this northern tree of life, as it were, rather than the dying branches.

Llamazares never assumes that broad stance which uses the rural as a romantic pretext. He writes as someone who knows the countryside intimately and understands the ways in which it supports human life. 'En la ciudad, como los árboles solo sirven para dar sombra, no son más de eso, árboles. Pero tu no oirás a un campesino que te diga "un árbol", dirá ese roble, o ese pino'.[8] There are few *árboles* or *flores* or *animales* in Llamazares' poetry, but many *abedules, urces, ciervos, grillos* and of course, *bueyes*. The plethora of plants and animals is reminiscent of earlier Spanish rural poetry, in particular Góngora. The use of a rich nomenclature was part of the baroque cornucopia, but such fertility plays another role here. It is indeed evidence of nature's plenty, but its purpose is not primarily to appeal to the senses – how could it be so, when few of his readers know any longer that *urces* are plants, let alone what they look like? Rustic poetry tends to be preconceived as familiar and unproblematic, we feel it will not be so complex and conceptual as urban verse, it will be emotional and instinctive and sensual. But not only does

Llamazares write sometimes obscure lines which are very open to interpretation, but he uses a vocabulary with which even the native speaker of his own generation will be unfamiliar. In this sense the poetry is doubly opaque. The 'soledad' so often mentioned may recall Góngora's and also Machado's usage of the term, but Llamazares' usage would have been unthinkable in the seventeenth or even the greater part of the twentieth century, for its meaning extends beyond the idea of wilderness and lonely places to include grieving and *aislamiento*, due to inheriting a field of knowledge that many people no longer share or care for. The poet is now in a wholly new situation, for an entire way of life is threatened with extinction, a vast amount of the vocabulary and knowledge of agrarian culture is being lost in the sense of passing out of use. The abandonment and silence of *La lentitud de los bueyes* not only refers to the land and the creatures left behind, but to the poet who wanders through an increasingly obsolete world. 'Lenguaje helado y gris que sólo yo conozco' (poem 26, MN) may be read in this context; an expression of pride but also of isolation.

Two consequences of the confrontation with radical change that Llamazares has in common with the *Novísimos* are the writing of metapoetry and an obsession with the roles of memory and forgetting. The former is far less marked in Llamazares' poems; perhaps the *novísmos* generation had already done enough work in this area, as mentioned above. But poem 2 (LB), for example, can be read as a metapoem, concerned with the negative connotations of language, the word as a barrier rather than the key to knowledge: 'Con la primera palabra nace el miedo y, con el miedo, se incendia la hojarasca del conocimiento y del olvido', these are constant *novísimos* sentiments, as is the poet's paradoxical attitude to knowledge, now an 'hojarasca'. The metapoetry is interspersed with social concerns, such as the hint of large machines clearing a way in this line: 'Qué importa, pues, que el paisaje se rompa antes de tiempo o que zarzales rojos obstruyan las salidas a los lados', and with lines which seem to be both: 'No quedará por tanto ninguna perspectiva de retorno: pues los espesos bosques de cucañas no pueden ser talados en un día'. Are the 'cucañas' clichés perhaps, thickets of easy words which accumulate and spread tenaciously, and which prevent the past being made present in the poem? And in poem 13 (LB) the theme of doubt and uncertainty in the word itself is again apparent:

> Pero es seguro que palabras absolutas, más absolutas que vasijas de aceite derramadas, me estarán esperando al otro lado del olvido.

> Y entre esas voces acuñadas sobre moldes de arcilla y certidumbre, mi voz sonará extraña como tomillo arraigado en las cuestas del amor.

> Mi voz será como un paréntesis de duda.

Memory and forgetting in these works are conceived as processes rather than ways of evoking the past. In the introduction to the 1985 publication of the two volumes together, Llamazares stresses that reading the poetry after a lapse of time is like looking at '*dos fotos viejas que el olvido ha sobado*', and suggests that 'el recuerdo sepulta lo que nunca existió'. Perhaps his intention *is* to save traces of the past, not impossibly eternalised, not romantically evoked, but in an open and temporal form which allows their significance to be interpreted, lending them a future. The creamy inner texture of the squashed holly berry, the custom of putting immature fruit in 'arcones de trigo' to hasten its ripening, the gullies and ditches and topographical details, the diversity of pots and containers; the richness of this culture is found more than sufficient to provide metaphors for its own disappearance. There is a desire to put what may otherwise be wasted knowledge to another use. The objects, tasks and practices which are threatened with extinction, in figuring their own demise provide themselves with another function. The context of the poems, in however small a way, provides a new adaptive environment. We are probably more familiar with the complexities of remembering and forgetting than with the objects and customs which figure them, and which thus emerge in our consciousness like *objets trouvés*; we are made to conceive them anew, or even see them for the first time. The poems are a consolation in the face of desertion and neglect, and the poet's 'memoria de la nieve' can be interpreted as the blankness of the page awaiting the written word; the symbol of snow changes from a sterile whiteness to a pregnant space, its emptiness becomes a virtue: 'ya la nieve sustenta mi memoria ... por eso puedo despedirme de mi amor sin llorar' (poem 10, MB).

In *La lentitud de los bueyes* a variety of disembodied voices merge into each other; the poet becomes his bardic ancestor, who becomes one of his 'bueyes', who becomes a 'vagabundo' or a past lover. As the human population is disappearing from the villages, so the human voice seems to be absent in many of the poems, as if the creatures that are left were speaking – the abandoned, domesticated creatures, or those that had adapted their way of life to human presence; the oxen which wander off, the dogs left tied up, the robins and storks and bees, even in poem16 (MB) the swifts, which '... trazan la urdimbre de su vuelo intemporal sobre la torre'. Indeed every plant and creature mentioned is connected to man's activities, even if only marginally, circling his towers or sharing his company. In the first poem of *La lentitud* the silence, slowness and meekness are associated with the *bueyes*, echoing lines from Antonio Machado and Juan Ramón Jiménez, but in Llamazares' poetry these creatures sometimes seem to speak for themselves, taking over the first person plural. The oxen have no value when there are no more carts or ploughs to haul, and they wander aimlessly through the poems, eventually committing suicide by drowning. But they are passive, with no minds of their own: '... ni habitan nuestra alma las oquedades del conocimiento' (poem 1, LB). Even the plants are abandoned: 'el grito desolado de las frutas silvestres', 'el grito de las urces negras', 'el gemido negro de las moras' (poems 9,16 & 27, MB). There are echoes of Eden, but it is no paradise. 'Man' ate from the tree of knowledge, but in his wisdom has neglected the animals he should have cared for, but 'men' were and are being forced to leave, the shadow of Cain still darkens these northern regions.

The conceit of such fragile structures as 'las oquedades del conocimiento' is reiterated throughout the first book. In poem 2 a similar concept is employed '... si la nada crece sobre el brocal de espuma de la historia ...'. In poem 3 we find the 'posos' of time, 'más ácidos y azules que el olvido', and the substance of solitude is this time as sweet as 'nata crecida'. In poem 12: 'Hablo de la tristeza que madura lentamente en el panal del corazón', in poem 17: 'Rezuma soledad el tiempo roto, como un panal de ausencia', and 'El conocimiento alienta en mí como una levadura cuajada de oquedades que se alimenta de tiempo'. These are all metaphors for various forms of knowledge or states of mind as fragile constructions which will collapse under pressure. The honeycomb, the foam or scum which milking and wine-making produce, the beaten cream, the risen dough, even the cavities and vessels of the human heart, all figure the frailty of human consciousness. In poem 18 the time is New Year's Eve, and the speaker could be dying, or drinking to forget. The connection between man and earth seems very close: '... uvas de sangre en esta noche amarga de San Silvestre'. Strange music and the voice of the 'vagabundo' reach him, and 'Lentamente el sonido cae sobre mí como un tejido de hierbas, y el corazón se esponja y se abandona a su alimento' – not *elemento*, but something like self-pity, that feeds its softness. Doubt, as opposed to these delicate confections of certainty, is 'nata derretida'. There is a further set of conceits of things spilled or scattered, accidental but indelible stains, '... palabras absolutas, más absolutas que vasijas de aceite derramadas' (poem 13) or things growing in the wrong places: 'El esparto ha crecido entre las grietas del placer y un círculo de angustia rodea los arbustos de mi alma' (poem 17, LB). They are metaphors of substance, the by-products of other activities, sticky excretions, liquids that ooze and set and melt and spill, marks and stains left in the poetry by the physical world.

The particular lexical set that Llamazares employs articulates a disappearing world which may be no more or less worth saving than any other, but which obviously forms an essential part of his identity and his relationship with his ancestors, made quite explicit in poem 4 (LB): 'Yo vengo de una raza de pastores que perdió su libertad cuando perdió sus ganados y sus pastos'. This statement expresses a measure of personal pride in his inheritance, but he also recognises not only the temporal distance from these and earlier ancestors, but also the contrast between the transience of urban living and the stability they enjoyed in living out their lives in one place. Yet again, this awareness of the 'escisión' is not manifest as a yearning; the desire to save the past seems more of a squirrel-like instinct than a romantic longing. His poems reveal a determination not to waste his inheritance, they are perhaps means of ensuring that the 'monedas verdes' (poem 4, LB) should not be a squandered investment:

> Qué lejos de mí la región de las fuentes del tiempo, el lugar donde el hombre nace y se acaba en sí mismo como una flor de agua.

> Ellos no conocían la intensidad del fuego ni el
> desamor de los árboles sin savia.
>
> Los graneros de su pobreza eran inmensos. La
> lentitud estaba en la raíz del corazón.
>
> Y en su sosiego acumularon monedas verdes de
> esperanza para nosotros.

Both books are more literary, less subjective and lyrical, and have more varied cultural allusions than is often acknowledged. In *Memoria de la nieve* many images are again redolent of Góngora: 'Las grosellas derraman granates en la nieve ...' (poem 2) and 'Rojo es el vino sobre los brezos, derramado en la tarde por arrieros sin nombre' (poem 15) recall his blood on snow, and several others echo the 'Soledad primera' in particular. The 'hojarasca' of poem 2 (LB), the signs written on the bark of the tree, the footsteps of the wanderer also call to mind Góngora's 'Soledades'. To read these books is to accompany the poet through a tract of countryside, where the repeated but changing images are like landmarks or trees or plants that we begin to recognise. More obviously crafted than *La lentitud*, in *Memoria de la nieve* the poet seems to have accepted his propensity to build fragile structures, and lends artificial substance to his ghosts by referring to Celtic myths and legends. But this is not to say that in this book Llamazares creates an idealised rural world, since throughout the two books we find broken branches, rotting trees and rusting metal and the threat of desolation. There is always a streak of realism, of social comment and commitment, an absence of bucolic melancholy.

The inclusion in *Memoria de la nieve* of reference to the world of his most ancient ancestors, those *celtíberos* described by Strabo in the epigraph, is related to Llamazares' emphasis on a *cultura del norte.*[9] By referring to this people and their rich culture of legends and symbols he is stressing this northern accent, counteracting the echoes of southern Spain which are inevitably associated with Góngoran and Juan Ramónian language. Likewise, the *cultura del norte* is emphasised over the Mediterranean world by this replacement of the more usual allusion to the classical culture of the ancient Greeks with reference to that of these northern pagans. Travelling north to a frozen snowy landscape accumulates positive connotations which are associated with the writing of poetry itself as the book develops. Llamazares is now inventing an identity rather than searching for authenticity, in the same spirit as he is creating his poems; he seems to see himself as a disenfranchised descendant of the Celtic bard, and it should not be forgotten that a large part of what Llamazares knows comes, as he admits, from an oral tradition, from listening to the reminiscences of the old people of his villages, from hearsay.[10] These points are implicit in lines such as the following, from poem 13:

> Los bardos llegaban con el verano. Por los verdes caminos vagaban de aldea en aldea.
>
> Y siempre había algún anciano que decía: vienen del país de la nieve, del país de los bosques y los lagos helados.

But most importantly, I think, Llamazares refers to this ancient world as to a time when everything was meaningful, when the differentiated rural culture was far more comprehensive than the traces he cherishes in his own precarious memory. For the pagan people: '... A cada río otorgaban un sonido distinto' and '... hubo un dios por cada hombre sobre la tierra' (poem 11). So the second book is full of trees and sacred plants – the mistletoe, the walnut, the henbane roots, and sacred rites – the burying of silver artefacts, and the capercaillie feathers thrown into the rivers to placate the water gods. But Llamazares is fully aware that: 'Inútil es volver a los lugares olvidados y perdidos, a los paisajes y símbolos sin dueño / ... / la mansedumbre helada del muérdago cortado, de los paisajes abrasados por el tiempo' (poem 21). In the final poem of *Memoria de la nieve* we find the poet – or is it the last surviving, abandoned ox? – listening to the apocalyptic sound of the hunting horn in the woods. It is finally uncertain whether the response to the disappearance of human culture from the land is wholly disastrous. In the first book the sound of the horn was melancholy but not entirely apocalyptic, the '... uva granate / ... no hallará su eclosión definitiva hasta ese día en que los últimos arrieros hagan sonar sus cuernos tristemente en los montañas' (poem 17, LB). Llamazares associates the antediluvian, symbolic spiral shape of the horn with time in this final poem. As opposed to the cyclical concept of rural life, this implies that nothing is ever really lost:

> ¿Qué espero aún de la espiral del tiempo, de esos cuernos epílogos que suenan en los bosques?
> [...]
> Solo estoy, en esta noche última, como un toro de nieve que brama a las estrellas.

Although Llamazares lives in and writes from the city, the sensitive nature of his relationship with the rural world of his childhood and his ancestors is reflected in all his work. But his poetry is not so distinct or distant from the work of his contemporaries and his predecessors as the rural theme may indicate, or as perhaps he himself would like. His desire to shun postmodernity is above all a reaction to his belief that many writers were disowning rural Spain, turning their backs on something that he considers to be still of primary importance. His statement that his work is romantic is a part of this same resistance, but to interpret Llamazares' poetry from this perspective is only justifiable in a limited sense, as has been discussed. No specific places are named, and neither are his poems anecdotal or evocative, but they are undoubtedly the product of a particular region and era. Llamazares assumes a contrastive, defensive position as a rural writer in an urban age, but his poetry subverts his defences, and can be appropriated more closely and comfortably than has hitherto been acknowledged into the contemporary Spanish scene.

NOTES

1. Julio Llamazares, *La lentitud de los bueyes/Memoria de la nieve*, Madrid: Hiperión, Edición conjunta (1985).

2. See, for example, Rafael Alfaro, 'Hacia una tierra deshabitada', review of *La lentitud de los bueyes*, in *Nueva Estafeta* 30 (1981) 103-5; Antonio García, 'Poesía del recuerdo', review of *Memoria de la nieve* in *Cuadernos del norte* 4 (22) (1983) 91-93, and José María Izquierdo, 'Julio Llamazares: Un discurso neorromántico en la narrativa española de los ochenta', which also discusses his poetry, in *Iberomania* 41 (1995) 55-67.

3. See José María Marco, 'Julio Llamazares, sin trampas', interview in *Quimera* 80 (1988) 22-29. Llamazares says that the *paisaje* is 'un espejo en el que te miras y te ves de diferente manera según tu estado de ánimo', that '... no hablo de montañas, la montaña soy yo', and that 'la literatura es lo que queda del tiempo que pasa', 25 & 29.

4. Luis Antonio de Villena, *Postnovísimos*, (Madrid: Visor, 1986).

5. Marco, *Quimera*, 25.

6. Ibid., 25.

7. Ibid., 25.

8. Ibid., 28.

9. Quoted by Antonio García, *Cuadernos del norte*, 92.

10. Marco, *Quimera*, 25.

PATRICIA McDERMOTT

University of Leeds

FROM HERE TO ETERNITY:
The Theatrum Mundi of Carlos Rojas, *Auto de fe*

(For Ronald, who first spoke to me of *kairos*. Forgive me if I have not understood.)

> 'We *believe* in the ultimate, but we *live* in the penultimate'
> (Bonhoeffer)

> 'To-morrow, and to-morrow, and to-morrow,
> Creeps in this petty pace from day to day,
> To the last syllable of recorded time;
> And all our yesterdays have lighted fools
> The way to dusty death. Out, out, brief candle!
> Life's but a walking shadow, a poor player
> That struts and frets his hour upon the stage
> And then is heard no more'
> (Shakespeare)

> '... then the Last Judgement begins, and its
> Vision is seen by the Imaginative Eye of
> Everyone according to the Situation he holds'
> (Blake)

> 'Bien predican los vivos: pero mucho mejor los muertos'
> (Palafox)

On 27 September 1700 Innocent XII, who would go down in the history of the Papacy as one of the best popes of modern times, died in the Eternal City of Rome. On 21 September of that same year of Our Lord, after a series of exorcisms which began in 1698, His Catholic Majesty Charles II, once 'The Desired' henceforth 'The Bewitched', had taken to his bed in the Alcázar of Madrid where he died on 1 November, the feastday of All Saints. It was the end of a line and of an era. For the second time in modern Christian history and in less than a century the death of the Pope and the King of Spain had occurred in the same year. At a time when the historical and the eternal orders, the human and the divine, were considered to be interconnected, the signs of the times were portentous and might be read as the interference of the demonic in the external events of history in order to frustrate the hidden drama of salvation at all levels, individual, national and universal.

The reputed last words of the last of the Spanish Hapsburgs – 'Yo no soy nadie' – are recorded in and reverberate through the text of Carlos Rojas' novel *Auto de fe*, winner in 1968 of the Premio Nacional de Literatura Miguel de Cervantes.[1] The *historicismo mágico* of this richly tragicomic fiction, which projects twentieth-century existential preoccupations back in time, is perhaps most truly historical when it gives the lie to the statement, ironically placed on the lips of the Bishop of Segovia Mendoza y Sandoval, now Inquisitor General, with respect to his suspension of the exorcisms of the king ordered by his predecessor Rocabertí: 'Estos fueron actos de política, no de conciencia. En España son siempre distintos.' (362). The historical novelist exercises poetic licence in his use of sources[2] and foregrounds the conscience of the king amidst the dynastic power struggles over the prostrate body politic: 'For what shall it profite a man, though he should win the whole worlde, if he lose his own soule?' (Matthew, XVI, 26).[3] Indeed one could apply to Carlos Rojas, as a creative re-writer of history, Jessie Lace's judgement of the author of St. John's Gospel, a major source of Rojas' biblical inspiration: 'This writer, even more clearly than the writers of the other Gospels, writes history so as to make it transparent and luminous – so as to show us the depths beneath it and the infinite vista beyond it.'[4]

The Catalan historian and professor of literature, one-time *lector* in the University of Glasgow, emerged as a novelist in the late fifties, consciously writing against the vogue of social realism in the creation of a philosophical novel that explores man's being in time with a nod in the direction of Unamuno: 'La historia, al decir de Unamuno, es el acontecer que pasa. La intrahistoria es la realidad intemporal que permanece por debajo del cambio y del fluir histórico.'[5] Like many writers before him Rojas distinguishes different kinds of time: the scientific measurement and linear progression of chronology, Bergson's *durée homogène*, and the dynamic flow of past into future of life, the *durée pure*. Rojas in his narrative imagination explores this *durée* not only in relation to individual consciousness of being, but also in relation to collective human being through history, in the belief that 'La humanidad es un ser único.'[6] On occasion he expands the idea of the dynamic order of time in a continuum to reverse the past and remember the future as in a dream. One thinks of the distinction made by Australian Aborigines between the 'clock time' of the white man and the 'dream time' of the Ancestors in which, as they re-sing the song-lines of their tradition, they engage both with the time of origins and the end-time. Like the primitive, like religious man everywhere, Carlos Rojas is particularly concerned with the relationship of time and eternity and the experience of those expanded moments which translate man into another dimension: '... todos los tiempos un momento indivisible... la eternidad el presente fugitivo de un instante.'[7]

Auto de fe is a duplex narrative: one third the post-resurrection story of the Lázaro of the New Testament, composed by a dwarf Fool in the court of his putative father Carlos II and named after the King's dead brother Felipe Próspero; two thirds the post-resurrection memoir of an unnamed *Bufón*, his putative half-brother, written at the instigation of the inquisitors who want a confession regarding his own possible bewitchment, that of his half-brother and the part played by both in the bewitchment of the King. Felipe Próspero has been burned at the stake for witchcraft in raising to life the *Bufón* who had died playing the part of Lázaro in a court mystery play *El autillo de Lázaro*, authored by the King, but whose authorship has been accepted by Felipe Próspero during his trial by the Inquisition. Hence the title *Auto de fe*, which conjures up the historical spectacle of trial and judgement in the exemplary drama of Christian salvation, resolved either by fire or symbolic representation in public arena or court theatre. The text signals its own intertextuality through the ages with references to Calderón, the incorporation of Castilian ballads and Old Testament psalms sung in Gregorian chant, the constant pastiche and parody of the New Testament. The Synoptic Gospels are the source for the reworking of miracles and exorcisms involving the Gerasene/Gadarene swine, the woman with the issue of blood and Jairus's daughter. St. John (XI) is the source of the key story of the raising of Lazarus, the prefiguring of the Resurrection and rebirth in the sacrament of Baptism, the crucial miracle in the sequence of events which led to Calvary: 'Al principio era la farsa, y ésta el *Autillo* de Lázaro' (92). In Rojas' parody the biblical source of inspiration is crossed with that of the modern Greek master Kazantzakis whose *The Last Temptation of Christ* provides Rojas' novel with its epigraph: 'Sentábase Lázaro en el rincón más oscuro de la casa porque la luz lo hastiaba'.[8] The synchronism of human experience through time and writing is further signalled by the introduction of anachronisms which interrupt the illusion of historicity in the two times of the narrative and the language of their telling. For example, Ortega's 'La claridad es la cortesía del filósofo' and 'Yo soy yo y mi circunstancia' are legends written in Chinese characters on kites flown by the young dwarfs at court; when Carlos on his death-bed speaks in foreign tongues, his quotation from *Macbeth* – 'Life is a tale told by an idiot, full of sound and fury, signifying nothing' – is translated by the Inquisitor General as 'La vida es una greguería [Gómez de la Serna], contada por un bellaco' (449).

The two tales told by a Fool in counterpoint and which finally merge into one are hypothesized in the end as the dream of an anonymous narrator in the future – the present of the author and his reader – dreaming the dreams of each other – in his and our past – of the two resurrected beings Lázaro and the *Bufón*:

> No me maravilla compartir los sueños con Lázaro de Bethania, a los cabos de largos siglos. El me soñara, yo lo soñé y alguien quizá me sueña soñándolo en otro tiempo. Será la suya época no habida, como no lo era ésta cuando Lázaro vivió en pesadillas mis desventuras. Cambiará el mundo; pero no sus mortales soñadores. Al mío en el porvenir lo imagino necio como Lázaro y bufón como yo, aunque vista de otra guisa y sea su talla mediada entre las nuestras. Nos envidiará precisamente cuanto más sufrimos: la resurrección, y en nuestras vidas pretenderá en vano perpetuarse. (438)

Auto de fe is a visionary novel which shares the character of prophecy, that 'seeing in "timeless sequence" events which are historically separated from each other',[9] whose significant relationship is only realized in the fullness of time. In this novel, which situates the enigma of being in time in Christendom, the fullness of time (post-Kierkegaard/post Tillich) is related to *kairos* as Christ time: the *Great Kairos*, the coming of Christ in history, the fulfilment of the waiting-time of the Old Testament prophets, and *kairos* in the life of every Christian, that opportune moment which transforms past and future in the light of the Last Things (Death, Judgement, Heaven or Hell) and the Resurrection: '... la resurrección que es siempre el comienzo de todas las cosas' (469).

Felipe Próspero's Lázaro experiences the *Great Kairos* in his lifetime, but misunderstands its significance in relation to himself, until he drinks the wine which is prepared every seven years when the desert cacti bloom and he is translated into the *Bufón*'s experience ('Y yo soy otro', 414 ff.). Seven was the number the Pythagoreans associated with *kairos*, understood in Antiquity as the decisive moment of crisis in which fate forces man to take up a position. In the Christological-cum-existential dimension of this text, the force of will power is emphasized alongside memory and understanding in the triad of mental powers associated with the human spirit. Lázaro has previously been immune to the effect of the mysterious vintage which robs the drinker of the capacity to sleep/dream (*sueño* is ambiguous here), but which promotes interior vision, and has received ambivalent replies to the questions he addresses to its drinkers: ' "¿Qué ves dentro de tus carnes? ¿Qué ves en el centro de ti mismo?" RESURRECCION Y MUERTE. NADA. EL SUEÑO DE LOS LOCOS MUERTOS, LAZARO EL NECIO, RESURRECCION Y VIDA' (415-416). It is as the *Bufón* that he will fulfil his *kairos* and will understand resurrection as life not death in the '*Epílogo También dicho Juicio Final*': 'Entre el sueño y la muerte sólo media el Juicio Final' (994).

The *Bufón* is both the conscience of the King – 'Soberanos y juglares nos requerimos unos a otros. No hay monarca sin bufón, ni bufón sin monarca' (19) – and the innocent eye which sees the truth – 'Pues los bobos y los niños afirman verdades, al sentir del vulgo' (424). In the final anaysis he is the (anachronistic) intellectual as scapegoat: 'Lázaro de Bethania, hermano mío, tú y yo, los supervivientes, los necios sabios, los bufones pensadores, *los intelectuales* como nos llama la corte, seremos acaso los únicos culpables hasta que perezca todo poder y resucite el hombre entre los hombres' (437). The Final Judgement bears witness as a novelistic act of faith in the saving grace of the sacrifice of love and transtemporal presence of Christ in an essentially humanist vision of Christ and the Communion of Saints as the brotherhood of man. The post-Christian secular scripture continues to broadcast the spiritual message of Christ as universal compassion and love. The recognition of self in other and of co-responsibility for human destiny from here to eternity is the personal truth that sets man free, but which in the historical vision of the novel is tempted into self-denial by the Holy Office as unwitting agent of the Devil it attempts to exorcize.[10]

This line of interpretation is the thread of Ariadne which guides the present reader through a re-reading of a novel which systematically confuses the trinity of identities and relationships in the universal drama of human redemption: the saving victim (Cristo/Felipe Próspero), the resurrected or redeemed (Lázaro/*Bufón*), the betrayer (Judas de Keiroth/Carlos II). The *Bufón* remembers playing at confession with the King and his baby half-brother in a toy theatre turned back-to-front: 'Sentí entonces – o siéntolo ahora, al recordarlo – que el mundo entero acababa de reducirse al teatrillo y nosotros tres' (132). The mythical biblical archetypes and the travesties of the court are brothers under the skin and the *Bufón* will retell their stories so that future listeners will recognize themselves in the eternal roles: 'Quiero que rían y se regodeen y quiero que se estremezcan bajo corpiños y pedorreras, como si les contase sus propias vidas' (439). The exploitation of the grotesque, which reaches its climax when the erect penis of the cataleptic King confesses the naked truth of his authorship of the *Autillo de Lázaro* and betrayal of Felipe Próspero – in response to the Inquisitor General's question after Pontius Pilate '- ¿Qué cosa es verdad?' (406) -, shocks the reader into a defamiliarized moral awareness of the human condition. As the conscious King advised the Bufón when he showed him the portraits of his ancestors the court dwarfs of the past: 'Recuerda, no obstante, que también para salvar gentes como ésas murió Cristo en la cruz' (243).

In *The Last Temptation*, Kazantzakis relives through his Christ the problem of the acceptance of the role of Messiah and the associated role of Judas. In *Auto de fe*, Rojas focuses on the role of the redeemed and the inter-dependence and inter-changeability of roles in the act of human redemption. The identification in the *Bufón*'s narrative of the King-father who betrays his son unto death as a Judas figure insinuates a disturbing analogy which is formulated in the interrogation of the mystery of Christ's Incarnation by Lázaro in Felipe Próspero's manuscript: '¿Quién podría justificar al propio Dios, razón del mundo, sacrificando a su Hijo para resucitarlo?' (267). In a dream the *Bufón* visits Felipe Próspero in jail during his trial and asks him why he does not reveal the King's authorship of the *autillo*:

> - El rey es un judas. Vendió a su propia madre. No se perderá por salvarte, ni confesará que al alzarme en el patio cumplías su letra y espíritu.
> - Si no se pierde por salvarme, lo haré yo por rescatarlo a él. Alguien debe morir para que otras vivan. Poco importa quién perezca; vistos desde el cielo parecemos todos el mismo. (155)

Rejecting the temptation to save his own life – "¿Por qué quieres destruir al rey, si todo poder perecerá para que resucite el hombre?' (156-157) -, Felipe Próspero traces in the dust the words 'RESURRECCION Y VIDA', Christ's first reported words in his Lázaro narrative: 'Yo soy la resurrección y la vida' (12). Felipe Próspero plays the role of Christ in the King's *autillo* and is the *figura Christi* in the *Bufón*'s narrative and visions. But before he is burned at the stake, he records the bewildering experience of the resurrected Lázaro up to the point when, after drinking the seventh-year wine and taking to his bed, he responds to the call 'Lázaro, ven fuera' and awakens to find himself in the Spanish court in the person of the *Bufón*, playing the role of Lázaro in the king's *autillo*. As the *Bufón*, in his final vision of the *auto de fe* and Last Judgement, he will assist Felipe Próspero to accomplish the sacrifice of his life for love of father and brother and proclamation of the truth, to the confusion of the Inquisition: 'For whosoever will save his life, shall lose it; and whosoever shall lose his life for my sake, shall finde it' (Matthew, XVI, 25).

In his initial interrogation regarding the King's siring of Felipe Próspero out of the English dwarfess Vivianilla, the *Bufón*'s stepmother, the dwarf declares to Inquisitor Rocabertí and the King's confessor Fray Froilán: '- Un bufón sólo debe creer en Dios, su rey, la iglesia y el diablo, decía mi confesor. Lo demás es burlería' (23). (The juxtaposition of the Church and the Devil in the text here is not without significance.)[11] If God is love, the Devil is solitude. Death is a mirror in which man confronts his action in time for all eternity, a terrible destiny if man has opted for the Devil: 'la muerte se me antoja espejo frente al cual permanecemos solos y parados, por siempre jamás, mirando quien fuimos' (438). When the resurrected *Bufón* ignores the request of the King's coachman Coca that he heal his wife who is suffering from an issue of blood, because he wants to be left alone in peace, the Moorish *converso* replies: '- Solo no puede ser [...] Quizá sea soledad el infierno; pero el mundo es compañía, y nos necesitamos todos unos a otros. ¿Comprendes, bufón? Todos los vivos somos hermanos' (215-216).

The Devil wants others to share his fate and during the Bufón's dream of death in the course of the King's *autillo*, in the guise of his animal emblem the monkey, tempts the Bufón with the royal crown and immortality on condition that he neither loves nor hates. The Bufón rejects the temptation and answers the call to life – 'Lázaro, ven fuera' – with a salutation of joy to his resurrected body: '- Mica, ¡soy mortal y libre! ¡Ni rey ni bufón, soy, al fin, hombre!' (111). Although at this stage he does not know what it is, he surmises as he reads his brother's account of Lázaro that there may be a purpose to their resurrection: 'A los dos nos desvelaron de la muerte y sus burlerías – tan falsas acaso una como otras -, voces que nos ordenaban dejar el osorio. Obedecimos, sí, *mas sigo preguntándome si con dejar la fosa cumplimos del todo lo mandado.* Nacimiento y resurrección precisan concurso ajeno. La vida, empero, como dicta la Iglesia, es albedrío. Somos libres por vueltos a mortal envoltura y yo, al menos, no sé qué hacer con mi carne visible y mi oculta libertad' (209-210). It will be given to the *Bufón*, and in him Lázaro, to realize the active purpose of their resurrection, fulfilling the King's prophetic words to his dwarf:

> - Carlitos, deliras. ¿Quién soy yo entre el demonio y la santa inquisición?
> - Puedes ser más fuerte que los dos. (74)

Lázaro sees his resurrection as an act of betrayal as he had no belief in life, only in death: 'No quise amar ni aborrecer desde el día que mortal me supe. Me reduje a ignorarme y a ignorar el mundo perecedero (196) [...] Yo no creí nunca en el cielo ni en la tierra. Sólo en la muerte (198)'. In his exchanges with Judas, who has betrayed Christ because he believed Christ had betrayed his Messianic mission to liberate the sons of Israel from political oppression, Lázaro defines Christ's mission as that of enabling man to pronounce the name of God and to call Him Father at the price of his own life. He expresses a belief in the necessity of love – 'No, hijo de Simón: es necesario amar y compadecer. Cuando toda nuestra piedad devenga amor, el hombre de Nazaret regreserá a su Padre, y yo habré logrado mi paz' (234) – but, he sits passively holding the heart of his mother which is mysteriously resuscitated at the time of Christ's Resurrection, withdrawn from the world. In a soliloquy addressed to his dead brother – 'No soy tu guardián, Felipe Próspero, pues tú ya nada eres' -, the *Bufón* questions what his role in life should be in relation to his dead brother and Lázaro: 'En los sueños más secretos y sutiles, los más inconfesables, pienso ser tu Lázaro, este Lázaro por quien volverían a quemarte si resucitases. El, como yo, regresó de la muerte por orden ajena. Soy quien tú me hiciste, pero no sé quién soy. Alguien tiene que vivir por ti – creo adivinarlo – y éste soy yo; pero ignoro cómo debo vivir; cómo lo harías tú en mi lugar' (133). Through a series of visions and strange experiences, linked by the symbolic motifs of blood and ashes, the *Bufón* will learn that he *is* his brother's keeper across the bounds of time and death.

But first the *Bufón* partly realizes his role in relation to the King, explicitly identified as Judas in Chapter 9. Because Coca's wife has been cured of her issue of blood, the *Bufón* is now credited with miraculous power and the King asks him to prolong his life in order to save the kingdom from a foreign heir. The *Bufón* attributes his desire to live to his fear of damnation and, in order to hurt the King, he defines Hell as eternal remorse: '- El infierno es eterna, penosa memoria. Allí verás siempre a tu hijo, como lo vi yo: amarrado a la estaca del quemadero, abrasándose vivo y sonriéndote' (251-252). This is followed by an act of God when lightning strikes the coachman. Coca's dying words, from the mouth of a *converso* who has eaten a surfeit of pork to prove the authenticity of his conversion, – 'Cerdos, os amo, sois mis hermanos y mis semejantes (256)' -, are a grotesque formulation of the fundamental message of the novel: the communion of man in flesh and spirit. The pity that is treacherously contained by the banks of the Manzanares is released beside the King's deathbed in the penultimate chapter in response to a plea for Christ's mercy: 'Cuando en el fondo del infierno tópeme con Felipe Próspero, empezaré eterno penar, sin tregua. Más allá del fin de los tiempos, quedaremos solos los dos: él meditando agravio y yo temeroso de su venganza. ¡Cristo, ten piedad de mis llagas!' (435) The *Bufón* reveals what he had previously kept hidden from the King, the existence of Felipe Próspero's Lázaro manuscript, discovered by the Inquisition, which would have been sufficient cause for his condemnation if he had not resurrected his brother. The King can now face death: 'En el juicio o en el infierno, sostendré su mirada y le diré: "Perdóname por hombre, no por padre, el mal que te hice. Por mortales, tú, bufón, y yo, rey, compartimos la carne y el ánima' (436). The *Bufón* believes the mission of his resurrection is accomplished in helping to reconcile the betrayer to eternity in a peaceful death: 'Lázaro de Bethania, soñaste tuya mi vida; pero no alcanzaste a soñar por qué me resurgieron. Yo lo sé ahora, y a ti, solamente a ti, te lo confieso: fue para que otro día ayudase a bien morir al verdugo de mi resucitador. Lázaro de Bethania, sueña otro sueño mío, te lo suplico: descuelga a Judas de Keiroth de su cinto, antes de que perezca, y dile que tarde o temprano hubiesen crucificado al Rabbí, sin aguardar su traición, porque él me había resucitado' (436-437).

White doves, emblematic of the Holy Spirit, spell out the message in the sky over Madrid 'LA MUERTE HA MUERTO' (440). But the full reason for the Bufón's resurrection remains to be revealed in the fantastic vision of the Epilogue: *'pero ahora, sólo ahora, comprendo por fin por qué me resurgió aquel día mi hermanastrillo, y por qué escribió antes su fábula de Lázaro y Judas.* Temía y sentíase solo: esto era todo (462). [...] Hasta un truhán y un bastardo necesita un hermano en este mundo. Felipe Próspero mío, quizá porque todos somos espurios, acaso porque todos somos hermanos' (463). In a scene that recalls the final scene of *The Last Temptation* in which Judas helps Christ accept his destiny on the Cross, the *Bufón* helps Felipe Próspero in the present to reverse a course of action in an alternative past, to take up his cross and follow Christ: 'Nunca hasta ahora lo supe, mas hoy te lo juro: en cada reo, sea quien fuere, revive la muerte de Cristo' (467).

In this vision Felipe Próspero had recanted at the stake and confessed that his brother's resurrection was the Devil's work; his death sentence had been commuted to life imprisonment, so that when Carlos' last testament naming him his son and heir is found, he is released in order to be crowned King as Felipe V. He is crowned by the Inquisitor Mendoza, before an assembled company of the living and the dead and of dancing devils, with a cardboard crown and seated on a wooden throne, symbolizing the ephemeral nature of earthly power. The Inquisitor requires the new King as the embodiment of justice to judge, not only Carlos and Judas, but also his own actions in speaking the words of Christ and bringing his brother back to life. The *Bufón* engages in a desperate battle for the eternal salvation of his brother's soul with the Inquisitor who threatens to execute Felipe Próspero if he does not declare his brother to be Satan himself:

> -Sólo soy tu hermano, y te traigo la vida que te debo. Me la diste de palabra en este patio y de palabra te la devuelvo. Diles que me amabas cuando me alzaste de entre los muertos y serás libre, ¿comprendes? Libre para siempre.
> - ¿Libre?
> - Sí, de morir quemado gritando la verdad que ellos dicen reniego. No cabe otra, Felipe Próspero, en esta tierra. (467)

The *Bufón* helps his brother overcome his fear of death, by presenting him with the choice of the vision of resurrection as either eternal death or eternal life: 'Todos la [resurrección] tenemos, Felipe Próspero: Lázaro, Judas, el rey, tú y yo. Vivir eternamente, con la conciencia por carne, devorada por los gusanos del ánima, sería el peor de los castigos. Salva la tuya en la hoguera y el verdugo será tu redentor. ¡Ven fuera! ¡Ven fuera, hermano mío!' (468). The *Bufón* in his turn assumes the role of Christ as redeemer, fulfilling his *kairos* by assisting his brother to fulfil his *kairos*. Man is not saved alone, but in the company of his fellow, his other, his brother. The Beatific Vision offered to the reader by Carlos Rojas in *Auto de fe* is a shared vision of mutual love for all eternity,[12] but the choice of that vision begins and continues in the communion of man in the here and now:

> Aquí, hasta en el soñar nos vemos otro a través de los tiempos. Si Lázaro y yo nos alzáramos en un mundo vacío de semejantes, sería nuestra resurrección idéntica a la muerte, y fuera dislate resurgir para ser solos. Ahora creo comprender el proverbio que mi hermano inventóse en mi sueño: TODO PODER PERECERA PARA QUE RESUCITE EL HOMBRE. Las tinieblas, hechas miedo, odio, egoísmo, soberbia, poder en suma, nos separan y aíslan como la misma muerte. Para que reviva en cada uno de nosotros la humanidad es preciso alentar para otros concebidos a nuestra imagen y semejanaza, pues con ellos compartimos la vida eterna: el pan, el vino y la resurrección de todos los días. (439)

NOTES

1. *Auto de fe*, Madrid: Guadarrama, 1968. Page references for quotations from this edition are cited within brackets in the text. An earlier novel, *La ternura del hombre invisible*, Barcelona: Plaza & Janés, 1963, bears a Cervantine epigraph: '- Yo sé quién soy – respondió don Quijote. – Mi nombre es Nadie: así me han llamado siempre mi madre, mi padre y todos mis amigos.'

2. His main secondary source for the life of Carlos II appears to have been John Nada, *Carlos the Bewitched*, London: Jonathon Cape, 1962. This work is cited in a previous novel, *Adolfo Hitler está en mi casa*, Barcelona: Ediciones Rondas, 1965, in which a fictional alter ego is writing a film-script on the life of *The Bewitched*. By the end of this novel, the reader begins to wonder if the author Carlos Rojas does not believe he *is* a reincarnation of Carolus Rex.

3. *The Newe Testament of Our Lord Iesus Christ*, Imprinted at London by the Deputies of Christopher Barker, Printer to the Queenes Maiestie, 1589, p.448.

4. *The Cambridge Bible Commentary on the New English Bible: Introductory Volume: Understanding the New Testament*, ed. O. Jessie Lace, Cambridge/London/New York/Melbourne: Cambridge University Press, 1965, p.84.

5. Quoted by M. García-Viñó, 'La nueva novela española', in *La nueva novela europea*, Madrid: 1968, p.73. Rojas, 'Problemas de la nueva novela española', ibid., p.123, writes: 'La literatura es siempre nueva, asegura Ezra Pound. Unamuno estaría de acuerdo, pues tal es su concepto de la intrahistoria: novedad eterna, bajo el caduco, por perecedero, acontecer histórico.'

6. *La ternura del hombre invisible*, p.121.

7. ibid.

8. In a letter sending his manuscript to Börje Knös in 1951, Kazantzakis wrote: 'I wanted to renew and supplement the sacred Myth that underlies the great Christian civilization of the West. It isn't simply a "Life of Christ". It's a laborious, sacred, creative endeavor to reincarnate the essence of Christ, setting aside the dross – falsehoods and pettinesses which all the churches and all the cassocked representatives of Christianity have heaped upon His figure, thereby distorting it. The pages of my manuscript were often smudged because I could not hold back my tears. Parables which Christ could not possibly have left as the Gospels relate them I have supplemented and I have given them the noble and passionate ending befitting Christ's heart. Words which we do not know that He said I have put into His mouth, because He would have said them if His Disciples had had His spiritual force and purity. And everywhere poetry, love of animals and plant life and men, confidence in the soul, certainty that the light will prevail.' (Helen Kazantzakis, *Nikos Kazantzakis. A Biography Based on his Letters* , Oxford: Bruno Cassirer, 1968, p.505). Kazantzakis had written to Renaud de Jouvenel from Madrid in November 1932 (ibid., p. 256): 'The two extremes of the Spanish spirit – *Nada* [Nothingness] and Passion – offer me the austere climate that suits me. Here, I breathe with ease. If I could, I would settle down in this old Castile, as my compatriot El Greco did. I love and admire the clarity and unbefogged rationality of the French race. But I feel rather stifled within their precise horizon. To stare straight into the *Nada* and to have a burning love of life (of the path leading to the *Nada*), this is what I love and find here in the earth, the air, the windmills of our Lord, Don Quixote.'

9. 'Eschatology', *The Encyclopaedia Britannica*, Cambridge: University Press, 1910 (11th edn), XI, p.762.

10. In 'Problemas de la nueva novela española', op. cit., p. 123 Rojas writes of the act of creation: 'Se hace lo que se es y lo que otros hicieran de uno. Escribir es perseverar, no sólo en esencia sino en propia conciencia. Cada título es una firma estampada con nuestra sangre y ésta debe ser tan fresca como auténtica.' In an interview published by José María Gironella,

100 españoles y Dios, Barcelona: Ediciones Nauta, 1969, pp. 531-534, Rojas replied to the question '¿La religión le ha influido de alguna manera en el ejercicio de su profesión?': 'La ha determinado, advertida e inadvertidamente, y la sigue determinando. El demonio, es decir: la eternidad del mal y su arraigo en las simas de nuestra conciencia es obsesión permanente en toda mi obra.' I thank Ronald for transcribing this for me a quarter of a century ago.

11. The Inquisitor Mendoza, born with the inscription on his brow 'La peor putada del demoni és fer-nos creure que no existeix' (360), is obsessed with finding the devil in whom he cannot believe. He formulates an ironic demonic inversion of Pascal's Divine wager: 'Si hay demonio e infierno, ellos serán mi bochero y mi castigo por descreerlos. Si no los hay, me condeno igualmente, pues aún no habiéndolos debemos creer en ellos mientras el cielo no disponga lo contrario' (365).

12. 'Beloved, let us love one another; love springs from God; no one can love without being born of God, and knowing God. How can the man who has no love have any knowledge of God, since God is love? What has revealed the love of God, where we are concerned, is that he has sent his only-begotten Son into the world, so that we might have life through him. That love resides, not in our shewing any love for God, but in his shewing love for us first, when he sent out his Son to be an atonement for our sins. Beloved, if God has shewn such love for us, we too must love one another. No man has ever seen God; but if we love one another, then we have God dwelling in us, and the love of God has reached its full growth in our lives. This is our proof that we are dwelling in him, and he in us; he has given us a share in his own Spirit' (I John 4: 8-11), *The Holy Bible*, Knox Version, London: Burns and Oates/Macmillan, 1957, p.255. Or as John Steinbeck's Casey puts it in *The Grapes of Wrath,* Harmondsworth: Penguin Books Ltd, 1951, p.24: ' "Maybe," I figured, "maybe it's all men an' all women we love; maybe that's the Holy Spirit – the human sperit – the whole shebang. Maybe all men got one big soul ever'body's a part of." '

FRANK SMITH

Madrid

THE SPANISH TRANSITION
An Historic Achievement Still Pending?

Spaniards are justifiably proud of their transition from dictatorship to democracy. None more so than the key political figures whose task it was to oversee the momentous changes that were enacted in Spain, following the death of General Franco in 1975.

Almost twenty years later, just after the fall of the Berlin Wall, I remember the late Francisco Fernández Ordóñez – then Spain's Foreign Minister – bubbling with enthusiasm about what had been achieved in Spain. In an interview with the BBC, he advocated with passion that the fomer Soviet bloc countries – at that time emerging slowly from the shackles of Communism – could do no better than take a leaf out of the Spanish book.

I was a producer on Radio Four's *Europhile* programme at the time. The story we were covering was about the Polish secret police and what should be done with those bastions of the former Communist regime as Poland tentatively tried to make sense of its painful democractic re-awakening. A decade or so earlier, Spain had gone through a similar experience. So it seemed valid to turn to Madrid in search of answers.

'We were careful not to exact revenge on people linked with the former regime', Fernández Ordóñez said. 'By and large, people were not booted out of their jobs and even shady characters who had worked in Franco's secret police were accommodated. To have done otherwise would have been to risk fomenting centres of resistance – even armed resistance – in the midst of our society. That would have been very dangerous.'

In many ways, Fernández Ordóñez's own political career – from chairman in Francoist times of the state holding company, INI, through portfolios in the UCD (Union of the Democratic Centre) governments of Adolfo Suárez, to cabinet minister in the Socialist administrations of Felipe González – was, in itself, a paradigm of the spirit of the Spanish transition.

It was a time when Spaniards seemed, for once, to have learned the lessons of their history. A time for people from different walks of like, from different ideologies and persuasions, from different nationalities even – Catalans, Castilians and moderate Basques – to join forces and work together in the common good.

It was no easy task. Iñigo Cavero, recently appointed President of the Council of State, was another cabinet minister in the governments of Adolfo Suárez, during the first years of the transition. I interviewed him for a series of programmes on democracy that the BBC broadcast to Russian audiences in the early 1990s.

'We were not all politicians', he said. 'Nor were we a homogenous bunch. But whatever our backgrounds and beliefs, we felt we had to chip in to ensure that the country got through this difficult period'.

The UCD *was* a disparate group. That explains why it disappeared, almost as quickly as it had been formed, after the Socialists first came to power in 1982. But, in the days immediately after Franco's death, the desire to overcome difficulties and resolve national problems mattered much more than political ideology.

People's past records counted for little. In fact, inside knowledge of the Franco years was considered a positive advantage when it came to the task of dismantling the *ancien régime*. The great architect of the transition, Adolfo Suárez had, after all, been Franco's Minister of the National Movement.

The Spanish transition was not, as John Hooper has succinctly pointed out in his admirable book *The New Spaniards,* a case of forgive and forget. 'Since no one in Spain was ever judged, no one was ever deemed guilty. And since no one was ever deemed guilty, forgiveness never entered into it. It was just a matter of forgetting' (p. 78).

From time to time, the spirit of Spain's transition resurfaces as a talking point in contemporary politics. This is particularly noticeable when the climate becomes brusque and the atmosphere rarified. After the past three years of what has been deemed *'crispación política'*, Spaniards are receiving constant reminders in the media of what is portrayed as a golden age of consensus politics.

Spanish Television (TVE) recently re-ran a documentary series on the transition and the book of the series, written by journalist Victoria Prego, has become a best-seller. The posthumous memoirs of the Archbishop of Madrid and President of the Spanish Episcopal Conference, Cardinal Vicente Enrique y Tarancón, have just been published. Entitled *Confessions*, they outline, from a unique vantage point, the Spanish church's crucial role in the political transition.

All of this looking back has righted one historical injustice in contemporary Spanish public life. Adolfo Suárez, who left politics under a dark cloud in 1981, amid the rattling of sabres, has at last been rescued from the dustbin of history.

The German writer, Hans Magnus Enzensberger (another regular in the early days of the BBC's *Europhile* programme) recognised Suárez's contribution to European history in a short radio talk in 1989. He described the task facing most countries in the new European order as one of orderly retreat. Political leaders such as Suárez, Gorbachov and Jaruselski were entrusted with guiding their countries out of the darkness of their immediate past.

According to Enzensberger, the three faced almost insuperable odds in their political careers. Borrowing heavily from military manuals, the German poet observed that it was far more difficult for a general to effect an orderly retreat than it was for him to order his troops to advance and attack.

Spain, Poland, and the Soviet Union were described as armies on the retreat, each requiring a leader prepared to perform the thankless task of withdrawing and, if possible, avoiding bloodshed.

Gorbachov, Jaruzelski and Suárez all succeeded, but they each paid a huge price in terms of popular support. Perestroika, martial law and the Spanish transition were not instantly understood by the majority of their respective publics. On the other hand, the political lot of more aggressive leaders (Margaret Thatcher was the model chosen in this second instance) was infinitely more easy.

Nowadays, in Spain at least, the lack of public recognition and gratitude has been rectified. Suárez has been restored to the place he rightly deserves in the annals of Spanish history, receiving last autumn the Prince of Asturias Prize for Concord, in recognition of his work during the transition.

The present discussions in Spain about the transition are not, however, a mere exercise in nostalgia about the immediate past. A much more profound debate is raging around the proposition that Spain's political transition is not yet complete.

That in itself is not new. The issue has resurfaced from time to time through the past two decades of democracy in Spain. In the early eighties, the political propaganda of the Socialists ran along the lines that the transition would not be completed until Spaniards elected a government of the left.

Almost a decade and a half later, after thirteen and a half years of Socialist government, the Popular Party of José María

Aznar resurrected virtually the same slogan before the general election of 1996. The transition would not be fully over, the conservatives claimed, until the right got back into power in Spain. Aznar even wrote a book entitled *The Second Transition.*

It is now almost a year since the right came to power, but the question 'Is the transition over?' has re-surfaced again, because the new Aznar government has got itself into an awful mess about what to do in connection with the secret papers relating to the "dirty war", allegedly waged by the Socialist government in the early eighties, against the Basque separatist organisation, ETA.

The courts investigating the GAL (the anti-terrorist liberation groups) want the government to declassify top secret papers of the Spanish secret service, CESID, in order to expedite legal proceedings and verify if orders were given by Socialist cabinet ministers – even by Prime Minister González himself – to carry out the illegal operations which resulted in the deaths of 28 people linked to ETA.

In opposition, the Popular Party seemed in no doubt about the ethics of the case. The papers – they argued then – should be declassified in order to establish the truth and bring any wrong-doing before the courts.

But what proved to be a fruitful line in opposition (it is an undoubted fact that the GAL scandal cost Felipe González a fifth successive term in office), has become something of a legal and constitutional minefield for the new government. Some members of the government have said that the papers should be declassified, but the cabinet decided against that option.

So, there appears to have been a radical *volte-face* as regards the GAL papers. The Popular Party achieved its main goal in defeating the Socialists at the polls last March but the new government seems embarrassed and angry that the GAL scandal just will not go away.

The courts have been persistently knocking on the administration's door to get the secret documents declassified. So far, their efforts have not been successful, but the whole issue has been referred to the Supreme Court.

At the time of writing, it remains to be seen what the court's ruling will be or what action the government will take if, as many believe likely, the Supreme Court does uphold the judges' right to have access to the secret papers.

The main arguments adduced by the government against releasing the documents are based on reasons of state security. It is argued that the government must protect state secrets.

The wholesale leaking of CESID documents to certain sections of the national press has already deeply compromised the Spanish secret service in the eyes of other countries. It is known that the secret services of friendly countries have been witholding information from Spain because of the scandal. By placing the originals of the CESID documents in the public realm, via the courts, the government would be further endangering the interests of, and heaping more opprobrium on, their own secret services.

As well as arguments of state security, Spain's new Defence Minister, Eduardo Serra, adduced another powerful reason why the government should not release the CESID documents. To do so, he argued, would be to break the conventions of Spain's transition, by flying in the face of the tradition of forgetting what people had done in the past.

On one level, of course, such arguments smack of political convenience. The judges investigating GAL are not likely to be deterred in their efforts to clean out the stables of Spain's murky past, by the thought that they may be embarrassing the political classes.

The confrontation between the judiciary and the executive, therefore, over the CESID papers seems likely to continue for some time to come. This struggle, what is alternately described in Spain as either the "judicialisation of politics" or the "politicisation of the judiciary", is a sure sign that, on one fundamental level, the transition in Spain is, indeed, not yet over. The separation of powers has not been fully achieved.

In that sense, Eduardo Serra *is* right. To rake up misdeeds, to call people to task for past political actions is still a dangerous exercise in today's Spain. There there are too many skeletons in the cupboard. If the courts were allowed *carte blanche* to investigate the alleged malpractices of recent Socialist administrations, what would stop them delving even further into the past?

Eduardo Serra has also raised another intriguing possibility. If the Supreme Court were to rule that the government must release the CESID papers, he said he would appeal to an obscure piece of Francoist legislation in order to countermand such a ruling.

Observers have been divided as to the probity of such a recourse. Would it be constitutional or not? No one seems to know the exact answer. Another clear example of the legal uncertainty that predominates in contemporary Spanish politics. Another clear example, by implication, that the transition is not yet fully over.

Nor is it accidental that it is Eduardo Serra who should be at the centre of this present imbroglio. For the new Defence Minister is another of those Spanish politicians whose career typifies how the transition has worked in Spain.

Now a Conservative cabinet minister, Serra served in the Socialist administration of Felipe González in the early eighties, in the Ministry of Defence, at the time – incidentally – when the GAL were at their most active.

Many people believe Serra's appointment as a cabinet minister was forced upon José María Aznar, in order to ease the right's passage into power after so many years in the political wilderness.

It is just possible that Aznar himself realised the need for someone who understood the ropes of the immediate past to make up for the lack of experience in what is essentially a young cabinet team.

Either way, Serra is a figure who stands for continuation in the sea change from a Socialist administration to a conservative one. He is a political figure in the mould of Francisco Fernández Ordóñez – the sort of politician still deemed essential to oversee Spain's not yet completed political transition.

It has been fashionable, in the democratic Spain of the past two decades, to use Montesquieu as a kind of barometer. His postulations on the separation of powers were first resurrected and then – some have claimed – buried again as the Socialists tightened their stranglehold on the Spanish state in the mid-eighties.

Felipe González has been depicted as a kind of all powerful Caesar figure. Some of his decisions have certainly smacked of omnipotence. One of his very first – the expropriation and sell-off of Rumasa – seemed to many to fly in the face of any legal safeguard.

As late as 1993, González achieved the remarkable coup of signing up for his party one of the most uncompromising judges on the Spanish bench to stand as an independent candidate in the general election of that year. Judge Baltasar Garzón – who believed he had a copper-bottomed guarantee from González to effect the elimination of corruption in Spanish public life – undoubtedly swayed the voters in favour of the Socialists, in an election that many believe González should have lost.

Garzón was quickly to be bitterly disappointed with his short-lived stint in politics. A year after the election, he resigned his seat in Congress amid acrimonious complaints that he had been sold down the river, tricked by González into putting his reputation on the line for a party that had no intention of cleaning up its act. Garzón is now back on the bench in the Audiencia Nacional where he has resumed his investigation of the GAL case with a vengeance.

The Garzón episode illustrates how ill-defined the dividing line remains in Spain between the executive and the judiciary. If anything the judge's brief sally into politics did irreparable damage to the endeavours of many within the Spanish judiciary to effect a total dissociation between themselves and the executive.

The close identity between executive and judiciary is not a problem that was invented by the Socialists. It was – it still is – a direct inheritance of the Francoist era. The dictator effectively disembodied the judiciary by splitting it up into sectarian areas. In what was a classic case of divide and rule, Franco handed over all military matters – including cases of terrorism – to the military courts. Ecclesiastical jurisdiction was handled by the Church and what little was left was given to civil lawyers. No wonder then that Spain's legal classes turned to government and parliament – a large number of the deputies in Congress are to this day qualified lawyers – in search of real power.

The battle between politicians and judges in today's Spain may have been enjoined but its outcome is still far from certain. Until such time as it is resolved, we will not be able to say that the Spanish transition is over, nor if it has succeeded.

If Tocqueville is right, the real transition will only be effected when the habits of the heart and spirit change. 'Je suis bien convaincu', he wrote to his friend, Francisque de Corcelle in 1853, 'que les sociétés politiques sont, non ce que les font leurs lois, mais ce que les préparent d'avance à être les sentiments, les croyances, les idées, les habitudes de coeur et d'esprit des hommes qui les composent, ce que le naturel et l'éducation ont fait ceux-ci'.

On that score, as far as Spain and its transition is concerned, the jury is still out.

(Frank Smith is Madrid correspondent for the BBC and *The Observer,* and a Lecturer in Journalism at the Universidad San Pablo-CEU, Madrid).

OWEN REES

University of Surrey

A SPANISH COMPOSER IN LISBON: THE POLYCHORAL MUSIC OF FRANCISCO GARRO

The era widely acknowledged as Portugal's 'golden age' in music – the late sixteenth century and the first half of the seventeenth century – corresponds rather neatly with the period of Spanish Hapsburg rule in Portugal (1580–1640). Unsurprisingly, one of the issues most often raised concerning Portuguese musical culture of this time is the strength and nature of the relationship between that culture and those of Spain and other countries.[1] During the sixty years of Hapsburg rule a number of Portuguese composers sought employment and patronage in Spain.[2] However, traffic the other way seems already to have been healthy during the reigns of João III (1521–1557) and Sebastião (1557–1578): several Spanish musicians dedicated publications to Portuguese royalty,[3] and others worked at the Lisbon court.[4] The first *mestre de capela* at Évora Cathedral was the Spaniard Mateo de Aranda, who went on to become Professor of Music at Coimbra University; another Spaniard – Dom Francisco de Santa Maria – was *mestre de coro* and *mestre de capela* at the Augustinian Monastery of Santa Cruz in Coimbra from the 1560s until the 1590s, having previously served João de Portugal (Bishop of Guarda) and João Soares (Bishop of Coimbra) as *mestre de capela*.[5] Under the Philips, members of the Lisbon Capela Real included a Spanish *mestre* (Francisco Garro, whose music is the subject of this study) and many other Spanish musicians. As early as 1581 Philip had summoned to Lisbon the organist Hernando de Cabezón (son of the famous Antonio de

Cabezón), and several other Spanish keyboard players served the Chapel in the late sixteenth and early seventeenth centuries: Sebastián Martínez Verdugo (from Madrid), Estácio Lacerna (from Seville), and Diego de Alvarado (from Vizcaya). Overall, a recent survey has revealed that more of the Chapel's musicians (thirteen) are identified as Spanish in chancery documents during this period than are identified as Portuguese (eleven).[6] Outside the Capela Real, one of the distinguished pupils of Filipe de Magalhães at the Colégio dos Moços do Coro attached to Évora Cathedral was the Spaniard Estêvão Lopes Morago, who went on to be *mestre de capela* at Viseu Cathedral from 1599 until 1630. In addition, the printed catalogue of part of the vast music library amassed by João IV provides vivid testimony to the continuing influence of Spanish musicians in the first half of the seventeenth century, at least upon this avid collector.[7]

An especially prominent place in João's library was taken by the Flemish composers of the Spanish Royal Chapel, such as Philippe Rogier, Géry de Ghersem, and Mateo Romero.[8] João had copies of no fewer than 243 pieces by Rogier alone;[9] he also commissioned works from Romero and Carlos Patiño (Romero's successor as *maestro* of the Spanish Royal Chapel) through his agent in Madrid,[10] and made efforts to acquire the complete works and musical library of Romero (who spent some six months at João's palace in Vila Viçosa in 1638).[11]

The existence of such multi-faceted musical contacts between Spain and Portugal raises numerous questions concerning the influence of particular composers (or 'schools' of composers) and repertories on others. The impact which the music of one Spanish composer – Francisco Guerrero – made upon the Portuguese Duarte Lobo is clear (since four of the eight parody Masses by Lobo for which the models have been identified are based on works by Guerrero), and Guerrero's influence has recently been recognised also within the work of

Filipe de Magalhães (whose *Missa Veni Domine* is based upon a Guerrero motet).[12] However, at present we have almost no equivalent evidence (i.e. the choice of models for parody Masses) pointing to the influence of other Spaniards upon Portuguese composers, although it must be said that the models of a significant number of parody Masses remain unidentified. It is particularly striking – given all that has been said above – that no Masses by Portuguese musicians are known to be based on works by the prominent members of the Spanish Royal Chapel, from Pierre de Manchicourt to Philippe Rogier and his successors mentioned above. It is thus difficult to assess the validity of the view expressed by Manuel Carlos de Brito, when he emphasises the role of the composers associated with the Madrid Royal Chapel in guiding the styles of Peninsular polyphony, and indeed sees their influence as a major cause of the stylistic conservatism of sacred music in Spain and Portugal in the late sixteenth and early seventeenth centuries: 'Poder-se-á argumentar com alguma razão que este florescimento tardio da tradição flamenga em Espanha, paralelamente com o isolamento cultural no qual toda a Península mergulhou depois da Contra-Reforma, são os principais responsáveis pelas tendências conservadoras que se podem encontrar na música religiosa portuguesa e espanhola até bem entrado o século XVII'.[13] A more specific claim for the influence of the Royal Chapel composers has been made by Rui Nery, when discussing the works of Francisco Garro, the Spanish *mestre* of the Royal Chapel in Lisbon from 1592 until his death in 1623. Nery sees Garro's output as displaying 'um gosto pela policoralidade que parece revelar alguma influência dos compositores flamengos ao serviço da Capela Real de Madrid'.[14]

Garro's music does indeed provide a fascinating opportunity to consider possible Spanish influence upon Portuguese musical culture. After all, Garro held perhaps the most prestigious musical position in Lisbon for over three decades, and

– according to one document – was also *mestre de capela* to Duke Teodósio II of Bragança. Since Garro's post in Lisbon was parallel to that of Rogier in Madrid, one can easily believe that he might have acted as a conduit through which the influence of Spanish Royal Chapel musicians spread to Lisbon. However, Garro's polychoral works (published in a single collection in 1609) which Nery identifies as revealing such influence remain largely unstudied (although the rest of Garro's output of sacred music has formed the subject of a dissertation[15]). We cannot therefore say at present either whether they reveal influence from Madrid or whether Portuguese musicians of the time were themselves influenced by Garro's music. Indeed, looking beyond Garro's output one can observe that the polychoral sacred music written in Portugal at this period has been in large part omitted from assessments of the country's musical culture in the sixteenth and seventeenth centuries,[16] resulting in an unbalanced view which hinders any evaluation of possible influences from Spain or elsewhere. The present study aims to right the balance somewhat by providing a preliminary survey of Garro's polychoral works and identifying possible influences of Garro's music upon Portuguese composers.

Garro's sacred music (or, at least, all that has so far been identified) is preserved in two publications both of which were issued in 1609 – they were the first books of polyphonic music printed in Portugal – by the royal printer Pieter van Craesbeeck.[17] One of these prints, containing all the surviving polychoral music, appeared as a set of part-books, that is, with each vocal part in a separate book.[18] No complete set of the thirteen original part-books has been located (an all-too-frequent situation with music published in part-books, which are of course more easily lost than substantial choirbook-format prints), but three partial sets are known to survive: these are in the British Library, the Biblioteca Geral of Coimbra University, and the Biblioteca Pública e

Arquivo Distrital in Braga.[19] In addition, the music library of João IV once contained a copy.[20]

Garro dedicated his collection of polychoral works to Philip III of Spain. The title-page of the books reads: 'FRANCISCI GARRI NATIONE NAVARRI; NUNC IN REGIA CAPELLA OLISIPONENSI CAPELLANI, ET IN EADEM MUsices præfecti opera aliquot: AD PHILIPPUM TERTIUM HISPANIARUM Regem, secundi Lusitaniæ. Missæ quatuor, octonis vocibus tres, & una duodenis. Defunctorum lectiones tres, octonis vocibus. Tria Alleluia, octonis etiam vocibus...' ('Certain works of Francisco Garro, a native of Navarre, currently Chaplain in the Royal Chapel at Lisbon, and Director of Music in that Chapel: to Philip III of Spain, II of Portugal. Four Masses, three of them with eight voices, and one with twelve. Three Lessons of the Dead, with eight voices. Three Alleluias, also with eight voices...'). The licences which follow show that the music was ready to be printed by the Spring of 1607. Garro's dedication to Philip III begins by recalling the composer's long service in the Lisbon Royal Chapel, and his appointment by the King's father. What follows indicates that the works published in the collection had been composed during Garro's years in Lisbon, that they were performed both in public and privately by the singers of the Capela Real, and that they had won the approval of both natives and foreigners.[21] Their publication is, says Garro, both a response to demands that they be made widely available and also an attempt to increase the honour of the Lisbon Chapel.[22]

Craesbeeck's work in publishing the volume can only be described as shoddy. The numerous errors include those which might well have caused problems in performance, such as wrong notes, the frequent misplacing of G2 clefs as G1 clefs, the omission of the flat signature from the last two staves of the first tenor part of *Parce mihi Domine*, the wrong positioning of *custodes* (the signs at the end of staves which tell the singer the pitch of the next note), and the common omission of a ledger line for notes on the first line above the stave. In addition, the placing of text under the music is sometimes very careless, text is omitted, and there are mistakes in the Latin (such as 'elegit' instead of 'elegi' in the title of the last piece, and the omission of a whole word ('homo') in the bassus chorus 1 part of *Parce mihi Domine*). It is clear also that Craesbeeck did not possess a music fount adequate for his task; specifically, he could not reproduce ligatures (symbols representing two or more notes), and had to add elements of these symbols by hand.[23] The result would have been particularly unclear to singers in the *Missa pro defunctis*, which makes extensive use of ligatures. One must conclude that the volume was never proof-read by the composer.

The print contains the following works:[24]

1	Missa Cantate Domino
2	Missa Fili quid fecisti nobis sic
3	Domine in virtute tua lætabitur rex
4	Missa pro defunctis
5	Parce mihi Domine
6	Responde mihi
7	Spiritus meus
8	Alleluia. Tanto tempore vobiscum sum
9	Alleluia. Vidimus stellam eius in Oriente
10	Alleluia. Ego vos elegi (with alternative verse: Assumpta est Maria)

The contents thus fall into three sections, which are at first glance apparently distinct:

1. four Masses (nos. 1–4 above);
2. three lessons for Matins of the Dead (nos. 5–7);
3. three Alleluia settings (nos. 8–10).

When one looks more closely, links between these sections become apparent. Thus, not only is there an obvious liturgical link between the *Missa pro defunctis* (no. 4) and the three lessons for Matins of the Dead (nos. 5–7; the texts are the first lesson of each nocturn of Matins),[25] but each of the first three Masses in the collection is linked to one of the Alleluia settings, as is indicated by the titles – 'AD I. MISSAM', 'AD II. MISSAM', and 'AD III. MISSAM' – given to the Alleluias. With regard to this facet of the collection, it seems likely that at least some of these pairs of works were composed as such rather than simply being presented as related for the purposes of publication. Thus, as far as we can tell from the surviving parts, the *Missa Fili quid fecisti nobis sic* and the *Alleluia. Vidimus stellam* used the same clef-combination.[26] In addition, all three Masses are in the same mode as their corresponding Alleluia setting, and there are motivic links between Mass and Alleluia setting in the cases of the first two pairs of works.

This pairing of Masses and Alleluia settings draws a substantial proportion of the volume's contents into what was a clear strategy of including pieces honouring the royal dedicatee. The most obvious reference to Philip (or his father) is the text of the first Alleluia verse (for Mass on the Feast of SS. Philip and James, Apostles): 'Tanto tempore vobiscum sum et non cognovistis me? Philippe, qui videt me, videt et patrem meum'. The last sentence, preceded by the words 'Ostende nobis patrem' and omitting the final 'meum', was to be used also by Manuel Cardoso as the text of an added voice-part in the *Agnus Dei* of his *Missa Philippina*, included in his book of Masses published in 1636 and dedicated to Philip IV.[27] There also exist several motets setting the portion of the text beginning 'Philippe, qui videt me' (which appears as the antiphon to the second psalm at Second Vespers for the feast just mentioned), but with 'alleluia' added at two points. Two of these motets are by composers associated with the Chapel of Charles V: Tomas Crecquillon (master of the Chapel) and Nicolas Gombert (a singer and master of the choirboys in the Chapel).[28] In addition, a number of composers set the complete Alleluia verse text (beginning 'Tanto tempore') as a motet, and these included a master of the Royal Chapel of Philip II – Pierre de Manchicourt. It is quite likely that this last piece and some at least of the *Philippe, qui videt me* motets were written in honour of Philip.

It is tempting to speculate regarding an occasion which might have prompted the composition of Garro's *Alleluia. Tanto tempore* and the Mass with which it is linked in the 1609 print: the *Missa Cantate Domino.* Unfortunately, the parody model (presumably a motet) upon which this Mass is based has not been identified. However, given its joyful title, one wonders whether it might have been written for the celebration in Lisbon of Philip III's coronation in 1598, or the King's first visit to Lisbon.

With regard to the third Mass in the collection, its title – *Domine in virtute tua lætabitur rex* – immediately suggests another compliment to the royal dedicatee. (In this respect it is notable that so unusually extensive a title is given in the print, presumably so that the word 'rex' was included.) Although, once again, no surviving parody model for this Mass has been identified, it is intriguing that there once existed a motet for twelve voices upon this same text, composed by Philippe Rogier and copied for Philip II's Chapel by Isaac Bertout in 1593.[29] Given Rogier's position and the fact that the piece was in the repertory of the Madrid Royal Chapel, together with the nature of the text, this motet was in all likelihood written in honour of Philip II. If this was the parody model for Garro's Mass (which seems likely, given both the identical number of voices and the parallel posts held by Garro and Rogier), then his Mass too was probably written for Philip, and printed as an act of homage to his son. When considering possible occasions for its composition, it is worth examining the text – from Psalm 20 – which Rogier (or the composer of Garro's model, if this was not it) is likely to have set. Palestrina's motet with this same incipit, a work which formed the parody model for Rogier's Mass with the same title, includes the first four verses of the Psalm in its *prima pars*:

> Domine in virtute tua lætabitur rex: et super salutare tuum exsultabit vehementer.
> Desiderium cordis eius tribuisti ei: et voluntate labiorum eius non fraudasti eum.
> Quoniam prævenisti eum in benedictionibus dulcedinis: posuisti in capite eius coronam de lapide pretioso.
> Vitam petiit a te, e tribuisti ei longitudinem dierum: in sæculum, et in sæculum sæculi.

Whether or not Garro's parody model included verse 3, with its reference to coronation ('thou hast placed a crown of precious gold upon his head'), the title of the Mass would have brought the whole Psalm to mind. There may thus have been a link with Philip III's coronation in 1598. Verse 4, on the other hand, would clearly have been more appropriate to Philip II's long reign ('He asked thee for life, and thou granted him length of days, for ever and ever') than to his son (born in 1578). The Alleluia with which this Mass is associated in the 1609 publication is provided with two alternative verses, of which the first has the following text: 'Ego vos elegi de mundo, ut eatis et fructum afferatis, et fructus vester maneat'. Once again, it seems very likely that Garro chose to publish such a setting not principally with the intention that it be used to mark the feast of St Barnabas (for which it is the Alleluia verse at Mass), but to honour his Hapsburg masters as God's 'elect', whose line would endure.[30]

The remaining Alleluia in the collection – with the verse 'Vidimus stellam eius in Oriente, et venimus cum muneribus adorare Dominum' – belongs liturgically to Mass on the feast of the Epiphany. Nevertheless one wonders whether the opening words of the verse might not have been intended in this context to mark the birth of another 'star in the East' (as viewed from Portugal), the future Philip IV (born in 1605). The Mass associated with this piece is entitled 'Fili quid fecisti nobis sic': it was presumably based upon a motet (so far unidentified) with a text similar to the following (found in a motet by Lassus, and taken from Luke 2):

> Fili, quid fecisti nobis sic? Ego et pater tuus dolentes quærebamus te. Quid est quod me quærebatis? An nesciebatis quia in his quæ Patris mei sunt oportet me esse?

There is no obvious textual connection between this and the Alleluia with which it is paired; nevertheless, there are musical links between the two works (as noted above) which suggest that they were composed as a pair. Perhaps then the Mass's title was intended to refer not only to the young Jesus but to the heir to the throne.

Whether or not there is any value in these last speculations, the connection between parts at least of the 1609 collection and Garro's royal masters seems clear. The final Mass – the *Missa pro defunctis* – and the lessons for Matins of the Dead provide no equivalent clues through their titles or texts.[31] In deciding to place a *Missa pro defunctis* at the end of the group of Masses in the print Garro was following the precedent of the most eminent Spanish composers of the previous generations: a *Missa pro defunctis* occurs at the end of the *Missarum liber secundus* (1544) of Cristóbal de Morales and both books of Masses by Francisco Guerrero (1566 and 1582).[32] The influence of Guerrero upon Garro is apparent in the latter's choice of the former's motet

Maria Magdalene as the source of material for his own parody Mass of that title.

Garro's arrival in Lisbon to take up a position in the Royal Chapel coincided quite closely with the convergence on the city of all three of the greatest Portuguese composers of the time: Manuel Cardoso, Duarte Lobo, and Filipe de Magalhães.[33] These musicians must have known the Spaniard's music well, especially Magalhães, who was a fellow-member of the Royal Chapel and who acted as Garro's deputy, directing the choir when the *mestre* was absent.[34] The possible influence of Garro's music on these men has not previously been considered; in fact, connections can be found between one work in the 1609 polychoral collection and a Mass by Magalhães, and it may be that a Mass by Lobo also makes reference to one of Garro's from the same collection.

Magalhães published just one book of Masses (in 1636), which he dedicated to Philip IV (as mentioned above). The volume contains eight Masses, of which two are based on chant. Until recently, no convincing model had been traced for any of the other six Masses,[35] but study of the polychoral Masses of Garro reveals what was almost certainly Magalhães's source for the head-motive of the intriguingly entitled *Missa O soberana luz* in the 1636 print.[36] The relevant passage is the setting of the words 'Domine Deus' in the 'Gloria' of Garro's *Missa Fili quid fecisti nobis sic* (ex. 1). This resembles very closely Magalhães's head-motive as it appears in the 'Sanctus' and 'Benedictus' (the former is shown in ex. 2). Besides this thematic resemblance, the two Masses are in the same mode, use the same basic clef-combination (although there are more voice-parts in Garro's Mass), and have the same overall range: three octaves, from *A* to *a"*.[37] The fact that this range is unusually wide for works of the period – which, when notated in *chiavette* clef-combinations as here, do not usually descend so low as do these pieces – increases the significance of this correspondence.

Two further points emerge from this discovery. First, we now have a convincing explanation of the fact that Magalhães adopted for the *Missa O soberana luz* a style – and, in particular, an approach to texture and rhythm – which contrasts strikingly with that of his other surviving works.[38] The principal aspect of the *Missa O soberana luz* which has made it appear so unusual is characteristic of Garro's Mass and indeed of his other polychoral works: the juxtaposition of passages moving in rhythmic values typical of the *stile antico* (the style often seen as most clearly represented by the works of Palestrina) with others employing shorter values and, frequently, syncopation. Such a juxtaposition may be seen, for example, in the 'Sanctus' of the *Missa O soberana luz*, where the long note-values and contrapuntal texture of the opening give way abruptly to homophony and declamation in crotchets and quavers at 'Dominus Deus Sabaoth' (ex. 3). In fact, this passage was probably inspired by the equivalent point in Garro's Mass (ex. 4): the change in rhythmic technique occurs at the same point in the text, and Magalhães retains Garro's falling triadic bass line at 'Pleni sunt cæli'. It must be pointed out that the type of writing observed here is by no means peculiar to Garro's polychoral works, and in other circumstances it would be rash to attribute Magalhães's employment of them in this Mass to Garro's direct influence; however, given the other connections between the *Missa O soberana luz* and the *Missa Fili quid fecisti nobis sic*, it seems probable that Magalhães's approach to rhythm and texture is here indebted to Garro's Mass.

The second point to emerge from the recognition that these pieces are linked concerns the title *O soberana luz*. As already noted, Garro's *Missa Fili quid fecisti nobis sic* is paired in the 1609 print with the *Alleluia Vidimus stellam eius in Oriente*, and the suggestion was made above that there may have been an association between these works and the birth of the future Philip IV in 1605. That the 'soberana luz' of Magalhães's title was intended to be understood as this same 'star in the East' is made all the more likely by the fact that Magalhães dedicated the 1636 book of Masses to Philip IV.

We turn now to the (admittedly more remote) possibility of a connection between one of Garro's polychoral Masses and a Mass by Duarte Lobo. Lobo's *Liber missarum* issued at Antwerp in 1621 was the first book of Masses by a Portuguese composer to reach print. Of the eight Masses which it contains, three are parodies of works by the Spaniard Francisco Guerrero and two of works by Palestrina, while two others are based on plainchant. The identification of borrowed material in the eighth Mass – the *Missa Cantate Donino* – is more difficult. Of the two motives which appear repeatedly in the work, one (ex. 5) may be derived from chant (although no particularly convincing identification of the chant concerned has yet been made).[39] The second motive (ex. 6) appears in Garro's eponymous Mass from the 1609 print;[40] moreover, although it is found in only one section of Garro's piece, that section is the 'Christe', which is also the site of its first appearance in Lobo's work. It might in consequence seem unlikely that the resemblance is wholly fortuitous; however, the situation is complicated by Lobo's use of a similar figure in two settings of Christmas responsories published in his *Opuscula* issued at Antwerp in 1602,[41] and thus printed (although not, of course, necessarily composed) several years before Garro's *Missa Cantate Domino*. The plot thickens further when one considers the other recurrent motive in Lobo's Mass (the first four notes of ex. 5). This occurs at prominent points in the first superius part of Garro's *Missa Cantate Domino*: at the opening of both 'Kyrie' and 'Gloria', and at 'et vitam venturi' towards the end of the 'Credo'. However, the same motive is also used frequently in another eight-voice Mass by Lobo, the *Missa Natalitiæ noctis*, which was – once again – printed in the 1602 *Opuscula*. In addition, the motive appears many times in the two sets of

Christmas responsories (for four and eight voices respectively) in that print.[42] This being so, it is far from certain that Lobo was making deliberate reference to Garro's *Missa Cantate Domino* in his own work of that title.[43]

* * * * *

The very considerable Peninsular repertories of polychoral music have not yet been adequately studied either in their own right or in the context of international polychoral repertories.[44] Until this is done, it is difficult to trace lines of influence, since one cannot state with confidence that a particular trait is, for example, an idiosyncratic feature of Garro's style, or likely to be derived from Rogier or another member of the Spanish Royal Chapel, or from another Spanish source, or from polychoral or other works by composers from outside the Peninsula (including the prestigious Flemish tradition from which Rogier and other Spanish court composers sprang). A good example is Garro's frequent use of syncopated rhythms at the level of the crotchet in, for instance, the *Missa Fili quid fecisti nobis sic*. This can certainly be found in the works of Rogier, such as the 'Kyrie' of the eight-voice *Missa Domine Dominus noster*,[45] but there are many other parallels to Garro's rhythmic practices beyond the music of Rogier: for example, Philippe de Monte (born in 1521, and thus some forty years older than Rogier) showed a fondness for syncopation of this type, and not only in the polychoral *Missa La dolce vista* but in single-choir works such as the *Missa Deus Deus meus* included in his *Liber primus missarum* published at Antwerp in 1587. Similar syncopated writing is likewise not difficult to find in the works of a still more famous composer – Lassus.[46]

One can see a comparable approach to rhythm in Portuguese music of the late sixteenth century (besides Magalhães's *Missa O soberana luz*, whose style may – as already noted – reflect the direct influence of a work by Garro): Duarte Lobo made heavy use of syncopation and of crotchet and quaver declamation in the settings of Christmas responsories published in his *Opuscula* of 1602. These works alone would be sufficient to upset the consensus regarding the technically conservative nature of Portuguese polyphony in the late sixteenth and early seventeenth centuries, but once again we are not yet in a position to identify the ancestry of such writing. It will, I believe, be through just such attempts to trace specific lines of influence and to distinguish and characterise the various Peninsular repertories of polychoral sacred music (as well as other compositional types) that we may become better able to judge the nature and extent of the impact which Hapsburg rule had on the musical culture of Lisbon and of Portugal in general.

NOTES

1. See especially Manuel Carlos de Brito, 'As relações musicais portuguesas com a Espanha, a Itália e os Países Baixos durante a Renascença', *Estudos de História da Música em Portugal* (Lisbon: Editorial Estampa, 1989), pp. 43–54.

2. These included Estêvão de Brito (d. 1641), António Carreira Mourão (d. 1637), Manuel Correia (d. 1653), Manuel Machado (d. 1646), Filipe da Madre de Deus (*c*. 1630–*c*. 1690), Francisco de Santiago (d. 1644), and Manuel de Tavares (d. 1638). In addition, Manuel Cardoso (1566–1650) travelled to the Spanish court in 1631, and was treated generously by Philip IV, who invited him to conduct the singers of the royal chapel; Cardoso subsequently dedicated his Third Book of Masses (1636) to Philip; this book includes a *Missa Philippina*, the composition of which had been proposed to Cardoso by the *maestro* of the royal chapel, Mateo Romero. Another volume published in the same year and dedicated to Philip is Filipe de Magalhães's *Liber missarum*.

3. Luis Milán (*Libro de música de vihuela de mano intitulado El maestro* (Valencia, 1536), dedicated to João III), Juan Bermudo (*El libro primero de la declaración de instrumentos* (Osuna, 1549), likewise dedicated to João III), and Francisco Guerrero (*Liber primus missarum* (Paris, 1566), dedicated to Sebastião; Guerrero travelled to Lisbon in that year to present a copy to the King).

4. For example, various members of the Sevillian Baena family of instrumentalists served João III and Sebastião. Of these, Gonzalo de Baena (who had entered the service of the Portuguese royal house between about 1496 and 1500) published in 1540 an *Arte novamente inventada pera aprender a tanger* – an anthology of pieces intabulated for keyboard – dedicated to João III. See Tess Knighton, 'A newly discovered keyboard source (Gonzalo de Baena's *Arte nouamente inuentada pera aprender a tanger*, Lisbon, 1540):

a preliminary report', *Plainsong and Medieval Music* 5 (1996), 81–112.

5. Biographical details on Francisco de Santa Maria may be found in the author's thesis, 'Sixteenth- and Early Seventeenth-Century Polyphony from the Monastery of Santa Cruz, Coimbra, Portugal', 3 vols (PhD diss., U. of Cambridge, 1991), III, 11–12.

6. Adriana Latino, 'Os músicos da Capela Real de Lisboa c. 1600', *Revista Portuguesa de Musicologia* 3 (1993), p. 12.

7. *Primeira Parte do Index da Livraria de Musica do Muyto Alto, e Poderoso Rey D. João o IV Nossa Senhor* (Lisbon, 1649); modern facsimile edition published as volume II of *Livraria de música de El-Rei D. João IV: estudo musical, histórico e bibliográfico*, ed. Mário de Sampayo Ribeiro (Lisbon: Academia das Ciências, 1967).

8. On these composers, see Paul Becquart, *Musiciens néerlandais à la cour de Madrid; Philippe Rogier et son école (1560–1647)* (Brussels: Académie Royale de Belgique, 1967).

9. See Lavern Wagner, *Philippe Rogier: opera omnia* I, Corpus mensurabilis musicæ 61 (American Institute of Musicology, 1974), p. XII.

10. As pointed out by Rui Nery, in Rui Vieira Nery and Paulo Ferreira de Castro, *História da Música* (Sínteses da cultura portuguesa) (Lisbon: Comissariado para a Europália 91/Imprensa Nacional – Casa da Moeda, 1991), pp. 61–2.

11. João's library contained about 100 works by Romero, as well as approximately 300 by Géry de Ghersem.

12. The author announced the identification of this model in a paper delivered at the VIII Encontro Nacional de Musicologia in Lisbon, 7 April 1997. See the author's forthcoming article

on the subject in *Revista Portuguesa de Musicologia* 7 (1997). The influence of Guerrero's *style* upon those of Lobo and Magalhães remains to be studied.

13. 'As relações musicais', p. 50.

14. Nery and Ferreira de Castro, *História da Música*, p. 60.

15. Adriana Latino, 'Francisco Garro, Mestre da Capela Real de Lisboa (ca.1590/1623): O Livro de Antiphonas, Missas e Motetes publicado em Lisboa em 1609', 2 vols (diss., Mestrado em Ciencias Musicais, Universidade de Coimbra, Faculdade de Letras, 1992). Garro's complete works, edited by Robert Snow, are to be published in the series Portugaliæ Musica.

16. One likely reason for this neglect is the incomplete survival of two of the three printed collections which concentrate on such music – Duarte Lobo's *Opuscula* published at Antwerp in 1602 and the Garro collection just mentioned. This has hitherto discouraged publication of modern editions, and hence study of the music (although the Lobo print and its contents are considered by Armindo Borges in *Duarte Lobo (156?–1646): Studien zum Leben und Schaffen des portugiesischen Komponisten* (Regensburg: Gustav Bosse Verlag, 1986), pp. 95–115 and at various points in Chapter 3 of Part II). The third collection containing significant quantities of polychoral works – João Lourenço Rebelo's *Psalmi, tum Vesperarum tum Completarum. Item Magnificat, Lamentationes et Miserere* (Rome, 1657) – does survive complete, and has been edited by José Augusto Alegria in the series Portugaliæ Musica. As a consequence, Rebelo's 'advanced' musical style does indeed feature in recent accounts of Portuguese sacred music in the seventeenth century.

17. A number of other works – psalm settings, Responsories for Christmas and Epiphany, and villancicos – are listed in the catalogue of João IV's library, but are apparently lost.

18. In this case another separate book contains the *guião* of certain works. This part consists of the lowest sounding line at each point, and was designed for use by an organist or other accompanying instrumentalist.

19. The British Library copies were acquired by the British Museum in (or very shortly before) 1899. A seventeenth- or eighteenth-century hand has added the words 'S. Bento' at the top of pages; a candidate for their original ownership is the Convent of São Bento de Saúde in Lisbon, an important house (the site of which is now the Parliament building) which possessed a fine library and which briefly became the home of the Lisbon Patriarchate after the earthquake of 1755.

    The part-books in the Biblioteca Geral of Coimbra University may once have belonged to Coimbra Cathedral, since a list of books of polyphony held by the Cathedral Succentor in 1635 includes the entry 'Outo Cartapacios de Garro'. See Jóse Augusto Alegria, *O ensino e prática da música nas Sés de Portugal (da Reconquista aos fins do século XVI)*, Biblioteca breve 101 (Lisbon: Instituto de Cultura e Língua Portuguesa, 1985), pp. 50–1. The reference to 'eight books' ('outo' presumably stands for 'oito') may mean either that the set was already incomplete (as indeed is the set in the Biblioteca Geral, which does in fact consist of eight books) or that the entry is inaccurate.

20. Garro's two published editions are listed on pp. 135–6 of the *Primeira Parte do Index* mentioned above.

21. 'Per hos igitur annos...opera aliquot de re Musica composui, quæ à M.V. Cantoribus publicè, & privatè decantata publicè, & privatè placuerunt; aliisque tum nostræ, tum exteræ gentis nationibus communicata cunctorum calculis sunt comprobata.'

22. 'Cúmque assidue efflagitarer, ut ea in communem omnium usum quantocyus dimitterem, consensi tandem; cum, ut urbis huius nostræ votis subscriberem, tum maximè, ut in orbis totius commodis inservirem, Capellæque nostræ decus, & gloriam augerem.'

23. Craesbeeck's son Lourenço, who took over the business upon his father's death in 1632, was still unable to print ligatures properly, as in shown by the Second Book of Masses of Manuel Cardoso, issued in 1636.

24. All works are for eight voices except the *Missa Domine in virtute tua*, which is for twelve. Since there is considerable inconsistency between part-books with regard to the page on which each work begins and ends, no folio numbers have been provided in the list of works here.

25. More will be said below concerning the growing practice in late-sixteenth- and early-seventeenth-century Spain and Portugal of including settings of non-Mass texts (and particularly texts from Matins of the Dead) when publishing polyphonic Requiem Masses.

26. It is likely that the clef-combination of both works was G2, G2, C2, C3 for choir 1 and G2, C2, C3, F3 for choir 2; it should be noted, however, that one part (a different one in each case) is missing from both works.

27. Modern edition by José Augusto Alegria in *Frei Manuel Cardoso (1566–1650): Liber Tertius Missarum*, Portugaliæ Musica 22 (Lisbon: Fundação Calouste Gulbenkian, 1973), pp. 195–6.

28. The other settings are by Ludovicus Louys, Jan Louys, Caspar Othmayr, and Ludwig Senfl.

29. See Becquart, *Musiciens néerlandais*, p. 46.

30. Not only is this Alleluia provided with an alternative verse ('Assumpta est Maria', for the Feast of the Assumption of the Blessed Virgin Mary), but Garro included in the print alternative versions of two sections of the associated Mass, *Domine in virtute tua lætabitur rex* (the sections being 'Domine Deus' in the 'Gloria' and 'Crucifixus' in the 'Credo'). One can imagine a scenario whereby the Mass and

Alleluia were originally composed for a specific event connected with Philip II or Philip III, and that when, subsequently, Garro provided a new Alleluia verse to allow the pieces to be used for the feast of the Assumption he then also took the opportunity to revise the Mass.

31. It is of course quite likely that Garro would have written music to mark the death of Philip II in 1597, but we have no way of knowing whether this was the origin of the Requiem Mass and/or the lessons for Matins of the Dead in the 1609 print.

32. Another Spanish book of Masses to follow the tradition of placing a *Missa pro defunctis* at the end is Juan Esquivel's 1608 *Missarum . . . liber primus.*

33. Garro was paid as *mestre* of the Chapel from 27 September 1592. Cardoso entered the Carmelite Convent (Convento do Carmo) in Lisbon on 1 July 1588. Lobo was *mestre da capela* at the Hospital Real de Todos os Santos from, probably, the early 1590s, and subsequently *mestre* at the Cathedral, a post he had secured by 1594. Magalhães became a Chaplain in the Royal Chapel at about the same time.

34. This emerges from Magalhães's letter of appointment to the post of *mestre*, which begins: 'Dom Phelipe & faço saber a vos dom João da Silva, que servis de mordomo mor de minha casa, que avendo respeito a boa informação que tive de Phelipe de Magalhães, capellão do serviço, e ter servido muitos anos em minha capella real ensinando aos ministros della a musica do canto chão e canto de orgão e ter cuidado da estante nas ausencias do mestre da capella...'; quoted in José Augusto Alegria, *Polifonistas portugueses*, Biblioteca Breve 86 (Lisbon: Instituto de Cultura e Língua Portuguesa, 1984), p. 68.

35. As noted above, the author recently identified the model (by Guerrero) of Magalhães's *Missa Veni Domine.*

36. Modern edition by Luís Pereira Leal in *Filipe de Magalhães (1565?–1652): Liber missarum*, Portugaliæ Musica 27

(Lisbon: Fundação Calouste Gulbenkian, 1975), pp. 148–71. Leal draws attention (p. XVIII of the same volume) to the similarity between the most important theme of this work and the theme upon which Cardoso based his *Missa Philippina* mentioned above. However, the fact that the two themes are in different modes suggests that the resemblance may not be significant.

37. Magalhães's Mass keeps to this range throughout except that there is one *G#* in the bass during the 'Kyrie'.

38. The editor of the modern edition (see note 36 above) reflected this anomalous character when he chose to retain the original note-values for this piece while using halved note-values for his editions of all the other works in the 1636 volume.

39. Armindo Borges notes that this motive is a retrograde form of the opening of the Alleluia verse 'Cantate Domino' for the sixteenth Sunday after Pentecost as it appears in the Lisbon edition of the *Graduale Romanum* dating from 1791; see *Duarte Lobo*, p. 140. This motive appears in the Mass in the form quoted by Borges only at the opening of the 'Kyrie', in the first bass part (shown in ex. 5), but a shortened four-note version of the motive (missing the final note seen in ex. 5) is heard at many points in the work: throughout the first 'Kyrie'; at 'voluntatis' and 'qui tollis' in the 'Gloria'; at the opening of the 'Credo', throughout the section from 'et ex Patre' to 'de Deo vero' in the same movement, and – still within that movement – at 'et incarnatus', 'sub Pontio Pilato', 'et unam sanctam', and 'amen'; at the opening of the 'Sanctus' and in the 'Hosanna'; and at the opening of the 'Agnus Dei'. Borges's hypothesis that the motive is derived from the chant mentioned above is somewhat weakened by the motive's appearance (noted later) in a number of other works by Lobo to which this chant has no relevance.

40. This was first noticed by José António Abreu, to whom I am grateful for sharing the information with me. The relevant motive occurs within Lobo's Mass in the 'Christe', in the

section of the 'Gloria' from 'laudamus te' to 'glorificamus te' and at 'in gloria Dei patris' in the same movement, and at 'et iterum venturus est cum gloria' and 'et vitam' in the 'Credo'. It will be noticed that the words 'gloria'/ 'glorificamus' occur in three of these instances.

41.   The figure occurs at the words 'et chorus' in the setting for four voices of *Quem vidistis pastores*, and at the words 'de cælo' in the eight-voice setting of *Hodie nobis de cælo*.

42.   It is particularly prominent in the first responsory for eight voices, *Hodie nobis de cælo*. Borges's derivation of this theme from the chant 'Hodie nobis cælorum rex' – which she achieves by selecting the necessary few notes from a substantial section of chant – must be treated as fanciful; see *Duarte Lobo*, p. 103. It should be noted that the position of tones and semitones is not always the same in the various appearances of this motive in the works mentioned.

43.   In other respects the two *Cantate Domino* Masses are less alike than are Garro's *Missa Fili quid fecisti nobis sic* and Magalhães's *Missa O soberana luz*, discussed above, in that – for example – they are in different modes.

44.   Anthony Carver's *The development of sacred polychoral music to the time of Schütz* (Cambridge: CUP, 1988) devotes very little space to relevant Spanish and Portuguese repertories.

45.   Modern edition by Lavern Wagner in *Philippe Rogier opera omnia*, vol. II, Corpus mensurabilis musicæ 61 (Neuhausen/Stuttgart: American Institute of Musicology, 1976), pp. 1–5.

46.   A good example is the last phrase of the motet *Timor et tremor*, published originally in 1564.

Example 1. Francisco Garro: part of 'Gloria' from *Missa Fili quid fecisti nobis sic*

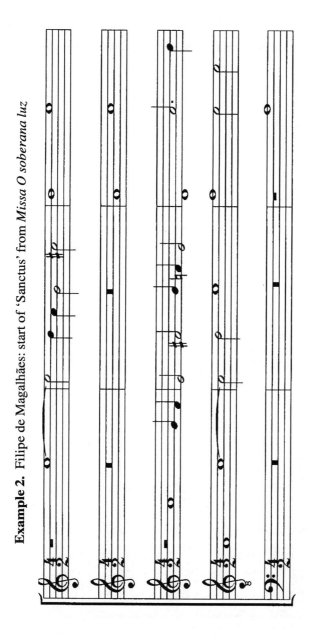

Example 2. Filipe de Magalhães: start of 'Sanctus' from *Missa O soberana luz*

Example 3. Filipe de Magalhães: part of 'Sanctus' from *Missa O soberana luz*

Example 4. Francisco Garro: part of 'Sanctus' from *Missa Fili quid fecisti nobis sic*

Example 5. Duarte Lobo: motive from *Missa Cantate Domino*

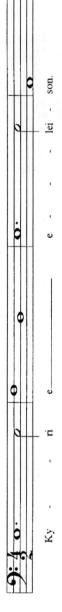

Ky - - ri - e - - - lei - son.

Example 6. Duarte Lobo: motive from *Missa Cantate Domino*

Chri-ste _____ e - lei - son

Example 7. Francisco Garro: motive from *Missa Cantate Domino*

Chri - ste e - lei - son

TABULA GRATULATORIA

John Alban Metcalfe

Steven Boldy

Federico Bonaddio

Marta Campomar

Ruth Christie

Françoise and Andrew Convey

Mike Crompton

Sister Wilfred Daly and
Sister Fidelis C.P.

David Davies

Gareth Alban Davies

Judith Drinkwater

Howard Evans and
Michelle Pepratx-Evans

Peter Evans

Edmund Fryde

Angel M. Garcia

Antonio Gil de Carrasco

Enriqueta Harris Frankfort

Daniel and Helga Huws

Instituto Cervantes,
Manchester and Leeds

Austen Ivereigh

Alvaro Jaspe

Gabriela Jones

John A. Jones

Margaret Kay

Sita and Laurence Keates

Jeremy Lawrance

Alex Longhurst

Patricia and Martin McDermott

John Macklin

Manuel Joaquín Montoro
Blanch

Rosemarie Mulcahy

Michael O'Brien

Terence O'Reilly

Carmo Ponte

Helen Rawlings

Ann Rees

Gwilym O. Rees

Owen and Gareth Rees

Rob and Annie Rix

Penny Robinson

Antonio Ruiz Hernando

João M. Saraiva de Carvalho

Erica Segre

Frank Smith

John Sullivan

Monica and William Tomkiss

Colin Thompson

Gerard Turnbull

Michael Williams

Patrick Williams

Clive Willis

Margaret Wilson

Anthony D. Wright